European Cohesion Pol

The European Cohesion Policy was established with the objective of decreasing the considerable disparities of wealth across the EU. It is put in practice through thousands of development projects across the Union and influences the daily workings of national ministries, local authorities and private contractors. Despite its significance, the policy is subject to many misunderstandings and there is much controversy as to its effectiveness.

European Cohesion Policy seeks to bring a much needed clarity to these issues. It is the first text to clearly present both the theoretical and practical aspects of EU intervention and to provide a systematic view of the various stages of the whole policy cycle, looking in detail at:

- the evolution of the problems;
- the design of the policy system;
- the implementation in practice;
- the evaluation of effects.

An authoritative analysis of the problems and debates involved, *European Cohesion Policy* is essential reading for students, policy makers, project promoters and researchers working in all aspects of European cohesion policy.

Willem Molle is Professor in Economics of International Integration at Erasmus University, Rotterdam and is Senior Adviser at ECORYS Research and Consultancy, also based in Rotterdam. His work focuses on problems of cohesion and regional development in the framework of European and global integration. He has much practical experience in each of the stages of the policy cycle and has published a great number of books and articles on the subject.

Regions and Cities

Series editors: Ron Martin, University of Cambridge, UK; Gernot Grabher, University of Bonn, Germany; Maryann Feldman, University of Georgia, USA

Regions and Cities is an international, interdisciplinary series that provides authoritative analyses of the new significance of regions and cities for economic, social and cultural development and public policy experimentation. The series seeks to combine theoretical and empirical insights with constructive policy debate and critically engages with formative processes and policies in regional and urban studies.

Creative Regions
Technology, culture and knowledge entrepreneurship
Philip Cooke and Dafna Schwartz (eds)

European Cohesion Policy
Willem Molle

Geographies of the New Economy
Peter Daniels, Michael Bradshaw, Jon Beaverstock and Andrew Leyshon (eds)

The Rise of the English Regions?
Irene Hardill, Paul Benneworth, Mark Baker and Leslie Budd (eds)

Regional Development in the Knowledge Economy
Philip Cooke and Andrea Piccaluga (eds)

Clusters and Regional Development
Critical reflections and explorations
Bjørn Asheim, Philip Cooke and Ron Martin (eds)

Regions, Spatial Strategies and Sustainable Development
Graham Haughton and Dave Counsell (eds)

Geographies of Labour Market Inequality
Ron Martin and Philip Morrison (eds)

Regional Development Agencies in Europe
Henrik Halkier, Charlotte Damborg and Mike Danson (eds)

Social Exclusion in European Cities
Processes, experiences and responses
Ali Madanipour, Goran Cars and Judith Allen (eds)

Regional Innovation Strategies
The challenge for less-favoured regions
Kevin Morgan and Claire Nauwelaers (eds)

Foreign Direct Investment and the Global Economy
Nicholas A. Phelps and Jeremy Alden (eds)

Restructuring Industry and Territory
The experience of Europe's regions
Anna Giunta, Arnoud Lagendijk and Andy Pike (eds)

Community Economic Development
Graham Haughton (ed.)

Out of the Ashes?
The social impact of industrial contraction and regeneration on Britain's mining communities
David Waddington, Chas Critcher, Bella Dicks and David Parry

European Cohesion Policy

Willem Molle

Taylor & Francis Group
LONDON AND NEW YORK

First published 2007
by Routledge
2 Park Square, Milton Park, Abingdon, Oxon OX14 4RN

Simultaneously published in the USA and Canada
by Routledge
270 Madison Ave, New York, NY 10016

Routledge is an imprint of the Taylor & Francis Group, an informa business

© 2007 Willem Molle

Typeset in Bembo by Wearset Ltd, Boldon, Tyne and Wear
Printed and bound in Great Britain by The Cromwell Press, Trowbridge, Wiltshire

All rights reserved. No part of this book may be reprinted or reproduced or utilized in any form or by any electronic, mechanical, or other means, now known or hereafter invented, including photocopying and recording, or in any information storage or retrieval system, without permission in writing from the publishers.

British Library Cataloguing in Publication Data
A catalogue record for this book is available from the British Library

Library of Congress Cataloging in Publication Data
Molle, Willem.
European Cohesion Policy
p. cm — (Regions and cities)
Includes bibliographical references and indexes.
1. European Union countries—Economic integration. 2. European Union countries—Economic conditions—Regional disparities. 3. Social integration—European Union countries—Regional disparities. 4. Political planning—European Union countries. 5. Regional planning—European Union countries. I. Title.

HC241.M62 2007
337.1'422—dc22
  2007004048

ISBN10: 0-415-43811-X (hbk)
ISBN10: 0-415-43812-8 (pbk)
ISBN10: 0-203-94527-1 (ebk)

ISBN13: 978-0-415-43811-7 (hbk)
ISBN13: 978-0-415-43812-4 (pbk)
ISBN13: 978-0-203-94527-8 (ebk)

Contents

List of illustrations	ix
Foreword	xii
Preface	xiv
Acknowledgements	xvi
List of abbreviations	xvii

1 Introduction: introducing the policy cycle   1

STAGE I
Assessing the problems and identifying their causes   13

  2 Disparities: general   15

  3 Economic disparities   36

  4 Social disparities   60

  5 Territorial disparities   83

STAGE II
Designing a solution-oriented intervention system   101

  6 Policy fundamentals   103

STAGE III
Specifying objectives and matching these with instruments   131

  7 Reaching objectives by financial support   133

  8 Reaching objectives by regulation and coordination   161

STAGE IV
Implementing actions and delivering results   189

  9 Implementation and delivery   191

STAGE V
Checking effectiveness and consistency   221

10 Evaluation   223

11 Consistency with other EU policies   254

STAGE VI
Drawing lessons   275

12 Conclusions and outlook   277

Notes   298
References   319
Index   342

Illustrations

Figures

1.1	The policy cycle	7
2.1	Convergence and divergence	16
2.2	Differences in GDP/P by country, 2004	27
2.3	Differences in GDP/P by region, 2001	31
2.4	Regional extremes in GDP/P (PPS) by country, 2000	32
3.1	Inflow of FDI (per capita) in the NMSs by country, 1990–2003	54
4.1	Unemployment by region, 2002	66
5.1	Accessibility by region, 2001	89
6.1	Structural policy for balanced growth	118
6.2	Projects and programmes as central elements of policy	128
7.1	Net position of member states as to the EU budget (2004) in percentage of GDP with member states ranked by GDP/P (in PPP)	148
7.2	Schematic view of financial flows for structural support	150
7.3	Structural aid per head of population in cohesion countries, 1989–93, 1994–99 and 2000–06	152
7.4	Regions eligible for support under the convergence and competitiveness objectives, 2007–13	154
9.1	Role of the different actors in the absorption of the SCF	202
10.1	Key elements in the evaluation of SCF programmes	227
10.2	SF allocation and GDP growth	234
10.3	Effect of the 4 per cent cap on SCF receipts for the NMSs	242
11.1	Cohesion impact of EU agricultural policy funding	257
11.2	Cohesion impact of EU transport policy funding	267

Tables

2.1	Summary view of theoretical approaches	23
2.2	Integration and wealth disparity indicators in Western Europe, 1830-1950	25
2.3	Development of GDP/P (EU = 100) by country, 1950–2004	28
2.4	Catch-up time (in years) for different levels of initial disparity (level in % of target) and differential in growth rates (%)	30

2.5 Evolution of wealth disparities (EU 15), 1950–90 — 33
3.1 Employment in manufacturing by technology class (% of total) and country, 2004 — 41
3.2 Production and trade patterns of multinational, multi-product companies under different trade regimes — 48
3.3 Geographical distribution (%) of direct investment between groups of member countries of the EU, 1980–2003 — 51
4.1 Development of unemployment (% of total active population) by country and gender; ratios of gender (women/men) and city size (large cities/national mean), 1990–2004 — 64
4.2 Percentage of population with a tertiary education degree by country and age group, 2001 — 69
4.3 Evolution of the number of migrants as % of total population by country (1980–2000) and ratio of large cities to national average (2001) — 73
4.4 Social exclusion by country (several indicators), end of 1990s — 76
4.5 Social benefits (expenditure) by country, 1960–2000 — 81
5.1 Evolution of the divergence of the regional GDP/P levels by peripherality class (index to EU 15 average) — 90
5.2 Top 40 airports by passenger numbers (in millions), 2001 — 91
5.3 Innovation indicators by country (100 is best) (around 2003) — 93
5.4 Top 40 regions (above EU average) ranked by their score on the innovation index (EU 15 = 100) — 95
6.1 Forms of redistribution at different levels of integration — 115
6.2 Changing roles of the major actors — 127
7.1 Development of cohesion policy; change of objectives and distribution of aid (billions of euro) by objective, 1989–2013 — 143
7.2 Allocation of SCF aid (2007–13) by objective and country (billions of euro of 2004) — 153
8.1 Maximum allowed aid intensities (% to total cost) in different types of regions (wealth level in % of EU) — 174
9.1 Main characteristics of the stages of the policy cycle on the systemic and delivery level — 195
9.2 Responsibilities and tasks of major institutions involved in the implementation — 198
10.1 Elements of the intervention logic — 226
11.1 Schematic view of the impacts of EU policies by policy area and type of region, 1985–2000 — 272
11.2 Schematic view of the impacts of EU policies by dimension of cohesion (2000) — 273
12.1 Main characteristics of the various dimensions of cohesion — 283
12.2 Regional disparities in MERCOSUR (around 2000) — 293

Boxes

3.1	The OLI paradigm for FDI	46
3.2	Adaptation to regime change; the case of Philips	48
3.3	Why car makers move East	58
4.1	Models of social protection	79
5.1	Polycentrism: a concept as yet impossible to make operational	85
6.1	Monetary Union and redistribution	116
6.2	Limited role for the EU in matters of social security	123
6.3	Groupings of major beneficiaries	126
7.1	Major turning points of the EU cohesion policy	141
7.2	Main characteristics of the main funds	144
7.3	The specific case of the dimension of territorial cohesion	145
7.4	Allocation methods for EU support	149
7.5	Creation of a R&D support centre in Basilicata (Italy)	155
7.6	Ethnic Minority Business Support Network London (UK)	157
7.7	INTERREG project in central Europe: enlarging opportunities for SMEs	158
8.1	Negotiations on eligibility and area coverage	164
8.2	The case of social inclusion	167
8.3	Authorized and unauthorized state aid	175
8.4	Social standards	176
9.1	Major components of the programming process	205
9.2	What type of organizations act as IBs?	209
9.3	The improvement of the River Danube as a main transport axis	211
9.4	Combating unemployment in the Gdansk region of Poland	212
10.1	Catching up: the case of Ireland	236
10.2	Italy's institutional restructuring to reach conformity with EU norms	246
11.1	Cohesion impact of CAP budget outlays	257
11.2	Impacts of EU expenditure in transport infrastructure	267

Foreword

Europe at the beginning of the twenty-first century faces significant challenges. Globalization is moving forward at an unprecedented pace, and technologies are evolving ever more rapidly. As a result, our economies have to cope with continuous structural change. Populations are ageing, the environment is under increasing pressure, and we need to ensure the security and affordability of our energy supplies. The fifth enlargement of the Union, completed with the accession of Bulgaria and Romania, means that regional disparities are greater than ever before.

Our overall challenge in this context is to ensure that Europe is a modern, dynamic and outward-looking economy. This is the aim of the Lisbon strategy which was relaunched in 2005. One of the innovations of this new strategy is the key role which cohesion policy and Europe's regions play in implementing it.

In order to play this role, cohesion policy has been radically reformed for the period 2007–13. We have increased our focus on those investments which are essential for economic modernization: research and development (R&D), innovation, entrepreneurship, human capital and information and communication technologies (ICT). We have put in place a new more strategic approach which integrates growth strategies at European, national and regional level. We have introduced new instruments involving European financial institutions to leverage in both private sector resources and expertise. And we have strengthened partnership: cohesion policy involves people at the regional and local level because it is here that we find the expertise and experience necessary to identify problems and appropriate solutions. These stakeholders are deeply involved in the design, implementation and follow-up of the policy. The ownership which results from this process greatly increases the effectiveness of what we do.

Europe's cohesion policy has come a long way since the creation, more than 30 years ago, of the European Regional Development Fund (ERDF). Over time, the European Union (EU) has become a case study in how to manage economic integration and the need to accompany it with measures to promote widespread access to the opportunities created. Other countries and areas around the world such as Russia, the Ukraine, China and Mercado Common del Sur (MERCOSUR) have taken an active interest in European cohesion policy and in some cases have adopted similar policies.

In this book Professor Molle charts the dynamics of cohesion policy in

Europe. He explains the principles of each of the stages of the policy: from identification of problems to evaluation of effectiveness. He exposes the practical side of the implementation of the policy and illustrates this with case studies.

This book makes a significant contribution to a better understanding of why we need cohesion policy, how it works, who is involved, what are its effects. It contains many stimulating ideas and discussions, constructive criticism and suggestions on how the policy might be improved. It constitutes essential reading for all those who are interested or involved in European cohesion policy.

Danuta Hübner
Member European Commission
responsible for Regional Policy

Preface

Since its take off I have been an active observer of and a modest contributor to European cohesion policy. In the early 1970s I was a young researcher at Netherlands Economic Institute (NEI) in Rotterdam and was particularly interested in the subject of cohesion. Under the stimulating drive of my directors Professors Leo Klaassen and Jean Paelinck we started a programme of work on cohesion issues. We did quite a lot of work for the European Commission (EC) and national and regional governments all over the EU and its candidate countries. We published the results of our collective work in books and articles. Since then NEI and later ECORYS (of which NEI has become part) have kept a stake in this subject with many studies.

These studies varied according to specific problems and circumstances.

- We pioneered the systematic analysis of disparities in the EU as a whole (Molle et al., 1980) and some of the causal factors such as the development of the economic structure including industrial migration (e.g. Molle, 1983; Klaassen and Molle, 1982).
- We participated actively in the analysis of the effectiveness of the different segments of the policy in a range of monitoring and evaluation studies.
- We made early contributions to the consistency of cohesion with other EU policies (e.g. Molle and Capellin, 1988).
- We worked on specific issues such as competitiveness; absorption capacity, choice of instruments, evaluation methods, etc.
- We built up an impressive statistical data base and a documentation with the main contributions to the literature.

In the course of the 35 years that have passed since I started my career, I became chairman of the Board of Directors of NEI and later of ECORYS. I also became part time professor in economics; first at Maastricht University and later at Erasmus University in Rotterdam. Over this whole period and in all these roles I have kept a keen interest in the subject of cohesion and actually stayed actively involved in concrete work on the subject. The disadvantage of having less time to spend to research, which my new roles implied, has been compensated by the advantages of access to the results of the work of excellent staff and colleagues, the broadening of views following the diversification of my interests and the stimulating exchange with students.

The fruits of the capital thus accumulated have been made available to a large diversity of audiences in the form of:

- concrete studies for the broad range of clients of ECORYS/NEI;
- participation in think tanks on the reform of cohesion policies; an example has been my participation in the 'Groupe de Prospective' that Commissioner Barnier convened in 2001–02 to prepare the ground for the recent reform of the Structural Funds;
- papers to academic and policy conferences;
- articles (published in refereed journals) and specialized books; and
- teaching material for courses for students.

Over the past decades the issue of cohesion has grown in importance and with it the literature on the subject. Several colleagues have drawn my attention to the fact that there was one major element missing in this literature, a thorough textbook that would be of help to both academics and practitioners. They thought I was well qualified to write it and they have stimulated me to devote time to do it. I started quite some time ago by making drafts of several chapters; drawing on work I was currently involved in. Most of these draft chapters have been presented in the form of papers at international seminars and conferences. Some draw very heavily on articles that have previously been published. Progress on the book was slow as I was too involved in other obligations. However, after having handed over my management responsibilities in ECORYS/NEI to my successors I have finally found the time to get to work on the project in a systematic way.

I hereby submit the result of my efforts to the public. I hope it will prove a useful contribution to the understanding of the anatomy of the problems, and a way to find effective solutions to them for all those professionally involved in the shaping and the delivery of the policy. I also hope that this book will be found useful for courses in all the universities that pursue an active interest in the subject of cohesion in Europe and that it will stimulate the work of the generation that will shape the future.

Willem Molle

Acknowledgements

In writing this book I have benefited from a lot of help. I am indebted to all those who have contributed to the final result.

Several colleagues (notably Peter Lloyd and Alberto Gianoli) have made suggestions as to the character of the book, which resulted in the adoption of the stages of the policy cycle for its main structure.

Many colleagues, too numerous to mention, have indicated relevant material to me in the areas of their specific specialist competences. In this way the book covers notions far beyond my main field of expertise, which is economics. Work in this interdisciplinary way has been stimulated in particular by colleagues from the Jean Monnet network.

Yet other colleagues have been helpful by making suggestions and critically reviewing (parts of) the manuscript. I mention here in particular Sjaak Boeckhout and Jan-Maarten de Vet of ECORYS, Alberto Gianoli of the Erasmus University (Institute for Housing Studies) and Jiri Blazek of Charles University in Prague.

I give a particular word of thanks to Walter Lutz of ECORYS and Astrid Ringeling of the Erasmus University for very effective research assistance during the final writing stage of this book.

Finally, I thank both the Erasmus University and ECORYS Research and Consulting for creating a stimulating environment for my work.

Of course all remaining errors and shortcomings are my responsibility. In order to make a possible next edition better adapted to the needs of the users of the book I here invite all users to let me have the benefits of their critical comments.

Willem Molle
molle@few.eur.nl

Abbreviations

AA	Audit Authority
ACFTA	ASEAN–China Free Trade Area
ALMP	Active Labour Market Policies
ASEAN	Association of Southeast Asian Nations
BEPG	Broad Economic Policy Guidelines
CA	Certifying Authority
CAP	Common Agricultural Policy
CCC	Cross Border Business Cooperation for Central Europe
CEEC	Central and Eastern European Countries
CF	Cohesion Fund
CI	Community Initiative
CM	Common Market
CoA	Court of Auditors
CoR	Committee of the Regions
CSF	Community Support Framework
CSG	Community Strategic Guidelines
CTP	Common Transport Policy
CU	customs union
DDR	Deutsche Demokratische Republik
DG	Directorate General
DI	direct investment
EAGGF	European Agricultural Guidance and Guarantee Fund
EBRD	European Bank for Reconstruction and Development
EC	European Commission
ECB	European Central Bank
ECSC	European Coal and Steel Community
EDIE	European Direct Investments in Europe
EEC	European Economic Community
EFTA	European Free Trade Area
EGTC	European Grouping of Territorial Cooperation
EIB	European Investment Bank
EMU	Economic and Monetary Union
ERDF	European Regional Development Fund
ESC	Economic and Social Committee

ESDP	European Spatial Development Perspective
ESF	European Social Fund
ESPON	European Spatial Planning Observation Network
EU	European Union
FDI	Foreign Direct Investment
FED	Federation
FIFG	Financial Instrument for Fishery Guidance
FP	Financial Perspective
FOCEM	Fondo para la Convergencia Structual del MERCOSUR
FRG	Federal Republic of Germany
FTA	Free Trade Agreement (Area)
GDP	gross domestic product
GDP/P	gross domestic product per head of population
GVA	gross value added
HR	Human Resources
IB	intermediate body
ICT	Information and Communication Technologies
ILO	International Labour Organization
IMF	International Monetary Fund
IPA	Instrument for Pre-Accession
JASPERS	Joint Assistance in Supporting Projects in European Regions
LDC	less developed country
MA	Managing Authority
MC	Monitoring Committee
MEANS	Methods for Evaluating Actions of a Structural Nature
MERCOSUR	Mercado Common del Sur
MNF	multi national firm
MTE	Mid-term Evaluation
NAP	National Action Plan
NDP	National Development Plan
NE	Northern and North Eastern
NEI	Netherlands Economic Institute
NGO	Non Governmental Organization
NMS	New Member State
NSRF	National Strategic Reference Framework
NTB	Non-Tariff Barrier
OECD	Organisation for Economic Cooperation and Development
OLI	Ownership, Location and Internalization
OMC	Open Method of Coordination
OP	operational programme
OVI	Objective Verifiable Indicator
PA	Payment Authority
PPP	purchasing power parities
PTA	preferential trade agreement (area)
R&D	research and development
RDP	Regional Development Programme

ROP	Regional Operational Programme
RSA	Regional State Aid
SCF	Structural and Cohesion Funds
SDP	Sectoral Development Programme
SE	South Eastern
SF	Structural Fund
SG	Strategic Guidelines
SGI	Services of General Interest
SGP	Stability and Growth Pact
SMEs	small- and medium-sized enterprises
SOP	Sectoral Operational Programme
SPD	Single Programming Document
SWOT	strengths, weaknesses, opportunities and threats
TA	technical assistance
TEN	Trans European Network
USSR	Union of Soviet Socialist Republics
VAT	value added tax
WB	World Bank
WTO	World Trade Organization

1 Introduction

Introducing the policy cycle

1.1 Why, what and for whom?

1.1.1 Why was this book written; what are its specific characteristics?

Much has been written about both the anatomy of the cohesion problems and about the best ways to attack them with adequate policies. In recent years the results of an increasing number of studies on EU cohesion issues have been published. So the question, 'What can a new book add to this?' is warranted. The answer is to take away some of the major shortcomings in the existing literature. The contributions of this book (its 'value added') are:

- *Comprehensive scope.* Much of the literature is about either regional economics, social policy, or about specific problems such as economic convergence or social deprivation. Another part is about the shaping of multi-level policy making. Some of this literature is only descriptive; other work is very econometric. This book covers both issues of economic, social and territorial cohesion problems and issues of various policies devised to solve these problems.
- *Integrated approach.* The book integrates the results of theoretical and empirical work on both the evolution of cohesion problems and on the fundamentals of policy design and implementation. It draws from different disciplines such as economics, political science, sociology, geography and public administration.
- *Clear structure.* It facilitates access to the vast material on complicated issues by providing a rigorous structure inspired by the policy cycle; identification of the problems (diagnosis); design of an intervention method; delivery and implementation (therapy); evaluation and feedback.
- *Long time frame.* Much of the available studies deal with the present situation only. As the cohesion problem is of a structural nature and solutions take time we have to look at the long-term development. So this book covers a period of more than half a century from the very beginnings of the EU up to the present time. This long time frame applies to both the analytical part and the policy part. It also applies to the theoretical foundations of both the development of the system and the influence of policy.[1]

2   *Introduction*

- *Open and critical attitude.* The book is based on an evaluation of the existing theoretical and empirical literature. It is non-partisan in the sense that it does not take a priori views and it does not set out to make a point. On the contrary, it acknowledges the results of the work of different schools. It substantiates positions by referring to authoritative studies made of the subject. It does not present the existing set up as self-evident but refers to other options that might have been chosen as well. It invites the reader to reflect critically on the foundations and modalities of the EU cohesion policy.
- *Extensive reference base.* The broad scope of the book means that it is not based on a small specialist part of the literature but on a wide range of contributions from very different disciplines and information sources. As many readers may be unfamiliar with the origins of the information given in the book that is outside their own specialist area we will give ample reference to the evidence that substantiates the views expressed in the book. This will moreover be of much help to those who want to use the book for more in-depth study of specific parts. We hope that the book will in this way contribute to the design of better policies and in doing so help to optimize welfare of the European citizen.

1.1.2 For whom is the book written? Which readership?

The book addresses primarily two groups of readers:

- *Students.* These include in particular students in economic geography, regional economics but also students in sociology, public administration, political science and European integration. In this book they will find a balanced view of the subject whereby issues are first of all analysed from the theoretical point of view, immediately followed by a presentation of the insights of empirical analysis. Ample reference to publications in the form of books, articles, documents and websites permits students to use it as a starting point for executing tasks on specific subjects. Although this book is not one that provides easy access to simplified notions and precooked exam questions, it should be of essential reading for advanced students (master level) of this fascinating field of EU policy making.
- All those who are *professionally interested* in European cohesion policy. This group includes, first, all those involved in the daily execution of cohesion policy. It also includes researchers, consultants and journalists who find here the essential framework for their specialist work. Although this book is not a popular 'How to' book it provides the essential information on the practical functioning of the EU policy machinery; essential for effective contribution in the definition of specific projects and the monitoring and evaluation of policy measures.

The material of the book has been organized to permit a fruitful study of individual subjects without having to work through the previous chapters. To facilitate deeper and more advanced study of the subjects treated we give ample references to more specific literature.[2] To facilitate the access of all readers from different target groups, the book has been written in such a way that it can be read with only a basic knowledge of one or other of the diverse disciplines cited before. Moreover the use of mathematics has been avoided.

1.2 European cohesion policy: a controversial subject

1.2.1 The controversy

The EU is confronted with very large disparities in wealth. These lead to social and political problems. To cope with such problems the EU has elaborated a cohesion policy. This policy absorbs the lions' share of the EU budget. It is implemented through thousands of development projects. It influences in a multitude of ways the daily work of hundreds of thousands involved in its delivery and subjected to its effects. And it arouses both admiration and contempt.

Admirers say European cohesion policy is the cement that holds the construction of the EU together. Without it the construction would fall apart. It would mean that the flow of benefits (for instance enhanced productivity and hence welfare growth) that one draws from integration would stop. In this view the cost of cohesion policy is the price we pay for earning the advantages of integration. Although many would agree with this major political statement there is not much agreement as to the actual performance of EU cohesion policy.

The dominant view is more or less positive. The premise is that without the EU cohesion policy the economic system would increase divergence between the rich and the poor. Those who hold this view consider that in the past the EU cohesion policy has been able to decrease the wealth difference between member countries. Moreover, they consider that the EU has increased the effectiveness of the joint efforts of the EU and the member states by setting up better intervention and delivery systems than the national ones. In other words: thanks to the EU cohesion has improved. We should be proud of it.

There are other views on cohesion policy, some of which are highly critical. Some consider that the European cohesion policy is the very opposite of what it says and realizes. Some find that cohesion policy is not appropriate: a good set of other policies producing the conditions for healthy growth would also lead to convergence of wealth levels. Others find that cohesion policy is not effective: they observe that during the years that the EU cohesion policy was very limited disparities decreased: following huge increases in EU cohesion spending, disparities have actually increased. Yet others find that the policy is inefficient; observing that the actual functioning of the policy takes up a lot of resources and just keeps an army of civil servants from doing better things. In short they consider EU cohesion policy a waste of money. We should be ashamed of it.

1.2.2 What to do to bring clarity?

Who is right, who is wrong in this debate? How good are the arguments of each of the antagonists? The answer to these questions is not easy. It requires a whole series of investigations. To begin with, one has to define correctly the problems and their possible solutions. Next, one has to take a closer look at the soundness of the theoretical foundations of the various strands of thought. Finally, one has to measure correctly the efforts made by the policy and observe empirically the effects it has realized. In other words one has to go in depth into the various mechanisms that produce cohesion, and into the way policies can support them. That is in essence what this book sets out to do.

In the rest of this introductory chapter we will start with some definitions: each of the three words in the title of this book merits a short introduction. Next we introduce the basic structure of the book followed by its main features.

1.3 Introducing the main notions

1.3.1 Europe: from small nucleus to almost complete coverage

The term Europe here designates the EU.[3] Now the EU has changed quite a bit in the course of the time period we cover in this book. This applies both to its area and subject coverage.

Area. The EU started in the early 1950s from a fairly small basis of originally six countries. In the course of the past decades the EU has been successful in realizing its objectives of providing an area of peace and economic growth. In this way membership of it has become attractive for other European countries. The number of member countries has gradually increased, as countries that fulfil the criteria for membership wish to share in the advantages of European integration. This has resulted in several rounds of enlargement. The EU now consists of 27 countries.[4] Even though the EU has not covered this area over the whole period of its existence, we will, as much as possible, describe developments for this larger area. However, due to data limitations we will often be constrained to smaller areas. This applies notably to the period before 1990; for this period comparable data for countries in Central and Eastern Europe are not available.[5]

Subjects. The EU started off as a common market (CM). At that moment the EU did have almost no competences in matters of cohesion. However, over time and with increased integration the need for an EU cohesion policy increased and the EU has been endowed with very extended competences in cohesion matters. We will go in detail into the way in which this process has been given shape.

1.3.2 Cohesion: from a political notion to operational indicators

The EU is confronted with very large cohesion problems. One of them is the existence of large disparities between its different parts. These disparities were already quite large in the former EU 15. To give an example: by the turn of the century the income per head in the richest region was about five times as high as in the poorest region. Since the recent enlargement the disparities in income have doubled; the average gross domestic product (GDP) per head in the ten new member states (NMSs) in Central and Eastern Europe is about half the average of the EU 27.

The capacity of regions and countries to do something about this disparity is not equally distributed. Some countries that are economically weak tend to stay so because their vulnerability in macro economic and monetary matters puts them at risk of having to adapt their policies to counteract important turbulence on exchange markets, with negative effects on economic growth. Large rich countries tend to be able to shield themselves, to a large extent, from such problems.

Next there are also differences in access to employment. These have also increased since the accession of the NMSs. In the EU 27 only 56 per cent of the population of working age held a job (around 2004), while the figure for the EU 15 was 64 per cent. Problems of unemployment are sometimes exacerbated by problems of social exclusion; people that have lost their job risk ending up in a vicious circle of lack of income (poverty) and exclusion from social contacts and from participation in social life. There are also big differences between parts of the EU in the occurrence of this problem. However, that is not so much a question of the less developed areas; social problems can be very acute also in the urban areas of the wealthier member states.

These large disparities are often felt as morally unjust and may lead to discontent. In some cases such discontent takes very violent forms, for instance riots in the suburbs of major cities. In other cases it takes the form of absence of support, which on the EU level may translate into a lack of progress for the European project. So for economic, moral and political reasons these disparities are a problem. The EU has realized, itself, that it cannot function well in cases where large segments of the European society are not part of the beneficial effects of integration. So it has set out to foster internal cohesion.

Cohesion is a concept that has been introduced in the EU policy without a precise definition. Over time such a practical definition has been developed. Cohesion is now understood as the degree to which disparities in social and economic welfare between the different regions or groups within the EU are politically and socially tolerable.

Whether cohesion is achieved is largely a political question. In general, one does not try to answer this question in the static way it is asked here. One rather looks at it in a dynamic way. That means that one looks at the change in disparity from one period to another. A decrease in disparity (convergence[6]) then means improved cohesion and an increase in disparity (divergence) means less cohesion. Any decrease in disparity is supposed to ease the situation in terms of political and social tolerance, any increase acerbates the situation on this score.

1.3.3 Policy: a multi-actor game in a cyclical framework

Cohesion does not come about by the natural processes that operate in modern socio-economic and political systems. As a matter of fact the very dynamics of the integrated economy of the EU may even increase cohesion problems. So, a policy is needed to bend the processes in such a way as to lead to targets: less disparity and more cohesion. Policy making involves the coherent use of a set of instruments to influence the determining factors of the target variables. So the essential elements of the policy are: the attribution of responsibilities to actors, the definition of objectives, the set up of a framework for intervention and the deployment of instruments. We will detail each element somewhat hereafter:

Actors. Given the scale of the problem the EU has taken responsibility for a significant part of this policy. It is not solely responsible, however. Member states play an important role. Moreover, the EU also involves local governments and representatives of the third and private sector. This multi-level governance of the EU cohesion policy involving many actors is set up to increase participation and hence effectiveness.

Objectives. The EU has set a number of objectives for its cohesion policy. The first is directly related to the main problem of disparity discussed in the previous section. The others have been added at certain points in time in EU development.

1   Improve cohesion (that is decrease disparities or generally the convergence of wealth levels) on three dimensions: economic, social, territorial.
2   Contribute to other EU objectives:

- Facilitate major advances in economic integration such as enlargement or the passing into higher stages of integration (e.g. the Economic and Monetary Union (EMU)).
- Contribute to major policy targets such as the increase in competitiveness or the stimulation of environmental sustainability.

Framework. Taxpayers and other stakeholders that contribute to the policy want to be assured that the policy is effective. To that end, one has to set up adequate institutions and intervention systems, implement in practice the policy and evaluate the results. The better understanding that is thus gained can be used to adapt the policy and make it better geared to its objectives.

Instruments. The EU now spends considerable financial resources to solve cohesion problems. And it regulates the actions of national and regional public authorities that pursue the same and related objectives.

This whole process can be conceptualized as a *cycle* (see Figure 1.1).[7] The EU has opted for a period of about seven years to complete a full cycle. The set up of the book follows fairly closely this cycle.

1.4 Introducing each of the stages of the cycle

1.4.1 The first stage: assessing the problems and identifying their causes

The policy cycle starts when people become aware of the existence of a socio-economic problem and start to voice claims on politicians to do something to solve it. However, in this initial stage the magnitude of the problem and its root causes are often ill understood. So the cycle starts with the analysis of the *cohesion problem*. This can be done by asking three questions:

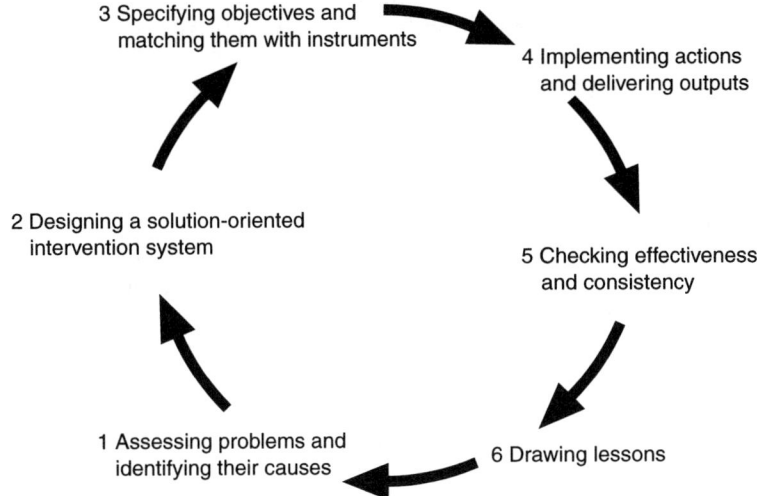

Figure 1.1 The policy cycle

1 How do you measure (the lack of) cohesion?
2 Has cohesion become better or worse over time?
3 What are the factors that determine disparities and thus cohesion?

In the first part of the book we set out to give answers to these questions.

The essential aspect we deal with here is *convergence*. Convergence of wealth is the main objective of cohesion policy and hence it is important to measure its development and capture the factors that contribute to either a positive or a negative development. To measure its development (first and second question) we will make a long-term analysis of a series of indicators. To identify and understand the causes of this observed development (third question) we will scrutinize the theoretical and empirical literature. This stage is essential as it permits one to identify the factors on which policy can focus so as to solve the problems.

The improvement of cohesion depends to a large extent on the increase in *competitiveness*. Competitiveness is defined as the ability of countries, regions, cities or social groups to generate, while being exposed to external competition, relatively high income and employment levels. As main drivers of competitiveness we distinguish:

- industrial structure (specialization in high-value-added activities, new products and services; clusters of related activities);
- human resources (employment rate, educational level, training and teaching facilities, adaptability of labour force, entrepreneurial talent);
- accessibility (telecommunication networks; transport infrastructure, urban services);
- innovation (R&D institutes; knowledge-based firms);

8   *Introduction*

- environmental quality (attracts high-level activities; devastation of the environment leads to bad image and hence can be a barrier to development.

We will study the problem and its causes in four parts. First, in general terms, that is with the help of the key indicator of wealth disparities which is gross domestic product per head of population (GDP/P).[8] Next we deal subsequently with the three dimensions of cohesion: economic, social and territorial. We will set each of these in its relevant policy context.

Economic cohesion is largely determined by development of the first item of the four competition factors given above, namely: the production structure (Chapter 3). Under this heading we detail the composition of the economy in low and high value added sectors. Moreover, we go into the issue of Foreign Direct Investment (FDI) as this is of much interest to public authorities. We will equally pay attention to industrial migration as the general public is much concerned about the relocation of firms from developed areas to the less developed areas of the wider Europe and of the rest of the world.

Social cohesion is not easy to capture. However, it is closely related to the second group of factors given under competitiveness. A whole series of indicators permit specific aspects of social cohesion to follow. We will analyse in some detail the aspect of employment (or rather its counterpart unemployment), the effects of migration and segregation and the aspect of social exclusion (Chapter 4).

Territorial cohesion is a concept that is even less easy to translate in concrete indicators than economic and social cohesion. Central in this respect are the notions of accessibility and peripherality to markets and innovation. These coincide largely with the competitiveness factors given in the last two bullet points above. We will elaborate them further in Chapter 5.

Some of the indicators used for measuring territorial disparities (such as accessibility) are in practice determinants of the location of industry and hence of economic structure, employment dynamics and finally wealth levels. So in practice they are all part of an integrated system. The EU cohesion policy has acknowledged this fact and has integrated the three dimensions (economic, social and territorial) in a common framework. We will follow that integrated approach in the elaboration of the following parts of the cycle.

The main *result* of this part of the analysis is that the disparity in wealth between EU member countries has gradually decreased. However, the development of disparities on the regional level is less positive; after a long period of convergence the trend has turned and indicates now quite some divergence.

1.4.2 *The second stage: designing a solution-oriented intervention system*

The assessment of the problems has led politicians to the conclusion that the situation in matters of cohesion is not satisfactory and that policy action is needed to do something about it. Once the question whether intervention needs to be answered in a positive way a whole series of other questions need answering, such as: who is in charge, what instruments can best be used, how is the process to be organized, where is action needed, what packages of measures have to been taken, etc.? We will deal with these issues in some depth in Chapter 6.

Giving a good answer to these questions involves the making of a few very fundamental choices as to the design of the intervention system. They are often decided at the constitutional level. In the EU tradition this means that they are codified in the various treaties.

The first question is about the level of intervention. We will first go into the rationale for EU involvement (the 'why' question). We will show that national governments are not capable of delivering cohesion on the EU level in an efficient way. So the EU has been given overall responsibility for it.

The next question is about the intervention system to be put in place and the type of instruments to be used (in other words the 'what' question). We will explain why the EU has opted for financial redistribution as its major instrument to foster cohesion. It has set up EU funds from which grants can be given to regions and social groups to alleviate particular problems. The second important instrument of the EU is regulation and coordination.

Finally, we will discuss the various partners involved (the 'who' question) in the EU cohesion policy. They assume different roles at different stages of the elaboration and implementation of the policy cycle. The Council has the decisive role in the decisions on the policy fundamentals and the multi-annual framework. The Commission has a pivotal role in all the stages of the application, daily management and evaluation of the policy. Regions play an increasingly important role as advisers in the design stage and operation managers in the implementation stage.

1.4.3 The third stage: specifying objectives and matching these with instruments

Next we deal with the translation of the constitutional and overriding policy objectives in major principles that guide the practical operations. This we will do in two chapters.

In Chapter 7 we will describe the multi-annual framework; specifying the major objectives and the *financial instrument*. Moreover, we will deal with the determination of the size of the funds and criteria for the allocation of financial resources (that is the definition of eligible social groups and regions).

The main objective of cohesion policy is convergence; in other words the decrease in disparity. A considerable share (some 80 per cent) of EU Structural Fund's (SF) resources is devoted to this objective. In order to enhance effectiveness, support is highly concentrated on the regions that are most in need of it (indicated by the lowest levels of wealth and the highest levels of social problems).

The EU cohesion policy has two other major stated objectives. One is to prevent new problems arising and to increase competitiveness and employment in other regions than those covered by the convergence objective. The other is to improve territorial cooperation of regions negatively influenced by border situations. The EU devotes smaller parts of the total package (together some 20 per cent) to these objectives.

In Chapter 8 we will describe the *regulatory instruments* the EU uses to influence the combined activities of EU, national and regional authorities. Regulatory instruments forbid certain actions of private and public actors that may have a negative effect on cohesion or prescribe other actions that may enhance cohesion. Important in this respect is coordination; both vertical and horizontal.

We will turn our attention first to vertical coordination, where the EU determines the framework for actions by lower forms of government such as member states and regions. In the group of vertical instruments the light form is 'open coordination'; which leaves most freedom to the member states. There are quite a few cases where such a light method is not sufficient to get to results. In those cases the legal instrument of the Regulation is used. With this instrument the EU defines in detail the joint efforts of the EU and the national governments in terms of targets, areas of intervention, intensity of support, etc.

Next we will orient our attention to the problem of horizontal coordination where the different services of the EU have to make sure that their policies are consistent and reinforce each other. We will describe how in the course of time some overarching objectives have been defined and methods to foster consistency have been introduced.

The analysis shows that the putting in place of these regulatory instruments is fully justified. However, it cannot prevent that in the daily practice multiple conflicts arise in practice in the pursuit of the different policies at various administrative levels.

1.4.4 The fourth stage: implementing actions and delivering results

The next point concerns the actual putting into effect of the policy by executing programmes and concrete projects. It means building roads, training people, etc. At this stage we deal with questions about governance.[9] Here too a number of basic principles are to be respected. We present the most salient features of these principles and of their implementation in the practice of the EU cohesion policy in Chapter 9.

Over the years the EU has identified the conditions that need to be fulfilled in order to realize a high-quality implementation and delivery system. We will describe how this system has been specified in basic principles, institutional structures, general rules and detailed administrative procedures.

One of the basic principles of the EU cohesion policy is *partnership*. Partnership implies that civil servants of the EC, national governments and regional authorities together with representatives of private and third sector (among them local business, labour unions and social action groups) collaborate closely and continuously in the design, implementation and evaluation of EU-funded programmes. In the previous chapters we have already dealt with the different roles the various actors play at the earlier stages of the policy cycle, here we will describe the distribution of the roles in the critical stage of implementation. We will show that the application of the partnership principle has the advantage of increasing the effectiveness of the efforts by involving all concerned; it has the disadvantage of a loss of efficiency due to uncertainties in the division of responsibilities and the high input of human resources that it mobilizes.[10]

A second principle is that of *programming*. Its application makes for a consistent and transparent implementation of the policy. It involves the definition and adoption of a multi annual framework that sets out the problems to be attacked, the instruments put in place, the priorities set, the EU and other funds to be deployed and, most important, implementation provisions. It takes account of the EU strategic guidelines and is made concrete in sets of clearly defined operations.

The *implementation* of these programmes is not done by the EU itself but has been entrusted to the national governments. We will describe how they have delegated this task to so-called management authorities, in turn supported by intermediate bodies. The latter are the first recipients of the project applications and select the ones that have the highest contribution to the realization of the objectives.

In order to make sure that the agreed programmes and projects are implemented according to agreed specifications and time schedules, *monitoring* is needed. In the governance model of the EU cohesion policy the responsibility for this monitoring is given to the member states that have entrusted it in turn to monitoring committees. They have to report annually on the progress.

The SF disburses very high amounts of money. *Financial management and control systems* need to be in place to make sure that this money is rightly spent on the agreed projects and on authorized expenditure. Internal and external audit complements the delivery system by testifying to all involved in the justification of the expenditure.

1.4.5 The fifth stage: checking effectiveness and consistency

The amounts of money that are involved in the cohesion policy are of considerable size and the EU has to satisfy its contributors that they are well spent. This is the principle of *accountability*. So the EU has to show the effectiveness of its actions through evaluation of the results and the use of its means in a coherent set.

We will first deal with *evaluation* (Chapter 10). In this part we will describe how the EU has devised standard methods for evaluating systematically its cohesion efforts. These involve checking whether results correspond to targets, whether instruments have had the expected effectiveness and whether the human and financial resources have been efficiently used. The effectiveness of the EU cohesion policy is not easy to establish due to lack of specification of targets and numerous methodological and data problems. We will deal with the way in which practical solutions to these problems have been found. A general conclusion from this evaluation of the *effectiveness* of the policy is difficult to establish, but we will find that a positive effect is very plausible. We will also review studies as to the *efficiency* (ratio outputs to inputs) and find a satisfactory situation; indeed the delivery of the cohesion policy entails high cost.

12 *Introduction*

Next we deal with the problem of *coherence* (Chapter 11). We will show that the EU has gradually acquired competences in a whole series of fields. Starting with its core competence 'market integration' it has moved in areas such as macro and monetary environment, etc. These policies can have a positive, a neutral or a negative effect on cohesion. We will analyse for each of these policies the way in which they have influenced cohesion and the end effect on cohesion. We will show that overall their beneficial effects on cohesion are not sufficient to make a cohesion policy superfluous. We will show moreover that some had a clear negative impact on cohesion. In the course of the past decades most of these policies have been redesigned so as to minimize their possible negative effects. At present the effects seem on balance neutral.

1.4.6 The sixth stage: drawing lessons from the past and preparing the future

The final part of this book is devoted to the last part of the policy cycle: drawing lessons from the past that can help to shape the *future*. In the last chapter (Chapter 12) we thereby move from a mainly descriptive, positive analysis towards a more predictive, normative approach.

We will do several types of analysis in this respect. First, we detail by stage of the cycle the main lessons. Next we speculate somewhat on the likely development of the EU as an organization in terms of deepening (more areas of competence) and widening (more countries). We will show how lessons from the past can be used to shape the future of the EU. Actually these lessons may be relevant for other countries and integration areas as well. For that reason we will finally give some experiences of the EU that may help the shaping of an effective and efficient cohesion policy for other countries.

1.5 Summary and conclusions

- Cohesion is an elusive concept. It has been made operational by selecting and defining indicators of disparity. Less disparity means more cohesion; more disparity means less cohesion.
- The EU has gradually extended its competences and its geographical coverage. In step therewith it has developed a very elaborate cohesion policy. This policy integrates the aspects of economic, social and territorial cohesion.
- The EU cohesion policy follows the standard *policy cycle* in which one distinguishes the following stages:
  1. awareness of problem;
  2. design of policy system;
  3. defining of objectives and elaborating appropriate instruments;
  4. delivery of the policy through programmes and projects;
  5. checking (evaluation) of effectiveness and consistency; and finally
  6. drawing lessons and giving suggestions for improvement.

Stage I
Assessing the problems and identifying their causes

2 Disparities: general

2.1 Introduction

Cohesion is usually measured with its negative; the lack of cohesion, in turn measured by the size of disparities. So the development over time of the degree of cohesion and thereby the answer to the key policy question: Has cohesion been improved or has it deteriorated? is usually measured by the development of the disparity in wealth levels between member countries, social groups and regions. Wealth also is an elusive concept. Many indicators have been tried out to measure it. They all have certain advantages and disadvantages. We will use GDP/P levels, the most usual indicator. So cohesion is said to improve in case disparities in GDP/P levels decrease and vice versa. The analysis will allow us to answer at a later stage two questions:

1   Which are the type of regions that show a poor situation with respect to the EU mean or a poor performance in terms of convergence and hence where policy action is needed?
2   Does the system tend to convergence and hence can policy focus on supporting natural tendencies or does the system tend to divergence and do policy makers face an uphill fight?

The present chapter is set up as follows: the first part is devoted to the analysis of the *theory of wealth distribution*. We will review the schools that have constructed theories that either lead to convergence (less disparity) or divergence (more disparity). We will identify the determinant factors for either development. Paramount among these are structural features that can only be changed in the long term.

Next we move to the results of *empirical research*. Given the long-term character of the problem we will describe very long-term trends. The first section will deal with the trends that prevailed up to the end of the Second World War. The following two sections will deal with the developments of GDP per head levels since the Second World War, both on national and regional levels.

The chapter will be rounded off with a brief summary of the findings.

2.2 Concepts and indicators

2.2.1 Policy-relevant concepts and definitions

The basic concepts about cohesion have been given already in the previous chapter. We recall here briefly that cohesion is understood to exist in case the disparities in social and economic welfare between different regions and social groups are politically and socially tolerable. Cohesion improves when disparities decrease. This is generally called convergence. The opposite occurs when disparities increase. This is called divergence.[1] Convergence is thought to prevail when the wealth levels of the different countries, regions or social groups (generally measured by income per head levels) tend to evolve towards the mean of the group to which they belong. In Figure 2.1 this is represented by the downward-sloping curve that indicates average percentage growth rates that are lower the higher the initial level of income per head. Divergence is the opposite; here the differences between the members of the group increase. In Figure 2.1 it is represented by an upward-sloping curve, the growth rates being higher the higher the initial income per head level.[2]

Several statistical indicators exist to measure degrees of convergence and divergence.[3] These indicators measure the differences between the elements of a set. However, in policy terms the notion of convergence relates in particular to the catching up of the poor with the rich, or at least with the medium. To that end one needs to study the trajectories of individual elements of the set.

2.2.2 Operational indicators

The most used indicator of disparities is the GDP per head, usually of population, sometimes (in case one wants to put the accent on productivity rather

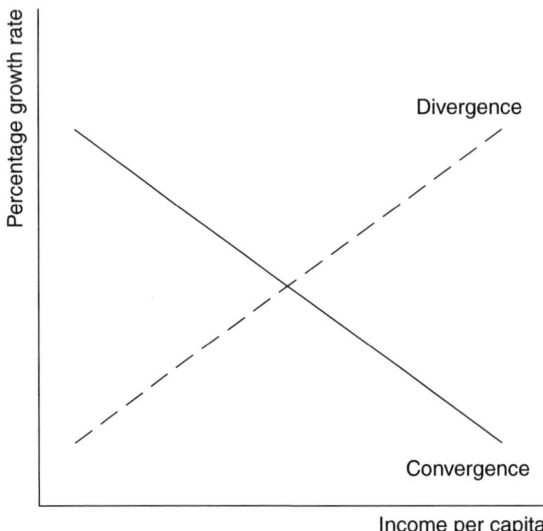

Figure 2.1 Convergence and divergence

than wealth) per employed person. Now this choice is not without drawbacks. One problem with GDP/P figures is that the monetary valuation of income categories may hide important aspects of the real situation. Several attempts (e.g. the set up of quality of life indicators) have been made to capture non-monetary aspects. One can thereby distinguish between two approaches:

- *Objective indicators*. These are factors that are assumed to determine welfare, such as income, health, education, housing, number of passenger cars, telephones, television sets or doctors per 1,000 inhabitants.
- *Subjective indicators*. These are established by asking people what they feel about their situation; that is whether they feel happy, or how they would describe their degree of life satisfaction.

Objective indicators tend to be highly correlated with GDP per head figures (Giannis et al., 1999). Subjective indicators on the contrary appeared to be fairly insensitive to variations in objective social economic conditions. Recent research on international differences among European countries (Fahey and Smyth, 2004) has changed that picture; it shows that there is a positive relation between on the one hand the mean life satisfaction and on the other hand the level and growth of wealth (as measured by GDP per head and the recent growth of GDP per head). In other words, populations in the rich parts of Europe have high and relatively equal life satisfaction, while those in the poorer parts of Europe have low and unequal life satisfaction.

Given these results and given the fact that the level of GDP per head is also highly correlated with a number of other aspects of cohesion,[4] it seems justified to take GDP/P as the main indicator of cohesion.[5]

2.3 Theory: convergence or divergence?

2.3.1 Convergence

The *convergence school* is of rather neo-classical inspiration. It assumes that markets do work efficiently.[6] There are different strands that we will shortly describe. First, we will give our attention to theories that discuss development on the national and international level.[7]

The theory of *international relations* holds that economic (market) integration through increased movements of products (goods, services) and production factors (labour, capital) tends to equalize factor returns and, hence, incomes. For instance migration of workers will bring equalization of wages. Capital movement through FDI in low-wage countries will increase the demand for labour and increase productivity. Multinational firms will transfer technology and management practices to low-wage countries, thereby increasing the capacity to sustain higher wages. National governments of these countries will match this with investments in training of labour and infrastructure. In other words, the economic process leads to convergence of income levels and hence wealth levels. The outcome of such models depends on many assumptions; the most

18 *Assessing the problems and identifying causes*

important being that markets function properly and that there are no impediments to movements.

Even in the absence of such factor movements, convergence may occur as the *theory of equalization of factor returns*[8] demonstrates. Openness to goods trade will lead to international specialization, which will in turn change the demand for production factors. In the relatively poor country demand will shift to the abundant factor labour and away from the scarce factor capital, which will lead to an equalization of wages (and hence income levels).

The theory about *growth*[9] states that production is characterized by diminishing returns. Marginal additions of units of capital will add less to total factor productivity in countries with abundant capital and a high level of income than in countries with a low level of income. So, rich countries tend to have lower growth rates than poor countries. Some other economic mechanisms tend to reinforce this tendency towards convergence. High wages based on high productivity in the export sector tend to increase the cost of locally produced goods, like houses and many services, like leisure. Countries with lower labour cost and a spatial structure that can be easily adapted to new opportunities have a competitive advantage over the high-cost countries leading to their higher catching up.

Transposing the neo-classical theory from international to *interregional relations*, one finds the following approaches.

Theories putting the accent on the *regional mobility of production factors* show that if wages are higher in the developed regions, labour will migrate from the less developed regions to the higher developed ones. Consequently, labour will become scarce in the first and abundant in the latter type of region, triggering a downward or an upward movement of wages. On the other hand, if wages and the marginal product of capital are inversely correlated, capital will move to labour-intensive sectors in low-wage regions, diminishing the trend for labour to migrate outwards. Thus economic growth would lead to convergence (poor regions catching up with rich ones).

The theory about *export-led inter-regional growth differences* takes again the openness of product markets as a point of departure. The expansion of a region's exports (relative to those of other regions) would lead to an expansion in the demand for factors supplies, the price of which will be bid up relative to those in other regions. This should encourage a fall in the region's rate of productivity growth, a decline in the competitiveness of the region's exports, as well as capital movements to lower-price regions.

Regional *growth models* often take the elements of openness of markets into account but add to these *geographical features that influence the location of economic activity*. Thus, just as neoclassical economists' primary analytical concept is the 'production function', linking a firm's (or nation's) output to key factor endowments (labour, capital and technology), so economic geographers saw the geography of production in terms of a 'location function' in which the location of economic activity was to be explained in terms of the geographical distribution of key 'locational endowments' (availability of natural resources, labour supplies, access to markets and so on). On the one hand, firms search for regions with a profile that matches, as well as possible, their requirements. On the other hand, regions 'compete' with one another to attract economic activity on the basis of their comparative endowments with 'locational factors'. Convergence comes about as the very success of regions as a location gradually deteriorates its position. High congestion costs tend to put a break on the further development of urban regions.

A theory that has both been operationalized on the country and the region level is the theory of *the life-cycle of the product*. It distinguishes four stages in the life of each product: (1) introduction, (2) expansion, (3) saturation and (4) decline. At each stage in this cycle, the companies that produce the product have different preferences as to their location. In the first stage they will need nearness to innovation so tend to locate in the most developed countries and regions; in the later stages they mainly seek low-cost locations hence will tend to locate in the less developed countries and regions.[10] This model can produce convergence. This is realized by poor countries and regions absorbing, gradually, the skills and know-how by benefiting from direct investment that develops production at the middle stages of a product's life-cycle. This permits these countries to develop, gradually, their own research and innovation and to upgrade the quality of the production, at the same time increasing the capacity of their productive system to sustain high wages and high profits.

Most of these theories have already been developed some time ago. In recent years interesting new developments have, however, been made to refine these theories. A number of concepts have been integrated into a new generation of (regional) growth and convergence models. The *new growth models* (see Aghion et al., 1999; Barro, 1997) incorporate such factors as education, good governance, etc., that stimulate economic growth. Convergence occurs when countries that were poorly endowed with such factors upgrade them. The fundamental tendency towards convergence (based on decreasing returns) is then reinforced by these growth factors (e.g. Barro and Sala-I-Martin, 1995).[11]

In *practice* not only convergence occurs, but also divergence. Can convergence theories also accommodate divergence? The answer is yes; divergence can occur because the assumptions on which the neo-classical theory bases itself are not fulfilled in practice, due to restrictive practices of private actors or to distortions of the market mechanism by public intervention. For instance, because (a) adaptation takes time; (b) mobility of factors of production is impeded; (c) free competition and entry are impeded by collusive practices of firms; (d) resources are not exploited in full; (e) technology is not easily transferable from one region to another, etc. So, for all those reasons the outcome of convergence cannot be taken for granted.

2.3.2 Divergence

The *divergence school* maintains that the system has built-in tendencies towards more disequilibrium. Technology and innovation together with scale economies play an important part in the divergence theories. The theories generally assume that factors like the cost of bridging spatial distance and overcoming differences in language and institutional factors inhibit factor (notably labour) movements. The divergence mechanisms apply on both the international and the interregional level.

The most well-known strand of these theories is that called *cumulative causation* (Myrdal, 1956, 1957). A system characterized by large initial disparities and the free play of market and social forces will tend towards an increasingly unbalanced development. This can be observed on the level of countries and regions. It is also relevant in an urban rural context (e.g. Perroux, 1955), where large urban centres tend to grow and areas with a deficient urban infrastructure tend to decline (polarization).

The *life-cycle of the product* can also lead to divergence. Advanced (core) countries or regions can perpetuate the gap separating them from backward (peripheral) ones by attracting to themselves in each new cycle the high-value products of that cycle, leaving to peripheral regions only those products that are in their maturity stage of the cycle; the production of which sustains only low incomes. The gap can even be accentuated in case the core manages to also keep the medium products for a long time within its borders, for instance through mechanization and automation.

Factor movements reinforce the tendency; highly qualified labour, not finding sufficient employment in peripheral regions, will migrate to the centre and so will capital. Thus labour tends to move to areas with the best career potential, in other words where the investment in human capital is likely to give the highest rewards (in general already developed regions) (Vernon, 1979; Hirsch, 1974). The technological advance of certain countries implies that they will always specialize in products with high value added that sustain high wages. Thus the wage gap that accompanies the technology gap is not only perpetuated, but even accentuated. The expectation of a continuation of this trend may lead to a situation where the expected returns on labour and capital are higher in the centre than in the periphery with the consequence that labour and capital will continue to flow from the latter to the former (Krugman, 1979). Government policy may consider that the returns to public investment in central regions are much higher than in others. So they will reinforce existing disequilibria. This may come to the point where government even stimulates the out-migration of people from regions with very poor potential to regions with high potential.

Some theories on growth reinforce these arguments and point to further cumulative effects. One is *economic integration* that implies exposing the country's economy to stronger international competition, which leads to increased movements of goods and factors.[12] Another set of developments concern *increasing returns models* (e.g. Romer, 1986). They recognize that many economic activities are subject to increasing returns to scale, and that many regions benefit from agglomeration economies (joint location of linked economic activities) and urbanization economies (location in an area with many and varied urban services, like education, leisure, R&D, etc.).[13] As a result rich developed regions tend to produce competitive advantages for the firms located there, leading to faster growth there than in lower level income regions with deficient infrastructure and limited economies of agglomeration and urbanization. The effect is of course divergence.

How can convergence, observed *in practice*, be explained under the divergence model? The answer lies in the weaknesses of the drivers of divergence such as economies of scale. Some products and services are not subject to economies of scale. Some production technologies require locations that are provided outside traditional centres (e.g. aircraft production and testing). Preferences of location of key groups of labour (e.g. well-educated labour is likely to go to places where leisure and quality of the environment are particularly good). These may lead to departures from the divergence model.

2.3.3 Consecutive divergence and convergence

There is much to be said for, and against, the theories of both convergence and divergence of national and regional wealth levels. So, they may very well turn out to be specific cases of a more general theory. Some have worked at a synthesis by assuming that divergence and convergence between groups and regions (countries) occur in a specific sequence; so consecutively.

The theories are concerned with the very long-term growth pattern.[14] The point of departure of these theories is the stage concept (Williamson, 1965). A country at an early stage of development will show a tendency towards more regional inequality because at that stage the Myrdalian divergence effects (described in the previous section) are likely to predominate. However, as growth proceeds and countries enter stages of higher economic development, the 'classical' mechanisms of convergence can be expected to regain strength and inequality is likely to level off. Finally, in highly developed economies, the market mechanisms are likely to function better, leading to more equality.[15] Moreover, transfer mechanisms attenuate much of the inequality in the distribution of primary income. However, for the highest stages, one may expect again divergence as liberal forces tend to be dominant (e.g. Amos, 1988).

How does the theory relate to *practice*? The diachronic or stage approach has been very popular, probably because it nicely accommodates both the convergence and the divergence schools of thought. The former finds its thesis confirmed as soon as the conditions are met,[16] the latter believes that conditions for convergence take a long time to fulfil and hence divergence will be with us for a long time to come. Moreover, the diachronic approach leaves ample room to the pragmatists (who observe the developments in practice); if the statistical indicators show convergence, they conclude that the country has entered the stage of developed nation; if divergence predominates, they conclude it is still at an infant stage of development. However, the approach has also aroused serious critics. The main criticism is that the stages have never been well dated and documented for groups of countries, nor has a satisfactory and systematic explanation been found for the fact that nations and regions apparently starting from similar positions nevertheless follow different development rhythms and paths (Aydalot, 1985).

2.3.4 Simultaneous convergence and divergence

The uncertainties that are left by answers to the basic question given by the three schools mentioned up until now have been resolved by a number of scholars that assume that, actually, convergence and divergence will occur at the same time. The system is thought to be essentially indeterminate.[17] The outcome of the processes depends on the balance between two opposing forces in practical circumstances that may differ very much over time and space.

- On the one hand we have centrifugal forces that tend to spread economic development to regions that initially are poorly developed and hence lead to convergence. Among these forces the diffusion of technological and organizational knowledge takes pride of place.
- On the other hand we have centripetal forces that favour central regions and hence divergence; we mention in particular the agglomeration advantages that central locations tend to provide.

The theoretical underpinnings of this view come from several strands of thought.

New growth theory identifies as determinants of differential growth differences in market access, human capital, technological change, international competitiveness, economies of scale, public infrastructure, institutional efficiency, etc.[18] Some regions and countries succeed in mastering good combinations of these factors and grow, others fail to do so and lag behind.[19]

Endogenous growth theory tries to explain why some economies have succeeded and others have failed. The key assumption of endogenous growth theory is that accumulation of knowledge generates increasing returns. Knowledge and know-how are not disseminated instantly – not between nations, regions, sectors or companies – but need to be acquired. This means that one has to account for market failures: markets do not necessarily yield an optimal result. Endogenous growth models[20] build upon the standard neo-classical growth model, but allow the possibility of non-diminishing returns to scale by making endogenous improvements to human capital and technological change. In a regional context, inflows of labour into a growth region are likely to be of the more skilled and enterprising workers, thus adding to the general quality of the region's stock of human capital and its productivity. In addition, technological spill-over appears to be geographically localized, so that once a region acquires a relative advantage in terms of innovation and technological advance, it is likely to be sustained over long periods of time.

New economic geography models of international trade and of growth can produce both convergence and divergence in the system. The decrease of transport cost combined with increasing returns to scale would lead to concentration of these economic activities in central regions, with negative consequences for the periphery. However, in case these factors are weak, and depending on hypotheses concerning the mobility of production factors, the opposite tendency may occur.[21]

The simultaneity school seems to come very close to the reality that one can observe *in practice*. Indeed, the considerable body of literature on the causes of differential national and regional development does account for a large variety of development paths.[22] Much depends on the initial situation, the capacity of

Disparities 23

regions to adapt, the growth effects of integration on all regions, etc.[23] So, the new theoretical constructs show an indeterminate system producing a fan of possible outcomes of remarkable diversity.

2.3.5 An overview

As evidenced in the previous sections there is a very wide and diversified fan of theoretical approaches. The main aspects of the various strands of theory discussed can be briefly summarized as follows (see Table 2.1).

2.4 Some history

2.4.1 National disparities up to 1950

As the theoretical analysis does not give a clear indication as to the likely development of the system, we turn to empirical analysis to see how things have worked out in practice. We will first turn to the very long-term trends.

Some 2,000 years ago, the disparities between the richer and the poorer parts of Europe were quite the opposite from the one we know today. The Mediterranean Basin was then considered in economic, technical and cultural terms the most developed part of Europe. In the Middle Ages and the Renaissance, the 'centre' of Europe was still in the Mediterranean (Venice, Genoa and the

Table 2.1 Summary view of theoretical approaches

	Convergence (C)	*Divergence (D)*	*Consecutive C–D*	*Simultaneous C–D*
Inspiration	Neo-classical (growth and trade)	Marxist	Stages	New economic geography; endogenous history
Basic tendency	Spread	Concentration polarization	First concentration, next spread	Indeterminate
Markets	Efficient	Deficient	Alternate	Monopolistic competition
Technology	Decreasing returns to scale	Increasing returns to scale	Pragmatic	Increasing returns to scale; transport cost
Dynamics	Catch up and fall back	Cumulative causation	Changing private and public preferences	Survival of fittest
Policy	Stimulating growth factors and efficient working of markets	Focus on highest returns on public investment in education; infrastructure, etc.	First strong bias on efficiency; next support for equity	Simultaneous stimulation of competitiveness in all regions; concentration of efforts on laggards

developing Spanish and Portuguese empires). However, economic activity shifted to the North, particularly to Flanders, later to Holland and England. The spatial configuration was upset by the Industrial Revolution, which fundamentally transformed the European economy. Remarkably, the Industrial Revolution got off the ground in a peripheral country of eighteenth-century Europe. Historians tend to explain that phenomenon by an institutional rather than a geographical factor. In their view, the critical factor in the emergence of leading economic powers in general, and the UK in particular, was the fixing of economic rights which gave private economic actors confidence in their capacity to capture future benefits of present risky undertakings (North and Thomas, 1973; North, 1991).

The Industrial Revolution went hand in hand with increased international trade. GDP/P growth figures, that up until that moment had been very low (a fraction of a per cent per year before the Industrial Revolution), rose to 2 to 3 per cent a year in the last part of the eighteenth and the major part of the nineteenth century. This led, however, to very unequal growth patterns. On balance there was an increase in disparity between European countries that was the result of three trends:

- The UK kept a paramount place with an income per capita above that of the other European countries; intermediate countries (Benelux, France and Germany) caught up in relative terms with the leading country, the UK.
- Mediterranean countries (Greece, Italy, Spain and Portugal) failed to take full part in the industrialization process and fell behind the rest. Detailed analysis of the factors determining national growth performances shows that the late development of these countries seems due to the lack of resources (natural and human) and bad economic (and military) institutions and policy rather than distance to the European core or exposure to external competition.
- Eastern Europe failed to develop; here the reasons are manifold but institutional factors seem to have played as large a role as lack of resource endowment or geographical distance.

As a consequence the centre periphery dichotomy in Europe is defined as a West–East rather than a North–South difference; indeed, in Eastern Europe, incomes were in general even lower than in the Mediterranean countries.[24] The various countries of Eastern Europe continued to have difficulties in keeping up with the developments in Western Europe during the period between the two world wars (so adding to divergence) (see, for example, Aldcroft and Morewood, 1995).

In Western Europe a major question has been whether the *development of international economic integration has influenced disparity* either in a positive (convergence) or negative way (divergence). To answer that question we have to measure the evolution of disparities and of the degree of integration and compare the two.

The study of the quantitative aspects of the long-term evolution of *national disparities* for the western part of Europe is hampered by data limitations. For a zone that is approximately comparable to the EU of 12 as it existed in 1990 we

Table 2.2 Integration and wealth disparity indicators in Western Europe, 1830-1950

	1830	1860	1913	1920	1929	1938	1950
Disparity[a]	0.14	0.32	0.60	n.a.	0.53	n.a.	0.77
Trade (as a % of GDP)[b]	n.a.	10	14	9	10	6	n.a.
Average protection (tariff) level[c]	n.a.	1	2	2	2	7	n.a.

Notes:
a Own calculations of the Theil entropy index based on data in Bairoch (1976). The higher the index the higher the disparity.
b Based on data (average value of imports and exports) in Mitchell (1981).
c Based on Messerlin and Becuwe (1986).

have calculated disparities of wealth differences among countries between 1830 and 1950 (see first row in Table 2.2). The table shows that disparities have gradually increased, notably up to 1913. The inter-war period (up to 1929) showed a slight decrease in disparity, which was due to the intermediate countries' further catch-up and the stabilization of the relative wealth level of the Mediterranean countries.

The next problem is the *measurement of integration*. We have done this with the help of two indicators: trade as a percentage of GDP and the decrease in protection measured by average tariffs. In the 1830-60 period, increasing industrialization led to progressive economic integration, which was manifest from the growth of trade based on international specialization. Depression slowed down the growth of trade to a sluggish pace between 1870 and 1914. The First World War interrupted the integration tendency, which was resumed afterwards on a lower level. The recession of the 1930s dealt another blow to integration (row 2 of Table 2.2). National solutions were resorted to, based on short-term economic thinking (unemployment) and military thinking (autarky was believed to be safer than interdependency). That tendency was reflected in the upsurge of protectionist measures. After a long period of relatively stable average tariff protection in most European countries, tariffs soared, increasing almost fourfold in the 1930s. Moreover, non-tariff protection rose, both in the period immediately following the First World War and in the 1930s (row 3 of Table 2.2).

The comparison of the data on economic integration and wealth disparity among European countries leads to a clear *conclusion*. Disparity rises when integration advances, and drops when integration lets up. A more detailed look at the underlying figures shows that the decline in disparity in the period between the world wars resulted from the drop in per capita income in the more affluent countries, which were hit harder than others by the downturn of the economic cycle and the ensuing protectionism in many countries.

2.4.2 Regional disparity up to 1950

Disparities among European regions are our next object of study. While international integration went through ups and downs, the integration of regions in a national economy seems to have increased steadily owing to technological (transport, communication) as well as institutional factors (centralization, unification, bureaucracy). Economic history has had some difficulty of getting to grips with the study of systems of regions; it is traditionally oriented towards either national development or to local history (Timar, 1992). However, the research by economic historians can provide a picture of the pattern of regional development in many European countries during the nineteenth century – the period of industrialization – and the early twentieth century. In this historical period the presently available sophisticated regional account statistics did not yet exist. So the various studies use a variety of indicators of economic and social cohesions such as relative wealth levels, wages or literacy. Most highlight the role of economic and geographical factors (ports, coal) for income distribution, but some put the accent on institutional factors (e.g. Chor, 2005), notably the role of property. Cities that exercised stronger institutional protection of private property experienced higher levels of both skilled and unskilled wages as well as lower inequality as measured by the skilled:unskilled ratio.

As few other Europe-wide studies exist we have to turn to evidence on a country by country basis. Annex 2.1 gives a review of the relevant studies.[25]

The *conclusion* of these analyses is that on the regional level both convergence and divergence of wealth levels have occurred. For the whole of the west European area, however, it seems as if, on balance, divergence has occurred. Spatial patterns of growth seem to depend most on political factors, e.g. internal peripheralization occurred in many countries only when conditions were organized by the government to the advantage of people living in the centre (Nolte, 1991). However, even here, there is no determinism; lagging regions have been shown to be able, at any stage, to develop their economy by making use of the transfer of technology and capital as well as their physical and human resources. Some regions have even developed by effectively turning a distance barrier to their advantage (Pollard, 1981).

2.5 National disparities

2.5.1 The present situation

The enlarged EU is confronted with considerable differences in wealth levels (see Figure 2.2).

The figure clearly indicates that there are mainly three groups of countries.

1. *Above average countries.* These are all in the northwest of Europe. The differences in levels of development between the members of the first group are very low.
2. *Below average countries.* This is a group that consists of the three western (Mediterranean) countries and the two most developed new member states.
3. *Far below average countries.* This third group consists of the NMSs with all GDP/P levels considerably below the EU average. Bulgaria and Romania are even significantly below the average of this group.

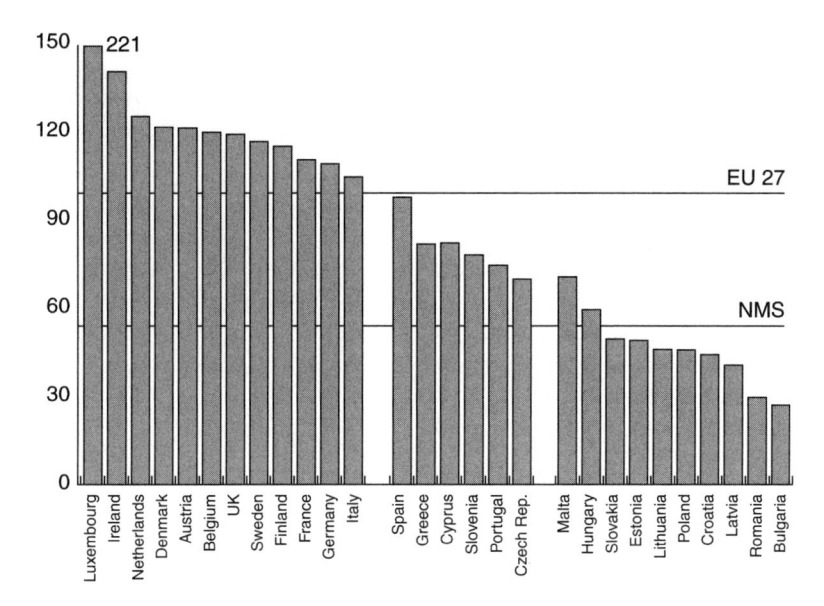

Figure 2.2 Differences in GDP/P by country, 2004
Source: Database Eurostat

The differences between the groups are considerably larger than they used to be with previous extensions of the EU. The extension with three Mediterranean countries in the eighties did introduce some disparity between member states (compare groups 1 and 2). However, the present round of extension introduced much higher internal disparities in income per head level. For illustration: the gap between the average of the EU and the Iberian countries at the time of their accession was about 30 per cent while today the gap between the average of the EU 15 and the NMSs is 60 per cent.

2.5.2 Past evolution

Many were afraid that European integration (by opening up markets) would lead to divergence. Others were rather of the view that it would help convergence. In the 1970s much uncertainty persisted as to which tendency actually dominated. So, better empirical evidence was needed. In a pioneering study we (Molle et al., 1980) showed that in the first decades of European integration disparities actually decreased.[26] Later studies for a wider integration area (Molle and Boeckhout, 1995) confirmed the tendency of convergence. Due to the accession of the Mediterranean countries the disparities did of course increase, but this was a one time statistical effect. Once in the EU countries like Portugal, Spain and Ireland have actually been able to catch up with the average of the EU.[27]

An idea of the *evolution of the GDP/P levels of European countries* is given in Table 2.3. The table shows, first, that immediately after the Second World War, some Western European countries were rather poor (Portugal, Greece and

Table 2.3 Development of GDP/P (EU = 100), by country, 1950–2004

Country	1950 €ᵃ	1990 €ᵃ	2000 €	2004 €	1990 PPP	2000 PPP	2004 PPP
Germanyᵇ	93	125	127	120	116	113	109
France	136	111	120	119	109	115	111
Italy	71	101	102	104	102	111	105
The Netherlands	100	100	128	135	100	121	125
Belgium	166	104	122	122	105	116	119
Luxembourg	201	149	245	253	150	217	223
UK	140	89	135	129	99	114	119
Denmark	153	132	162	161	104	126	122
Ireland	81	71	139	164	74	127	141
Spain	35	69	79	88	77	93	99
Portugal	35	37	60	58	61	80	73
Greece	30	43	57	67	58	72	82
Austria	58	109	133	130	105	127	122
Sweden	170	142	148	139	108	119	116
Finland	114	143	128	128	102	114	115
EU 15	**100**	**100**	**115**	**114**	**100**	**110**	**109**
Poland			24	23		46	47
Czech Rep.			30	38		65	70
Hungary			25	36		53	61
Slovakia			21	28		47	52
Slovenia			52	58		73	78
Lithuania			18	23		38	48
Cyprus			72	75		86	82
Latvia			18	22		35	43
Estonia			22	30		43	51
Malta			54	48		77	71
Bulgaria			13	8		38	23
Romania			15	8		36	24
EU 27			**100**	**100**		**100**	**100**
North	120	111	129	126	107	115	115
South	53	80	86	91	86	98	98
East			22	22		46	45
CoV	50	33	68	67	23	45	45

Notes:
PPP = purchasing power parities.
a Estimate.
b In 2000, inclusive of former DDR.

Sources: OECD National Account Statistics, several years; Eurostat, National Accounts (ESA) Review, several years; Statistics in Focus 1996/5. National figures on GDP made comparable with exchange rate figures; EC, European Economy, No. 70, 2000, Tables 8 and 9.

Spain, to a lesser extent Italy, and initially also Germany) while others (Belgium, Denmark, the UK and France) were relatively well off. The table shows next that these disparities have decreased considerably in the 1950–2000 period.

So one can draw here as a major conclusion that on the national level convergence prevailed. This was due to two developments:

- Member countries with an income level below the EU average, notably the so-called cohesion countries (less than 75 per cent of EU GDP/P), showed above average growth rates. The total of these countries grew by 3 per cent a year, the total of the EU by about 2 per cent (EC, 2004a).
- Rich member countries (GDP/P levels above the EU mean) such as Belgium and the UK showed below average growth rates.[28]

A case to highlight is Ireland that has successfully fought its way into the league of above average countries over the past decades. The three Mediterranean countries that joined in the 1980s have all adapted their industrial structure by taking advantage of the access to markets that the EU offered and by attracting FDI. This much resembles the development path of Italy about a decade earlier. The accession of the NMSs has drastically changed the situation. Their wealth levels are significantly below those in the West. This thus leads to a one-time statistical effect of increase in disparity.

In the bottom part of the table we give the evolution of the averages of the three broad geographical areas; the North, the South and the East. The growth of the North has been relatively slow; which contributed to lesser disparities. The catching up of the second (Mediterranean) group with the average of the EU 27 is now complete, although quite important deficits in wealth levels of some countries (e.g. Portugal) still persist.

The picture, as given up until now, shows very stark differences. These have to be corrected for a number of specificities of GDP as an indicator of relative wealth levels. Indeed GDP per capita has indeed a *number of drawbacks*:

- First, it does not take into account that the *cost of living* is quite different in different countries and regions. It means that the same euro can buy more wealth in one country than in another. In order to correct for this difference so-called purchasing power parities (PPP) have been calculated. GDP figures corrected for PPP have been given in the last three columns of Table 2.3. As one sees, they tend to attenuate the differences in wealth.
- Second, GDP does *not measure all production and income creation*. Some elements are excluded by definition, so we will not go into that here (e.g. the value of work that is done by housewives). Other elements are not included because they have escaped registration. That is the case for the so-called black, grey, shadow or underground economy. They comprise both illegal activities (such as drugs trade and prostitution), and legal activities that have not been reported to avoid taxes (fairly common in construction). The underground economy is much more important in low-income countries than in highly developed countries. Recent studies (Schneider, 2003) estimate that it was about 15 per cent in the countries of the North, 25 per cent in those of the South and 30 per cent in those of the East. The implication is of course that absolute differences in wealth are less outspoken than the GDP/P figures indicate.

In Table 2.3 the detailed picture, with data by country, permits one to analyse convergence/divergence tendencies, but fails to capture these tendencies in one indicator of disparity. As such we use the coefficient of variation (applied to the figures in the upper part of the table it produces the figures given in the bottom part of the table). These figures leave no room for doubt; they show a significant decrease in disparity over the study period for the EU 15. This decrease has been steady all over the period, as data for intermediate decennial benchmark years show (Molle and Boeckhout, 1995).

2.5.3 Time needed for catching up

The major differences in wealth between countries, regions and social groups are associated with long-standing structural differences, such as deficient levels of education or infrastructure. Changing such factors takes time. The time lag needed for catching up is dependent on two factors (see Table 2.4): the difference in wealth level at the outset (per cent with respect to the EU mean) and the difference in growth rate during the catching-up period (per cent points difference with mean EU growth rate).

The NMSs are more or less around the level of 50 per cent of the EU 27 average (see Figure 2.3 and Table 2.3). Over the past decade their growth rates have in general been several percentage points above the one of the mature economies of the developed northwestern part of the EU. One sees from the upper line of Table 2.4 that if this differential can be maintained over a prolonged period, the catching-up process of the NMSs will take about a generation. This may look long to some but it is realistic by historical standards. Some doubt whether the NMSs may indeed outperform the old member states for such a prolonged period and with a significant margin. However, the experience of the southern cohesion countries, such as Portugal, Spain and Greece (see Table 2.3) has shown that such a process is indeed feasible.

2.6 Regional disparities

2.6.1 The present situation

The differences between member states are very significant as we have shown in the previous section. However, within member states very big differences exist

Table 2.4 Catch-up time (in years) for different levels of initial disparity (level in % of target) and differential in growth rates (%)

Level/growth	1	2	3	4
50	71	36	24	18
60	52	26	18	13
70	36	18	12	9
80	22	12	8	6
90	10	5	4	3

Source: Adapted from Vaneecloo (2005).

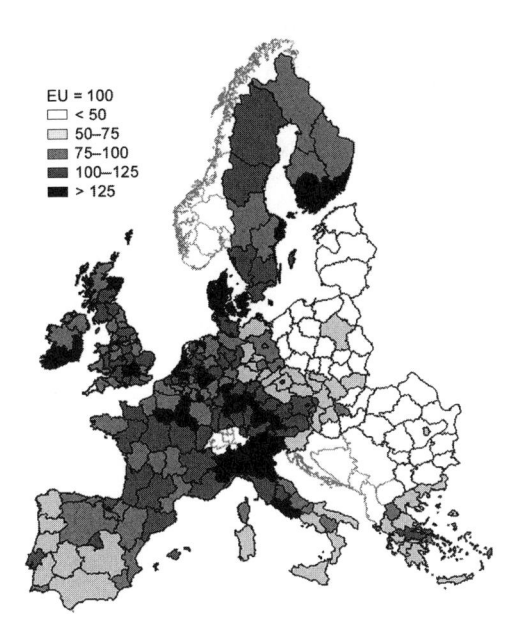

Figure 2.3 Differences in GDP/P by region, 2001

which means that the overall differences between the wealth levels of the regions of the enlarged EU are indeed very significant (Figure 2.3).

The map shows that within the poorest countries there are regions that are even worse off than the national average of the country to which they belong; an example is the Eastern border regions of Poland. On the other hand, one sees that certain urban regions in member states in the rich northwest have income levels that considerably exceed the national average (for instance Paris). So the regional disparity in the EU (measured by the ratio of the two extremes) far exceeds the national disparity. The present disparity of the regions with respect to their national level and the EU level is given in Figure 2.4.

The disparity measured in terms of ratio between extremes has much increased due to the latest enlargement. The ten least-favoured regions in EU 15 had a wealth level that was only one-third of that of the ten 'richest' (measured in GDP per head, but also by level of infrastructure, capital endowment and so on). Now the same ratio exists not between the ten poorest regions and the ten richest, but between the ten poorest and the EU 27 average.

2.6.2 Evolution of the regional disparities: convergence or divergence?[29]

At the start of the EU there was much concern about the possibility of a *divergence* in wealth levels. There were few who believed that the convergence tendencies would prevail. Again the dispute could only be settled by empirical analysis.[30]

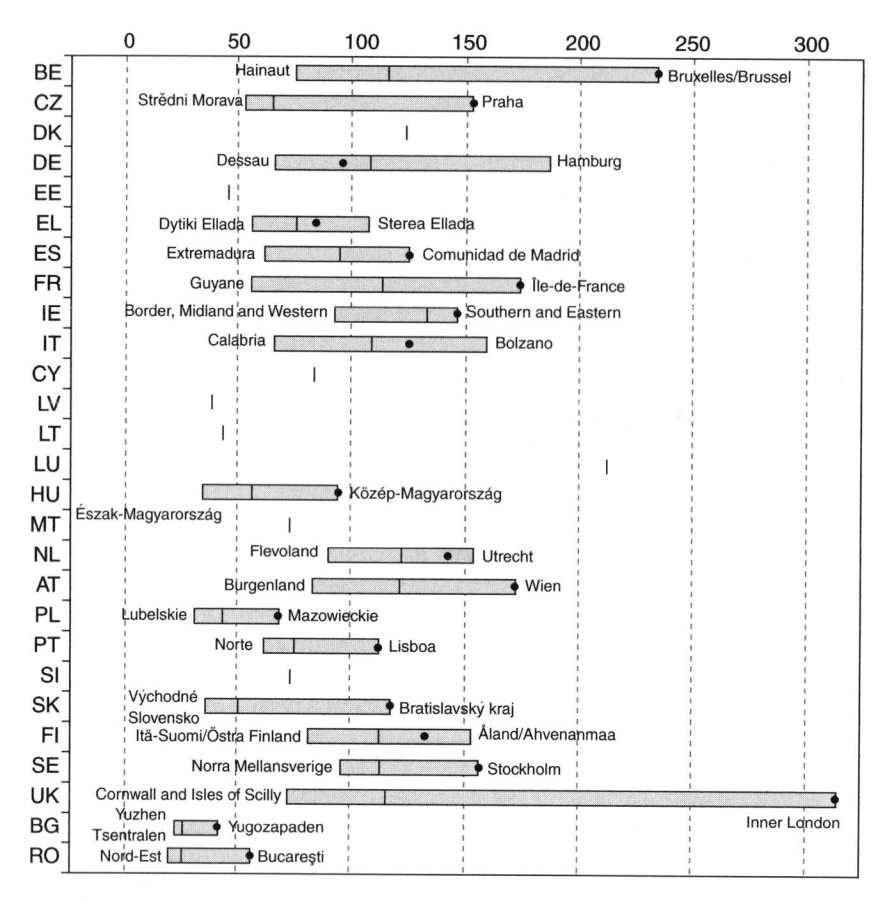

32 *Assessing the problems and identifying causes*

| Average of all areas of the country
• Capital city area of the country

Figure 2.4 Regional extremes in GDP/P (PPS) by country, 2000
Source: Eurostat

We can illustrate the evolution with Table 2.5. Here we use Theil entropy indices to measure the evolution of total disparity. The choice of this index allows us to decompose disparity in a national and a regional component. The lower the Theil index, the lower the disparity. The figures of Table 2.3 show that convergence prevailed in the early decades of the existence of the EU. Indeed, the disparity between all Western European regions decreased considerably over the third quarter of the previous century, after that more diverse patterns can be observed.[31] Convergence of regional income levels seems however, to have levelled off in the 1980s and even have turned into divergence in the 1990s.

Table 2.5 shows (row 3) that the decrease in the disparity in regional wealth levels (row 1) is to a large extent determined by the disparities that exist

Table 2.5 Evolution of wealth disparities[a] (EU 15), 1950–90

		1950	1960	1970	1980	1990
1	disparity among regions	0.124	0.100	0.079	0.058	0.057
2	disparity among countries	0.096	0.080	0.063	0.043	0.040
3	2:1 in %	77	80	80	75	70

Note:
a Theil entropy indices of Gross Regional Product by head of population based on exchange rates.

Source: Molle et al., 1980; Molle and Boeckhout, 1995: additional estimates based on various Eurostat and national publications.

between the countries of the EU (row 2). The underlying factors, such as resources, the level of schooling of the labour force, the access to markets and, in particular, the social and economic institutional infrastructure, are national rather than regional characteristics. So the improvement of national factors is an important condition for the catching up of the lagging countries and, subsequently, regional cohesion.[32]

Studies for *individual countries* show similar patterns by group. We will distinguish between the old and the new member countries or in other terms between North/South on the one hand and East on the other.

- In the old member countries (North/South) a fairly strong and consistent tendency towards convergence prevailed for the post-war period (evidence[33] for Austria, Spain, Italy, Sweden and Finland). On the contrary the intra national disparities had actually started to increase in the 1990s (evidence for all member countries with the exception of France, Germany and Austria (EC, 2002a, 2004a)). This may very well be the price member countries have paid for the fast development of their total value added.
- For the new member countries (East) on the contrary divergence dominated recent (post transition) developments. In the second half of the 1990s disparities between regions indeed increased considerably. Cities that are well attached to the international economy tend to grow faster, because they can overcome, very quickly, the constraints for their development, often by mobilizing the resources of their direct surroundings. FDI is the main engine for growth. This tends to be concentrated in capital cities and intra-EU border areas. Regions with traditional state industry in the East have a very difficult transition problem, which is comparable to the problem of the regions that traditionally specialized in mining and heavy industry in the West.[34] Consequently many NMS countries face a very problematic choice: Should they use to the best their limited resources for a fast catching up with the West and accept increasing disparities within their country, or should they limit their possibilities for development to a certain extent in order to go for more equity?[35]

The ranking of European regions by their level of prosperity evidences a remarkable stability. Indeed, throughout the 1950–2000 period, the 'peripheral'

34 *Assessing the problems and identifying causes*

regions of Mediterranean countries were always in the lowest positions, while some urban regions in Northern Europe were consistently at the top. Only two significant shifts in the first half of this period are recorded: (1) all German regions moved strongly upward, and (2) all regions of the UK and Belgium fell back.

2.7 Summary and conclusions

- Theory does not give a clear answer to the question whether the economic system produces convergence or divergence. The end result depends on the balance of a multitude of contradictory tendencies.
- Empirical analysis has thus to bring the answer to the question whether convergence or divergence prevails. This analysis is commonly done with the help of indicators of the development of the disparity in wealth, in practice mostly GDP/P figures.
- These indicators show very diverse developments both on the national level and on the regional level. For the period after the Second World War cohesion has tended to improve. National disparities have consistently decreased. The same is not true for regional disparities. Although the system showed for some time a fairly general trend towards convergence, it has recently produced quite a few cases of divergence too.
- These highly diversified reactions are a function of diversified initial conditions, economic structures, geographic location, institutional and administrative systems and reactions to various policies.
- The socio-economic system does not by itself produce convergence so a policy is justified that aims at decreasing the disparities and thus improve cohesion. The policy will not only have to support natural convergence tendencies but will have to be able to counter a multitude of different tendencies, some divergent, others convergent.
- The regions and countries that are the farthest below the EU mean, in terms of GDP/P, will be the main beneficiaries of such a cohesion policy. At the moment these are notably located in the Mediterranean area and in NMSs.

Annex 2.1 Review of historical studies into the development of regional disparities

We give here a review of the studies that have been made on the national level into the development of disparities. We will use a large variety of indicators; given the paucity of data we will use whatever indicator is available.

In the *UK*, divergence occurred. Wage differences among British regions tended to sharpen in the 1760–1914 period. Once established, neither the substantial migration of persons, nor important shifts in the industrial structure could undo the disparities. Only with the changes following the 1930 recession did they begin to diminish, partly as a result of large-scale government policy (Hunt, 1986). However, whether these wage data are good indicators of regional per capita wealth levels is questionable. For another important indicator, viz. income tax receipts, the differences between England, Scotland, Wales and Ireland decreased for the 1803–1921 period, probably due to the spread of industrialization to regions with good natural and human resources (Hechter, 1971).

In *Germany* wages of workers in the cotton industry at five different locations (states) varied considerably in the nineteenth century owing to the tremendous changes brought about by the Industrial Revolution (Kiesewetter, 1981), but a clear-cut tendency towards either convergence or divergence could not be seen. Other studies produced indications of widening disparities in wealth (GDP/P) among German regions in the nineteenth century (Fremdling and Tilly, 1979; Borchardt, 1968).

For *Austria-Hungary* (which did cover quite a different area as at present) indicators could be established for five series on prices (for instance, for goods: wheat, beef; for capital: interest rates) and for regional income (deposits in saving banks, number of physicians per 10,000 inhabitants and literacy rates). They showed a persistent tendency for regional income inequalities to reduce in the second half of the nineteenth century (Good, 1981).

For *France*, more comprehensive statistical data are available for a very long period. The variation in GDP values and other wealth indicators for the 21 regions into which France is nowadays divided[36] showed some clear-cut trends (Toutain, 1981). First, the *concentration of* economic activity (which in practice centres on Paris) went on for at least 100 years. This went hand in hand with reduced regional inequality in incomes per head and in productivity (overall as well as for agriculture and industry). That movement towards convergence should not let us forget the permanent contrast between poor and rich; indeed, the same regions continued at the lower and upper ends of the income per capita scale for a century and a half, while intermediate regions often changed places.

Italy achieved its national unity only a century ago. Before that time, it consisted of seven independent states, with rather closed economies. There is much debate as to the regional effects of that integration. The north is found (Eckhaus, 1961) to have acquired a competitive lead already at the time of unification. Since then the divergence has been accentuated, partly because of Myrdalian 'backwash' effects (Esposto, 1992), partly because of an unfortunate choice of external policies (Massacesi, 1965).

The evidence for *Spain* is less easy to interpret; the causes for the development of some regions (e.g. Catalonia and the Basque provinces) and the underdevelopment of others (e.g. Andalusia) are very complex. There has been a gradual tendency of convergence of real wages between the Spanish regions from 1850 to 1914 (Roses and Sanchez-Alonso, 2004). However, regional differences have tended to be accentuated by trade policies, choices of regional political elites, etc. (Sanchez-Albornoz, 1987).

For *Sweden* a very clear tendency towards convergence in GDP per head levels between the provinces can be observed since 1911 (Persson, 1997).

3 Economic disparities

3.1 Introduction

Cohesion is a multidimensional concept. One of these dimensions is economic in nature. The concept of economic cohesion is not well defined. In this chapter we therefore start by operationalizing the concept in the light of the policy demands. We will find that economic cohesion cannot be captured in one single indicator. For that reason we will have to work with a series of relevant indicators. The major ones are to be found in the factors that determine the GDP/P levels; in practice the factors that determine the adaptation of the structure of the economy.

For each of the indicators used we will describe, in concise terms, the theoretical approaches that have been developed to make them operational and the results of empirical studies into their factual development. These will permit us to identify the regions that are confronted with the biggest problems and draw indications for the type of policy action that might be used to incite enterprises to invest in those regions.

The rest of the chapter is structured as follows:

1   We will devote our attention to the constant change in the industrial (sectoral) structure in terms of composition in high value added and low value added activities. We will pay particular attention to the aspect of the knowledge economy.[1]
2   We will make an analysis of the patterns of specialization of regions and the concentration of economic activities over the European space.
3   We will make an analysis of the behaviour of multinational firms in terms of direct investment. This indicator is particularly well suited to highlight the changes that take place over time in terms of industrial location patterns.
4   We will indicate the movement (migration) of industries that makes the picture even more specific as it deals with concrete moves of plants.

As usual we will round off the chapter with a few short statements that summarize the main findings.

3.2 Concepts and indicators

3.2.1 Policy-relevant concepts and definitions

The concept of economic cohesion is not well defined. Neither the academic literature nor the policy documents give clear definitions. The concept can, however, be approached from the context in which it is often used. This suggests that *economic cohesion is assumed to exist if all segments (notably regions) are inserted in the total European economy where they can stand up to international competition*. Economic cohesion is thought to have improved in case the disparities on the components of competitiveness have decreased; in other words in case the weakest regions have been able to catch up.

3.2.2 Operational indicators

In a number of documents the notion of economic cohesion is assimilated to the disparities in GDP. It implies that GDP is taken as the main indicator of economic cohesion. We have discussed in Chapter 2 the disparities in general on the basis of this indicator. GDP/P is a synthesis indicator. GDP/P levels are subject to changes in the different components (economic factors) and these in turn are influenced by a whole series of other factors that determine competitiveness.

Competitiveness is conventionally measured by the level of productivity (which is the main determinant of GDP/P levels). Now differences in productivity in turn are highly dependent on two elements:

- *Production structure*. This can be illustrated with some examples. Some branches have a low productivity and sustain only low value added, one need but think in agriculture of hill farming or in the manufacturing sector of standard products such as ballpoints. Other branches have a high productivity and sustain high value added. One need but think in manufacturing of aircraft or in services of specialist advice for mergers and acquisitions. Regions that specialize in high value added activities will show high income levels. For example, the high productivity in financial and business services contributes to the good performance of many urban areas. Regions specializing in low value added activities will sustain only low income levels. For example, the high degree of dependence on agriculture explains the relatively poor performance of many rural areas.
- *Production environment*. We can illustrate this also with some cases. A high quality of the labour force will positively influence the productivity in all branches of activity. The same holds for other regional characteristics such as the level and quality of transport and knowledge infrastructure. Other important elements are the factors that determine the degree of innovation, the dynamics of entrepreneurship, etc.

For seizing the development of *economic cohesion* we will concentrate on the first set of factors: the production structure. Elements influencing the productive environment will be dealt with in the subsequent chapters as they tend also to influence mainly social and territorial cohesion.

The correct appraisal of the determinants of economic cohesion is very relevant for policy makers. Indeed, the objective to increase the productivity in regions with below-average levels can be fostered by stimulating the development of branches with high value added. Essential in this respect is to understand the locational preferences of enterprises from these branches.

3.3 Economic restructuring

3.3.1 Some theory

The present structural characteristics of an economy tend to determine the chances for future growth,[2] which can be explained as follows. If a very dynamic sector of activity is well represented in a region, it can be assumed that this region has better chances for growth than another region where the industrial base is composed of branches that show little dynamism or are even in straightforward decline. This insight has given rise to the so-called *shift-share analysis* (also called components of change analysis). This approach decomposes the regional employment growth in several elements.

- The first is the share element; also called the structural component. It indicates the theoretical growth a region would have had in case all its sectors had grown with the national growth rates for that sector. The size of the share element is dependent on the degree to which one details the sectoral composition. Within metal manufacturing there are large differences between high-value-added high-tech branches (such as medical electronic equipment) and more traditional low-value-added branches (such as metal-bashing activities). In services a similar effect can be observed, e.g. tourism services in general do show medium productivity levels compared to high productivity levels of financial intermediation. So the level at which the industrial structure is analysed does influence the indicators of regional performance.[3]
- The second is the shift element also called the locational component. It indicates the differences between the theoretical growth component and the real observed growth. This difference is attributed to factors that are specific for the region (also called its locational profile). They tend to lead to differences in productivity that cut across all sectors.[4]

The distinction between the two is not as clear as one would think at first sight. Indeed, some of the factors that stimulate productivity are also related to the production structure. 'The indicator for the skills of the regional work force, the broad level of educational attainment, is closely associated with the structure of economic activity – market services, especially the high-value-added sectors, tending to employ relatively highly-educated people – and the level of innovation' (EC, 1999a: 85).

3.3.2 Sectoral change

In the past 40 years the economies of the EU have gone through a profound economic transformation that has fundamentally changed the branch structure of the EU economy. The constant process of restructuring is driven by technological change and leads to the rise of new (e.g. Internet services) and the fall of old (e.g. textile weaving) activities. All EU countries and regions have participated in this long-term change. But the change has not been uniform. Major shifts have occurred in the regional distribution of low- and high-value-added branches of activity. A shift/share analysis for the post war period (Molle, 1997a) for the EU 15 showed three features:

1. Highly developed (central) regions have constantly performed less well than could be expected from their industrial structure.
2. Low developed (peripheral) regions have constantly improved their industrial structure.
3. Intermediate regions tend to take intermediate positions on this scale.

Together these tendencies have produced *convergence*; on average the distribution of high- and low-value-added activities is now more balanced than 40 years ago. There are many factors that have together contributed to this result. We will come back to a number of them in the following sections. However, one major contributing factor can be highlighted here already; it is increased economic integration. Indeed, the improved access to markets that the EU has given to firms in backward countries and regions has made it possible for them to exploit in full their advantages in cost base and on that basis build up the necessary know-how that is an essential prerequisite for successful restructuring and hence for growth of productivity and catching up. Illustrative in this respect is the Italian white goods industry (refrigerators, washing machines, etc.), which in the 1960s and 1970s was capable of exploiting its cost and innovation advantages through the access it gained to the markets of other member countries (Owen, 1983). In matters of services the thriving tourist industry has done much for many peripheral countries to move from agriculture (with low value added) to services (with medium value added per person). These processes of change in the location of the various categories of economic activity in the EU area have continued over the past decades and the larger area of the EU 27 (e.g. Molle, 1997a, 2006).

This change has been particularly marked for the NMSs. The old structure inherited from the communist period (mainly based on forced industrialization) has been revolutionized by the transition to a market economy and the access to EU markets.[5] In many regions that had concentrated on heavy industry the adaptation of such industries to the market has led almost invariably to significant redundancies; in many cases it even implied closure and complete lay-off of employees. In the traditional labour-intensive industries a considerable reshuffling has been made so as to make them competitive on the EU market. The most dramatic shift, however, is within the service sector. The former bureaucratic structures have been replaced by market-oriented services that are essential for the good functioning of modern economies.[6] Moreover, new foreign direct investment has moved in helping to increase the technological level and hence the average productivity (see later sections of this chapter).

So we may *conclude* that the speed of the renewal of the industrial structures of the backward regions is an important explanatory factor of the convergence of the wealth levels of the national and regional economies in the EU.

3.3.3 The knowledge economy

The EU has set itself the target to become the most competitive knowledge-based economy in the world. This ambitious objective triggers several questions (Cooke, 2002).

What is a knowledge-based economy? To answer this question we can best compare the knowledge economy with the traditional economy. The latter is characterized by the transformation of natural resources (agriculture and mining products) into manufactured products. The automation revolution has led to a perfection of this material-based economy; and it has led to tendencies of economies of scale and hence concentration (see later section in this chapter). The knowledge economy has been made possible by the information and telecommunication revolution. It has created an environment where information is very widely and easily available.

What economic activities are the most specific representatives of the knowledge economy? The question does not have an easy answer. Knowledge is a very pervasive element. It is essential now in traditional industries, such as food processing, where the new insights of bio-medical sciences are applied. However, the original segments of the knowledge economy are in activities which are largely dissociated from a material basis such as software design and Internet-based services. It is not easy to describe the knowledge economy in statistical terms as there are no good statistics on the various components. The data that come closest to our definition of the knowledge economy are for employment in the sectors that are knowledge intensive. We will use data for these sectors to show the differences that exist in the EU between the countries and regions with a high participation in the knowledge economy and those with a low participation.

The picture on the *national level* is given in Table 3.1. The manufacturing activities have been grouped by three technology classes: high, medium and low. One sees a very clear pattern in the specialization of the various member countries of the EU. The countries of the North have de-specialized from the low-tech manufacturing, the countries of the South are halfway to that process, while the East is still concentrating on low-tech manufacturing. The data for the category medium are less telling; they indicate (as expected) a slight specialization of the North. The data for high tech are somewhat difficult to interpret as the percentages are very low. However, if one does the rounding at tenth of percentage points one sees that the North is almost twice as specialized in this group than the other two areas.

On the *regional level* the data are much less complete. We can, however, base

Table 3.1 Employment in manufacturing by technology class (% of total) and country 2004[a]

Country	Technology class			
	High	Medium	Low	Total
Germany	2	9	12	23
France	1	6	10	17
Italy	1	6	15	22
The Netherlands	1	3	9	13
Belgium	1	6	11	17
UK	1	4	8	13
Denmark	1	5	10	16
Ireland	3	4	9	16
Spain	1	4	12	17
Portugal	–	3	16	19
Greece	–	2	11	13
Austria	1	5	12	18
Sweden	1	6	9	16
Finland	2	5	12	19
Poland	–	5	15	20
Czech Republic	1	8	18	27
Hungary	2	6	15	23
Slovakia	2	7	18	27
Slovenia	1	7	20	28
Lithuania	1	2	15	18
Cyprus	1	1	10	11
Latvia	–	1	15	16
Estonia	2	3	19	24
EU 27	**1**	**5**	**12**	**18**
North	1	6	10	17
South	1	5	13	19
East	1	5	16	22

Note:
a No data for Luxembourg, Malta, Romania and Bulgaria

Source: Eurostat (2006) EU integration seen through statistics, p. 100

ourselves on data for the EU 15 that give the distribution over the West European space of the sectors 'high technology manufacturing' and 'knowledge-intensive services'. This produces three main categories of specialization: high, medium and low (Cooke and de Laurentis, 2002). We will detail the two extremes.

Among the *regions that score highest* in the knowledge economy we find in Northern Europe:

- Capital cities (metropolitan areas) that are leading national and international centres for finance, media and technology (e.g. Stockholm, London, Helsinki, Brussels).
- Regions with modern industrial and centres of research; regions with a considerable component of automotive or Information and Communication

Technologies (ICT) engineering activities (e.g. Piedmont, Gothenburg, Midlands).

On the other end, *regions that score lowest* in the knowledge economy, we find (without exception) regions in Southern Europe that are dominated by:

- Agriculture. Regions with cities that are specializing in farming and traditional resource-based manufacturing (food, textiles) production (Central Greece, Northern Portugal, Central Spain).
- Tourism. Regions with beautiful landscapes and seascapes (e.g. Algarve, Murcia, Thessaly). The more remote these regions the lower their scores (notably the island regions near the international borders of the EU (e.g. Balearics, Dodecanese).

Unfortunately there is insufficient good data to describe in the same detail the situation in the NMSs but the indicators that are available show that some of their central regions (capital cities) have moved into knowledge activities, whereas remote regions where traditional activities still dominate have not yet been linked to the knowledge economy.

So to *conclude*, one sees important differences in the development of the knowledge economy over the EU space. Unfortunately one cannot establish whether the disparities increase or not as comparable data are not available.

3.4 Concentration

3.4.1 Some theory

Economic activity is not evenly spread over space. On the contrary we see areas of concentration and areas that are almost empty. It is clear that if the concentration would increase economic cohesion would be negatively influenced. So it is important to know whether the system tends towards more or towards less concentration. There are several strands of theory that try to explain the concentration of economic activities in specific regions. We give a succinct description here of the salient points of the most important schools. Some of them are actually refinements of the more general theories we have discussed in the previous chapter.[7]

Traditional trade theory suggests that economic integration will increase the specialization of countries and regions on a limited set of industries. The type of distribution over space is then determined by the endowments of the various countries in terms of production factors, natural resources and technology (comparative advantage). Countries with a high potential of qualified labour and hence with a high labour cost will tend to specialize in the capital-intensive sectors, on the other hand countries with low labour cost will specialize in the labour-intensive industries. The result is concentration of the high innovation industries in countries with high endowments and a concentration of the more mature industries in the more peripheral countries. Economic integration creates a larger economic area and industries will relocate to the member country that has the best endowments with respect to the new market situation. So, integration is likely to increase the specialization of regions on specific sectors. However, it depends on the specific demands that the firms that compose these sectors put to their productive environment (e.g. labour force), whether integration will also lead to higher concentration.

In *new trade theory* a switch in emphasis occurs from exchange efficiency to productive efficiency. The latter is influenced by, for example, labour force skills, level of technology, increasing returns to scale, agglomeration economies and strategic actions of economic agents in technological and institutional innovations. This new trade theory suggests that a comparative advantage can be acquired by sustained actions. It is no longer 'natural' or 'endowed' as assumed by traditional trade theory. There will be a concentration in high-income countries of industries that are characterized by high degrees of innovation. This concentration has several causes: technology (economies of scale), demand-side factors (concentration of the major industrial clients in these countries) and supply-side factors (concentration of R&D organizations, concentration of specialized labour). Countries with similar endowments will specialize but according to the logic of intra-industry trade, some will specialize in one type or brand, others in another type or brand of the same product category.

Regional export-based and export-multiplier models assume that a region's economic performance depends on the relative size and success of its export-orientated industries (tradable sector). The simplest model is the economic base model, in which a region's comparative growth depends simply on the growth of its economic base (export sector of the local economy). More sophisticated versions seek to formulate export demand and supply functions (Armstrong and Taylor, 2000; McCann, 2001). Demand for a region's exports is assumed to be a function of the price of the region's exports, the income level of external markets, and the price of substitute goods in those external markets. On the supply side, all factors having a significant effect on production costs can be expected to affect a region's competitive position in world markets. These will include wage costs, capital costs, raw material costs, intermediate input costs and the state of technology. This model does lead to a concentration of industries in regions where the demand and supply factors are more favourable than in a competing region.

The New Economic Geography approach is ambiguous as to the prediction of industrial concentration (e.g. Krugman and Venables, 1990; Krugman, 1991). On the one hand there are agglomeration (centripetal) forces that are based on the economies of scale and on forward and backward linkages.[8] On the other hand there are de-glomeration (centrifugal) forces (such as trade costs and factor price differences). In case trade is liberalized (decrease in trade cost) the latter may become dominant. This gives rise to the idea of a U-shaped curve. In a situation with high trade barriers we see that activity will be rather dispersed. When trade costs are reduced industrial location choices may lead to concentration. A further fall in trade cost will bring again de-concentration, as the periphery offers lower cost of production factors.

Cluster theory takes it inspiration more from business strategy economics. This micro-economic theory departs from the notion that firms, in order to stay competitive, must continually improve the operational effectiveness of their activities while simultaneously pursuing distinctive rather than imitative strategic positions. The existence of geographical clusters enhances firm competitiveness on both scores. This occurs notably through the formation of regionally based relational assets external to individual firms.[9]

So, overlooking this large variety of theoretical approaches one can only *conclude* that they are pointing in different directions as to the possible effect of structural change on concentration of economic activity.

3.4.2 What empirical evidence?

As theory is inconclusive in matters of concentration empirical evidence is very much needed. Unfortunately empirical research in this area has up until now suffered from lack of data.[10] Indeed, for a good analysis one cannot work just with data at the level of the total economy. On the contrary, one has to go into much detail by economic branches as these tend to differ in their locational behaviour. Some of them are heavily orientated towards their markets; others depend very much on low-cost labour, etc. Moreover, one has to detail as much as possible by regions to reveal specific patterns. In the following sections we will give the main features and results of the most relevant contributions on branch concentration at the national level and on the regional level.

3.4.3 Concentration at the national level

On the national level the empirical studies into concentration tendencies do lead to rather contradictory results.

Some find *concentration tendencies*. In the study of Amiti (1999) concentration was measured by calculating with the help of national data for detailed branches of activity, so-called Gini coefficients. These measure the inequality of the distribution of a specific sector with respect to a reference measure; in this case total economic activity.[11] The concentration is in general higher the more the industry is subject to scale economies and the more it depends on intermediate goods from other industries. The coefficients of many industries have increased in the 1980s, indicating a higher concentration.[12]

Some find *de-concentration tendencies*. For example, in the study of Bruelhart (1998) concentration was measured by making a correlation analysis between the share of a particular branch of manufacturing industry in the total economy of a country and the centrality index of the country for the period 1980–90. The centrality index is a measure that describes the location of a country or region in the European space with respect to the main centres of economic activity. The closer to these centres the higher the index, the farther away (that means the more peripheral) the lower the index (see Chapter 5, notably Figure 5.1). The analysis showed that there are broadly three categories of branches:

1   positive relation (scale-intensive industries are concentrated in core countries);
2   negative relation (labour-intensive industries are concentrated in peripheral countries);
3   neutral relation (other sectors that tend to be concentrated in intermediate regions).

The correlation coefficients decrease over time suggesting a decrease in the importance of centrality for concentration.

Some do not find *clear tendencies*. For example, the study of WIFO (1999) found that the geographical concentration of industries did fall in only a number of cases. This was mostly due to the fact that a number of the smaller countries (some of them in the periphery) did grow faster than the EU average.

Theory did not give clear-cut predictions as to concentration of economic activity. Empirical analysis shows diversified patterns. In trying to *link the empirical results to specific theories* a few observations can be made:

- The EU is likely to be in the last stage of the U-curve as proposed by the New Economic Geography theory.
- The most important determinant of industrial concentration in Europe seems to be the location of demand (Haaland et al., 1998). This suggests a home market effect as postulated by the new economic geography theories and a proximity effect as suggested by the cluster theories.
- Other significant forces are differences in factor intensities, suggesting that the classic theories are still of relevance too.

3.4.4 Concentration at the regional level

On the *regional level* the empirical analysis is even more hampered by the paucity of data than at the national level. The few studies that have explored branch concentration at the regional level do also conclude to a diversified pattern.[13] We highlight three major features:[14]

1   For most of the 17 branches the spatial concentration decreased continuously through the 1950–2000 period (Molle, 1997a).
2   High-value industries that were initially concentrated showed a tendency of dispersal; while low-value industries relocated to the periphery, which in some cases increased their concentration level (Midelfart-Knarvik et al., 2000).
3   Looking specifically at the manufacturing sector there is not much evidence of clustering. Clustered concentration seemed to prevail only in branches that used to be dependent on specific raw materials that were only available in specific locations.

These *results* seem to reinforce some of the theories that we have depicted in the previous chapter, notably those about the life-cycle of the product. Increasing return models seem to be of little relevance in the EU space.

3.5 FDI

3.5.1 Some theory

The *definition* of FDI is: the transfer of capital by a company in one country to another country to create or take over an establishment there, which it wants to control. FDI mostly involves the transfer not only of capital but also of other resources, such as technological know-how, management and marketing skills.

The most important underpinnings of the theory dealing with FDI are of a micro-economic nature. Central to it are the incentives that a firm has to internationalize its production and marketing. Several approaches have been tried (Carson, 1982) that have been welded together into an eclectic approach (Dunning, 1979, 1980, 1988, 1993). This approach has become known as the ownership, location and internalization (OLI) paradigm. Each of the letters stands for a word that is central to a major question related to FDI (see Box 3.1):[15]

Box 3.1 The OLI paradigm for FDI

O. *Which* firms undertake FDI? Firms investing abroad must possess specific *ownership* (O) advantages over local firms to overcome the extra costs of operating in a different, less familiar environment. These ownership advantages largely take the form of the possession of intangible assets – a technological lead, for instance – which are, at least for a period of time, exclusive or specific to the firm possessing them. These advantages are generally costly to create, but can be transferred to a new location at relatively low cost. The analysis of 'O' advantages draws on industrial organization, resource-based, evolutionary and management theories, with advantages residing mainly in firm-specific technology, brand names, privileged access to factor of product markets or superior technological or management skills.

L. *Where* do firms choose to exploit their advantages, in the home country (by exports) or abroad, and in which foreign locations? They select sites with *location* (L) advantages that best match the deployment of their 'O' assets. Location advantages consist of some factor inputs (including natural resources) outside its home country; otherwise foreign markets would be served entirely by exports and domestic markets by domestic production. The analysis of 'L' advantages draws on trade and location theory. The main factors determining comparative costs are factor and transport costs, market size and characteristics and government policies (e.g. stability, predictability, tariffs, taxes and FDI regulations). Asset-seeking FDI is drawn to locations with strong technological, educational or information-creation activities.

I. *Why* do firms choose to internalize their advantages by an extension of their own activities in preference to selling them to other firms through licensing and similar contracts with foreign firms? The analysis of *internalization* (I) draws on transaction-cost theories of the firm. It centres on the feasibility of and returns to contracting the sale of intangible advantages to other firms. The most valuable and new advantages tend to be internalized, since these are the most difficult to price and contract over time. The more mature ones are easier to price, less subject to uncertainty and less valuable to the owner: these are licensed more readily.

The modern multinational firm can be seen as a *functionally differentiated organization* (NEI/E&Y, 1992). It will internationally orient its investments by looking for optimal locations of its various functions. Headquarters will be located in central cities with good international communications. R&D facilities will be located in an environment that will stimulate innovation through contacts between researchers and the quality of the living environment. Distribution will be located at places from where relevant market areas can best be serviced. Production facilities again follow their own logic where cost and market access reasons meet.

There are two main — and quite distinct — reasons why a firm goes multinational:

1 To better serve a local market. This is often called 'horizontal' FDI, since it typically involves a duplication of the production process by establishing additional plants. This form of FDI usually substitutes for trade. This type of FDI typically involves investments in advanced countries, such as the establishment of Japanese car manufacturing and electronics plants in the USA and Europe in the 1980s.
2 To acquire low-cost inputs. This is often called 'vertical' FDI, since it involves relocation of specific activities of the value added chain to low-cost locations. Unlike horizontal FDI, vertical FDI is usually trade creating. This typically involves investment in developing countries and emerging markets (such as today's large-scale relocation of production activities in textiles and many other manufactured goods to China). Such vertical FDI is only done in the presence of internalization advantages; otherwise the part of the production process would have been subcontracted to independent suppliers.

The pattern and magnitude of direct investment flows depend on the characteristics of a country. The more the firms in a country show entrepreneurial competitiveness (related to ownership advantages) the higher will be outward direct investment (DI), as these firms will want to cash in on their advantages by investing abroad. The higher the locational attractiveness of a country, the higher the inward DI, as firms will have advantages in producing there rather than elsewhere (Sleuwaegen, 1987).

The model described here has no predetermined outcome in as far as the concentration tendency is concerned. On the one hand, it leads to a flow from the rich capital-intensive countries to the less well-to-do countries that have much cheap labour, which will lead to deconcentration of activities. On the other hand, different multinational firms (MNFs) may take the same location factors into account (e.g. infrastructure or international schools), which may lead to concentration within the same regions. However, the literature suggests that the core periphery model related to the life-cycle of the product theory (described in Chapter 2) may be very relevant for explaining FDI patterns.

3.5.2 Economic integration and MNF strategy

Strategy and internal organization of multi-product, multinational companies differ under different trade and direct investment regimes (see Table 3.2). In the left-hand column of this table we give these regimes. Their order is based on the chronology in which they have occurred in the past century. In the central part of the table we give the choices as to location of production units that are optimal for the regime in question. In the third column we give the effects on the internal organization of the firm.

These different cases can best be illustrated with a specific case. Philips is a good example of a firm that has experienced these changes in environment. Box 3.2 describes how its strategy has evolved over time (Muntendam, 1987; Teulings, 1984).

Table 3.2 Production and trade patterns of multinational, multi-product companies under different trade regimes

Trade regime	Location of production units for each product	Dominant part of firm
Free trade	One plant (usually home base)	Production and export
Protectionism	Numerous plants (one in each major national market to jump behind tariff walls)	National companies
Integration	Limited number of plants (at good locations)	Matrix of national and product organizations
Free internal market	One plant (optimal location)	International product divisions

---

Box 3.2 Adaptation to regime change; the case of Philips

Taking advantage of the *liberalist trade environment* from the first decade of the twentieth century, Philips rapidly increased its production of light bulbs and other products, such as radio sets and domestic appliances. As early as 1910, Philips had established sales companies in 18 European and in eight other countries of the industrialized world. Most were supplied by the home base, built for low-cost, large-scale production.

In the 1930s, the surge of *protectionist measures* compelled the company to change its strategy thoroughly. It switched to the exploitation of ownership advantage. Its direct investments became of the tariff-jumping type. First, assembly lines for each of the major products were set up in every individual country in whose market Philips was well established. Next national Philips companies were created, which became responsible for the production and local marketing of all Philips products. Quite naturally these national companies, having to gear their production to local taste, also acquired responsibility for product development. Conditions during and after the Second World War reinforced the system of geographically decentralized combined production and selling units.

In the 1960–90 period characterized by the *opening of the EU markets*, all national companies were integrated in a centralized international system based on product division. This reflects investment behaviour of the optimal location type. The major plants, which used to produce a whole array of products, were now made to specialize in only one or two products.

Recently this European strategy of specialization and product division has been given a worldwide dimension under the impetus of global trade liberalization. Now production is split over the various parts of the world according to the optimal location type; low-cost production in countries with very low labour cost; high value added productions in countries with good R&D environments.

3.5.3 Growth and composition of intra-European FDI

Direct investment flows within the EU have been completely free since the 1970s. On theoretical grounds we may expect that direct investments will increase as soon as companies become convinced of the advantages of selecting optimum locations within an enlarged market area (see Table 3.1). In line with this, we have seen a particularly rapid growth over time of European direct investments in Europe (EDIE). In the 1966–70 period, intra-EU FDI (between the original six member states) increased by 63 per cent (Pelkmans, 1983). In the period 1970–83, double-digit percentage growth continued. However, the real boom came after 1985, when EDIE doubled about every two years under the impetus of the 1992 programme. This is again in line with the optimum location hypothesis, as the taking away of the many remaining non-tariff barriers (NTBs) has a similar effect to the taking away of tariffs.[16]

The *industry pattern* of EDIE has been very stable over the past decades; services accounted for nearly two-thirds. This high share reflected two features of the service sector: first, its dominance in all advanced economies; second, the difficulty of trading its products compels them to serve foreign markets by local supply through FDI. The manufacturing sector came in second place (accounting for the remaining one-third); the EDIE of other sectors like agriculture, energy and construction was insignificant. Within the service sector, the branch of finance and insurance took the lion's share. Much of this investment was made as part of the creation of a geographically diversified production and distribution network (involving both vertical and horizontal FDI). EDIE was largely

50 *Assessing the problems and identifying causes*

of the inter-industry type, whereby manufacturers of country A invest in country B, and vice versa (for example, Cantwell and Randaccio, 1992). The liberalization of markets and the privatization of companies in branches such as energy, telecom, etc., have made apparent a considerable need for international rationalization of these industries. As a consequence, at the turn of the century, FDI in these industries has risen explosively.

3.5.4 Geographical (national) pattern of intra-EU FDI

The pattern of the flows of DI among EU countries (EDIE) has changed over time. Picturing these changes for all member states of the present EU gives many details but little insight. Therefore we have grouped the countries by geographical area. The three broad areas distinguished earlier (North West, South West and East) provided too little information. Inspired by the core–periphery model as suggested by theory we have grouped the EU countries into three classes by degree of centrality/peripherality (see Chapter 5).[17] Table 3.3 gives the importance of the FDI flows between these three classes (core, intermediate and periphery). The table invites the following remarks:

- The internal relations of the core group of countries (mainly Germany, France, the Benelux and the UK) dominate the picture.[18]
- The flow from the core to the intermediate zone of the EU (mainly Spain, Portugal and Greece) is of considerable importance.[19]
- The flow from the core to the periphery (most of the NMSs) has quickly picked up during the period immediately preceding membership of these countries.
- The flow in the opposite direction (periphery–core) is fairly modest.
- The net flow of capital from the core (high GDP/P) towards intermediate and peripheral zones (the relatively less developed EU countries) confirms that private investment supports the convergence of wealth (see Chapter 2).
- The flows between the intermediate and peripheral areas are very small or negligible.

Membership (or non-membership of the EU) has a considerable influence on the magnitude of the flows of EDIE. We will illustrate this with three examples:

1   The accession of Spain and Portugal in 1985 has triggered important FDI flows from the core countries to these countries.[20] Apparently the concentration effects, which the divergence school had feared, have not materialized. On the contrary, the intra-EU pattern of FDI showed a net 'core-to-periphery' pattern, which leads to more convergence of wealth levels.
2   Two countries that joined the EU in the middle of the 1990s (Sweden and Finland) are non-typical peripheral countries (high income; strong MNF structures with 'O' advantages). They have been very active in FDI both in the traditional core of the EU and in other EU countries. Hence a strong

Table 3.3 Geographical distribution (%) of direct investment between groups of member countries of the EU, 1980–2003

	1980–84	1984–88	1988–92	1993–96	1997–2000	2001–03
Core to core	77	80	71	79	76	56
Core to intermediate	20	16	22	16	11	25
Intermediate to core	3	4	5	3	4	8
Intermediate to intermediate	–	–	2	2	5	5
Core to periphery					3	5
Periphery to core					0	0
Intermediate to periphery					1	1
Periphery to intermediate					0	0
Periphery to periphery					0	0

Note:
1980–96: EU 12, 1997–2003: EU 25

Source: Morsink (1998); based on Eurostat and OECD statistics and a number of unpublished sources, Eurostat: *EU Direct Investment Yearbook*. Eurostat, *EU direct investment flows, breakdown by partner country and economic activity* (2005)

change in relative shares in the last column of the table. Since their accession the flows between these countries and those of the rest of the EU have become more equilibrated.[21]

3   The case of the NMSs that joined in 2004 merits some more attention. We will devote a special section to it.

The core periphery model is very instructive as to the general pattern of FDI but does not give much detail as to the relative importance of the various *determinants* of the detailed flows. To capture these factors a more detailed analysis has to be made whereby the FDI is compared to the scores of the member countries on a number of indicators suggested by theoretical approaches, such as the OLI paradigm. Such an analysis into the determinant factors of EDIE flows revealed some clear patterns.[22]

- Most important is the financial strength of a country: the largest EDIE flows occurred when the country of origin showed a net financial resource and the receiving country a high borrowing requirement.
- Almost equally strong influences come from the ownership advantage (high R&D leads to high outward DI, and vice versa).
- Intermediate influence comes from several factors. The higher the size of the target market, the higher FDI. The higher the distance (transport) cost between the home and host country the lower the EDIE flow. The integration of goods markets (trade intensity) stimulates that of capital markets; this relation highlights the point that EDIE is of the optimum-location type. Monetary integration, creating stable exchange rates, influences the EDIE flows positively.
- Limited influence came from some other factors, e.g. differences in culture and taxation.

3.5.5 Geographical (regional) patterns of FDI

FDI can be an important stimulus for the regeneration of regional economies. So there exists a keen interest in attracting such DI. To be effective one needs to know on the one hand the demands that MNFs put forward to select their location and on the other hand a region's locational ('L') advantages. This interest is both on intra-EU FDI and on incoming FDI from non-member countries of the EU. The main question is thus: 'What factors determine the choice of the location of the investment project?' There are no EU-wide studies made to answer this question. So we will deal with the evidence that can be provided by studies made for individual countries.

For France the analysis of over 4,000 FDI projects made over the past ten years (Crozet *et al.*, 2004) found a clear trend towards agglomeration of industries. The sectors that were influenced most by such tendencies were computers, car parts and machinery. Previous establishments tend to increase the probability of later investments significantly. An interesting aspect of the location pattern of FDI in France is the proximity of the home country. This is not only a question

Economic disparities 53

of geographical distance but also a question of sharing attributes with the home country (for instance German investment in Alsace).

For Italy the inflow of FDI over the past 15 years has been fairly low. The location patterns of FDI over this 15-year period (Roberto, 2004) show that both takeovers of existing firms and creation of new firms were positively influenced by the usual factors: low labour cost, good infrastructure, industries of the same type (clusters) and the presence of other FDI (uncertainty of investors about certain aspects of their location leads them to follow a leader). The congestion in the Northern cities was found to generate on balance centrifugal forces, notwithstanding a significant number of locations in those areas. So contrary to other EU countries with the same welfare levels the backward regions of Italy have not benefited much from the positive external effects of FDI.[23]

For *Portugal*: the study of the location of some 750 FDI projects (Guimaraes et al., 2000) has revealed very clear patterns of agglomeration. Urbanization economies thereby far outweighed industry-specific localization economies. In practice this means that most newly created foreign-owned plants located close to the major cities. Only in a small number of cases labour cost seemed to be of relevance.

For *Ireland* much of incoming FDI came from the USA (Barry et al., 2003). US firms locate close to each other, which is a demonstration of efficiency-seeking behaviour. Moreover, the existing location of a FDI sends strong signals to newcomers as to the reliability and attractiveness of the host country and region. This finding leads to the policy recommendation to stimulate take-off by promoting a flagship location and to stimulate further development by the building up of clusters.

Overlooking this evidence we can conclude that agglomeration tendencies are fairly strong and that regions that do not provide urbanization advantages have an uphill fight to attract FDI. However, such a fight can be won as some investments are more interested by low cost than high urban services and these can later serve as focal points for related investments.

3.5.6 The changed position of the NMSs

In the 1990s the countries in Central and Eastern Europe (CEEC) have changed over from a command economy to a market economy. Since then the EU has gradually integrated them by offering access to its markets and pre-accession support. This has sparked off a strong movement of European FDI towards the accession countries. FDI from the EU 15 to the NMSs has surged to arrive at some €15 billion a year at the end of the 1990s. EU FDI in these countries accounted for about 80 per cent of their total FDI. The motives for EU firms to invest in accession countries varied by type of activity. On the one hand, some firms (e.g. in the food industry and in insurance) have moved in to capture local markets (horizontal FDI). On the other hand, firms in branches such as textile, machinery or automobiles effectuated DI of a rather vertical, efficiency-seeking type. Quite a considerable part of this FDI was in the form of the takeover of firms that the state wanted to privatize and where foreign ownership was felt necessary to bring them quickly up to the necessary level of competitiveness. Next to that a considerable part of greenfield investment (new firms created at a new location) took place.

The pattern of these FDI from the EU 15 countries into the NMSs reveals some interesting features that we will shortly discuss.

- The *sectoral composition* of the FDI that flows from the EU 15 to the NMSs has been dominated by the tertiary sector. Part of this preponderant position can be explained by the interest of EU 15 firms for investment in utilities (water, telecom, electricity). Within the manufacturing sector there is at this stage no clear specialization trend discernible. The only branch that stands out is the food sector.
- The *geographical orientation* has been very uneven as is evidenced by Figure 3.1. The largest flow in absolute terms (40 per cent of all accession countries) went to Poland.[24] There are several underlying factors to this pattern. First it seems that these flows follow a gravity type model; they seem to be largely determined by the mass of the recipient and donor country and the distance between the two. Other determinant factors found were the quality of the infrastructure, of human resources, of institutions and regulation and the absence of corruption.[25]

Is there a *displacement effect*? In other words: Has the FDI in the NMSs by firms of the core regions of the West been to the detriment of the FDI of the core to the periphery of the EU 15? Up until now little influence has been

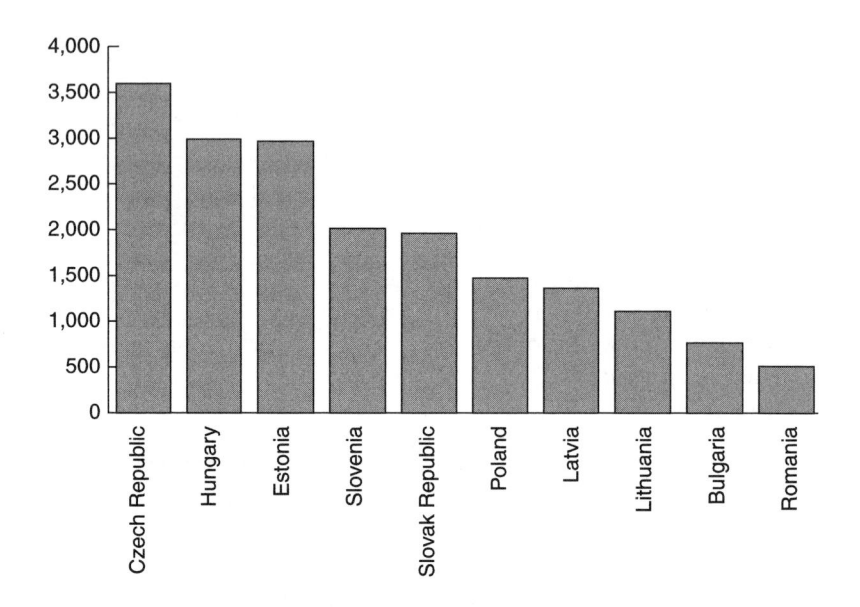

Figure 3.1 Inflow of FDI (per capita) in the NMS by country, 1990–2003

Source: Eurostat

found (e.g. Brenton et al., 1999); so empirical results are not in agreement with the political concerns.

3.5.7 Empirical estimates of welfare effects

FDI is supposed to have a positive net welfare effect on the host region. In empirical studies (see Blomstrom and Kokko, 2001) they were found to depend on the policies of the host country or host region. We analyse here three aspects: growth, technology and labour.[26]

FDI has been shown to stimulate *productivity growth*,[27] particularly so in the NMSs (Campos and Kinoshita, 2001). There are, however, factors that may inhibit that growth. For instance, if the quality of labour (skills of the workforce) is not up to a certain minimum level FDI does not seem to bear positively on GDP growth (Borensztein et al., 1998).

The transfer of *technology* determines to a large extent whether the outcome of the FDI is divergence or convergence. There is a positive effect with respect to developed countries (Crespo and Velasquez, 2003). Such a positive (convergence) effect is evident for the NMSs where technology transfer through FDI has been the main motor for productivity increases (Tondl and Vuksic, 2003). Moreover, there are spillover effects on the rest of the economy through backward linkages (that is contacts between foreign affiliates and their local suppliers in upstream sectors) (Smarzynska-Javorcik, 2004).

The *labour market impact* of FDI comes about as FDI shifts labour demand across countries. FDI raises the wage in the host country and lowers the wage in the source country.[28] The few studies that have analysed the effects of free internal flows of European direct investment have been limited to the employment effects in both source and destination countries. The latter seems invariably to have benefited from DI. The effect on the former varies from negative, when exports from the home bases are replaced, to positive, when the penetration into a foreign market actually increases home employment (Buckley and Artisien, 1987). More generally, FDI will be low in case unit labour costs are too high compared to competing locations; this may be responsible for welfare losses due to high unemployment. The opposite will be the case for countries where wages have been relatively low (given a certain productivity level) (Hatzius, 2000).

So in general we may *conclude* that the welfare effects are positive and that FDI does contribute to cohesion.

3.6 Industrial migration

3.6.1 Some theory

The total development of the growth of a regional economy can be broken down in several components that reflect the demography of firms. A first one is the growth (or decline) of establishments that existed for the whole period. A second one is new creations (births) and its counterpart closures (deaths). Finally, we can identify both immigration and out-migration of plants. Of course there are also some hybrid forms, for instance, the opening up of a branch plant in a region that partly takes over the activities of an establishment in another region.

On the national level a number of the phenomena that are the subject of migration studies overlap with the subjects of FDI studies (discussed in the previous sections). Indeed, on the national level immigration will overlap with incoming FDI; emigration will overlap outgoing FDI. However, on the regional level, many more cases of migration will find their origin in other regions of the same country. For that reason we will focus in these sections on migration on the regional level.

New investments, be they immigrant or new endogenous creations, have attracted most attention.[29] Theory has provided several approaches to explain the patterns of location of these new firms. Traditional location theory tends to highlight the cost factors of the manufacturing firm, such as the cost of shipment of the products to the market and the price of labour. Modern theory also recognizes the importance of factors that influence the location of other economic activities such as services (for instance access to customers and information).

These theoretical set ups have been set to empirical tests; usually in the form of firm surveys. The results of such surveys tend to be influenced by the conditions under which they were held. For instance, in a period of boom, firms will be tempted to stress the factors that constrain their development in their present location as the main factor for migration (such as lack of space). Moreover, the results are influenced by the type of activity of the firm (NEI/E&Y, 1992; Ernst and Young, 2005).

- Traditional manufacturing is highly influenced by cost factors, such as labour cost.
- Modern knowledge-based activities (such as high-tech manufacturing and R&D) tend to be strongly oriented to non-cost factors, such as quality of life.
- Headquarters are particularly attracted by metropolises, with good air connections and relations to the financial sector.
- Services are influenced by a wide variety of factors: market proximity, transport links, telecommunication and quality of life factors.

3.6.2 The boom period: 1955–75

The *patterns* of industrial migration over the post-war period in the major countries of the EU have been dominated by outward moves from the major conurbations (such as Paris, London, the Ruhr area) to the more peripheral regions of these countries. Only in Greece one has observed a centripetal force (concentration or agglomeration) instead of a centrifugal (de-concentration) one (Klaassen and Molle, 1982).

The major *motive* for such moves was that firms required extra production capacity for realizing their growth. They spread out from congested central areas (with a tight labour market characterized by high cost and low availability) to areas with abundant supply and low labour cost. The most common option chosen was the establishment of a branch plant. As a matter of fact such a strategy has the advantage of low cost and managerial ease, routine activities being gradually shifted while the firms' other functions are kept as much and as long as possible in the original location. As many areas in Europe could provide labour and space, the competition for mobile investment between them was done on the basis of other factors of location, such as infrastructure, support from local authorities, etc.

The *effects* have been significant. Various country studies give evidence of the fact that 'for quite a number of regions, especially peripheral agricultural ones, the whole industrial base consists of plants that ... moved to the area. Many immigrant plants were small at the moment of moving, but have subsequently grown considerably.' 'The industry created in regions that at the end of the war were virtually without any industrial base at all ... introduced a certain industrial culture, opening the way to the gradual upgrading of skills and the take off of local initiatives. As a consequence the sectoral composition of the economy came to be more and more equal' (Klaassen and Molle, 1982: 420–2).

3.6.3 *The slack period: 1975–90*

With the two oil crises at the end of the 1970s a new era began of slow growth. It was to have a considerable impact on the volume (net decrease) and the pattern of industrial migration (Klaassen and Molle, 1982).

- More global moves. The difference in wage level between the 'cheap labour' countries in Europe and Third World countries has become so great that many establishments are looking for cheap labour outside Europe. That implies a speed up of international emigration, showing up in European statistics as closures.
- Less traditional internal moves. The government's policy in many countries changed to withdraw gradually both the stimulants in the periphery and the controls on developments in the centre.
- More modern moves. Most new high-technology activities want to go to places where the location environment is characterized by pleasant living conditions.

3.6.4 *The recent period: 1990–2005*

The most recent period is characterized by the acceleration of the relocation of a number of activities to Central and Eastern Europe (see Box 3.3) and to the low-cost countries in emerging markets such as China and India. This movement is generally called de-localization. It is most important in manufacturing but also increasingly so in services (Djarova, 2004). Even in its highest segment R&D delocalization is now coming off the ground (Amiti and Wei, 2005).

> Box 3.3 Why car makers move East
>
> The automotive industry is one of the most expressive examples of an industry's move towards emerging markets. In about a decade (1990–2000) almost all car makers present on the Western European market had invested in production facilities in one of the NMSs. Many of the plants were established in regions relatively near to the border of the old member states (Poland, Hungary, the Czech Republic and Slovakia are cases in point). Volkswagen alone had, by 2002, invested some €4 billion in the Czech Republic and some €1.5 billion both in Slovakia and Hungary. This drive towards the NMSs has been caused by two investment objectives: market expansion and the reduction of cost. Locating in the NMSs permits car makers to optimize costs, suppliers, product portfolio and production.
>
> Most investors benefited from investment incentives or special investment packages offered by the countries. In return the country received an investment programme entailing production growth, new job creation, upgrading of the local labour force and development of the supply base.
>
> *Source:* Djarova (2004: chap. 6)

Politicians and trade unions have often alarmed the public about this phenomenon, as it would destroy existing jobs without creating any new jobs. This view is, however, distorted. Actually de-localizations tend to be only a small part (8 per cent) of the total job losses due to restructuring in the EU. Moreover, although they do have a negative direct effect on employment in the home country,[30] there are some positive indirect effects on the home country economy (e.g. Pennnigs and Sleuwaegen, 2000). These stem from the fact that MNFs that restructure through de-localization seem to specialize their remaining home units on competitive, dynamic and innovative activities. This is in stark contrast to firms that are independent, remain in the home country, start to suffer from a loss of competitiveness and are finally forced to close down with a permanent job loss to the home country.

3.7 Summary and conclusions

- The most important explanatory factor of the convergence of the wealth levels of the national and regional economies in the EU is the renewal of the *industrial structures*. Over the past all composite parts of the EU have seen a continuous and profound change in their industrial base.
- Theory is inconclusive as to the tendency of certain activities to *concentrate* in parts of the EU. Empirical analysis shows that there is rather a tendency of de-concentration. This would be positive for cohesion.
- *Capital movements* in the EU have on balance contributed to convergence of wealth levels. On the national level the 'poorer' member states are net importers of DI, while the 'richer' member states are net exporters. On the

regional level DI (partly through industrial migration) has in many cases gone from central to peripheral areas of the member countries.
- Notwithstanding these positive effects on convergence important disparities remain and new ones threaten constantly to emerge. So a policy aiming at improving the conditions for successful operation of high-value-added firms in the least favoured regions is warranted to improve economic cohesion.

4 Social disparities

4.1 Introduction

The EU is confronted by many social problems that impede cohesion. The issue of social cohesion refers to the balanced participation of different groups in social life. To measure such an elusive concept as social cohesion is not an easy task. Like economic cohesion the concept 'social' cannot be captured in one basic indicator. This is in line with European social policy that deals with a fairly large number of rather dispersed issues. So, in the present chapter we will describe the development of social disparities in the EU with the help of a set of indicators.

In a first section we will discuss first the concept of social cohesion and select the indicators that are most apt to describe social disparities. In the rest of the chapter we will concentrate on the measurement and the analysis of the five indicators that are most common in the literature. We will successively deal with unemployment, level of education, migration and segregation, social exclusion and social security.

For each of these five indicators[1] we will shortly describe their theoretical and conceptual foundations and then give the national, regional and, where possible, urban picture[2] of disparities.

The analysis is of very high policy relevance. It permits first to identify the groups that in social terms are less well off than the EU average and hence would qualify as target groups or as prime beneficiaries of the EU cohesion policy. It permits next to see on what type of problems policy interventions would have to concentrate so as to have most effect in improving social cohesion.

The chapter will be rounded off by a short summary and some conclusions.

4.2 Concepts and indicators

4.2.1 Policy-relevant concepts and definitions

Social cohesion has as little a well and clear definition as the other dimensions of cohesion. The notion refers often to the existence of harmonious relations between different social groups in society. A further elaboration of the concept in positive terms is difficult to give. Impressive attempts have been made to come to operational definitions on a wide range of indicators including fundamental aspects such as values or bonds, but also concrete aspects of access to employment and health (Council of Europe, 2005). However, the consistent quantification of these indicators runs far behind their conceptualization. This situation can be illustrated with two approaches.

A fairly recent attempt is the measurement of the *social capital* of an area (country or region). Social capital can be defined as 'the norms and social relations embedded in the social structure of a group of people that enable the group or individuals participating in it to achieve desired goals' (de la Fuente and Ciccone, 2003). An increase in social capital is supposed to have a positive influence on both economic growth and social inclusion. The use of the concept of social capital is not easy in practice; most of the indicators are difficult to measure in an internationally comparable way such as 'trust' or 'associational activity'.

An interesting notion that has a much older history than social capital is *industrial relations*. Indeed the consensual or harmony model of relations between employers and trade unions is often thought to lead to less strikes and thus to a more stable growth than the conflict model. Analyses for European countries of this indicator suffer from the poor comparability of the national situations. Where quantification has been possible, one finds, in general, a positive relation with growth and thus with the catch up of backward groups and regions. We will not pursue the issue further.

Social cohesion is often indicated by its mirror picture, the *absence of cohesion*. Clear examples of the absence of social cohesion are eruptions of violence. These can be of a religious nature, such as the armed conflict between Catholics and Protestants that has ravaged Northern Ireland for so long. They can also be of an ethnic nature; a case in point is the occurrence of riots that devastated the suburbs in major urban agglomerations. Many observers would say that the basis of these outbreaks of violence are not so much religious or racial but are the effect of causal factors such as lack of access to jobs and to culture, leading to bad housing and health conditions and in some cases to social exclusion. This too seems difficult to grasp in statistical terms.

The various academic and policy documents dealing with social cohesion use a variety of practical indicators to describe the actual situation and its development over time. The ones that we have just described (social capital, industrial relations and social violence) are not very prominent in these documents. On the contrary, a number of others appear. This puts us on the track of a practical definition for social cohesion permitting the empirical measurement of social disparities.

So, social cohesion is supposed to prevail when disparities on a number of social indicators are politically sustainable.

It is practically impossible to determine the point where disparities are no longer politically sustainable. So in line with the reasoning we have followed in the previous chapters we will consider that social cohesion improves in cases where the disparities decrease and vice versa.

4.2.2 Operational indicators

Employment and its mirror picture *unemployment* are among the most used indicators of social problems. Indeed, since the early 1980s unemployment overshadows all the other social problems in Europe. Moreover, the access to employment is highly associated to other determinants of social cohesion.

The *quality of employment* is also often used as an indicator of social cohesion. Indeed, with the growing relevance of knowledge-based activities the qualification of the labour force for such activities is evermore critical. We will try to capture this by an input indicator (level of education).

Quite a few social problems, notably those in urban areas, are related to the lack of *integration of immigrants* and their descendants. So we devote a separate section to this aspect.

Next, we go into the problem of *social exclusion*; a term that covers many aspects of social deprivation and poverty.

Finally, we also mention national policy variables. Countries with a highly developed *social security system* will insure their citizens against a number of risks that may bring them into situations of deprivation; the higher the level of protection the lower the chances of exclusion. Differences in coverage thus represent social disparities on the EU level.

4.3 Unemployment

4.3.1 Concepts, general facts and theoretical foundations

Overall, unemployment has shown ups and downs over the post-war period. Until the end of the 1970s unemployment was fairly low in most member countries. Thereafter, under the influence of the two oil crises, it increased dramatically. In the second half of the 1980s it declined mainly due to the economic upswing that was created by the completion of the internal market. In the early 1990s unemployment started to rise again; mainly under the influence of inadequate responses to increased competition. At the end of the 1990s the trend turned; unemployment showed a rapid decrease in many member countries, which is the positive effect of the growth of their economies, itself spurred by a combination of EU and national policies. In recent years unemployment has tended to grow again in most countries of the EU 15. In the NMSs unemployment is also a very big problem; the switch over from a command to a market economy has made considerable numbers of workers redundant, many of whom have had difficulty finding a new job.

There are a lot of theories that help us to understand the root causes of unemployment. These refer on the one hand to the determinants of the supply and demand for labour and on the other hand on the institutional aspects of the functioning of the labour market. Empirical testing of these theories has produced the following set of *causes* for the relatively high levels of European unemployment:

- *Adverse developments*. These are, in particular, movements in the terms of trade (increases in energy prices), the effects of counter-inflationary demand

policies and of the stiffened competition due to the increased openness of the EU economies. Propagation mechanisms make that such temporary shocks tended to have persistent effects.[3]
- *Low responsiveness of the European labour markets.* This European labour market does not function well due to rigidities coming from 'over'-regulation and generous schemes of unemployment benefits.[4] Shocks have larger negative effects on employment the higher the protection level.
- *Cost of labour.* There is a chain of cause–effect relations here. The rise in labour cost has induced firms to substitute capital for labour (Daveri and Tabellini, 2000). The increase in labour cost is in the first instance due to the growth of the taxes on labour. These in turn are a consequence of two factors. First, the increasing demands of the welfare state. Second, tax competition has shifted the tax burden from taxes on mobile factors such as capital and goods to taxes on the immobile factor: labour.

4.3.2 National differences

There are considerable differences between countries in their relative levels of *total unemployment* (left-hand side columns of Table 4.1). Unemployment is particularly concentrated in some of the new member countries (Poland and Slovakia), relatively strong in some countries of the southern part of the EU (Spain, Greece) and still problematic in some countries of the centre north, such as Germany (new *Bundesländer*). The differences between countries can be explained by the differences in three factors just described. Countries with persistently high unemployment tend to score high on labour cost and labour market rigidities; this group includes some of the largest EU member countries (Germany, France). On the other hand, countries that have more flexibility in labour market institutions showed low unemployment (e.g. the UK); the introduction of more flexibility resulted in a decrease in unemployment rates (e.g. the Netherlands). Of course the factors mentioned are not the only ones that explain the difference in unemployment. The sustained growth of the economy in terms of catching up with the EU average has been the primary driver of the decrease in unemployment in Ireland for example.

The *NMSs are a special case*. The table shows that they have in general a much higher level of unemployment than the countries of the West (North and South). The transition from command to a market economy has meant that in all of these countries certain groups were ill-adapted to the new demands. So unemployment has tended to increase everywhere. However, some countries have managed to overcome, relatively quickly, the problems; among them those that have made an early start with reforms had a diversified economic structure, are located in proximity to the West and have flexible labour markets (e.g. Slovenia and Hungary). Countries that score negatively on many of these factors are in the opposite case (e.g. Poland and Slovakia).

Over the years the *disparities* in total unemployment between the EU 15 countries have shown a rather changing picture. However, since 1993 the disparity has decreased[5] which implies that social cohesion as measured by the indicator of unemployment has improved.

Table 4.1 Development of unemployment (% of total active population) by country and gender; ratios of gender (women/men) and city size (large cities/national mean), 1990–2004

Country	1990			2004			Ratio[a] Women Men		Ratio large cities to national mean
	Total	Men	Women	Total	Men	Women	1990	2004	
Germany	5	4	7	10	9	11	1.8	1.2	1.8
France	9	7	12	10	9	11	1.7	1.2	1.6
Italy	13	6	16	8	6	11	2.7	1.8	1.4
The Netherlands	8	6	12	5	4	5	2.0	1.3	2.8
Belgium	8	5	13	8	7	9	2.6	1.3	1.4
Luxembourg	2	1	3	5	3	7	3.0	2.3	n.a.
UK	6	7	6	5	5	4	0.9	0.8	n.a.
Denmark	8	7	9	5	5	6	1.3	1.2	2.3
Ireland	16	15	17	5	5	4	1.1	0.8	6.4
Spain	16	12	24	11	8	15	2.0	1.9	1.3
Portugal	5	3	6	7	6	8	2.0	1.3	1.8
Greece	8	4	12	11	7	16	3.0	2.3	2.9
Austria				5	4	5		1.3	1.9
Sweden				6	7	6		0.9	1.7
Finland				9	9	9		1.0	2.8
EU 15				8	7	9		1.3	1.7
Poland				19	18	20		1.1	n.a.
Czech Republic				8	7	10		1.4	1.7
Hungary				6	6	6		1.0	1.7
Slovakia				18	17	19		1.1	1.7
Slovenia				6	6	7		1.2	n.a.
Lithuania				11	10	11		1.1	1.1
Cyprus				5	4	6		1.5	n.a.
Latvia				10	9	10		1.1	2.3
Estonia				9	10	8		0.8	n.a.
Malta				7	7	8		1.1	n.a.
Romania				8	9	7		0.8	n.a.
Bulgaria				12	13	12		0.9	n.a.
EU27				**9**	**8**	**10**		**1.2**	**1.5**
North	10	9	12	11	10	12	1.4	1.1	1.6
South	13	7	17	9	7	12	2.2	1.8	1.7
East				14	14	14		1.0	n.a.

Notes:
a Due to rounding of the original figures in the % columns, the figures in the ratio columns can differ from the ones that would result from a division of the figures in the % columns
b ratio large cities/national average: Urban Audit (2006)

Source: Unemployment by country and gender: Eurostat

Gender equality is an ideal that is still far from reality as far as access to employment is concerned. Indeed the figures in Table 4.1 show very clearly that women have a much higher propensity than men to be unemployed (ratios higher than 1). This is true for almost all member countries of the EU. Fortunately the situation seems to improve over time; as the last two columns show the ratio decreased substantially between 1990 and 2004 for all EU 15 member countries. For the NMSs historical data are difficult to produce. However, the data for the year 2004 show that the male–female situation in many member countries in the East is about equal to the level in the North. In many Mediterranean countries, on the contrary, women have actually much higher unemployment rates than men. This is generally traced back to cultural and institutional factors.

4.3.3 Regional picture

The regional picture of unemployment is, in large part, determined by the national one; Figure 4.1 shows very clearly that unemployment is particularly high in all the regions of countries that show high unemployment on the national level such as Poland and Bulgaria. On the other hand, there are also regional situations that distinguish themselves from the national one. These tend to coincide with the regions that suffer from disparities in terms of overall (see Chapter 2) and of economic cohesion (Chapter 3). Cases in point are the Mezzogiorno of Italy, the former DDR in Germany and the south of Spain.[6]

The disparity between regions in unemployment is considerable. Moreover, the disparity has tended to widen since the middle of the 1980s. By 1995 the dispersion of unemployment in the old member states was three times what it had been in the late 1970s. This reflects a structural weakness of high unemployment areas; they are much more vulnerable to cycles than other regions; in times of upturn they become alternative locations for many activities; in times of downturn firms tend to concentrate on the best locations.[7]

The development of unemployment has thus followed different trends in different sets of regions. However, this should not hide a very important phenomenon: that of the persistence of the problems in most regions. This is revealed by the high correlation of the rank orders of regions (at any spatial level) at different moments in time (Martin, 1998a). The causes of this persistence are generally sought in the poor functioning of the labour markets of the European countries. They reflect sluggish adaptation of the labour supply (insufficient migration) or of labour demand (insufficient capital movements to problem regions) or of the regional wage levels (national collective agreements). This applies both to relatively centrally located regions that are confronted with a decrease in their competitiveness (old industrial regions) and more peripheral regions that are characterized by traditional agriculture.

High unemployment means a low contribution to GDP and hence a relatively low position in matters of economic cohesion. The same is true for a low participation rate. So there is a double negative effect as on the regional level high unemployment tends to go hand in hand with low participation (Elhorst, 1996). Indeed the worst-performing regions showed participation rates of about 50 per cent while the best performers showed rates of around 75 per cent.

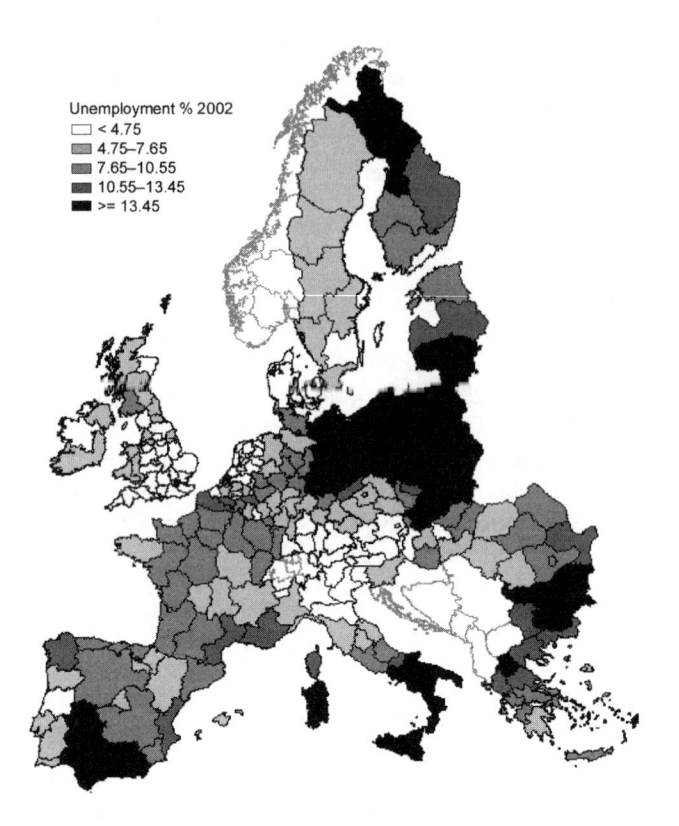

Figure 4.1 Unemployment by region, 2002

4.3.4 Urban issues

Unemployment is also often concentrated in cities, particularly in large cities. A picture of this phenomenon is given in the right-hand column of Table 4.1. One, indeed, sees very clearly that in almost all member states the unemployment rate in cities[8] is much higher than the overall rate in the country. As cities are concentrations of people it means that in absolute quantitative terms the unemployment problem of big cities is much larger than the one in low-density rural areas. Table 4.1 shows that the data for quite a few of the NMSs are missing; the detailed data for some countries not represented here show that in these countries some of the cities are not the worst in terms of unemployment (here unemployment is high in the smaller cities and rural areas).

Unemployment is not only concentrated in cities, within cities it is concentrated in certain neighbourhoods. In countries such as the UK, France and the Netherlands cases where some 40 per cent of the local population is out of employment is no exception. These compare to some neighbourhoods of the same cities where unemployment is very low. So disparities in unemployment between neighbourhoods within many of the largest cities are much larger than those between regions of the same country (ECOTEC et al., 2007).

4.4 Level of education

4.4.1 Theory and concepts

The level of education of the population plays a crucial role in the growth of the economy.[9] As the improvement of education leads to an increase in the quality and quantity of human capital it can give an important contribution to productivity, hence to competitiveness and finally to economic cohesion. However, education has also a direct role to play in social cohesion. Education is supposed to decrease the disparity between social groups in terms of access to knowledge, in terms of allegiance to common norms and in terms of the sense of belonging to society. Education creates benefits to the individual and to society that are difficult to capture in economic terms but that come through lower cost of public health, less crime, better care for the environment and more community participation, that may all improve social cohesion. In turn the increase in social cohesion tends to have a positive influence on the economic performance (e.g. Gradstein and Justman, 2001).

The realization of these positive effects depends on the way the increased human and social capital is put to use. This applies, first, to the individual who has to find the optimal conditions for the deployment of his capacities. Next, it applies to firms that have to create such conditions by putting in place both the hardware, the software and the 'humanware' by adequate management techniques. Finally, it applies to regions and countries that have to make sure that the wider socio-economic environment is conducive for optimal use. This implies that countries and regions need to make investments in education that match the technologies employed now and in the near future; it is no use going far beyond that, as the capital will not be put to use. In the framework of the EU that implies a strong investment in the higher brackets, given the level of sophistication that the EU economy has reached and given the policy objective of competitiveness in the knowledge economy. However, there are internal differences in emphasis between large geographical areas of the EU; the pressure for high levels is strongest in the North West and least in the East. This, of course, is also applicable to regions within the countries of each geographical area. To give an example: the main role in the catch up of Italian regions in the last quarter of the previous century has been played by medium-level human capital that was most effectively exploited by the economic system (Baici and Casalone, 2005).

4.4.2 National differences in education

Table 4.2, hereafter, gives a picture of the development of education over time. We have taken here as the indicator the share of the population with a tertiary

68 *Assessing the problems and identifying causes*

education. Given the problems of comparability of the basic data the results have to be interpreted with care. However, the following salient features stand out:

- There is a very pervasive trend of gradual upgrading of the education level. This is evident in the increase of the shares as one moves from the older age brackets to the younger ones. This trend does indeed apply to all EU countries, although it seems to level off in recent years in a few of the highest developed countries.
- There are considerable differences between member countries and between geographic regions. The areas and countries that have the highest level of economic development also show the highest shares in tertiary education. However, we observe that the level of education is in general higher in the East than in the West. So provided this human capital is well used it means that at least one condition for a fast catching up of the East is fulfilled.
- The disparity between the countries (as measured by the coefficient of variation) is highest for the older age brackets, lesser for the younger ones. It seems to stay fairly stable over time. One might have thought that it would have decreased as countries with low shares tend to catch up with the EU average.

4.4.3 *Regional and urban aspects*

The regional patterns tend to show the effects of two phenomena:

1 National features dominate regional ones. For instance, all Spanish, Italian and Portuguese regions tend to show relatively low educational attainment levels. On the other hand, all regions in the Nordic countries Sweden and Finland show fairly high educational attainment levels.
2 Intra-country variation is based on the urban–rural split. Urban centres tend to be concentrations of people with higher education. This is evidenced in the right-hand column of Table 4.2 that gives the ratio large city/country (people with higher education as part of total population). One sees that in all countries the ratio is largely in excess of 1.0. In some countries, notably the NMSs where the national level (N) is fairly low, the ratio even exceeds three. As is evidenced in the bottom part of the table the ratio is higher the lower the level of development.

Apart from the urban picture it is difficult to see other clear-cut patterns on the regional level. This changes if one does not only look at education levels per se but if one compares these figures with those of other indicators of disparity. The following patterns emerge (EC, 2004a):

- *Wealth.* In regions with a GDP/P level substantially below the EU average[10] the proportion of the population attaining tertiary education tends to be low. Furthermore, there is little sign that the divergence between these regions and the well-to-do regions in the EU is narrowing.

Table 4.2 Percentage of population with a tertiary education degree by country and age group, 2001[b]

Country	Age group[a]				City/ N ratio
	25–39	40–54	55–69	25–69	
Germany	23	24	17	22	1.3
France	28	19	10	20	1.6
Italy	13	11	6	10	n.a.
The Netherlands	25	23	16	22	1.2
Luxembourg	21	17	10	17	n.a.
UK	28	22	15	22	1.3
Denmark	25	26	17	23	1.2
Ireland	39	22	14	27	1.3
Spain	13	8	3	9	n.a.
Portugal	20	12	7	14	3.0
Greece	23	18	8	17	1.8
Austria	15	15	10	14	n.a.
Sweden	25	25	18	23	1.1
Finland	37	30	20	30	1.4
EU15	**22**	**17**	**10**	**17**	**1.7**
Poland	17	12	10	13	2.4
Czech Republic	13	12	11	12	2.2
Hungary	15	15	11	14	2.0
Slovakia	14	14	9	13	3.2
Slovenia	20	16	12	16	n.a.
Lithuania	31	28	16	26	2.1
Cyprus	38	26	13	28	n.a.
Latvia	15	17	13	15	1.3
Estonia	32	33	24	30	n.a.
Romania	11	11	7	10	2.9
Bulgaria	23	21	15	20	2.1
EU27	**20**	**16**	**10**	**16**	**1.7**
North	27	21	13	22	1.4
South	14	11	6	11	1.9
East	16	14	10	14	2.3
CoV	36	36	39	34	–

Notes:
a Belgium and Malta not included in original data
b Data from microcensus Eurostat

Source: Urban audit

- *Unemployment.* People with a low degree of education are more likely to be out of work than people with a high education. This gap tends to be wider in regions where the overall unemployment rate is relatively high.

4.5 Migration and segregation

4.5.1 Some concepts and theory

In matters of migration we have to make a distinction between intra-EU migration and migration from other parts of the world into the EU. Migration within the EU is fundamentally free. Internal flows in the North and South are very limited and are not seen as a threat to social cohesion. With respect to migration from the NMSs to the old there is more unrest but this is likely to be solved over the transition period. However, immigration from other parts of the world is perceived as a problem. Many observers agree that the migration of people with a different racial and cultural background and with little chance on the EU labour market do form a threat to social cohesion. So we have to see what drives such migration and what determines the reaction.

The theoretical foundations that explain migration all tend to focus on a few basic notions: push, pull and resistance factors.

- On the push factor side we find the reasons why people want to leave their home country; these are often combinations of problem situations of which the components are unemployment, poverty, unrest and insecurity.
- On the pull side we find the reasons why people are attracted to a country; factors such as freedom, employment opportunities, social protection, etc.
- In terms of friction one sees a number of elements that increase the cost of the move to the migrant; such as distance, culture and language difference, restrictive immigration policies, etc.

The EU economy has changed over time and is now characterized by persistent high unemployment. Under the influence of the increased globalization many low-skilled jobs are now transferred to low-wage countries. That means that many jobs that traditionally were filled by low-skilled immigrants no longer exist in the EU. Moreover, the integration of the previous immigrants into society reveals itself much more problematic than was initially thought; unemployment hits, more than proportionally, second- and third-generation immigrants. Claims on welfare benefits are mounting. The conditions for integration in the receiving countries have deteriorated (lack of job opportunities and increasing cost of social integration). So the general feeling is that the EU does not need any more immigration apart from some selected for their capacity to fill skill shortages of strategic importance (e.g. knowledge workers).

As a consequence of the upsurge in migratory pressure on the EU, voices grew loud in a call to severely *limit immigration* into the EU.[11] In practice, the governments of all member countries have now resorted to a policy of restriction of immigration. Notwithstanding a clear convergence of national policies with respect to their targets and their instruments, it has not yet been possible to complete a common EU asylum and immigration policy.[12] However, some features of it are discernible. They concern harmonization of rules, close cooperation between national immigration authorities and the setting up of a Union agency for border issues.

The pressure on the EU from the non-EU countries is, however, mounting. Political and social unrest in many areas of the world increases the number of asylum seekers. Unsatisfactory employment opportunities at home push many to try to enter the EU as workers. Others try to enter illegally. The estimates of illegal immigrants are very wide ranging between several hundreds of thousands and a million for the larger member states and several tens of thousand and a hundred thousand for the medium member states. Most of these are employed in the informal economy. The demand of EU employers in the black and grey economy (motivated by lower cost, flexibility, avoidance of safety rules, etc.) is thus an important pull factor that is often disregarded.

Now the presence of many migrants is often seen as a threat to social cohesion as they can lead to a high degree of intolerance and ethnic exclusionism on the part of the majority population. A theory that is used to explain this phenomenon is based on 'competition' or 'conflict' over scarce resources. In other words: people that experience real or perceived competition for jobs, housing, welfare, etc., will collude with their peers and try to exclude the others. In the case of majority populations they react to such threats from non-nationals by constructing obstacles against integration of minorities into society. This then creates problems of segregation; the newcomers are trapped in a situation of low access to housing and jobs and find themselves concentrated in some areas where there chances of escape from the circle are low (see Section 4.5.3).

4.5.2 The national picture

The total number of labour migrants has increased over the past decades. The official figures indicate that they amounted to some three million in 1973 and to some five million in 2000 (Molle, 2006). However, in terms of the share of the labour force the increase is less visible; from somewhat less than 3 per cent then to somewhat more than 3 per cent now. However, these figures under-report very significantly the real picture. This is mostly due to illegal migration and work on the black economy. Indeed, recent migrants often go to the informal, sometimes even illegal, labour market (Pugliese, 1992). So countries with a high share of the informal economy (black and grey) in the total economy also show a high share of illegal immigrants in the total employment, and vice versa (Djajic, 2001). An example of the high end is Italy, and an example of the low end is Denmark.

These migratory flows are very different from the ones that prevailed in the 1960s, for several reasons.

First, they concern more *sending countries* over a much wider geographical area. Apart from the traditional immigration from the countries of North Africa, countries in Latin America, Asia and sub-Saharan Africa now send people to the EU in significant numbers. The causes of this migration tend to become more complex (intertwining of political, security and economic factors), leading to increased pressure. Two cases in point can be mentioned: the migration from Argentina to Spain after the crisis in the former country and the continuous flow from migrants of black Africa that try to reach the shores of EU countries by all sort of means.

Second, they concern more *receiving countries*. The developed northwestern countries of the EU have traditionally been immigration countries and this continues due to so-called follow up migration (members of families, brides) and new migration attracted by the (perceived) opportunities in these countries. But

72 *Assessing the problems and identifying causes*

immigration concerns also the southern European countries that up to the mid-1980s had almost no immigration; they have now become the host countries of millions of third-country immigrants. This is due to their improved economic situation but also to their location on the southern borders of the EU that makes them the points of access for many immigrants. Smaller countries such as Malta even fear serious destabilization due to the pressure of immigrants that come to their shores. Even the NMSs have become immigration countries attracting people from their eastern neighbours such as the Ukraine.

Although, in this way, almost all EU countries have become immigration countries; the relative importance of the immigrants in their population is quite different (see Table 4.3).

The percentage number of migrants is still significantly higher in the northwestern group of countries than in the southwestern group of countries. Differences in wage levels may explain this to a large extent.

The characteristics of the migrants do reflect the socio-economic situation in the host country. Indeed, in the high-income countries in northwest Europe the percentage share of people with less than upper secondary school education is much higher among immigrants than nationals of these countries, which is an indication of the influx of low-educated people mostly filling in low-paid jobs. In the low-income countries of the east the share of the highly educated is higher among foreigners than nationals, indicating that in these countries foreigners mostly fill vacancies as managers or experts. The countries of the southwest take an intermediate position, with diversified situations that do not permit to describe clear patterns (OECD, 2005).

The question is then: Does a high proportion of migrants (as prevails in most countries of the northwest and increasingly in the countries of the southwest of the EU) lead to a lack of social cohesion? The answer is yes (EUMC, 2005) for countries where this high proportion goes hand in hand with high levels of unemployment and low levels of income. This underscores the importance of the GDP/P indicator we have taken in Chapter 2 for overall cohesion and of unemployment we have taken for social cohesion in this chapter.

4.5.3 *Some concepts and theory about segregation*

Most of the immigrants have only little education and low levels of professional training. So they tend to go to urban agglomerations where most low-skilled work opportunities exist in the manufacturing and service sectors (both in the official and in the black economy). There is a second reason why migrants concentrate there. Migrants will seek to rely, in the first instance, on people from their country of origin who have migrated earlier and who have already found their way in the highly complex administrative and legal environment that characterizes modern societies.

The concentration of migrants in urban areas is followed by a further concentration in specific areas of these agglomerations. Here, it is not so much job opportunities that drive the phenomenon. It is a highly complex interplay between social networks, availability of low-cost housing, access to certain ser-

Table 4.3 Evolution of the number of migrants as % of total population by country (1980–2000) and ratio of large cities to national average

Country	Migrants/population[a]			Cities/N ratio
	1980	1990	2000	2001
Germany	7.2	8.2	8.9	1.8
France	n.a.	6.3	5.6	1.6
Italy	0.5	1.4	2.3	1.4
The Netherlands	3.7	4.6	4.2	2.8
Belgium	9.0	9.1	8.4	1.4
Luxembourg	25.8	28.6	36.1	n.a.
UK	n.a.	3.3	4.4	n.a.
Denmark	2.0	3.1	4.8	2.3
Ireland	n.a.	0.8	3.3	6.4
Spain	0.5	1.0	2.2	1.3
Portugal	0.5	1.1	1.9	1.8
Greece	2.2	2.3	7.3	2.9
Austria	3.7	5.9	9.4	1.9
Sweden	5.1	5.6	5.4	1.8
Finland	0.3	0.5	1.7	2.8
Poland	n.a.	n.a.	0,1	n.a.
Czech Republic	n.a.	0.3	2.2	1.7
Hungary	n.a.		1.1	1.7
Slovakia			0.5	1.7
Slovenia			2.1	n.a.
Lithuania			1.1	1.1
Latvia			1.2	1.3
EU	**2.0**	**3.8**	**4.5**	**1.5**
North	3.3	6.0	6.4	1.6
South	0.6	1.3	2.7	1.7
East	n.a.	n.a.	n.a.	n.a.

Note:
a No data for Bulgaria, Cyprus, Estonia, Lithuania, Malta and Romania

Source: Percentage migrants: http://www.migrationinformation.org/GlobalData/countrydata/data.cfm; OECD (2003) Large cities: Urban Audit 2006 (figures for non EU nationals)

vices, etc. This leads to spatial segregation of, on the one hand, the poor immigrants that often are of a different race than the nationals of the country of immigration and on the other hand the well-to-do. This segregation is explained by three sets of theory.[13]

1   *Competition for urban space.* The people with the highest income will be able to occupy the areas with the best access to urban and other amenities. This leads to the concentration of the well-to-do in the urban centres and in the urban fringes.
2   *Neighbourhood externalities.* Poor immigrants will concentrate in areas where they can rely on social and family ties. This tendency towards segregation is exacerbated by the more successful people leaving these areas. The ensuing

74 *Assessing the problems and identifying causes*

concentration of poverty and unemployment in certain neighbourhoods often leads to crime and violence. In this way such urban neighbourhoods may become stigmatized. This stigma may then lead to a sort of poverty and misery trap, as people living in such an area may be discriminated against in the labour market only on the basis of their address and name. These lesser opportunities may then lead to high percentages of drop-outs from the educational system and hence, low aptitude to the formal labour market.

3   *Housing policies of local authorities*. The relatively decentralized structure of local government in most countries of the EU means that some do favour the private sector development, while others tend to put the accent on the publicly subsidized social housing accessible to the less well off and the poor.

The major economic changes that occurred over the past decades (see Chapter 3) such as the loss of manufacturing jobs (due to delocalization and globalization) and the rise of high-quality service jobs (due to further specialization into high-value-added sectors) have hit, in particular, the immigrant labour traditionally concentrated in blue-collar manufacturing jobs. It led to high levels of unemployment of immigrants notably in cities where the new service jobs were either insufficient in number or inaccessible as to the level of qualification. These became actual pockets of problems in cities where urban (housing) policies were not well developed.[14]

4.5.4 Regional and urban aspects

The proportion of *migrants* in the total population is in general much higher in large cities than on average. This rule holds for almost all member states (see right-hand column of Table 4.3). The concentration of migrants in cities is exacerbated by the further concentration within certain neighbourhoods of these urban agglomerations. This tends to lead to problems of segregation.

Segregation is a factor that prevails in most major cities of the EU, in particular the metropolises of northwestern Europe. However, notwithstanding the importance of the problem it is not very well documented. It is notably difficult to know whether the problem has become smaller or larger over time. We will illustrate this with a few case studies.

For *France* an analysis has been made by type of function people have, ranging from high (managers) to low (poorly skilled blue-collar workers). In the urban agglomerations studied the segregation levels between these groups have been rather stable over the past decades. Only in Paris did one observe a trend towards increasing socio-spatial polarization between high and low strata of the functional hierarchy (Gachet and Le Gallo, 2005).

For the *UK* the patterns of segregation depend on the indicator chosen, although there is some overlap. The unemployment indicator shows that problems are widely spread, with a strong concentration in the older industrial towns of northern England and the Midlands. There is no evidence that segregation has declined over the past 20 years (Meen *et al.*, 2005)

In *Sweden* there is only one major agglomeration: Stockholm. Here the segregation between foreign born and natives has increased over the past decades. The latter are increasingly concentrated in deprived neighbourhoods. This process is notably due to selective migration processes, the simultaneous inflow of the weaker and marginalized (often foreigners) into these areas and the outflow of relatively well-off residents from these areas (Andersson and Brama, 2004).

So one may conclude that segregation is an important problem in the EU and that over the past decades the situation has probably further deteriorated.

4.6 Social exclusion

4.6.1 Concepts; theory

In the EU the term social exclusion has quickly been widely accepted. In the course of time it has been used both in a static and in a dynamic sense. The first denotes a certain degree of deprivation, the other a process of increasing deprivation (see Vleminckx and Berghman, 2001).

Important aspects of social exclusion are mutual reinforcement and entrapment. We may illustrate this as follows. A prolonged situation of unemployment may lead to durable loss of qualifications as skills become obsolete due to changes in technology. The resulting lack of capacity to earn sufficient income inhibits people from investing in new skills. Poverty often goes hand in hand with ill-health, poor housing and low participation in civic life. Adverse situations may lead to indebtedness. Despair can lead to problems such as alcoholism and crime. The latter will make it very difficult for anyone to find a good job. This vicious circle means that social exclusion often equals durable and multiple deprivation.

Social inclusion or exclusion is thus a multi-dimensional concept. The two main dimensions concern the labour market (access to jobs) and the capacity to consume; or the access to goods and services. Other important dimensions are the participation in social relations normally available to the average citizen.

Unlike the term 'cohesion', that has been made operational with the use of statistics on disparity in income between regions and social groups, the term 'social exclusion' has not yet found a simple translation in statistical terms.

Central to the notion, however, is the aspect of unemployment and low capacity to earn income (wages, education). We have already discussed that in the previous sections. Another more direct indicator is poverty. Indeed it has been shown that poverty does negatively influence the capacity of people to participate in culture and society in general and, therefore, is a lead indicator for social exclusion. Poverty has many definitions. Some start from absolute standards, as to availability of food, shelter and clothing (Sen, 1983). However, such notions are not very relevant in highly developed societies. So, in the EU a relative concept of poverty is in use, whereby the position of certain groups is defined as poor in case they are below a certain percentage of the average situation in the country. These thresholds are often defined in terms of income or capacity to consume certain goods.[15]

4.6.2 The national picture

In the past the member states of the EU have all used very different concepts in matters of social exclusion. These reflected different levels of economic development, different social preferences and different institutional choices to cope with problems. These differences have precluded, up until recently, a comparative analysis on the EU level. In the early 1990s a start was made with comparable statistics on poverty (Eurostat, 1990, 1994). These data show that:

- Countries with high income levels and elaborate welfare states show low poverty rates; countries with low income and less developed welfare states show high poverty shares.
- The most vulnerable groups in all member states are households headed by an unemployed person (a fortiori where no one works), a single elderly, a single parent, a female, or a poorly educated.

By the end of the 1990s comparable data have become available from the European Community Household Panel surveys. These allow us to heed several dimensions of social exclusion that are given in Table 4.4. Unfortunately they do not yet cover the whole of the EU 27, nor the urban dimension. They show that:

- *Poverty* (defined as income below 60 per cent of the national mean) tends to be high in countries with high levels of income inequality and low in countries with low-income inequality.[16] The former is the case in the countries

Table 4.4 Social exclusion by country (several indicators), end of 1990s[17]

Country	Income; poverty	Non-monetary indicators			Persistence of problems Cumulative disadvantage
		Living conditions	Necessities of life	Social relations	
Germany	10	6	11	4	6
France	18	7	14	4	9
Italy	16	9	15	7	10
The Netherlands	11	4	10	5	5
Belgium	13	8	11	9	8
Luxembourg	11	5	8	6	6
UK	22	5	18	2	14
Denmark	13	3	6	3	4
Ireland	15	10	16	1	9
Spain	19	8	16	2	9
Portugal	23	21	15	5	17
Greece	21	10	32	2	16
Austria	11	7	11	6	7
Sweden	–	–	–	–	–
Finland	14	4	12	3	6

Source: Tsakloglou and Papadopoulos (2002)

of Southern Europe and in the UK; the latter in the countries of northwestern Europe. These differences go hand in hand with cultural differences in the ideas about the causes; people in southern countries feel that poverty is largely inherited and they tend to be in that situation for a long time. People in the UK see poverty more related to personal condition. Finally, people in the last group of countries think that poverty is associated with some unfavourable life event (Gallie and Paugam, 2002).

- *Living conditions* (defined as the average of a range of indicators on aspects such as housing conditions and access to durable household goods) vary much more than poverty between EU countries. Even though the indicators are relative to the national mean we see that they are low in low-income countries (such as Greece, Italy and Ireland and, particularly, Portugal).
- *Necessities of life* (defined as the average of indicators with respect to the possibility to keep the home warm, to leave for a week's holiday a year, etc.) show a less clear-cut picture, although here too one observes that the highest problems are felt in the low-income countries and the UK and the lowest problems seem to exist in the highly developed welfare states (Nordic Model).
- *Social relations* (meant to capture the non-material aspects of exclusion such as contact with friends, participation in clubs and associations) do not seem to be the most differentiating factor between countries.

The indicators: 'accumulation' and 'persistence' of problems tend to show very similar patterns in the EU. For that reason we have taken them together in Table 4.4 into one indicator. The figure of that composite indicator (last column of Table 4.4) shows a very high correlation with the poverty indicator: very high figures are shown for the UK, Portugal and Greece, while low figures are shown for the developed welfare states of the North (DK, NL, FRG, Lux). Sudden drops in income are the main origin of people falling into the poverty trap. The main instrument to prevent this happening is the welfare benefit system. Differences in welfare regimes thus tend to determine, to a large extent, the differences between EU countries in vulnerability to poverty and in persistence of poverty (Layte and Whelan, 2003; Whelan and Maitre, 2005).

4.6.3 The regional picture

Poverty can be measured by the share of people (households) who are dependent on low-income levels. The sparse internationally comparable figures available (Stewart, 2003) show a quite clear centre-periphery dichotomy (see next chapter). The highest poverty rates are found in the peripheral areas of the EU; the lowest poverty figures are found in the heartland of Europe (the Netherlands, Belgium, Luxemburg, part of western Germany and eastern France and northern Italy). If one compares these results with those of Figure 2.3 about average income, one remarks that low poverty shares are correlated to high income and vice versa. This need not surprise, as a matter of fact; low average income regions are likely to have a proportionately higher share of poor inhabitants than regions with a high average income.

Now one may argue that the comparison of household income to the national average is not that adequate. There are actually two reasons why a comparison to regional averages might be more adequate. First, the cost of living can differ a lot from a highly urbanized central region (e.g. Paris) with a more dispersed population and less centrally located region (e.g. Bretagne). Second, poverty is a relative notion, so the reference group should be rather other people in the same area than the national mean. If one takes regional averages as benchmarks the centre-periphery dichotomy is almost imperceptible. Moreover, some central capital regions such as Paris, Madrid and Vienna show up as average problem regions. Actually these results corroborate earlier findings that in large conurbations there is a real problem of poverty for significant segments of the population.

4.7 Social protection

4.7.1 Some theory and concepts

People are confronted with a large range of uncertainties and risks; forces beyond their control that can have a very strong influence on their capacity to earn an income. The loss of income due to accidents (becoming disabled), etc., can push people into poverty. Traditionally such problems were alleviated by solidarity based on family bonds and/or local charities. In the course of the nineteenth century the state started to take a certain responsibility for welfare, in particular, schemes of old-age pension. These schemes were not based on charity but on entitlements; state social transfers were: need based, means tested, non-contributory and tax funded. They reflected solidarity of the citizens of a national society with the unlucky among them.

The reasons for such actions were often of a political nature; for instance, in Germany the social security system reinforced the bonds of the citizens with the newly unified state. In other countries, however, theoretical arguments about productivity effects played a role. People who know they are insured against basic risks of becoming poor tend to make higher contributions to the national wealth by being more innovative, more productive, etc. Mind that the opposite can also be argued in terms of the risks of becoming unemployed; the higher the protection, the lower the incentive to accept a job for which cost needs to be made in terms of geographical or professional mobility.

After the Second World War all member countries of the EU have elaborated their national systems of protecting their citizens in general, and their workers in particular, against loss of income due to unemployment, sickness, accidents, old age and so on.[18] Many of them included a system of minimum income to those who did not have the means to earn one. This implied a considerable increase of the items of the national budgets devoted to social security, paid for by the taxpayers of that country.

Social security is thus based on national solidarity. Now European integration has eroded the bases of such solidarity in many instances, starting with the free movement of workers (see Ferrera, 2006). The EU member states have reacted to this not by accepting an increased involvement of the EU in such matters, but by limiting the inroads of European regulation to that system to the very essentials. They have jealously kept the development of their systems to themselves and have dealt with the complications of EU integration by specifying the cases where non-nationals can draw upon their social security schemes.

So, from a European policy point of view social protection is an exogenous factor. For that reason we do not deal with it in the policy chapters of the book but treat it already here as it influences disparities as perceived on the EU level.

4.7.2 The national picture

The national systems have been elaborated independently of each other in very different institutional and cultural settings. Thus, it is not surprising that they are very idiosyncratic and differ from each other on a very large number of points. However, on closer investigation, one can see some clear patterns (see Box 4.1).

Box 4.1 Models of social protection

On the basis of a clustering of characteristics of a whole series of indicators of social protection systems it appears that in the EU five types of welfare state exist.[19] They tend to be associated with specific geographic areas of the EU.[20]

- *West*. This type is of liberal inspiration. Public sector financed protection is limited to groups that have no other options; all others are supposed to take private insurance against such risks. The state stimulates the latter by tax incentives. Examples of this group are the UK and Ireland.
- *North*. A type that is dominated by socio-democratic views. Large groups of the population are collectively (via public finances) insured against a broad range of risks. Benefits are rather generous. In order to maintain the financial sustainability of the system it is coupled with many stimuli to reintegration into the labour market such as active labour market policies. Typical representatives in this group are the Scandinavian countries Sweden and Denmark.
- *Central*. This system has many intellectual sources. Its most salient feature is that many different professional groups have their specific provisions. Public sector finance and regulation support sectoral financing and rule-setting. The system is often characterized as corporatist. Examples are Germany, the Netherlands, France and Belgium.
- *South*. The countries in this group have a limited safety net in terms of access to general schemes of income support. Labour market policy is not very developed. On the other hand, there are high pension

> schemes (based on old habits as patronage). Examples are Greece, Spain and, to a lesser extent, Italy.
>
> - *East.* These countries had before the transition very elaborate systems that were characterized by very high levels of protection. Since transition the capacity of these countries to finance even rudimentary systems is very limited. So for the time being this group has low scores on all indicators (e.g. Poland and Hungary).

A good indicator of the various systems is the level of expenditure on social protection. We depict in Table 4.5 the evolution of the protection in terms of benefits per head of population and in terms of share in total GDP. The two indicators used reflect fairly well the general picture described in Box 4.1.

Social security payments per head figures show the existence of several categories of countries.

1   Very high levels, these are the traditional welfare states of the developed part of the EU. We cite here in decreasing order the group of Scandinavian countries and the group of core countries of the EU (D, F, NL, B, L, A).
2   About average, where we find two types: the UK that has relatively low protection levels compared to other high GDP/P countries due to its choice of system and Italy due to its lower than average level of development.
3   Below average levels; all due to low development levels (Med).
4   Very low levels particularly NMSs (based on rudimentary data not taken up in the table).

Social benefits as a percentage of GDP indicates also that protection is much less well developed in the less well-off member countries than in the richer countries. Table 4.5 shows also that the level of protection seems to follow a so-called S curve; initially it rises more than proportionally as income rises but from a certain level onwards it tends to level off. The table indicates that for some countries the point of saturation seems to have been reached. The reason for this levelling off is twofold. First, systems take into account that very generous benefits may have a negative influence on the flexibility of the labour market. Second, systems leave the insurance against other than basic risks to the private sector.[21]

The level of protection influences the degree to which the systems are able to reduce poverty. In the richer member countries social transfers (including old-age pensions) reduce poverty with some 50–60 per cent while in the less well-off (EU 15) member states this figure is around 40 per cent. This effect is also visible in the very neat negative correlation between the risk of poverty and the level of social expenditure per capita (EC, 2002b: 200).

An analysis of the development of the coefficient of variation shows (for the EU 15) that disparity in access to social security between countries of the EU has systematically decreased over the period 1960–2000.

Table 4.5 Social benefits (expenditure) by country, 1960–2000

Country	€1,000 per head[a]			% of GDP[b]				
	1980	1990	2000	1960	1970	1980	1990	2000
Germany	5.3	5.5	6.9	13	14	17	16	17
France	4.4	5.2	6.6	13	15	19	21	24
Italy	2.6	5.0	4.4	10	12	14	18	20
The Netherlands	5.0	5.5	6.2	7	13	20	18	18
Belgium	4.4	4.6	6.0	11	14	21	21	21
Luxembourg	4.4	5.7	9.1	n.a.	n.a.	n.a.	n.a.	n.a.
UK	3.0	3.8	6.4	6	8	11	11	13
Denmark	5.4	6.6	8.4	6	9	15	18	17
Ireland	2.0	2.2	3.3	4	8	12	15	14
Spain	1.4	2.7	2.7	4	6	12	14	15
Portugal	0.6	1.3	2.2	2	3	7	8	13
Greece	0.7	2.9	2.4	5	8	9	15	16
Austria	n.a.	5.2	6.9	8	11	15	15	16
Sweden	n.a.	8.9	8.5	6	8	14	16	16
Finland	n.a.	6.3	5.8	6	7	9	14	19
EU 15	**3.4**	**4.3**	**5.4**	**7**	**10**	**14**	**16**	**17**
Poland	n.a.	n.a.	0.5	n.a.	n.a.	n.a.	n.a.	16
Czech Republic	n.a.	n.a.	0.8	n.a.	n.a.	n.a.	n.a.	12
Hungary	n.a.	n.a.	0.5	n.a.	n.a.	n.a.	n.a.	12
Slovakia	n.a.	n.a.	0.6	n.a.	n.a.	n.a.	n.a.	12
Slovenia	n.a.	n.a.	1.8	n.a.	n.a.	n.a.	n.a.	17
Lithuania	n.a.	n.a.	0.4	n.a.	n.a.	n.a.	n.a.	11
Cyprus	n.a.	n.a.	n.a.	n.a.	n.a.	n.a.	n.a.	14
Latvia	n.a.	n.a.	0.4	n.a.	n.a.	n.a.	n.a.	13
Estonia	n.a.	n.a.	0.4	n.a.	n.a.	n.a.	n.a.	n.a.
Malta	n.a.	n.a.	1.5	n.a.	n.a.	n.a.	n.a.	12
EU 25[c]	**n.a.**	**n.a.**	**4.6**	**n.a.**	**n.a.**	**n.a.**	**n.a.**	**15**

Notes:
a Expressed in 1995 euros; data from Eurostat
b Data from Cornelisse and Goudswaard (2002); Eurostat
c No data for Bulgaria and Romania available

4.7.3 The regional picture

There exists very little systematic evidence about the way the transfers from the social security system do contribute to the regional distribution of wealth. The ones that exist for individual countries do, however, tend to show that this effect is very substantial. Mind that the redistribution from rich to poor regions is not only entailed by social security benefits in the strict sense, but also by public insurance systems against health risks, etc. Similar effects do even exist for all welfare state policies.[22]

4.8 Summary and conclusions

- Theory on social cohesion is very fragmented. The fragments tend to explain specific phenomena but do not come to conclusions about development of the factors that determine cohesion. Unfortunately the long-term evolution of social disparities is difficult to measure due to serious deficiencies in the data. So it is not possible to draw very strong conclusions about social convergence or divergence.

- In matters of *unemployment* important disparities persist. Notably the new member states suffer from high levels of unemployment. In the old member states the situation is diversified. Regional unemployment is fairly persistent depending on institutional (country) and geographical factors. Unemployment has become, increasingly, an urban phenomenon.
- *Education* levels differ much in line with GDP/P levels. This relation holds for countries, regions and cities. The disparity seems to decrease only slightly over time.
- *Migration* tends to increase pressure on social cohesion, notably where the influx adds to already existing problems of unemployment. Segregation (racial and professional) has tended to increase in many of the EU member countries.
- *Social exclusion* has several causes, one of which is *poverty*. The latter indicator shows quite a strong disparity along centre periphery patterns. The lowest figures appear in the richer countries in the EU heartland, the higher figures in the poor countries in the East and South.
- Many countries protect their citizens by different schemes of *social security*. These tend to vary much in line with the level of wealth of the country. Disparity in access to social security has systematically decreased.

5 Territorial disparities

5.1 Introduction

Next to economic and social disparities the concept of territorial disparities has come to the fore. The latter is even less well crystallized than the former. To bring as much clarity as possible we will devote the first section to its policy context, its definition and its measurement.

Next we will go into three major aspects of territorial disparities.

First, we discuss the disparities in *access to markets*. We indicate the areas that have good connections to markets via high-quality transport (and other) infrastructure and others where the *access to markets* in other regions is a real problem.

Next, we discuss *access to know-how and to innovation*, key to participation in the knowledge economy. Some productions require only simple, others very sophisticated technologies. Access to the various sources of innovation is of essence; one may think here of knowledge centres such as universities and specialized R&D organizations.

Finally, we go into *lack of access*, in particular the problems that national borders create to communication and the care for the environment and hence to a balanced development of the European space.

The basic findings will be given in a concluding section.

5.2 Concepts and indicators

5.2.1 Policy-relevant concepts and definitions

The concept of territorial cohesion is a relative newcomer. It has not yet got a clear let alone a formally adopted definition. On the contrary, it is in many respects still fairly ambiguous.[1] The concept 'territory' refers in general to clearly delimited spatial units, often coinciding with discrete political and/or administrative entities, such as regions and cities.

The *theoretical notions* of territoriality come from different strands. In one strand of thought the notion is mainly associated with the institutional barriers that ensue from the bounding of spaces. Such bounding has in general been realized by a sovereign that wanted to exert exclusive power over the subjects living in a territory, over the material goods present in that territory and over the relationships between subjects and objects. The bounding has often been done in a hierarchical way; local authorities being subsidiary to regions that in turn are subsidiaries of the nation states (Sack, 1986).

Another line of thought refers more to geographical features, in practice, handicaps. Examples of such handicaps occur in mountainous areas that lack flat land for economic activities or in peripheral areas that are restricted in their access to resources in the more central areas where activities tend to be concentrated. This seems to become the dominant view.

To understand the meaning of territorial cohesion better we will look at some major EU documents where the term is used. The term has been introduced in legal texts only in 1997.[2] The term has been introduced in *policy statements by* the second cohesion report of the European Commission (EC, 2001), where it was loosely linked to notions about a more balanced development of European space. It has been made more specific by the Community Strategic Guidelines 2007–2013 (EC, 2005). This document confirms that the *objective* of territorial cohesion is to *achieve a more balanced spatial development*. The major *ways* in which this objective is to be reached are in:

- the building of sustainable communities in both urban and rural areas;
- reducing the effects of (ultra) peripherality (due to such factors as insularity, sparse population, etc.), in particular with respect to services of general economic interest;
- improving the situation of cross-border and broader trans-national areas. This also involves improving territorial integration and encouraging cooperation between and within regions.

The official EU documents are not our only source for tracing the meaning of territorial cohesion. In a diversified set of documents we encounter the normative view of territorial cohesion meaning that people should not be disadvantaged by wherever they happen to live or work in the Union. Following these strands of thought we can then define *territorial cohesion as a situation whereby people and firms are not unduly handicapped by spatial differences in access to basic services, basic infrastructure and knowledge.*

To find an operational meaning of the concept of territorial cohesion we have to turn to documents on *spatial planning*. Spatial planning visualizes the consequences of autonomous developments and of policy choices on a specific territory and helps to create the conditions for a balanced development by integrating in one framework the various elements (industry, transport, infrastructure, ecological parks, etc.) and prioritize the claims of these users on space.[3] Spatial planning has for a long time been considered as a purely national competence. And national traditions about spatial planning differ a lot. Some take a minimalist view, limiting the concept to land use planning. Others take a maximalist view whereby spatial planning is the integrative framework for all policies with a spatial impact. Up until now the EU has not been given powers in this domain, notwithstanding clear relations between, for instance, regional development and spatial planning. However, with the growing integration the need for some sort of coordination at the European level has become apparent. This coordination has initially been done in the Council of Europe.[4] In this forum ideas of spatial planning have gradually matured. In 1997, after some ten years of work, the European Spatial Development Perspective (ESDP) was adopted.[5] This document has been elaborated with the support of the EU but not in the formal framework of the EU.

It defines three major aims of territorial cohesion:

1. Accessibility: to safeguard equal access of all EU regions to infrastructure and know-how.
2. Polycentrism: to maintain a balanced urban system for the EU as a whole and for its constituent parts.
3. Trusteeship: to achieve prudent management of the cultural and natural heritage.

5.2.2 Operational indicators

The previous sections have highlighted the lack of a generally accepted definition of the concept of territorial cohesion. From this follows of course a considerable difficulty in operationalizing the concepts in the perspective of the policy objectives. In the literature one sees two approaches:

1. *Minimalist.* This approach covers only the aspects of polycentrism (see Box 5.1) and accessibility (see ESDP). Territorial cohesion can be operationalized by specifying the disparities in, for example, accessibility between (types of) territories in statistical terms and follow over time their development.
2. *Maximalist.* The approach aims at achieving sustainable development that is based on the increase in a region's competitiveness by mobilizing its indigenous resources. The operationalization of this broad concept can no longer be based on simple indicators but has to try to work with composite indexes based on a whole series of indicators.[6]

In order to avoid overlap between the discussions on territorial cohesion and economic and social cohesion we will interpret territorial cohesion in an even stricter way than the minimalist approach. It means that we will work with only a few policy-oriented specific indicators. We are compelled to this approach as some of the notions that are high on the political agenda cannot be translated into operational concepts. This is notably the case for the battle horse of territorial cohesion: polycentrism (see Box 5.1).

Box 5.1 Polycentrism: a concept as yet impossible to make operational

The concept of polycentric development lacks a clear, generally accepted definition. It shares this characteristic with other notions that have a strong normative political dimension and where the very vagueness of the concept permits many to use it to their proper aims (compare the term cohesion in its infancy). Arguments for polycentric development often take as their point of departure the assumed prevalence of divergent tendencies.[7] Key in the concept of polycentrism is to avoid this and to foster a *balanced spatial distribution* of urban centres. Urban centres are concentrations of services and are nodal points of infrastructure and their distribution over space determines disparities in access to such services and in development potential. So balance in this distribution is of essence.

Polycentric systems are considered to bring such a balance. They are desirable as they are supposed to be more efficient and more equitable than either monocentric systems or systems with very many dispersed smaller centres.[8] One can illustrate both assumptions as follows:

- The assumption of *efficiency* is based on the large diseconomies of agglomeration (congestion) that characterize the large urban concentrations and of untapped potential in the poorly urbanized parts of the EU.
- The assumption of *equity* is based on the split between parts of the population that live in urban centres and have access to services and those that live in rural areas and suffer from the high cost of links to essential services (e.g. hospitals) but also to quality jobs.

The concept of polycentricity is difficult to put into practice. Indeed, the following three elements are essential for operationalization:

1 *Size*. There is a certain urban hierarchy. In the largest cities (metropolises) one finds concentrations of services that are sold over a very wide area (e.g. the financial services in the City of London). In the smaller cities one finds functions that reach only a local service area (so-called proximity services).
2 *Location*. The distribution of cities over the territory needs to be balanced. Now there is no clear definition of balance. Some consider that the balance is best in case one finds an increasing number of cities the more one goes down the urban hierarchy.
3 *Connectivity*. Smaller centres that are well connected to larger ones are likely to be better placed than smaller centres that are isolated. Such connectivity can be measured by the importance of interaction (telephone calls, passenger traffic, etc.) between such centres.

Application of such measures produces detailed maps and complicated sets of tables that depict aspects of the situation. However, up until now the research community has been unable to make a practical synthesis that can be translated into a simple indicator of a balanced situation. So there is no way to indicate deficiencies in territorial cohesion by measuring how far the situation in different countries and regions deviates from a norm (e.g. the EU mean). Consequently there is no way either to answer the question whether the situation as to polycentricity has improved (and hence whether territorial cohesion has improved) over time.

So we have to limit ourselves to the notions that can be operationalized in statistical indicators. Only in this way can we follow the evolution over time and assess whether territorial cohesion has improved or not. In line with the stated objectives of territorial cohesion we will opt for the indicators that appear in different words and slightly different meanings in most documents.[9] The one that is traditionally most used is the accessibility to markets. The second one is access to innovation and R&D that we will adopt in view of the aims of the EU to foster the knowledge economy. Finally, we will go into the problems that borders cause for a balanced development of the EU space.

5.3 Accessibility to markets

5.3.1 Concepts and theory

Territorial systems can also be seen as nodes and networks.

- The *node* can be defined as a centre of economic activities and decision making; in practice it will often be the main urban centre of a region.
- *Networks* can be defined in physical terms or in relational terms. In the first physical meaning the term defines the links in infrastructure that exist between the nodes; for instance the road or telecommunication network. In the second, relational meaning it indicates the strength of the links between the actors in each node. In practice the degree of interaction decreases with distance as bridging distances involves cost. Each link in the network is therefore characterized by its length and other aspects that determine the cost of passing that link, such as average speed.

The differences in strength of the nodes and in quality of the network determine together the differences in *accessibility* to main markets, knowledge centres, etc. So improvements in infrastructure lower the distance cost and thus increase accessibility, which in turn increases competitiveness and growth.[10]

There are several ways to operationalize the notion of accessibility with statistical indicators. Most take the following two elements into account:

1   *Market size.* For this part one can work with regional indicators such as population or GDP. The higher the inter-regional differences in wealth, the more the latter has to be preferred over the former. One may, however, also use specific other measures of markets dependent on the objective. In discussing for instance the accessibility of the market for steel products as seen from the various production regions, one may want to use the size of the steel-consuming sectors such as the metal working and car industries.
2   *Cost to reach the markets of the other regions* in the EU from the region under study. This second part requires a description of the network between the nodal points of all regions. Given the importance of the road haulage for intra-EU goods transport it has become usual to use the road network in this respect. Of course in a number of cases (notably islands) such a system

88 *Assessing the problems and identifying causes*

needs to be complemented by equivalent sea links (ferries) making it multimodal. It moreover requires the distance decay element; showing in which way the cost of bridging distances influences the attractiveness of extra-regional markets.

The intermediate step to operationalize the accessibility indicator is the calculation of the *regional potential*. To that end one calculates first for each origin region the attractiveness of each destination region based on its market size, the distance between origin and destination and the cost function to bridge the distance. Next one aggregates for each origin region all values of destination regions. As the 'potential' value that thus results does not have a clear meaning the results are finally scaled and usually expressed as an index (percentage difference around the EU mean). The higher the value of the 'potential' the higher will be the accessibility; the lower the value the lower the accessibility.

Regions with a high level of accessibility (potential) are also called central or core regions; regions with a low level (potential) are called peripheral.[11] The concept of *core-periphery* has in the course of time been enriched in the sense that it is no longer seen as purely market/distance determined. The centres are seen as the locations of decision making; it is here that the head offices of the large multinationals are located and also the centres of national and international public policy. Consequently the periphery is perceived as an area that is dominated by the centre.

5.3.2 Disparities

Based on figures on relative accessibility one can distinguish in the EU system several categories of regions. They are organized around the *core*, which is the multinational highly urbanized conglomeration area in northwestern Europe. On the opposite side we find the *periphery*. This category is loosely defined as the areas at the largest distance from the core. In between we find the *intermediate* areas. These seem to fall into several categories depending on their proximity to the core area. The EU has calculated the values of accessibility of each region and scaled them according to the average for the whole EU (see Figure 5.1).

On the basis of the figures represented in the map the following five categories can be distinguished:

1 The *centre* (core) of the EU that is constituted by the western and southern Benelux, northern France, central West Germany and the southeast of the UK. This core is delimited by five major cities, namely London, Paris, Milan, Munich and Hamburg. Hence its name the Pentagon (penta = five and gon = lines). It encompasses a series of other metropolitan areas, viz. the Ruhr in Germany, the Randstad in the Netherlands, and the Brussels agglomeration in Belgium.
2 A *ring* around the centre constituted of *above average intermediate* areas such as the rest of the Benelux, England, France and Germany, plus the north of Italy.

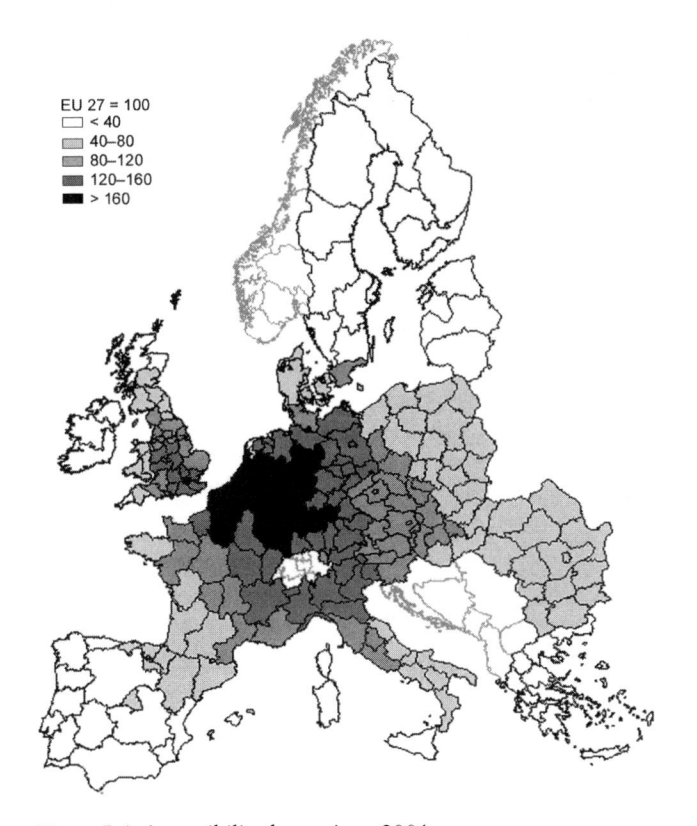

Figure 5.1 Accessibility by region, 2001

3   A loose band of *below average intermediate* regions, that are rather well connected, consisting of the rest of the British Isles, most of Spain, most of continental Italy, Slovenia, Slovakia, the Czech Republic, Denmark and southern Sweden
4   The *peripheral* zone consisting of Portugal, southern Spain, the Italian Islands, Greece, the southeastern Balkans, Poland, the Baltic and most parts of the Nordic countries. Within this zone there is an outer periphery. It consists of the regions at the eastern border of the NMS, making a band from northeastern Poland to southeastern Hungary, Romania and Bulgaria.
5   *Ultra peripheral* regions, sometimes also called outermost regions (not represented on the map) are composed of the French overseas departments such as Guadeloupe, Martinique and la Reunion, the Portuguese islands of Madeira and the Azores, and finally the Spanish Canary Islands.[12]

5.3.3 Development of disparities

In Chapter 3 we have discussed the tendencies in the economy to concentration. Such concentration happens often in the core regions that, thereby, tend to become the poles on which things converge: a phenomenon that has been labelled *polarization*. It implies not only the aspect of geographical concentration but also the accentuation of the differences in endowments, equipments and hence disparities in wealth between the core and the periphery. The question does then come up: Is there a phenomenon of polarization (divergence) in the EU or are developments rather marked by convergence?

The answer to that question on the level of the EU 27 (encompassing all the categories of regions just described) cannot be given as the data for such an analysis are not available. However, for the EU 15 the analysis is possible for a very long period. For this part of the EU we have grouped the regions in six classes (1 most central; 6 most peripheral). The classes are broadly comparable to the first four classes distinguished in the previous section whereby the 'core' and 'ring' classes have both been divided into two more detailed classes.[13] Next we calculated average GDP/P levels for these six classes at different benchmark years (see Table 5.1).

The results show that since the 1950s a continuous process of long-term convergence between the core and the periphery has taken place. The convergence of the GDP/P levels of the various categories of peripherality is most marked for the two extreme categories, still clearly visible for categories 2 and 5 and rather blurred for the intermediate groups (3 and 4).

Although it is not yet possible to describe in a similar manner the development in the EU 27 for the more recent years, we can give some indications as to the development of the categories on both extreme sides.

- The Pentagon used to be marked by a 20–40–50 series: it comprised 20 per cent of the EU 15 territory, 40 per cent of its population and 50 per cent of its GDP. In the EU 27 the Pentagon is much less dominant; the percentages are 14, 32 and 47, respectively.
- The peripheral regions as on the new eastern frontier of the EU form the 'Eastern wall' of the EU or the 'Dead end' of central Europe (Gorzelak, 1996; Sokol, 2001). Due to their disadvantaged geographic position and the very low economic dynamism on the other side of the 'wall' (Belarus and the Ukraine) these regions show slow transformation processes, low levels of FDI and, consequently, a poor growth record. So here divergence tendencies prevail.

Table 5.1 Evolution of the divergence of the regional GDP/P levels by peripherality class (index to EU 15 average)

Class	1950	1960	1970	1980	1990
1	153	143	136	127	126
2	120	124	127	117	116
3	103	111	105	110	111
4	97	98	95	102	102
5	97	89	90	93	95
6	32	32	41	47	46

Source: Own calculations

5.3.4 Air connections

For many economic activities the accessibility by air has become of utmost importance. This is due to the increased importance of personal contacts and swift delivery of essential parts for equipment that characterizes many high-value-added activities. So connectivity in modern times means air connections. The quality of the accessibility by air of a region is indicated by the number of connections and the frequency of flights from its major airport. Both indicators combined tend to reflect the same picture as the aggregate indicator total number of passengers. Table 5.2 gives, for a recent year, this figure for each of the major airports in the EU 27 separately. It shows very clearly a number of salient features:

- A considerable concentration of connectivity in the Pentagon of northwest Europe. The top four of the list are all in that area and together they account for some 28 per cent of the total traffic handled by the airports in the list. If we take all airports in the Pentagon together they account for half of the total traffic of those in the list (which is identical to the Pentagon's share in GDP).
- A high rank of tourist destinations. As there is now less difference between scheduled flights (business) and charter flights (tourism) it means that many of the peripheral regions are actually fairly well connected to the central parts of their countries and of the EU.

Table 5.2 Top 40 airports by passenger numbers, 2001 (in millions)

Rank	Airport	Number of passengers	Rank	Airport	Number of passengers
1	London/Heathrow	60	21	London Stanstead	14
2	Frankfurt	48	22	Vienna	12
3	Paris CDG	48	23	Helsinki	10
4	Amsterdam	39	24	Malaga	10
5	Madrid	34	25	Berlin	10
6	London Gatwick	31	26	Hamburg	9
7	Rome	25	27	Lisbon	9
8	Munich	23	28	Gran Canaria	9
9	Paris Orly	23	29	Tenerife Sur	9
10	Zürich	21	30	Nice	9
11	Barcelona	21	31	Birmingham	8
12	Brussels	20	32	Stuttgart	8
13	Manchester	19	33	Geneva	7
14	Palma Mallorca	19	34	Glasgow	7
15	Milan	18	35	Milan	7
16	Stockholm	18	36	London City	7
17	Copenhagen	18	37	Alicante	7
18	Düsseldorf	15	38	Lyon	6
19	Dublin	14	39	Prague	6
20	Oslo	14	40	Edinburgh	6

Source: Airports Council International, 2001 (Parkinson *et al.*, 2004)

- The absence of airports in the NMSs in the list. Some of these airports (e.g. Warsaw) have figures that just fall short of our cut-off point.

5.4 Access to knowledge and innovation

5.4.1 Concepts and theory

The EU strives to become the most competitive and dynamic knowledge-based economy in the world. In order to track the progress of the EU and its member countries on this matter the EC has developed the European Innovation Scoreboard. It focuses on high-tech innovation and provides data on some 20 indicators (on the national level). These indicators refer to the creation of new knowledge (e.g. R&D expenditure, patents); the transmission and application of existing knowledge (e.g. investment); and the marketing of products in which innovation has been materialized.[14]

The interrelations between public and private actors in an innovation system are very important factors for competitiveness.[15] That is also the case for the quality and density of business network structures; entrepreneurs in knowledge-based firms, when compared with traditional firms, invest more time in networking and also build more focused networks.[16] One strand of theory suggests that strong regional innovation networks stimulate the performance of individual firms in those networks. Other strands suggest that globalization and the Internet make inter-regional networks as effective as regional ones. Empirical research shows that the former thesis is relevant for knowledge-intensive small- and medium-sized firms; proximity of partners is a determining factor for their performance (Arndt and Sternberg, 2000).

It is likely that the patterns of disparity that will be revealed by the indicators of the knowledge society and innovation will show a high correlation with the indicators of economic and social disparity that we discussed in the previous chapters. This is suggested by the results of an analysis based on a pan EU household survey into the determinants of the adoption of two ICT items: the Internet and computers. Positive influences came from the level of income, access to university education, and links to R&D activities. Unemployment did have a negative influence (Vicente and Lopez, 2006).

5.4.2 The national picture

In Table 5.3 we present for five basic indicators and for an aggregate index the performance of the member countries of the EU in terms of innovativeness. This information is limited to the present situation; lack of comparable data for the past prohibits the analysis of the developments over time. The basic data for all indicators have been recalculated so as to produce a maximum of 100 and a minimum of 0.[17]

One sees that there is a clear split in the EU between large geographical groups. The North invariably shows the highest values, followed by the South and finally the East. There is a real problem for the South: as a matter of fact the

Table 5.3 Innovation indicators by country (100 is best) (around 2003)

Country	Public R&D expenditure	Business R&D expenditure	EPO high-tech patent applications (per million population)	Innovation expenditures (% of total turnover)	Internet access (composite indicator)	Summary innovation Index
Germany	70	51	38	29	72	56
France	77	40	26	26	34	46
Italy	47	15	6	19	43	31
The Netherlands	74	30	77	13	77	45
Belgium	49	48	23	28	67	47
Luxembourg	0	48	6	10	61	29
UK	53	37	26	17	69	49
Denmark	70	52	37	0	89	54
Ireland	25	23	22		51	44
Spain	37	15	3	9	37	30
Portugal	53	8	0	28	27	30
Greece	34	5	1	20	28	20
Austria	57	36	19		53	39
Sweden	92	100	62		100	76
Finland	100	71	100	26	69	75
EU15	**62**	**38**	**26**	**22**	**57**	**44**
Poland	36	2	0	17	27	14
Czech Republic	37	21	0	7		27
Hungary	58	9	3	11		25
Slovakia	14	8	0	100		24
Slovenia	54	26	3	10	45	32
Lithuania	45	2	1	16	7	26
Cyprus	14	0	0		44	17
Latvia	13	3	0	27	0	18
Estonia	46	5	2	12		34
Malta		1	0			25
Romania	2	5	0	10	105	15
Bulgaria	30	1	0			28
EU27	**60**	**36**	**20**	**21**	**52**	**42**
North	67	45	36	23	63	51
South	43	14	4	16	38	29
East	35	8	0	18	25	21

Source: EC European Innovation Scoreboard (2004)

innovation potential of the East seems to be higher than the one of the South. Let us recall that the NMSs also performed better with respect to human resources and investment in equipment (previous chapter).

Two countries are top performers in innovation, namely Sweden and Finland. Both are high-income countries that are not part of the core area and both have decided some time ago they wanted to step up innovation in order to stay abreast of the competition. These countries have adopted a new governance

94 *Assessing the problems and identifying causes*

model whereby government science policy, university research and industry innovation operate with a greater degree of synchronization than before.[18]

5.4.3 The regional picture

On the regional level the database is less complete than on the national level. It means that we are constrained in terms of time period, area coverage and type of indicator. The patchy information for specific indicators tends to produce fairly disparate results. So we have opted for the presentation of a comprehensive picture based on an aggregate index (being the average of a set of indices of the type given in Table 5.3). The regions that perform best on this index are given in Table 5.4.[19] Three salient features stand out that seem to determine performance:

1   EU centrality. Half of the regions in the top 40 and six out of the top ten are located in the regions that fall in the two highest categories of accessibility (see Figure 5.1). Not a single region from the periphery nor from the ultra periphery shows up in this top group.[20]
2   National centrality. A large number of national capital cities show up in the list (in total 11, of which six are among the 12 regions with the highest score). Moreover, there are many regions in the list that are traditionally most dynamic, such as Rhone-Alps in France, Catalonia in Spain, etc.[21]
3   National choices. Many of the best-performing regions are in Sweden and Finland; two countries outside the Pentagon that have been pursuing a very deliberate innovation policy (see previous section).

All regions of the NMSs and those of Greece and Portugal do show low figures on innovation type indicators (see note 19). In line with the picture given above their central cities stand out as poles of innovativeness.

So, this analysis conveys *two important messages*. First, the regional differences in innovation are to a large extent determined by centrality. Second, this is no reason for despair for regions outside the central areas; indeed a long-term policy can bring such regions up to top levels of innovation performance.

5.5 The problems of borders

5.5.1 Concepts and theory

The EU territory, notwithstanding half a century of integration, does still not function as one organism. The cause is simple. The different governance systems of the member states create barriers to a balanced development of the EU territory. The regions that suffer most from such problems are in a disadvantageous position and the ones that suffer least are in a relatively well-off position. These disparities indicate a lack of territorial cohesion. Border problems are generally classified in the following three groups:

Table 5.4 Top 40 regions (above EU average) ranked by their score on the innovation index (EU 15 = 100)

Rank	Region		Index	Rank	Region		Index
1	Stockholm	S	225	20	Vlaams Gewest	BE	112
2	Uusimaa (Helsinki)	SF	208	22	Lombardia	I	112
3	Noord-Brabant	NL	191	23	Kärnten	A	111
4	Pohjois-Suomi	SF	161	23	Région Bruxelles	BE	111
4	Eastern	UK	161	23	Rhone-Alpes (Lyon)	F	111
6	Ile de France	F	160	26	Lazio	I	110
7	Bayern (Munich)	D	151	27	Piemonte (Turin)	I	109
8	South East	UK	150	27	Zuid-Holland (Rotterdam)	NL	109
9	Comunidad de Madrid	E	149	29	Hessen	D	108
10	Baden Württemberg (Stuttgart)	D	146	29	Southern and Eastern	IRE	108
11	Sydsverige	S	143	32	West Midlands (Birmingham)	UK	108
12	Berlin	D	140	33	Groningen	NL	107
12	Östra Mellansverige	S	140	33	Comunidad Foral de Navarra	E	105
14	South West (Bristol)	UK	147	33	Noord-Holland	NL	105
15	Västsverige	S	146	33	Limburg	NL	105
16	Mid-Pyrénées (Toulouse)	F	141	36	N-West (Manchester/Liverpool)	UK	104
17	Wien	A	126	37	Hamburg	D	103
18	Etelä-Suomi	SF	124	38	Scotland	UK	102
19	Utrecht	NL	123	39	Cataluña (Barcelona)	E	101
20	Flevoland	NL	114	39	Gelderland	NL	101

Source: European trend chart on innovation; technical paper no. 3, EU regions, 2002 (Parkinson et al., 2004)

96 *Assessing the problems and identifying causes*

1   *Cross border.* Areas divided by national borders are in a disadvantageous position because any cooperation among parts on different sides of the border has to overcome many barriers of a legal, political and administrative order that stem from differences in national systems. One need but think of customs tariff structures for economic cooperation, of differences in insurance and social security coverage for transborder access to health services, etc.
2   *Transnational.* Some problems tend to be international but not limited to regions on the borders. We may cite here common problems of the management of river basins that extend over several countries (e.g. Rhine or Danube). Other problems are those that are posed by common geographical features (such as the management of tourism and environment in Alpine regions).
3   *Inter-regional.* Some types of problems are specific for only one region in a country. Solutions often involve the cooperation of the private and the public sector. In the past such cooperation was pursued within national frameworks. The cost of understanding the problems and the design of solutions can then be very high. A lowering of the cost can be realized by cooperation among regions confronted with similar problems abroad. Such cooperation is, however, hampered by uncertainties about potential, about procedures to follow once fruitful opportunities have been identified, etc.[22] So, lack of such inter-regional international access to knowledge is a serious territorial problem.

We will elaborate the first two problems in the following sections.

5.5.2 Cross-border disparities

In the course of history the nations of Europe have gradually extended their grip on the national territory. For security reasons they have tended to discourage the location of economic activities in their border regions. Later concentration tendencies of the type described in Chapter 3 have reinforced the marginalization of many border areas. A good example of such a situation are the border areas between Spain and Portugal, two countries that are said to have, for a long time, turned their back to each other. Less pronounced but of a similar type are the problems of the border areas between the Netherlands and Germany, as these areas are closer to major conurbations. But more pronounced are the problems of areas on borders that are very difficult to pass; such a situation that existed before 1989 between the border areas of the two parts of Germany. In general one may say that economic activity in border regions is mainly of the traditional agricultural type, that the urban infrastructure is weak and hence transport infrastructure is very poorly developed. So it is clear that borders did create significant problems and that at the start of the EU territorial disparities were very important.

Due to these tendencies problems occur for cross-border cooperation. Initiatives that are easy to realize within one member state encounter very big problems as soon as two member states are involved. An example in public services is the fire brigade. Cross-border cooperation can be highly profitable because of cost sharing. However, in practice such cooperation is very difficult and hence costly. Telephone connections over small distances are billed at international tariffs, technical solutions are to be found with the agreement of national central administrations, financial compensation for cross-border interventions needs complicated authorizations, etc.

How have these border-related problems developed into disparities and how have these disparities developed over time? Is the problem of cohesion now better or worse than 50 or ten years ago? Unfortunately, quantification is not possible but the following qualitative aspects can be mentioned:

- The *security threat* has been taken away by EU integration, so countries have no longer reason to maintain physical barriers.
- *Integration* also took away many economic barriers (such as customs duties with respect to the exchange of goods) and legal barriers (such as residence permits for migrant workers). The most important decrease in such barriers has of course occurred where a system change from a command to a market economy was involved; examples are the reunification of Germany and the access of the NMSs in central and eastern Europe.
- *Transport infrastructure* has been gradually improved under the influence of increased exchanges between countries. This was in many cases due to the natural cooperation of the two neighbouring member states. In other cases EU policy has moved in by the realization of the so-called missing links in the EU infrastructure (see Chapter 11). As a consequence many regions on the inner borders of the EU are now actually well linked into national and EU infrastructure.
- *Legal and administrative barriers* have increased due to the different choices that the various member states have made in the development of their welfare states (Ferrera, 2006). This would have tended to increase territorial disparities as it would make any cooperation and exchange across borders much more involved. However, at the same time a series of measures of both the national governments and of the EU have been taken to decrease these difficulties. Bilateral agreements, EU regulation and verdicts of the European Court of Justice have improved the situation and eased cross-border exchange and cooperation. Moreover, EU cohesion policy has moved in to support cooperation (see Chapters 7 and 8).

The weight of the various factors is uncertain but it is very likely that on balance the tendency has been towards greater cohesion and less territorial disparity.

5.5.3 *Transnational problems*

The socio-economic situation in countries and regions cannot be seen in isolation. Under the influence of internationalization and even globalization activities in a country or region can only flourish if the conditions for an effective access to the rest of Europe and to the world at large can be guaranteed.

98 *Assessing the problems and identifying causes*

A first point to be considered in this respect is transport and communication. Lack of connectivity due to inadequate infrastructure can hamper the development of a region. Within national states coordination mechanisms are in place that set the priorities for investment and realize the links most needed. These coordination mechanisms are much weaker at the international level which implies that investment in important links between countries tends to be low on the priority list. Hence, bottlenecks far away can limit the growth potential nearby.

A second point that is important in this respect is the environment. Many modern activities require locations with a high environmental quality. Now developments outside a region can negatively influence this quality. We give here some examples:

- *Air.* Among the main contributors to climate change are greenhouse gases. Emissions are high in metropolitan areas (in particular in the Pentagon, the urban heartland of northwest Europe). Climate change increases the risk of river floods and sea levels rising. Regions bordering the sea and major rivers have to invest in infrastructure that diminishes such risks, thereby limiting their investment capacity for other purposes. So they are interested in cost sharing or in agreements about increased abatement in neighbouring states.
- *Water.* The environmental quality of the lakes and sea basins is endangered by pollution brought by the rivers of the coastal states. A good example is the Baltic Sea that suffers heavily from pollutants from Denmark, Sweden, Finland, Estonia, Lithuania, Latvia and Poland. Another example is the Rhine river basin, where France, Germany, the Netherlands (and Switzerland) have to join forces to manage disaster protection (floods[23]), traffic management and water quality in the River Rhine.

Given the complexity of the issues it is difficult to measure how far the (extra) territorial effects described here have increased over time and it is near impossible to describe the evolution in one or a few disparity indicators. However, the examples given may suffice to illustrate the (lack of) territorial cohesion that ensues from these tendencies.

5.6 Summary and conclusions

- Territorial cohesion is a relatively new concept. It lacks at this stage clarity, both in theoretical and political terms. The quantification of indicators that would permit the measurement of its development over time is not very far advanced. As a consequence it is as yet impossible to say in general terms whether territorial cohesion has improved or whether it has deteriorated.
- As far as *accessibility to markets* is concerned things have much improved over time. The development of the EU transport infrastructure has decreased the disadvantages of the peripheral regions. In line therewith their relative position in terms of wealth has improved. However, important disparities continue to persist.

- *Access to knowledge and innovation* shows many differences that tend to vary with wealth and centrality. However, the influence of the latter factor is not dominant as some peripheral countries show by their very high scores on these indicators.
- All countries in the EU suffer more or less from the barriers that national borders create for the development of border regions.

Stage II
Designing a solution-oriented intervention system

6 Policy fundamentals

6.1 Introduction

In the previous part of the book we have dealt with the first stage of the policy cycle. We have found that the socio-economic system of the EU can lead to considerable differences in wealth and in access to employment. In other words, it may lead to considerable problems in terms of economic, social and territorial cohesion. Disparities on these scores are often considered as morally unjust and economically inefficient. So a policy is needed to counteract the negative tendencies and make sure that a better distribution of wealth is realized.

In this chapter we will deal with the second stage of the policy cycle; that is the way in which the institutions for such a policy can best be designed and actually have been designed. In other words, we address here the systemic options and choices made at the highest (constitutional) level.[1]

The structure of this chapter is as follows.

First, we will address the *why* question. We will deal in theoretical terms with the factors that justify an involvement of the EU in cohesion policy, then describe how these factors change under the influence of changing circumstances; following that, we will describe the actual political and legal foundations for an EU cohesion policy.

Next, we answer the *what* question. We will deal with the way in which a cohesion policy can be given form and substance by providing instruments adapted to the objectives. These fall into two categories: finances and regulation. For each we will detail the design options available, the factors that determine the choice and the choice actually made by the EU.

The answer to the *who* question will be given in the next set of sections. We describe the multilevel government situation (EU, national government, region), the different institutions at each layer (e.g. at the EU level the Commission, the Council and the Parliament), and the assignment of competences to each actor.

The *how* question is the subject of the last section. Here we deal with the fundamentals of the detailing of a policy in terms of programmes and projects and the different stages of the policy cycle.

As usual the chapter will be concluded with a short summary.

6.2 Why is intervention needed?

6.2.1 Role of cohesion in the overall policy framework

Economic and social systems do not always produce outcomes that are in line with political preferences. In order to change the outcomes of the system policies are pursued. In the literature on policy interventions (notably by national governments) it has become common practice to distinguish between three overarching policy objectives. These are: (1) the improvement of the efficiency of the system; (2) the creation of stable conditions; and (3) the safeguarding of reasonable levels of equity (Musgrave and Musgrave, 1989; Sapir et al., 2004).

The EU model is defined by the way the EU has given form to these three socio-economic policy objectives. The EU choices have been shaped by the basic ideologies that prevailed in most member states at the start of the EU integration process and that have been confirmed since. The first one is a liberal view to markets that has led to objective 1 (allocational efficiency) and objective 2 (macro economic stability). The other ideological component of the model is an interventionist view to social justice (objective 3). Hence the choice of redistribution (cohesion policies) to take away or cushion the potential negative side-effects of policies that pursue the first two objectives.[2]

The way the EU has given substance to these three overarching policy objectives can be described as follows:[3]

- *Allocation* (efficiency). This set of policies consists in the improvement of the functioning of the EU market with the objective to enhance competition, to boost productivity, international competitiveness and thereby economic growth. In this respect we mention in particular the removing of barriers to internal trade and movements of production factors. Equally important are competition policies to prevent private and public actors inhibiting fair competition.
- *Stability*. The objective of this set of policies is to create stable macro economic conditions. These are essential for a smooth functioning of the economy. After a hesitant start the EU has made a very big step forward with the creation of EMU, introducing the euro as the common currency. Stability in the recent period has been considerably improved by the low inflation policy of the European Central Bank, the absence of turbulence on the foreign exchange markets, and internal and external balance. In order to maintain such conditions the EU sets the so-called Broad Economic Policy Guidelines (BEPG) for member states.
- *Redistribution* (equity). The objective of this set of policies is to promote the harmonious development of the EU as a whole. The EU has set up its policy to foster economic, social and territorial cohesion. An essential aspect of this is the redistribution of resources from the wealthy to the poor. The EU has devised several schemes for that and now cohesion is one of the biggest items in the EU budget.

Next to these policies the EU pursues many more. Some of them can be categorized in one of the three socio-economic policies specified above. Examples are employment policy, industrial policy and R&D policy that fall mainly under allocation. Others pursue different objectives and form rather a category of their own, e.g. policies on environmental sustainability, external identity and security (see Chapter 10).

6.2.2 Theoretical foundations for intervention on cohesion on the national level

Cohesion policies involve the redistribution of resources. Why would the wealthy pay for redistribution? On the national level redistribution schemes often have the character of insurance. We may think here of social security (e.g. against the loss of income due to unemployment). As people are ignorant about what will happen to them personally, in future it is rational for them to participate in redistribution schemes. These schemes have become public schemes because the markets have not been able to provide efficient solutions. Another reason for governments taking responsibility for redistribution is that economic systems, when left to their own, are often unable to recover from shocks. It takes government involvement to steer segments of the economy through restructuring.

Traditionally two reasons for such intervention are given:

(1) *Efficiency*. This argument, of an economic nature, says that measures of economic, regional and social policy help towards the efficient allocation of resources by taking away bottlenecks and barriers to development. Total welfare increases, as resources that are badly utilized, or not utilized at all, will participate (better) in production. Some examples may illustrate this.

- *Regional* (economic and territorial). Where labour is rather immobile, unemployed human capital will not be put to work by private investors unless conditions for a profitable operation in that region (for example, in terms of infrastructure) are met. A government programme for such infrastructure removes the obstruction to development.
- *Social*. A programme for the retraining of workers that have been made redundant in an industry that had lost its competitive position will adapt this human capital to new conditions. Private initiative would not have taken this up. More generally the existence of a redistribution scheme can act as a growth factor because it is considered as an insurance against risk and thereby stimulates investment in labour and labour mobility.[4]

(2) *Equity*. This argument, of a socio-political nature, says that large groups of the population feel that inequality is morally unacceptable. Total welfare would increase if the inequalities between groups and regions were removed. Again we may give some examples.

- *Regional* (economic and territorial). Minimum standards of provision of public goods may be set for all regions (for example, number of hospital beds per inhabitant). The government's budget then transfers the money to regions that do not have the capacity to generate sufficient revenues themselves.
- *Social.* Minimum personal income standards may be set. Transfer payments from the most to the least affluent can take the form of detailed schemes of social security: old-age pensions, unemployment benefits, health insurance – schemes generally associated with the welfare state. Another way is the definition of basic social rights of workers, including minimum standards for the quality of occupations (safety, health, hours of work, length of paid holidays and so on) and industrial relations (such as collective bargaining, strikes and employee co-management).

There are interrelations between the two arguments of efficiency and equity:

- Application of the equity argument will have a positive side-effect on efficiency. On the one hand, measures of social security for instance will make sure that employees will be prepared to invest in the formation of their human capital. On the other hand, too high a level of security will take away flexibility and the willingness to adapt to new circumstances.
- Application of the efficiency argument will lead to higher growth and hence to a higher capacity to finance equity measures.

6.2.3 Application of theoretical arguments for intervention to the EU case

Can the arguments for redistribution as put forward in a national setting be transposed to the EU setting? What factors would motivate national governments of wealthy member states to pay net contributions to the EU budget to subsidize poorer member states? The insurance argument does not play much of a role. Indeed, the motivation of an individual to pay his social security contribution cannot be compared to the motivation of the government of a wealthy EU member state to contribute to an EU redistribution scheme. As a matter of fact, the risk of getting into a situation of distress from which it is difficult to recover seems much less likely for countries than it is for individuals. However, the other two arguments for intervention via redistribution do have a European dimension.

The *efficiency argument* has been central in each of the stages of its development. An example from the crisis period of the late 1970s may be illustrative in this respect. The lack of alternative activities in 'steel regions', where substantial cutbacks in employment were necessary, has induced certain member states to give heavy support to the established industry, to which other member states responded by threatening to close their frontiers to these subsidized products. Now that would mean a direct violation of the founding principles of the EU (free market and international specialization), so the lack of an effective policy to help the regions develop new activities put the allocation function of the EU in jeopardy.

The *equity* argument has only gradually come to the fore in the EU policy setting. Until the mid-1980s, neither the social dimension[5] nor the public support for a fiscal contribution to assist development in a different EU member country had developed much. For some time the EU put more emphasis on the social and human aspects of integration as necessary complements to the mainly economic ones that dominated the initial stages.

6.2.4 Justification of EU intervention: the stages approach

Traditionally the task for cohesion policies has been assumed by national governments together with regional authorities in regional matters and specialized agencies in matters of social policy. There are indeed good reasons for this as claims for redistribution are generally restricted to participants in schemes of social cooperation for mutual advantage. Since such schemes coincide traditionally with nation states, claims can be made only by citizens of the specific state involved.

However, with increasing economic and social integration the question comes up *How far Union authorities should play a role in matters of redistribution?* The answer to this question is positive. The arguments in favour have to do with the loss of instruments that occurs to all member countries each time the integration enters a new stage. This can be illustrated as follows:

- In the *first stages* economic integration concerns the internal liberalization of trade (intra Union) and the development of a common foreign trade policy. Both deprive member states of the trade policy instruments by which they had supported activities of certain social groups (e.g. farmers by import duties on food imports) or of regionally concentrated industries (e.g. by quota on textile imports). In the process of international specialization that is stimulated by further integration, resources (such as labour) are set free that need to adapt to other occupations. This often entails the loss of expertise, costs of moving and so on. For some countries the adjustment costs occur immediately while the benefits may take a long time to materialize. For others, such cost may be limited, while gains may be quick to come about. In other words, costs and benefits may be very unequally distributed among countries.
- In the *higher stages* economic integration involves the setting up of an economic and monetary union. This further curtails the instruments available to national states. They are losing, for example, on the monetary union side the possibility of influencing the equilibrium with partner countries by exchange rate and monetary policies. So, an economic and monetary union will increase the allocational efficiency by decreasing the transaction cost for all those who use the common currency, while it decreases the use of macro economic policy instruments to cope with distributional problems.

The distribution over member states of the cost and benefits of integration may be very unequal. A country that is a loser in the integration game may be inclined to opt out. If it does, it would imply that its partners lose the advantage from integration. So they will be inclined to accept some form of Union redistribution whereby the losers are compensated in order to keep them in the scheme and thereby preserve the essentials of their gains from integration. This economic argument is reinforced by a political argument. For countries that participate in an economic integration scheme (such as the EU), the boundaries of cooperation will extend beyond the national framework. So, it is logical to extend also equity considerations beyond that framework, in practice, to citizens of other member states of the union.

These arguments lead to the conclusion that there should be an EU involvement in matters of cohesion and that it is likely to be stepped up with increased integration. Now, neither theory nor empirics is able to determine the exact optimal amount of EU involvement needed at each stage; so practical solutions will have to be worked out in agreement with these general principles that can follow a more political inspiration (Breuss and Eller, 2004).

6.2.5 Limits to public support for EU solidarity

The promoting of the internal cohesion of the EU requires a union redistribution policy, transferring resources from the rich to the less well-off member countries, which means an appeal to international, intra-EU solidarity. The question is then: How strong is the basis for such a policy (compare Padoa-Schioppa *et al.*, 1987 and Findlay, 1982)?

Traditionally the framework for financial claims to solidarity has been the national state, where people feel they belong to one social system. Empirical evidence shows that there existed a firm basis for inter-regional transfers within each member state of the EU (EC, 1983). A large majority of citizens thus favoured the social or moral argument over the efficiency or economic argument. Indeed, in the entire EU, there were nearly twice as many supporters of aid to regions most in need of it, as supporters of aid to regions making the best use of it.

How does European solidarity among regions of different member countries compare with national solidarity among regions of the same country? The attitude of the EU citizens has changed in the past decades. In the 1980s the support was still limited. While four out of five respondents to an EU-wide survey accepted to pay a fiscal contribution for aid to regions in their own country, only one in three felt the same about aid to regions in other EU countries (EC, 1983). More recent surveys (EC, 1991b and c, 2002c) showed considerable support for common EU redistribution policies (over two-thirds). There was also support for the objectives of EU cohesion policy; on the one hand, to raise the standard of living, and on the other hand, to increase the competitiveness of the problem regions. Firm comparable data on the attitudes of the public after the extension of the EU to 27 member countries are not yet available but one may assume on the basis of anecdotal evidence that on average support is still substantial.

So, the European public is in favour of an EU cohesion policy that transfers resources from the rich to the poor (redistribution) and that is worked out as a structural policy, more specifically as a regional socio-economic policy.

As yet, there is no support for further-going claims on international, intra-EU solidarity. On the contrary, the idea of a European social security system is consistently rejected by a considerable majority (about two-thirds) of respondents.[6]

6.2.6 *The objectives*

The reasons given in the previous sections have urged the EU to adopt and gradually elaborate a cohesion policy. This political decision has been translated into constitutional obligations. In the EU case this means that cohesion has been taken up in the basic treaties (see Annex 6.1). The treaties set out the objectives of the EU cohesion policy (in its three dimensions) only in rather vague terms. This very vagueness is typical for the constitutional level. It permits the EU to give substance to it in policy in ways that can adapt to changing views and circumstances. Some clarity is given in the following specification of the objectives:[7]

> *The Union shall aim in particular at reducing disparities between levels of development of the various regions and the backwardness of the least favoured regions or islands, including rural areas.*

The objectives have been worked out in various policy documents that we will discuss in the subsequent sections and chapters. They rejoin to a high degree the specifications of the terms economic, social and territorial disparities that we described in the previous chapters.[8]

6.3 What is needed: providing the tools for reaching the objectives

6.3.1 *Forms of intervention on cohesion (instruments)*

The two *main instruments* by which public policies (be they cohesion or other policies) can be put into effect are:

1 The provision of financial means that permit payment for the resources that are needed as inputs for the policy.
2 The setting of rules that oblige economic and social actors to take specific action that is conducive for the reaching of policy goals or refrain from certain activities that may impede the reaching of such goals.

The mix of the two types of instruments and the amount of each differs considerably between policies. Some use very little finance, but much detailed regulation, for instance, competition policy. Others use much of finance and little regulation; for instance, infrastructure policy. The EU cohesion policies use both. The degree to which the EU uses both instruments is the result of two factors. On the one hand of some systemic thinking on the effectiveness and efficiency in policy design and delivery (see the following sections). However, in the end much has also been the result of political horse-trading.

The *main instruments to realize the objectives of the EU cohesion policy* also fall into two categories:

1   SF (finances). The EU pursues a redistribution policy allocating funds to the disadvantaged regions for the improvement of their structure and to social groups to improve their employability and to avoid their social exclusion. (This aspect is dealt with in the next chapter.)
2   *Coordination of national policies* (regulation). As cohesion is a matter of shared responsibilities between the Union and national authorities such coordination is vital for effectiveness. This applies equally to national cohesion policies as to other national policies, such as environment, etc. (This aspect is dealt with in the subsequent sections of this chapter.)

On top of this the cohesion policy also uses the instrument of coordination of other Union policies. Some of these policies can have negative effects, others may have positive effects on cohesion. The EU will, where it can, already take possible negative effects on cohesion into account while devising these other policies (see Chapter 11).

6.3.2 The specific position of territorial cohesion

The instruments mentioned are notably relevant for reaching the objectives of economic and social cohesion. To reach the objectives of *territorial cohesion* there is at present only the instrument of coordination available. In this respect one needs to recall (see Chapter 5) that the status of this ESDP is highly informal; it has been elaborated in an intergovernmental set-up external to the EU legal framework. The European Commission has only served as the secretariat. So formally the EU legal and financial instruments are not applicable. However, in many policy documents on the future role of the ESDP one takes a broader view.

There has been an attempt to develop a specific instrument in the so-called *Territorial Impact Assessment*. This concept has been borrowed from the tradition of spatial planning in some member states and seems to have its relevance mostly in cases of large infrastructure projects and the management of environmentally sensitive areas. An attempt has been made to apply it also to the European sectoral and structural policies. But this has stayed at an embryonic stage without policy consequences.[9]

Many claims have been voiced to put the EU SF (see Chapter 7) at the disposal of the objectives of territorial cohesion. Those claiming this generally use a wide concept of the meaning of territorial cohesion that tends to overlap with economic and social dimensions. It puts at the heart of territorial cohesion the concept of competitiveness instead of that of balanced spatial distribution.[10] We have not followed that broad definition.

Policy fundamentals 111

There is a tendency towards a stronger linkage of ESPD and the EU. On the one hand, the involvement of the Commission in the territorial cohesion debate becomes stronger. On the other hand, the guidelines of the SF stipulate that the regional strategies (programmes) shall take account of the ESDP.[11]

6.3.3 Adapting the tools to the needs: applying the subsidiarity and proportionality principles

All over the past the EU has been struggling with the question whether on certain issues it needed to have more involvement or not. Theory gives us a number of reasons why the EU should be modest; policy is best executed at the lowest level of government because:

- differences in needs and in preferences will be better taken into account; implementation cost will be lower and the accountability of the institutions for their actions will be higher;
- innovation and experiment will be given more latitude. Competition between jurisdictions will bring forward the best solutions.

Yet it can be advisable to centralize certain policy issues. The three main reasons are (Molle, 2006):

1. *Transaction cost.* The diversity of national rules (e.g. on product specifications) brings high extra cost to economic actors and loss of competitiveness.
2. *Economies of scale.* The production of a public good may be subject to decreasing cost or increasing benefits with larger size. An example is trade policy.
3. *Spill-overs.* In cases where outsiders bear the cost of non-observance of certain standards (e.g. pollution that is carried over national borders); international standards may be needed.

In the EU these economic principles have found their political complement in the so-called subsidiarity and proportionality principles (e.g. Pelkmans, 1997, 2006). Once the first is applied with a positive result the second comes into play.

The *subsidiarity principle* gives the justification for EU action. It says that a matter has to be assigned to the lowest public authority level that can effectively deal with it. In practice the member state or its constituent parts (regions). Assignment to the EU can be done in case:

- there is a need to act (that means the problem cannot be solved by market forces or by private organizations);
- the EU is better qualified than others: cases in point are corrections of market failures, compensation for externalities and economies of scale (as mentioned before).

The application of this principle leads indeed to EU involvement in matters of cohesion. One important aspect here is finances: the EU can mobilize and provide funds of bigger size and at far better conditions than could the poor member states. Moreover, it can give long-term predictability about the availability of resources to all beneficiaries. This means that investors will be more inclined to invest and hence growth is likely to be enhanced. Another important aspect is regulation; the EU determines the architecture and the operations of the policy system but leaves to member states the application of the eligibility criteria and the selection of projects within the EU priorities.

The *proportionality principle* deals with the optimal use of instruments. Here effectiveness to realize the objectives of the EU is the norm. In case the matter can be dealt with by less constraining instruments (such as coordination) these have to be chosen; in case these are not effective, more constraining instruments such as the EU legal instrument 'regulation' have to be chosen. A regulation actually unifies the regime in the whole EU. We discuss this instrument later in this chapter. The EU has chosen to use the 'regulation' tool for the design of its cohesion policy system, specifying the principles and major aspects of operations such as objectives, the system of delivery, the financial reporting requirements, etc.

6.4 Finances: redistribution by the Union

6.4.1 Why are Union[12] redistribution policies necessary?

Traditionally the task for redistribution policies has been assumed by national governments together with regional authorities in regional matters and specialized agencies in matters of social policy. There are indeed good reasons for this, as claims for redistribution are generally restricted to participants in schemes of social cooperation for mutual advantage. Since such schemes coincide traditionally with nation states, claims can be made only by citizens of the specific state involved.

However, with increasing integration the question comes up in how far Union authorities should play a role as well. Indeed, for participants in economic integration schemes the boundaries of cooperation tend to extend beyond the national framework, so it is logical to extend equity considerations and distributional justice to citizens of all member states of the Union.[13] There are, however, also good economic reasons. The first is the increase in efficiency of allocation engendered by redistribution. Theory (Casella, 2005) shows that while countries of unequal levels of development and characterized by differences in centrality (or peripherality) integrate, efficiency is likely to require both national and international transfers and coordination on international transfers. Theory further observes that countries are inclined to opt out from an integration scheme in case they judge that the benefits they draw from it are insufficient (Molle, 2006). If they do, it would imply that the other participants in the integration lose the advantage from integration. Although solidarity with integration schemes is not marked solely by immediate economic gains, for some countries the absence of such gains may become a political factor important enough to ask for compensation schemes but on the other hand, the occurrence of big gains for certain countries may be sufficient reason to justify some form of compensation or redistribution.

Countries participate in integration schemes because they expect welfare gains from them. However, there are also costs involved in progressive integration. Countries lose a number of instruments at each stage of integration that could be used for improving cohesion. Now, as more instruments are foregone to national governments, the need for a Union policy increases. This can be illustrated as follows.

Customs union (CU). The internal liberalization and the development of a common foreign trade policy deprives member states of the trade policy instruments by which they had supported activities of certain social groups or of regionally concentrated industries. In the process of specialization, resources are set free that need to adapt to other occupations. This often entails the loss of expertise, costs of moving and so on. For some countries the benefits may take a long time to materialize, whereas the adjustment costs occur immediately. For others, gains may be quick to come about, while the costs are limited. In other words, costs and benefits may be very unequally distributed among countries.

CM. In the CM stage the need for redistribution increases. First, because disequilibria become more likely aggravated when the free movement of production factors is introduced, and labour and capital begin to flow to the regions offering the best locations for investment. Now production factors may not always move in such a way as to bring about a better equilibrium. Capital in particular tends to move to those areas that have already secured the best position. Labour may move from low-wage to high-wage countries, but that may entail high social and personal cost. So these movements aggravate the risk of an unbalanced development.

Second, because the capacity of national states to cope with them is decreased as they no longer have instruments that impede the free flow of goods services and production factors at their disposal. At the same time the capacity to set up redistribution schemes improves, as the CM is more likely to be endowed with institutions that are capable of handling elementary redistribution schemes.

Economic and monetary union. The setting up of an EMU further curtails the instruments available to national states. They are losing, for example, on the monetary union side the possibility of influencing the equilibrium with partner countries by exchange rate and monetary policies. In an EMU this requires the moving of production factors (Giersch, 1949; Williamson, 1976; Molle *et al.*, 1993). Furthermore, with the progress of the economic union, increased harmonization occurs, especially on the industrial and social planes. So, an EMU will increase the allocational efficiency while diminishing the use of macro economic policy instruments to cope with the distributional problems.

6.4.2 *What form could international redistribution schemes take?*

Where countries integrate their policies the question comes up whether redistribution needs to be integrated and if so in what way. The theory of integration is not very explicit about these issues (Molle, 1997b, 2002). But many elements that are needed are actually provided by the 'Fiscal federalism' school. This school deals with the optimal organization of public finances, for instance, with the question at which level of government taxes can best be levied (Oates, 1972, 1977). In matters of redistribution this school offers several options (see, for example, Ahmad, 1997). Redistribution relies on fiscal transfers to correct the outcome of the market forces. Transfers may go through two channels:

1 *Interpersonal.* Income is generated by, for example, progressive income taxes, which means that the rich pay relatively more than the poor. The spending of these funds may be concentrated on the most disadvantaged: e.g. in the form of social security benefits. The system requires the definition of a minimum standard for all citizens, based on equity considerations.
2 *Inter-regional.* Poor regions may receive more for central state to finance their programmes of public works and of public services, than their contribution to receipts. This too is dependent on certain ideas of equity; for instance in access to infrastructure or to health services.

The schemes drawn up in groups at different levels of integration (ranging from free trade areas (FTAs) to federations and unitary states) for the inter-regional redistribution of resources differ as to the combination they use of income instruments (tax and social security) and expenditure instruments (grants and programmes) (MacDougall *et al.*, 1977).

There are two main ways to handle the redistribution of funds through the expenditure side of the Union budget (Musgrave and Musgrave, 1989):

- *General-purpose grants.* The union provides the member state with a certain amount of money that is supposed to cover all its needs. These needs are evaluated for each individual state against a standard for public-sector programmes and the capacity of the member state to finance them. So they are essentially equity oriented. They carry no conditions and the union has no control over the actual use of the funds transferred, which risk being used in a way not expedient to structural improvement.
- *Specific-purpose grants.* These are essentially conditional on the use that is made of them. Here the union decides on the type of programme that should be set up and to which it is prepared to give financial aid. Its inspiration is of the utilitarian type: such grants are considered to lead to optimum welfare in the long run, because they lead to a better allocation of available production factors to whole sections of the economy. So, there is both an efficiency and an equity argument.

6.4.3 Stages of integration and instruments of Union cohesion policies

The form redistribution takes changes as the integration process passes into higher stages.[14] Higher-stage integration in general means stronger common institutions as more and more complicated tasks have to be fulfilled. It also

Table 6.1 Forms of redistribution at different levels of integration

	Low PTA/FTA	Medium CU/CM	High EMU	Full FED
Expenditure:				
Compensation	★			
Specific purpose		★	★	★
General purpose			★	★
Receipts:				
Compensation	★			
Contribution		★	★	
Taxes			★	★
Social Security				★

means a stronger solidarity between the constituent parts of the integration area as interdependence has grown. These factors determine largely the type of instrument that can best be used for international/inter-regional redistribution schemes at different stages of integration. We have given these differences in Table 6.1. In the columns we have given the various stages of integration: low ones such as preferential trade agreements (PTAs) and FTAs, medium ones such as CUs and CMs, high ones such as EMUs and complete ones such as federations (FEDs) and unitary states. In the rows we have given the income instruments (tax, social security) and expenditure instruments (grants, programmes).[15]

During the *lowest stage of integration* (PTAs, FTAs) redistribution is often absent from the policy toolkit, for two reasons. First, because at these low stages the institutional set up is too weak to be able to handle complicated systems of redistribution. Second, because solidarity among constituent parts is too weak to mobilize sufficient popular support for redistribution. If these barriers can be overcome, the next step is a simple system of compensation. This can take the form of an agreement whereby payments are made to member states that do not benefit from integration by member states that are net gainers. This can also be in the form of a simple fund into which the gainers pay contributions and from which the losers receive payments.

Schemes for the international/inter-regional redistribution of resources under medium and higher stages of integration (CU, EMU) differ as to the combination they use of income instruments (tax, social security) and expenditure instruments (grants, programmes) (MacDougall *et al.*, 1977).

During the medium *forms of market integration* (CU/CM), redistribution occurs rather through the expenditure instruments involving different layers of government because (1) expenditure can be tailored to specific needs (including compensation of negative integration effects, and (2) governments are generally reluctant to let unions decide on interpersonal redistribution matters. Here the Union decides on the type of programme that should be set up and which it is prepared to support financially. Such specific purpose grants are considered to lead to optimum welfare in the long run, because they promote a better allocation of available production factors. International financial transfer through a common budget is the adequate mechanism for promoting equity in these integration schemes.

The setting up of an EMU brings the need to help member countries to deal with problems resulting from external shocks. The most adequate solution is a Union redistribution policy. Its aid can be a combination of specific-purpose and general-purpose grants. The former are likely to prevail for some time. The latter, taking the form of block payments from the Union to a member country, will take some time to be introduced. The reason is that the Union has no control over the actual use of the funds transferred, these funds are thus at risk of being used in a way that is not expedient to structural improvement and may erode the solidarity on which it is based.

Finally, at the stage of the *Full Union* (FED), solidarity among member states is likely to have grown sufficiently to justify extensive Union redistribution, using instruments dealing directly with the individual, like discriminatory personal income taxes and transfers to such low-income individuals as elderly persons, unemployed persons, etc. These are most effective as federal powers over income taxes and social security are substantial, and the federal budget represents a considerable portion of GDP. As problem groups are often concentrated in specific countries or regions, inter-personal income transfer policies work out as inter-national and inter-regional transfer policies. From an economic development viewpoint these policies have a drawback, however, as they have only a very indirect influence on the improvement of the productive capacity of the recipient country or region.

So, we can *conclude* that the way redistribution for cohesion is done depends on the stage of integration. The EU has in the past moved through the various stages of integration. It has attained the stage of EMU. It has constantly adapted its system of redistribution and elaborated its cohesion policy in line with these theoretical predictions. We will come back to that in later chapters.

Box 6.1 Monetary Union and redistribution

The EMU as set up by the EU leaves the responsibility for fiscal policy with each of the national governments within the constraints set by the Treaty and the Stability and Growth Pact. This means that each member state has to cope, itself, with specific problems that may come up (e.g. asymmetric shocks) and that the EU will not set up a system of financial transfers from one country to another (but it will use the Structural and Cohesion Funds (SCF)). The question is whether this choice is the optimal one.

In the case of *fiscal policy in general* there is on balance no reason to centralize. Indeed, recent reviews of theoretical and empirical studies (Breuss and Eller, 2004; Letelier Saavedra, 2004) find that the evidence is inconclusive, which may be interpreted as a stalemate between the various pros and cons of decentralized government.

What is valid for fiscal policies in general may not be true for specific aspects (segments) of fiscal policy. There is ample evidence that centralization is not the best option for the quality of the provision of public goods such as health and education (Letelier Saavedra, 2004). But there is less evidence in as far as the installation of a system of redistribution (transfers) is concerned. In order to judge we will again hear both the theoretical and the empirical arguments.

From a *theoretical point* of view there are strong arguments for a centralized (EU) fiscal system with redistribution over member states and citizens via automatic transfers (see, for example, Persson and Tabellini, 1996). However, in the EU case, the premises of the above-mentioned theory do not obtain. The first reason is that the EU has no competence in essential areas; e.g. in tax matters national governments are not willing to give up their autonomy. The second reason is that in cases where the EU has powers its complicated decision-making process precludes further advances in contentious matters such as fiscal policy.

The *empirical evidence* leads to two views:

1 There is a real need for an additional redistribution mechanism. The arguments of those who hold this view are twofold. First, EU member countries are often hit by shocks that, given the institutional circumstances in most of them, tend to have persistent negative effects. Left to themselves countries have difficulty to recover from such shocks (Breuss, 1998). Second, redistribution mechanisms as used in federations such as the US and Canada are very effective in coping with such negative effects (see e.g. Sachs and Sala-I-Martin, 1992; Bayoumi and Masson, 1998).
2 The present set-up is able to function in a satisfactory way. The arguments of the proponents of this view are the mirror picture of the previous one. First, they argue that the frequency and the severity of shocks are much smaller than suggested by some alarmists (e.g. Vinals, 1998). Second, the effectiveness of centralized systems of redistribution is often exaggerated (e.g. von Hagen, 1992; Fatas, 1998).

So, the evidence provided up until now does not lead to a *clear-cut conclusion* as to the need for a type redistribution mechanism as suggested by the fiscal federalism school in order to cope with the effects of the creation of the EMU. Given the uncertainty of the outcome of the research and given the institutional constraints of the EU, the present set-up seems to be adequate (see also, for example, Alesina and Perotti, 1998).

6.4.4 The EU option: redistribution via structural policies

Cohesion policies that work out through the redistribution of funds can be shaped in different ways. The form of support that is most suited in the stage of integration the EU has come to is the specific-purpose grant. This is indeed the system adopted by the EU. The EU has not acquired a sufficiently high degree

118 *Designing a solution-oriented intervention system*

of political solidarity to justify the use of general-purpose grants. The question then becomes to what sort of purposes these grants should be directed. In economic terms the best option is to use specific-purpose grants to the poorer countries, regions and disadvantaged social groups and territories. These have to be financed by sums from the richer countries and regions. The criterion for selecting purposes is that they should enable the disadvantaged region or group to recover and catch up with the rest. So after some time the beneficiary should no longer be dependent on aid. The efficiency orientation of these grants means that they are largely oriented towards the improvement of the supply side of the economy (demand side measures would be rather more equity oriented).

Creating a viable basis for competitive future oriented activities in the presently backward countries and regions implies the improvement of the structural features of the regional economy (both the industrial structure and the production environment) and of the active population (participation degrees; unemployment, etc.). In practice that implies that the conditionality of the redistribution policy is worked out as a regional economic and social policy.

The redistribution scheme in this option will then be designed in such a way as to help along (or, alternatively, to do the least possible harm to) the achievement of the targets of allocation and stabilization policies. This implies that they must help to create a viable base for future-oriented economic activities. Examples of this type are financial aid programmes for specific social groups, designed to retrain workers who have become redundant because of the structural changes of the economy due to integration. While such schemes are mostly short term, others are of a structural nature. An example of the latter is a programme for the improvement of the infrastructure in regions that are far below the average level of development, aimed at creating the conditions required for self-sustained regional growth.

The rationale for and the equalization effect of such structural policies are illustrated by Figure 6.1. Suppose income growth (Y) is determined completely by increases in production factor availability and productivity, together called P_f. Suppose further that country B is not only a slow-growth but also a low-level income country (OB_1), while country A is not only a fast-growth but also a

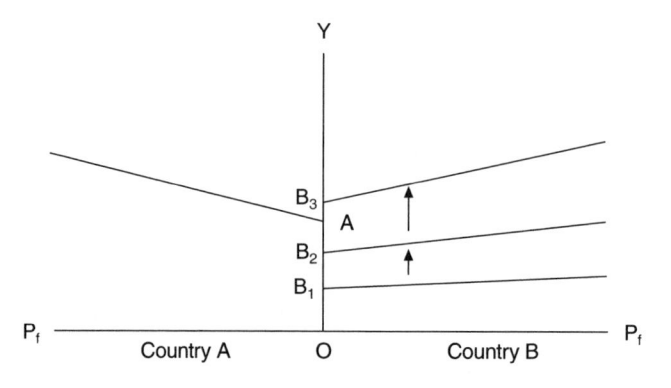

Figure 6.1 Structural policy for balanced growth

high-level income country (OA). To make income levels in the Union converge, the curve of country B has to move upwards, with the intercept moving from point OB_1 through OB_2 to OB_3, which is beyond point OA (the structural growth in country A).

6.4.5 Competitiveness is key

The graph above gives the essentials of policy intervention. However, it does not specify to what elements the policy should be directed. As a matter of fact, that is dependent on the specific goals set and the understanding one has of the working of the system. The former have been fairly constant over time (see Chapter 7), the latter on the contrary have changed under the impetus of different theories (see Chapters 2 to 5) and the perceived effectiveness of the various interventions (see Chapter 8). With respect to the theoretical foundations the accent has clearly shifted (see also Bachtler and Yuill, 2001).

In the post-war period the policy oriented towards economic and territorial cohesion focused on the attraction of (foreign) direct investment to designated (disfavoured) regions and on the improvement there of certain location factors such as the price of industrial land, transport links, etc. Social problems (due to redundancies) were attacked by (re)training of workers for jobs in modern industries. Both policies were often supported by growth poles that were set up to create sufficient agglomeration and concentration advantages and palliate the lack of urban services in the region.

In recent decades the accent has shifted to the factors that determine growth. They were brought together under the heading of *competitiveness* (EC 1990b, 1995b). So the policy focused on the factors that determine competitiveness in each element in the regional system. In one region, that could be a combination of support to innovativeness, entrepreneurship and training of the labour force; in other regions, the support to infrastructure and the environment. In yet other regions support to good governance, in other words to the improvement of the quality of its institutions, is an essential prerequisite for growth. All regions of the system have to contribute to the overarching EU goal of enhancing the competitiveness of the EU economy in the knowledge society (see later chapters).

6.5 Coordination and regulation

6.5.1 Some basics on vertical coordination

An important aspect of constitutions is the distribution of roles over the various layers of multilevel government. Now, the EU treaties and the draft constitution only deal with the relation of the EU institutions and those of the member states. It does not provide for relations with either constituent parts of the member states (regions) or social groups (trade unions).

Cohesion policy is a case of shared responsibility between the various actors at different levels of public authority (see next section). Such vertical coordination is of essence in order to make sure that the actions of the various layers do not contradict each other. On the contrary, they should support each other. We distinguish four different ways to put this into effect:

1 *Inform.* A rather passive way, in which one hopes for a behaviour adaptation of the partner on the basis of better knowledge.
2 *Coordinate.* Active consultation is sought and arguments are exchanged so as to bring both partners to the conclusion that concerted action is in their common interest.
3 *Cooperation.* Partners agree on common objectives and on concerted action to reach such objectives. They actively support each other's initiatives.
4 *Coerce.* This is mostly done in a hierarchical situation, where orders are given, or standards are set to which units have to comply.

Over the past half century, the EU has used all four types of vertical coordination in matters of cohesion. In the early days of the policy (see next chapter) the accent has been on the first two instruments. Later the other instruments have come to the fore. One can draw a parallel here with the discussion about finances (Table 6.1). The higher integration the stronger the instrument.

6.5.2 The importance of horizontal coordination of EU policies

Policies need not only be vertically coordinated; horizontal coordination is also necessary. This applies notably to horizontal coordination at EU level. In practice it means that one needs to make sure that the effects of other EU policies (such as competition) do not have a negative bearing on cohesion. The rationale for such coordination can be illustrated as follows.

The more the workings of the EU socio-economic system and the effects of the other EU policies (such as internal market or sustainability) contribute to convergence of wealth levels, the less need there is for cohesion policies per se. The first element (socio-economic development) is rather autonomous. The second, however, is a policy variable. So it is important to design these policies in such a way that they contribute a maximum to cohesion. Unfortunately this is not always easy. Market integration, for instance, can lead to unequal spatial development and hence may increase disparities.[16]

At the start of the EU it was presumed that most effects of integration would be rather neutral. In the seventies the idea was accepted that the effect could be negative and a policy was set up to improve cohesion. In the 1980s the EU became aware of the fact some of its policies, in particular the Common Agricultural Policy, tended to increase the disparities between the regions of the more developed countries in northern Europe and those of the less developed regions in southern Europe. This sparked off a considerable concern with the potential negative effects on cohesion of all EU policies. A number of studies have been made into the problem. An overview of these studies (Molle and Cappellin, 1988) showed that there was a significant risk that the end effect of a series of EU policies on the problem regions would be negative.

The EU has set itself the task to coordinate its policies so as to obtain maximum effect for cohesion. This is even a constitutional obligation of the EU:[17] 'By stating and developing Community policies and activities and developing the internal market, (cohesion) objectives shall be considered, participating in their achievement.'[18]

In the early years of the development of the EU the coordination problem was fairly simple, as EU policies were restricted to those immediately functional to the realization of the CM. Moreover, in the fields that fell in the EU competences, the objectives were relatively few and the instrumentation of the EU (apart from the Common Agricultural Policy) was often weak. Over the past half century the EU has considerably extended its fields of competence, e.g. in the field of environment much EU regulation has been issued. These extensions have increased the horizontal coordination problem.[19] The EU has also intensified its involvement in fields where it had already competences. This has led to a very strong increase, both in the number of objectives that are pursued in each field and in the number of instruments that can be used.

It has also led to a further complication, which is the combination of horizontal and vertical coordination. One major example of an extended policy area where this occurs is employment.[20] A European Employment Strategy (defining the EU objectives and the coordinated action of the member states) and the so-called Lisbon Strategy (defining the EU objectives in terms of competitiveness and the national action to promote such competitiveness) have been set up. Both are also subjects of cohesion policy.

So the conclusion is that the number, the type and the potential strength of the impact of EU policies have increased over time (Molle, 2006). It means also that the present coordination problem is now considerably more difficult and intricate than it was in the start-up years. The EU has realized this and has stepped up the analysis of the impact of its policies on cohesion (compare EC, 1996b, 2001, 2004a).

6.5.3 Regulation

The term 'regulation' covers essentially a whole hierarchy of formal rules (legal and other) that range from constitutions to by-laws and contracts. The constitutional level defines relations and ways of settling conflicts between actors with different rationales. These can be private–public relations, such as property rights, or public–public relations, for instance the distribution of functions between federation, member state and region. The higher their rank the more they have the character of frameworks, the lower their rank the more they specify allocation mechanisms.

Rules are set because they bring predictability in behaviour, efficiency in contracting and conformity with social values. In so doing they lower transaction cost for all concerned and contribute to an efficient economic and policy system.

The EU has specified various legal forms of regulation:

- A Regulation is general in its application; it is binding in its entirety and directly applicable in all member states. This means that national legislation (if existent) is overruled by EU regulations; indeed European law takes

precedence over national law. The national governments have no right or need to take action once a matter has been settled by a European regulation for it is automatically valid in all member states.
- A Directive is binding, as to the results to be achieved, for the member states but leaves the national authorities the choice of form and methods. So to implement directives, action of member states is needed in the form of national laws and decrees.

In line with the principles of subsidiarity and proportionality the EU should use, where possible, open forms of coordination and only if needed use Directives or even Regulations. The practice of the EU is, in broad outlines, in conformity with the principles. The EU cohesion policy uses two major types of instruments:

1 Uniform EU rules (regulations) govern its financial instruments (see Chapter 7).
2 EU coordination governs national regional and social policies (see Chapter 8).

In many cases these instruments are used in parallel; for instance to foster social inclusion the EU uses both the financial instrument (the European Social Fund (ESF)) and the coordination of national policies. The same is true for regional policy; to foster convergence and competitiveness the EU uses both the financial instrument (the ERDF), for example, to pay for infrastructure and the method of coordination, for example, to exchange best practices about networking.

The EU policy practice about horizontal and vertical coordination can be illustrated once more with the case of cohesion and competition policy. For state aids the constitution sets the main principles and general rules. These are worked out in regulations. There is regular coordination between member states and the Commission (Directorate Generals (DGs) responsible for competition and for cohesion) on the interpretation of these rules in concrete cases (see Box 8.2).

6.5.4 Involvement of the EU in matters of social security regulation

The major concern of the average European citizen in matters of cohesion seems to be with the sustainability of social security systems given its rising cost and the limitations to the capacity to pay. Hence, the question whether the EU should not be involved in this. The application of the subsidiarity principle (see next section) to social security has given rise to considerable debate (see Box 6.2) but has led finally to a negative answer as to the involvement of the EU.

We recall that in line with the fundamental features of the present EU given in Table 6.1 (a pre-FED) the EU does not have *financial* instruments, in other words, it has no power to use income tax and social security benefits for redistribution purposes. These instruments remain the domain of the member states. However, the EU has been endowed with *regulatory* instruments. The original reason for at least some EU involvement in social security matters is that differences in national social security systems impair the mobility of labour within the

EU and thereby the smooth functioning of the internal market. Following the principle of proportionality the involvement of the EU has initially been limited to a light form of harmonization of migrants' rights (Regulation 1408 of 1958). Under the influence of Court Decisions and political activism it has since been extended to all citizens that migrate. Present rules are very detailed and complicated and cover a wide range of benefits. In essence, they cover the right to export entitlement to social security benefits to other member states and the entitlement of migrants to the system of the host country.[21]

Box 6.2 Limited role for the EU in matters of social security

In the past there has been a lot of controversy over the degree of involvement of the EU in social protection in general and social security in particular. In this discussion broadly two views can be distinguished: the 'economic or liberalist' and the 'social progress or regulators' view (Holloway, 1981; Dearden, 1995, Brown *et al.*, 1996).

In the *economic view*, the social security systems need only be harmonized as far as necessary for the proper functioning of the CM. In modern times this view has been reformulated to limit the harmonization of labour market legislation to what is clearly needed to safeguard the fair competition within the internal market. The EU should favour a competition between rules and refrain from any major policy action.

In the *social progress view*, the EU is more than a CM, and has the clear task of enhancing welfare. This view has led to claims for standards to avoid a downward spiral and even to claims for upward alignment, eliminating at least the gravest shortcomings of the systems in certain member states. Proposals for redistribution from the rich to poor member countries by means of a European Social Security Fund have been put forward, too, but owing to the obvious lack of political support they have not been realized.

The outcome of the debate between economists and social progressists has changed over time. Initially the economists won. The Commission, which had associated itself with the social progress approach, was forced, in 1966, to adopt the economic line advocated by all member states. This line was followed during the period 1965–90. In the 1990s, things changed to some extent. The European Social Charter established that any citizen of the EU is entitled to adequate social protection, including social security; the determination of the level and form is, however, to be arranged by each member state.

The choice for only a very general EU standard and national autonomy as to level of security and modalities of execution has been maintained. Each country has to strike the balance between two considerations. First, a highly developed social security system strengthens investments in human capital. Second, the further improvement of social protection depends on long-term productivity growth, in turn, dependent on increased competitiveness on world markets.

6.6 Who: the intricacies of multilevel government[22]

6.6.1 Shift of competences from nation states to EU and regions

The EU is generally seen as a special case of multilevel governance. Usually this is set against the traditional view of the national state that in principle has full sovereignty within its borders. This also applied in the past to cohesion (regional) policy. National governments of member states used to be sovereign in matters of cohesion policy: setting objectives, selecting instruments, determining eligibility of regions and projects and deciding on the allocation of resources. This role has changed a lot; central government has lost its exclusive competence due to the simultaneous occurrence of three trends:

1 *Upwards*. In the past the EU has moved through the stages of integration as depicted in the previous section. As a consequence the scope of EU policy making has increased very considerably. This dynamics was motivated by good economic reasoning.[23] As a consequence of the European integration process the EU institutions have become actors in their own right. They do not behave like agents of national governments as is the case in many intergovernmental international organizations.

2 *Downwards*. In many countries the regional level has become increasingly important due to the devolution of competences from central government. Devolution (regionalization) is very evident in a number of member countries (e.g. Spain, see Moreno, 2002). That means an increased role for the regional and local government authorities. Such an increased role has been favoured by the very demands of the EU cohesion policy in terms of partnership that has induced many countries to empower the regions more than in the past.[24]

3 *Sideways*. Due to the tendency of privatization a number of organizations are now in the private sector and associations such as private-public partnerships have been formed. Moreover, there has been a tendency to empower non-governmental organizations (NGOs) that defend collective interests (such as the environment).

As a consequence the traditional separation of competences has become blurred. We see now many new forms of international associational activities among actors with different backgrounds at different levels. The EU has enshrined these forms of cooperative governance in the so-called *partnership principle* (see Section 9.4). As competences are shared by different actors, new modes of collective international decision making have emerged. In most countries a range of auxiliary institutions have developed – some of them in the public, others in the private and still others in the semi-public domain. This makes for a complex and sometimes opaque structure.

The three tendencies described above have been reinforced by two non-economic, political forces:

1 The wish of the European institutions (such as the Commission and the Parliament) to improve their legitimization. The EU wants to show that it

does indeed care for the needs of all its citizens, its companies and the representatives of the third sector. It wanted to wash out the image of an EU as a heartless organization caring notably about the regime of free trade with the implication that only the strongest companies can draw profit from it. This tendency bears a certain risk; due to such pressures the EU is in danger of becoming too lenient towards new demands on its cohesion policies that thereby may go out of hand in terms of effectiveness and efficiency.[25]

2   The pressure from a large variety of actors (such as local authorities, firms and interested organizations from the third sector) eager to escape from the tutelage of the national governments and to participate in the aura and manna from Brussels (Pollack, 1995). Sometimes this is to the benefit of all as regions may become victims of inadequate national policies. However, this pressure also bears a risk in so far as it reflects rent-seeking behaviour of regional actors.[26]

The combination of the building of institutions, the confirmation of cultural identity and the demands of economic development have given rise to a whole range of strengthened platforms on the regional level for networking, interest representation and decision making (Bukowski *et al.*, 2003). Some of these extend beyond traditional borders (Balducci, 2003).

6.6.2 EU institutions involved

The institutional set up of the EU is a complex one. Here is a shortened scheme of the most important institutional actors:

- *Commission.* The major tasks of the EC are threefold: the initiation of actions; the execution of policies; and the implementation of the budget. One of the members of the EC is responsible for cohesion matters. Cohesion policies take up a very large part of the budget. To perform its task the Commission has a European staff of civil servants organized by DGs (comparable with Ministries). The responsibilities for cohesion are divided over several DGs (mainly DG Regio and DG Employment). The Commission is accountable to the European Parliament.
- *Council and Parliament.* Together, these institutions have the task of legislation. The Council is the arena of the representatives of national governments.[27] On the one hand, through the broad guidelines set by the European Council of heads of government. On the other hand, by the negotiations about new legislation and financial frameworks in the Council of Ministers. The Council meets in a changing composition; for cohesion it regroups the ministers responsible for that matter in their national government (often the ministers for economic affairs). These ministers are accountable to their national parliaments. The European Parliament has an important say in legislation and in budget matters.
- *Committee of the Regions (CoR).* In the 1980s the Commission sought to create new platforms and networks to shoulder the extended cohesion

policy. As a result the Advisory Council for Local and Regional Authorities was set up in 1988. This function was strengthened with the set up of the CoR as one of the official institutions of the EU in 1993. The CoR permits the EU to hear directly the opinion of the lower layers of government. The CoR has the right to give its advice on EU policy proposals. It is intended to smoothe the coordination of more general issues between the EU and the regions. The CoR has not acted as a crystallizing point of political change. Membership is extremely diverse and this makes it difficult to come to strong common positions. The debates held and the counsels given tend to favour an ever more detailed interventionist policy for all European regions (with an important role for the interface EU/regions) rather than a limitation to essential redistribution matters.

- *Economic and Social Committee (ESC)*. The ESC is composed of representatives of employees and employers, professionals and consumers. It advises the Commission and the Council on their policy plans. The role of the ESC is notably relevant in matters of social cohesion.
- *Expert committees*. Many organizations are involved in the EU policy in the stages of design and delivery. Most of this is in a formal way through participation in advisory committees or management committees. Traditionally the employers' organizations were most important, later joined by trade unions and NGOs. Now (groups of) regions have come to the fore as the most important partners of the Commission (see Box 6.3).

Box 6.3 Groupings of major beneficiaries

Many regions have become aware of the fact that they compete with others in a European and even global context. They want to mobilize maximum support for their efforts to improve their competitiveness. With the growth of the European involvement in cohesion matters the European bargaining area is now of very high relevance. To lobby the EU many regions have opened offices in Brussels. To strengthen their lobby they have entered into trans-national networks. Most of these[28] regroup local authorities that have similar characteristics or common policy problems. Examples here are: ultra-peripheral regions; frontier regions and regions (often cities) in industrial decline. They lobby the European institutions to obtain a special constitutional status (which was realized by the ultra-peripheral regions); to obtain specific programmes with funding attached (which was realized by among others the border regions (INTERREG) and the urban regions (URBAN)) or to bend existing policy packages further in their favour (industrial regions). In a number of cases such associations are actively promoted by the EC in order to make sure that regions take a wider than national perspective and increase the effectiveness of the policies.

6.6.3 Changing roles and influence at different stages of the cycle

Among the actors described three assume particularly important roles in the various stages of the process. These are the Commission, the member states (acting in the framework of the Council of Ministers or of the European Council) and the regions (either acting alone or through their lobbies, national governments and the CoR). The competences of these three main actors, and hence the power balance between them, changes in the course of the policy cycle. An idea of this change is given in Table 6.2.

Among all these actors the Commission stands out, in practice, as the pivotal one. Indeed it is involved in the preparation, delivery and evaluation of the policy. The Commission has a formidable advantage over the other institutions in the sense that it controls much of the information flows. The role of the central governments of the member states has changed over time. Nowadays their role is rather one of negotiation and strategic decision making in the legislation stage and one of coordination, facilitation and arbitration in the implementation stages. The role of the regions has changed also. They can exert a certain influence by their direct access to the Commission in all stages of the cycle.

The Commission has over time intensified the dialogue with territorial institutions. To that end the Commission organizes hearings at the occasion of the presentation of its work programme. The Commission hopes that these institutions will provide it with advice and will act as a relay for communicating to their members any proposals or directives of the Commission. This means that they will not only play a role of adviser in the upbeat to major septennial decisions, but will increasingly play a role in the monitoring of strategic developments and the monitoring and evaluation of the practical implementation.

Table 6.2 Changing roles of the major actors

Stage in the policy cycle	EC	National governments (Council)	Regional authorities	Chapter in book
2 Basic design	strong	dominant	insignificant	6
3 Financial packages	modest	dominant	weak	7
Definition of objectives and of eligibility criteria				
3 Institutional framework and delivery system	strong	strong	modest	8
4 Implementation	very strong	variable	variable	9
5 Evaluation	strong	variable	strong	10

Source: Author, inspired by Hooghe and Marks (2001: 94)

6.7 How: the framework

6.7.1 Three levels

A policy can only be made effective by specifying further the actions to be undertaken and the resources to be put in place. In this respect it has become common practice to distinguish between the following three levels:

1   *Policy.* A set of activities, directed towards common, fairly general goals. Each policy may have several different direct beneficiaries. A policy usually consists of several programmes. Given the broad objectives there is often only a fairly widely defined financial framework for a policy. Unlike more detailed programmes and projects a policy is usually not specified in terms of budget and time schedule.
2   *Programme.* A set of organized but often varied activities (encompassing several projects) directed towards the achievement of specific policy objectives with a clear commitment to devote specified financial resources to it that may be mobilized from several sources.
3   *Projects.* Dividable intervention with a fixed time schedule, a dedicated budget and a designated organization that is responsible for carrying out the necessary tasks for its realization.

The success of projects and programmes (in terms of relevance, effectiveness, efficiency, impact and sustainability) depends largely on the broader context in which they take place. These have been specified in Figure 6.2 in the form of rings: the outer one is the political, institutional and legal context (this chapter);

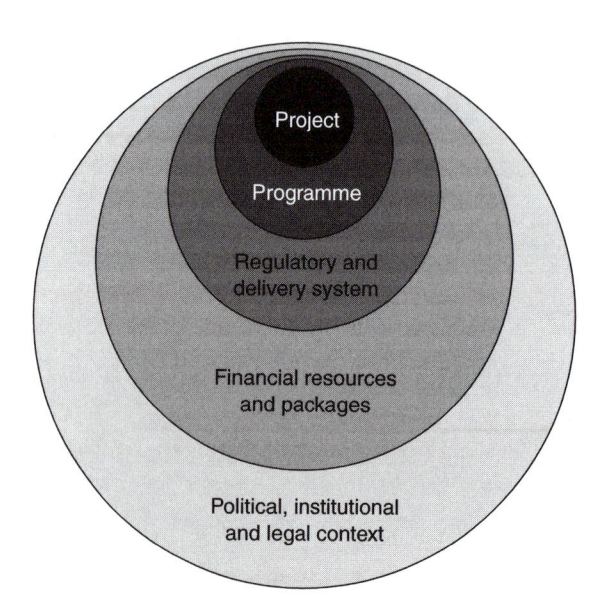

Figure 6.2 Projects and programmes as central elements of policy

the next ring is the financial package (Chapter 7); and the inner ring is the regulatory and delivery system (Chapters 8 and 9).

6.8 Summary and conclusions

- In the first stage of the policy cycle we have found that the considerable economic, social and territorial disparities have negative influences on the welfare of the EU. So, *a policy to alleviate them would be in order*. In the second stage of the policy cycle (described in this chapter) we have given the main design features of such a policy.
- The national governments are not capable of providing a cohesion policy at EU level in an efficient way. So, *the EU has assumed responsibility for it*. Cohesion is fundamental to the EU and cohesion policy has therefore been made a constitutional obligation for the EU.
- The major instrument the EU has put in place to foster cohesion is *financial redistribution*. It has set up EU funds from which grants can be given to regions and social groups to alleviate particular problems. These grants are to be used in programmes that aim at improving the structure of the production system, the productive factors and the production environment (infrastructure). The overall aim is to decrease disparity by increasing competitiveness. Given the stage of integration the EU has made a rational choice as to the fundamentals of the financial dimension of its cohesion system.
- The second important instrument of the EU is *regulation and coordination*. In order to preserve the effectiveness of support to the least developed areas the EU sets limits to national state aids. It moreover sets standards, for instance for preventing the loss of social protection for migrant workers. Finally it coordinates the cohesion policies of the member states.
- *Many actors* are involved in the EU cohesion policy. They assume different roles at different stages of the elaboration and implementation of the policy cycle. The Council has the decisive role in the decisions on the policy fundamentals and the multi-annual framework. The Commission has a pivotal role in the stages of the application, daily management and evaluation of the policy. Regions play an increasingly important role as advisers in the design stage and operation managers in the implementation stage.
- The EU puts its cohesion policy into practice by *concrete programmes and detailed projects*.

Annex 6.1 Legal (constitutional) foundations

Cohesion policy is one of the oldest policies of the EU. The legal basis for it is very disparate and differs according to each of the three dimensions of cohesion. It consists of a series of treaties that provide the constitutional basis for the various forerunners of the present EU.

Social cohesion policy has its foundations in the 1952 Treaty on the European Coal and Steel Community (ECSC). It created the ESF that could help the retraining of people whose jobs were made redundant by the restructuring of the coal and steel sector due to market integration. The experience of the ECSC proved profitable when the social policy paragraphs of the European Economic Community (EEC) Treaty were devised.[29] However, the preparatory discussions for this treaty did not produce a clear-cut view on such a policy, so that the relevant articles did not refer to an explicit redistribution objective.[30] The discussion assumed a different perspective when in the 1980s the plans for the completion of the internal market were set up (EC, 1988). There was much concern that the putting into practice of these plans would entail considerable social problems, for two reasons. First, the adaptation to new circumstances would lead to unemployment. Second, the competition from low-wage (low social protection) countries would lead to an erosion of the high social protection in the richer countries. This led to the insertion in the Social Charter and Single European Act of an explicit reference to cohesion. With the introduction of the Social Chapter by the treaties of Maastricht and Amsterdam the scope of the action of the EU in the social field was considerably widened (minimum hours of work per day, social security, health and safety requirements and so on). The Treaty of Amsterdam, moreover, introduced a European policy to promote employment in the form of guidelines for national policies.[31]

Economic cohesion policy developed later. In the 1950s and 1960s, a hesitant start was made. Real political commitment to a European regional policy was achieved at the 1972 Paris Conference of the European Council.[32] In the following 15 years the policies were given shape and substance. They involve, notably, the support from a Regional Development Fund to the improvement of the economic structure of regions in distress. With the adoption of the Single European Act (Art. 158), confirmed by the Treaty on the European Union, economic cohesion has become a constitutional obligation: 'In order to promote its overall harmonious development, the Community shall develop and pursue its actions leading to the strengthening of its *economic and social cohesion*' (Art. 130A).

Territorial cohesion is of much more recent development. Some of the origins can be traced back to the agricultural policy set up in the 1960s (that is the parts financed by the Orientation section of the Agricultural Fund). Implicit in economic cohesion has been some notions of territorial cohesion (e.g. on ultra-peripheral regions). However, it is only with the 1997 Treaty of Amsterdam that territorial cohesion was given an explicit constitutional position. The meaning there is limited; Art. 299.2 gave a special support status to the so-called outermost or ultra-peripheral regions. This article has been dropped in the draft constitution where territorial cohesion refers to a more general policy objective, thereby broadening its application to all spatially disadvantaged areas.

The treaties of course give only the basic objectives, principles and means (e.g. funds). They have been given substance in a series of regulations, specifying the way in which these are put in daily policy practice.

Stage III
Specifying objectives and matching these with instruments

7 Reaching objectives by financial support

7.1 Introduction

The EU cohesion policy, as framed by constitutional provisions during the second stage of the policy cycle, has to be worked out in more concrete terms. One does this in the third stage of the policy cycle. At this stage (that we address in this and the following chapter) the elaboration is done at the level of broad outlines and basic principles. They have an important status as they form together with the constitution (previous stage and previous chapter) and the delivery system (next stage discussed in Chapter 9), the framework for the more day-to-day implementation.[1]

Cohesion policy addresses major structural problems. For that reason it needs to have a long-term outlook that in turn requires a multi-annual framework. Indeed, annual rounds of budget and policy decisions with all their uncertainties would form too shaky a basis for such a policy. The EU has opted for a multi-annual framework that it revises every six to seven years. In the rest of this chapter we will describe how the EU has adapted this framework, taking account of the lessons drawn from the experience gained in the previous period and adapting it to new needs and challenges that it faced in the upcoming period.

The rest of the chapter is structured as follows:

We start with a description of the major problems and the ensuing priorities for policy making and their translation in concrete objectives.

Next we describe the development of the major financial instruments that have been put in place to attack the problems. We describe the main characteristics.

The main question will be addressed in the next section; that is how much money must be devoted to cohesion and on what basis does one need to make the distribution of the total packages over different potential beneficiaries.

Lastly we will discuss in some detail the distribution over categories of investment (the eligibility to aid for different types of beneficiaries).

The chapter will be concluded with a brief summary of the main findings.

7.2 Problems, priorities and objectives

7.2.1 Identification of problems

There has been a remarkable stability in the assessment of the problems and of the objectives. Over time the first objective of the EU cohesion policy has been to reduce the problem of internal disparities in wealth levels. To that end a selection of the areas and social groups has been made of the countries and regions where the level of wealth as measured by GDP was lowest and where unemployment was highest.

In the past the description of policy categories has been done in terms of *types of problems*. The objectives were defined as solving the problems of each of these policy categories. So, objective 1 was to improve the situation in the most important problem category: the backward areas. Next to this a whole panoply of more or less specific types of problems have been identified and (often after considerable political struggle) been accepted as eligible for support. In this respect the EU has defined as a second objective to solve the problems of the areas that have to cope with industrial restructuring. Examples of this objective 2 are regions facing decline due to the loss of a major industrial base (e.g. textiles, steel). Some other areas have been made eligible in the past because of their specific geographical characteristics (e.g. sparsely populated rural areas, polar areas or ultra-peripheral areas).[2] Many times the suggestions for such a new problem type came from member states, on other occasions it was the Commission (supported by regional pressure groups) that took the initiative.

For the present period this idea of denoting eligibility by the very specific character of problem has been put aside on the level of the design of the policy. Now the categories are directly defined in terms of objectives. Within these objectives there is much room for initiatives of all partners to address a whole range of problems.

7.2.2 From main problem to main objective and to points of intervention

The EU shows a considerable diversity in problem situations. Nevertheless, the major ones have been somewhat similar over time. The present situation in terms of (1) major problems and (2) their corresponding objectives is as follows:[3]

- *Lagging region: objective convergence*
  1. Most of these regions are traditionally backward, have failed to develop sufficient manufacturing or service industry and are still oriented to agriculture. This type of region is generally characterized by a peripheral situation, a deficient infrastructure, a meagre endowment with business services and a lack of skilled labour with a good industrial and service tradition. The main indicator of problems here is the wealth level.
  2. The first objective of the EU cohesion policy is to support structural improvement of the conditions in these long-standing problem regions

and thereby speeding up their convergence to the EU mean. All regions with a GDP less than 75 per cent of the EU average are eligible for aid under this objective.

- *Restructuring regions: objective competitiveness and employment*
  1. Some regions that have played a leading role at a certain stage of economic development by specializing in one or other sectors have landed in difficulties as production conditions for these sectors changed. Some of these changes are due to integration; others are the result of the continuous changes that occur in technology, in environment, in social values and in world politics. This type of region is generally marked by inadequate infrastructure and by serious problems in old industrial areas. They have often specialized manpower whose skills are, however, at odds with modern requirements. Their GDP per head levels are often above the EU average and anyway above the 75 per cent of the EU mean threshold. High unemployment is the main indicator of distress here.
  2. So the second objective of EU cohesion policies is to prevent such regions sliding away by strengthening the regions' competitiveness, attractiveness for investment and thus employment. Regions eligible for aid under this objective used to be very strictly delimited; now many regions can qualify provided they propose actions from a short list of themes related to the overall objective of the EU to become the most competitive knowledge-based economy in the world.

The main points on which the policy attacks these problems (scope of assistance in the EU jargon) are, in part, common to the two objectives but differ on essential points. The common ones are the improvement of the quality of human capital, the development of innovation and of the knowledge society and the protection of the environment. Specific for the convergence objective are the investment in physical capital, notably the adaptability to social and economic changes and administrative efficiency. Specific for the competitiveness objective are the accent on the improvement of accessibility, the adaptability of workers, entrepreneurship and the anticipation of economic and social change including the further opening to trade.

The EU has identified a third type of eligible region: *territorial cooperation*.

1. These are characterized by a deficient connectivity; in other words they are not well linked into the EU economic system. One group of such regions consists of border regions.[4] Their problems stem first from differences in administrative systems and traditions and second from deficient infrastructure between the EU member states. Cooperation with regions on the other side of the border is therefore difficult. Similar problems may also occur for functionally linked regions that are not contiguous. Finally, they occur for regions (often islands) that are located at a considerable distance from the mainland.
2. So the third objective is the strengthening of territorial cooperation at the

cross-border, transnational and inter-regional levels. Under this objective the whole area of the EU is in principle eligible. The objective is justified from the subsidiarity point of view as the national governments cannot cope with the problem without revolutionizing their institutions and their administrative organization.

The scope of assistance covers joint local and regional initiatives, the support for inter-regional cooperation and the exchange of experience at the appropriate territorial level.

7.2.3 Political side objectives

Next to the stated objectives that have been discussed in the previous section the EU cohesion policy has had as a side objective to ease the reaching of important compromises in the Council about the *progress of integration*. Major decisions have to be taken by unanimity and that means that a member state that considers that its interests are harmed can effectively block the negotiations and prevent the reaching of an agreement. The member states that stand most to benefit from such further integration will not want to forego these benefits. So they generally accept to compensate the member state that stands to lose by some other advantages. In this respect the cohesion policy has often been used. This type of horse trading or package deal making has been done both for the entering into higher stages of integration and for the further enlargement of the Union.[5]

The *moving into higher stages* can be illustrated by two cases. The first is the completion of the internal market programme in the middle of the 1980s. It meant a stronger competition and the weaker countries have accepted this only after having obtained in the negotiations the stepping up of their entitlements to the SF. The second case is the creation of the EMU. Political agreement on this project could only be obtained by providing extra means to the weakest member countries (Greece, Spain, Portugal and Ireland) via the establishment of a new instrument. This instrument was created in 1993 and was called the CF. It is specifically oriented towards the solving of problems that were supposed to suffer most of the introduction of the EMU.

Examples of compensation for the effects of *enlargement* are many. The first one is actually also the first round of enlargement, where the UK could only agree to become a member if it were to stand to benefit from an ERDF. Such a fund was indeed created. The second case deals with the enlargement of the EU with the Iberian countries in 1985. It could only be realized after agreement on compensation of the existing Mediterranean member countries that feared to lose out to the newcomers. A later negotiation on the accession of the Nordic countries could only be made after the EU had accepted to create a new objective (sparsely populated areas) under which the peripheral regions of these countries would be entitled to ERDF aid.

7.3 Putting in place the instruments

7.3.1 *The major instrument: financial support through funds*

The spending on cohesion operates mainly through three types of channel:

- The SF. These now consist of the ERDF and the ESF. The SF comprised, until 2006, of two other funds. The Guidance section of the European Agricultural Guarantee and Guidance Fund (EAGGF) helped the development and the structural adjustment of rural areas whose development was lagging behind. The relatively small Financial Instrument for Fisheries Guidance (FIFG) supported restructuring in the fisheries sector. These funds are called 'Structural' Funds because they support measures that aim at the improvement of the structural aspects of the economy. To favour such structural adjustments the funds have to respect the principle of partnership, which means the involvement of regions and private sector actors.
- The CF. Beneficiaries are the member countries with below EU average (actually 90 per cent) GDP per head figures, with a programme of economic convergence to EMU conditions (Art. 104 of the Treaty). The CF finances environmental and transport projects in a framework that is different from the SF on several scores. First, it is managed in close cooperation between the Commission and the national governments without applying the principle of partnership that would have brought the involvement of regional authorities and private actors. Second, it delivers national, not regional funding and the programming is simplified compared to the SF.
- *Various.* Under different headings similar funds are set up to facilitate accession states to become full NMSs. Eligibility to these funds is phased out as soon as the accession state becomes a full member. Support to NMSs is then mainstreamed under the conditions set out for the SCF.[6]

The multitude of funds can be explained by historical reasons. They had all different operational rules. So, in cases programmes covered several objectives and hence had to be supported by several funds; this gave rise to considerable coordination and compliance cost. As one sees from Table 7.1 there was in the past a multitude of objectives and some five instruments (ERDF, ESF, CF, FIFG and EAGGF).[7] In order to be more effective and efficient the EU has tried to simplify the set up. For the 2007–13 period there are only three objectives and three instruments.

7.3.2 *Long-term predictability and operational flexibility*

Uncertainty is a barrier to investment. So it is important that the funds have a multi-annual framework. It gives the beneficiaries of aid the advantage of predictability. They can plan for structural measures that improve the conditions for convergence and competitiveness that require prolonged efforts without having to worry about possible future cuts in resources. Such cuts often occur in practice due to sudden budget problems or due to the change in priorities when government changes after elections. This predictability enhances the willingness to invest and thus the growth capacity of the region in question.

The disadvantage of this multi-annual framework is, however, the lack of flexibility. In some cases new problems come up fairly quickly that need a quick response. During the early stages of the multi-annual frameworks it appeared that the lack of possibilities to react quickly and adequately to such adverse regional development was a serious handicap for improving the effectiveness of the policy. Moreover, the standard set up of the SF was very much orientated towards the standard approach and left little room for experimenting with new methods and approaches.

In order to cope with these problems the EU created a special section of the SF to be used for so called 'Community Initiatives' (CIs). These CIs used to claim some 6 to 10 per cent of the total resources. Of particular importance were INTERREG, which emphasizes the transborder, transnational and inter-regional dimension and URBAN, that had as its objective the economic and social conversion of urban areas. We will return to this later.

In the evaluation of the experience of the 1994–2006 period it appeared that the appropriateness of many of the CIs had in the meantime been established. It was decided that the mainstream programmes would take account of the most important of these CIs and that the new rules of implementation would permit a greater flexibility as to the choice of projects. So there was no longer a need for the CIs and these have been discontinued (mainstreamed) for the 2007–13 period, where flexibility is provided by the new rule for the selection of eligible areas and projects for the objective 'competitiveness'.

The evaluation of the past cycles made apparent that some beneficiaries have become somewhat lenient towards the quality of the implementation. They considered that they were entitled to the money earmarked for them. In order to stimulate the final beneficiaries to perform as well as possible, a new rule has been introduced in the 2007–13 regulatory framework that permits the Commission to keep some 4 per cent of total assignments as a performance reserve. This will be reallocated mid term to the best-performing programmes.

7.4 Financial resources and their use

7.4.1 The institutional framework

A redistribution policy can in principle operate through the expenditure side, the receipt side or both. On the national level, one sees on the receipt side the mechanism of the progressive income tax; high incomes pay a higher percentage than low incomes. On the expenditure side one sees targeted expenses for the groups that are most in need. For the EU interpersonal redistribution is not on the cards as we explained earlier. However, inter-country redistribution might follow the same ideas. Let us thus see how the EU budget is functioning with respect to cohesion.[8]

The EU does not use the receipt side of the budget for redistribution purposes. The contributions of the EU member states to the budget are largely in line with the economic size of each country. This stems from the fact that four-fifths of the receipts of the EU are based on the criteria of GDP and Value Added Tax (VAT) and these tend (in terms of percentage of their GDP) to be fairly similar for almost all member states.[9] So the real redistribution is in terms of the various items of expenditure.

The decisions on the total amount of the various items of expenditure that are dedicated to cohesion are taken in the framework of the multi-annual Financial Perspectives (FPs). The Commission makes a proposal that translates the ambitions as formulated by the Council into programmes with the associated cost. It derives from that the total amount that needs to be contributed to the budget. Decisions on these proposals are taken after intergovernmental negotiations by the member states. They have to be taken by unanimity. Since 1988 four such FPs, each covering a period of some five to seven years, have been agreed (1988–92; 1993–99; 2000–06; 2007–13).

The FPs comprise, on the one hand, the fixing of the level of total receipts and the contributions of each of the member states to these receipts and, on the other hand, the allocation over the various expenditure items, such as agriculture, cohesion and other items such as running costs. Member states are particularly interested in the share of the cake they get from the EU. They tend to give a very high weight to their net positions in budgetary matters ('juste retour'). The principle that is generally accepted here is that the poor member states get more from the budget than they contribute while the richer member states are net contributors. It means that the criteria for eligibility to the various programmes (that determine the share each member state has in total EU expenditure) are part of the same negotiations of the FPs.

The SF has become extremely important for the main beneficiary countries. Moreover, it is also very attractive for the more prosperous countries. As a consequence each discussion about a recast of the SF becomes, immediately, of the highest political relevance. As many countries think that there is a significant imbalance to their disadvantage between their receipts from and contributions to the EU budget, qualifying for additional EU aid becomes an extremely interesting option to rebalance their situation.

7.4.2 How much money for cohesion: needs versus limits to solidarity?

The discussions in the previous chapters and sections have given an idea of the magnitude of the problem and of the type of measures applied to improve cohesion. They leave open the question of how much redistribution is needed to obtain the policy goals. To give an answer to that question one needs to make detailed economic calculations, on the one hand, and evaluate the chances of major political trade-offs, on the other (Okun, 1975; Padoa-Schioppa *et al.*, 1987).

However, the theoretical and empirical basis to determine the amount of money a country should spend on cohesion is very thin. This is even more so in the case of a group of countries such as the EU. So the decision is essentially of a political nature and will depend on matching the demands of the recipients and the donors' willingness to pay. These can be approximated as follows.

The *needs* can be approximated by such measures as the cost of bringing (within say ten years) the infrastructure up to a level of 80 per cent of the EU average. One sees that very quickly normative elements creep into the analysis, for instance about the speed of the operation (ten years) and the degree of real convergence needed (80 per cent). The needs can, moreover, be approximated by the capacity of a country to absorb the aid it receives. This cap has a foundation in economics in the sense that empirical studies have shown that significant higher support percentages tend to lead to several types of unbalances. The first is of a macro economic nature; and bases itself on the empirical evidence that high levels of aid lead to inflation, loss of competitiveness (due to undue wage increases) and a series of distortions. Moreover, weak member states have often difficulty in mobilizing sufficient budget to meet the EU requirements of co-financing. The other unbalance is of an institutional nature and stresses the limited capacity of economically weak countries to manage effectively the process as described in the previous chapter. The EU has done some studies as to the level beyond which such problems do occur and has set a cap to total support to cohesion countries of some 4 per cent of their GDP per year.

The *willingness to pay* can be approximated by evaluating the gains that the more well-to-do countries draw from integration, gains that would come into jeopardy in case the groups that feel they do not get a good deal from integration would withdraw from it. In practice it is very difficult to determine the inter-country differences in advantages of integration. So a much more practical and step-by-step procedure has been followed. In the course of time member states have gradually attributed more tasks to the EU and in step therewith the total budget has gradually increased in importance. For some time the total budget of the EU is capped at some 1 per cent of the total GDP of the EU. This figure has no economic foundation whatsoever.[10] An increase of this ceiling does require a unanimous decision, in other words, it needs the consent of all member states. It is extremely unlikely that this is going to take place, given the ideological positions of some member states. The income ceiling determines the maximum expenditure of the EU because its budget rules require annual income and expenditure to be in balance.

7.4.3 Increased money for cohesion: the effects of political trade-offs

The total amount needed for cohesion is thus difficult to establish on the basis of the stated objectives of the policy (reduction of disparities) and the willingness to pay for solidarity. The outcome of the process is essentially political. Now the political trade-offs in the EU are not restricted to the cohesion issue per se, but are part of larger packages. Over time the development of cohesion policy and the resources devoted to it have thus also evolved under the influence of major political decisions in other fields. In order to obtain consent of those countries for which the balance of advantages and disadvantages of the package of policy measures could not be equilibrated, another way of compensation had to be found. In practice this has often taken the form of a stepping up of the size of the cohesion budget from which side payments could be made to the potential losers of the increased integration by the beneficiaries of it (often the strong and rich member countries).[11] These stages of increased integration can be defined in terms of deepening, in other words, the passing into higher stages of integration (from a CU to an EMU[12]). It can also be seen in terms of widening, in other words the enlargement of the Union with more members (Molle, 2006). The increase in size has been triggered mostly by the effects of such strengthened integration of the EU and in line therewith to the increase in the eligible areas.[13] The major moments when such historical trade-offs have been made are given in Box 7.1.

Box 7.1 Major turning points of the EU cohesion policy

- *1955*. Regional imbalances were already debated at the Messina Conference where the Treaty of the EEC was elaborated. The founding fathers of this forerunner of the EU were well aware of the regional problems; this is evident from the preamble of the EEC Treaty, according to which the member states were 'anxious to reduce the differences existing between the various regions and the backwardness of the less favoured regions'. Notwithstanding this, the EEC Treaty made no provisions for a European cohesion policy in the proper sense.
- *1965*. A timid beginning with structural support was made as it was felt that Germany with its strong manufacturing industry would benefit more from integration than France, whose economy was still dominated by agriculture. The EAGGF was created of which the Guidance section financed measures to adapt agricultural structures of which notably France benefited.
- *1973*. The first enlargement of the EU increased the regional imbalances. The UK was afraid of several problems. The first, that some of its regions would not be able to withstand their continental competitors. The second, that it would suffer from an unfavourable distribution of receipts from and payments to the EU budget. Much of the budget went to agricultural support and agriculture was not important in the UK economy. To compensate for the latter and to support the economy in its problem regions, the UK had obtained in the negotiations of accession that a European regional policy would be set up. The main instrument of that policy, the ERDF, became operational in the second half of the 1970s.
- *1988*. The enlargement with three less developed NMSs increased the demand on SCFs. These were stepped up again to obtain the agreement of the three Mediterranean member states (that acceded in 1981 and 1985) to the completion of the internal market. This agreement was later complemented by a further increase to permit Germany to incorporate the former DDR. To improve the economic and social

142 *Specifying objectives*

- cohesion in a wider and deeper EU, the resources devoted to regional development were doubled, the target groups restricted, the procedures improved and the instruments refocused (EC, 1990a).
- *1993.* The fear of the southern member states to lose out under the influence of the creation of the Monetary Union has been taken away by a package deal that increased the size of the SF and created the new CF. These new funds should also ease the coping with international developments like the further decrease of external trade protection. The extension with Sweden, Finland and Austria did not constitute a major new challenge for EU regional policy, given their relative wealth.
- *2000.* The recent eastern enlargement of the EU did increase, considerably, the demands on the EU budget for cohesion. A further stepping up of cohesion efforts was decided upon to make sure that countries at risk of losing out due to the enlargement of the EU with the central and eastern European applicant states would agree to that enlargement (EC, 1999c).
- *2007.* The cohesion policy is to cope with new demands as it is put at the service of the Lisbon (knowledge) and Gothenburg agendas (environment). However, in view of the constraints that many member states have in meeting the criteria of the Stability and Growth Pact and hence are hesitant to agree to budget increases, the total amount of the budget is not increased by much.

7.4.4 *Main features of the last cycles*

The EU policy cycle in matters of cohesion has followed a periodicity of some six years. In 1988 the cohesion policy had been reformed whereby it had received many of the features that still characterize it today (such as the principles of partnership and of programming). Since then four cycles have been defined (compare Box 7.1). The main features of these cycles have been brought together in Table 7.1. They concern, on the one hand, the main objectives (see rows). For each of these objectives we have detailed in the columns the financial instruments available and the amount of money devoted to it. For the period 1994–99 the table gives less information because in that period neither the objectives nor the instruments differed from the situation in the previous period (with the exception of the CF).

A number of efforts that could be called cohesion have been made in the past that notably targeted the countries that had obtained the status of accession country (CEECs). These funds (such as Phare and Sapard) had objectives that were similar to the ones of the SF but had operating rules that were quite different. However, their mechanics have over time been brought in line with the SF. The new Instrument for Pre-Accession (IPA) resembles the SF to an even higher degree (Reg. 1085/2006).

Table 7.1 Development of cohesion policy; change of objectives and distribution of aid (billions of euro) by objective, 1988–2013

1988–93			1994–99 2000–06			2007–13		
Objective	Instruments	Amount	Objective	Instrument	Amount	Objective	Instrument	Amount
1 Lagging	CF ERDF ESF EAGGF	43	1 Lagging	CF ERDF ESF EAGGF FIFG	102	1 Convergence (and competitiveness)	CF ERDF ESF	251
2 Restructuring	ERDF ESF	9	2 Restructuring	ERDF ESF	22	2 Regional competitiveness and employment	ERDF ESF	49
3 Unemployment	ESF	8	3 Social (former 3 and 4)	ESF	15			–
4 Social 5 Agriculture 6 Ultra-peripheral	ESF EAGGF ERDF	5						
Other programmes Community initiatives Innovative programmes			INTERREG URBAN EQUAL LEADER, etc.	ERDF ESF EAGGF Cohesion Fund	11 10 1 18	3 Territorial cooperation	ERDF	8
Adaptation to EMU conditions		–	EMU		10			
Accession	Phare, Cards, ISPA and Sapard	x	Accession	Phare, Cards, ISPA and Sapard	x	Accession	IPA	x
Total resources		65			159			308
SCF					213			

Notes:
n.a. non applicable
x only for completeness of the picture; no figures as designated sums are not part of internal cohesion efforts of the EU
Figures for the 2007–13 period in 2004 euros

Sources: EC (1999c, 2005a), EU (2005a)

7.4.5 The various categories of expenditure

Cohesion policy is the second largest item on the EU budget. It is the largest one with explicit redistributional objectives.[14] The expenditure for cohesion objectives is done via the SF, notably the ERDF, the ESF and the CF (see Box 7.2). There is a certain specialization according to the dimension of cohesion. The ERDF and the CF tend to cope with problems of economic cohesion (dealt within Chapter 3); the ESF tends to cope with problems of social cohesion (see Chapter 4). The problems of territorial cohesion (see Chapter 5) have not been matched by a specific fund but are taken care of by the ERDF (see Box 7.3).

Box 7.2 Main characteristics of the main funds

The ERDF[15] is the largest one of the EU funds with a cohesion objective. The ERDF was created in 1975. The tasks of the ERDF are to grant subsidies to stimulate investment and promote innovation in productive economic activities; develop the infrastructure and the endogenous potential (innovation) in regions designated as European problem areas. As such areas have been recognized notably as regions whose development is lagging behind and regions undergoing economic conversion or experiencing structural difficulties (Reg. 1080/2006, Art. 2/3).

The ESF[16] is the oldest of the EU funds; it was created in 1952. Its tasks have been continuously changed under the influence of new political demands and new economic and social circumstances. The ESF is the EU's financial instrument that supports measures aiming to achieve full employment, improve the quality and productivity at work and promote social inclusion. In short, an instrument for investing in people. Its organization has a specific aspect: it is administered by the Commission, assisted by a committee of representatives of governments, trade unions and employers (Reg. 1081/2006, Art. 2).

The CF was established in 1994. It gives assistance to infrastructure investment (notably in Trans European Networks (TENs)) and also supports projects that improve the environment (notably those that come under the EU priority areas) (Reg. 1084/2006, Art. 2).

The CF has initially been set up to help countries to deal with the exigencies of the EMU including the constraints put upon them by the Stability and Growth Pact in terms of budget deficit. This is still the case. Of the present members of the euro zone, Portugal and Greece still qualify for the CF, while Spain gets transitional (phasing out) CF support. All NMSs have agreed on accession to strive for the adoption of the euro and hence qualify for cohesion policy support. Of them Slovenia has entered the euro zone in 2007.

> *Box 7.3* The specific case of the dimension of territorial cohesion
>
> Territorial cohesion pursues mainly the objective of *improving accessibility*.[17] This major policy objective has, to some extent, found its concretization in specific programmes for regional development that aim at two of the three objectives of the present cohesion policy:
>
> - *Convergence.* There is a considerable correspondence between the regions that are eligible for support (because of their low income per head and their deficient economic structure and infrastructure) and the regions with the highest degrees of peripherality. So, implicitly, many of the resources for cohesion policy tend to go to areas that score high on peripherality and hence contribute to alleviate problems of territorial cohesion. There is only one case where separate financial resources are specifically earmarked for territorial cohesion purposes: the ultra-peripheral regions with a special constitutional status.
> - *Territorial cooperation.* This objective is specially designed to help out regions that are not sufficiently linked into networks that stimulate the competitiveness of their specific economic structure.

7.5 What match between objectives and resources?

7.5.1 Some basics

In the EU there is a strong current stipulating that the cohesion expenditure should be made largely in line with the *needs* of a country. That would mean that the low-income member states would benefit more than proportionally from the EU expenditure. This moral criterion seems to have indeed been applied in as far as the expenditure from the SF is concerned. Indeed for some time the lion's share of this expenditure item is concentrated on the segments of the EU population with the lowest per capita incomes. However, this needs criterion is amended by the capacity to absorb criterion; countries should only receive as much aid as they are capable of absorbing without creating major macro economic or institutional unbalances.[18]

There is another view that contests the needs hypothesis and says that it all depends on *power* politics. Empirical evidence that the latter factor plays a strong role is not far away; one needs to look at the UK rebate and the receipts of rich countries on budget lines such as research and transport. How can this be explained? Constitutional economics considers that the distribution of voting rights determines, to a large extent, the power of the various member states. However, this cannot be the sole factor as the EU treaties stipulate that the distribution of the funds is to be decided by unanimity. It is foreseen that decisions will be made in future by qualified majority.

To answer the question whether the determinant factor is *power* or *needs* researchers have regressed receipts from the budget on factors such as power (votes) and needs. Both seem to be important.[19]

7.5.2 Concentration on problem categories

The EU has set *concentration* as a main policy principle. It implies that the EU support should be concentrated on the most important problem regions (those scoring worst on various indicators of regional welfare), as the main aim has always been to diminish the disparity between countries and regions. So it was only logical that the bulk of the SF is spent in regions with a level of development (GDP/P) below the EU average. However, the EU also wants to avoid other regions falling back into that position. So, some of the SF money is spent on programmes in regions in structural difficulties.

There is no economic way to establish the shares that each category had to have in spending. So this has largely been a political decision. In the past about 75 per cent of the SF has been spent in regions with the largest gap in wealth (<75 per cent of the EU mean), which meant a considerable concentration as they represent only some 25 per cent of the EU population. A significant part of the remaining quarter was spent in regions with GDP/P levels between 75 per cent and 100 per cent of the EU averages (see Table 7.1). Only a small part has been devoted to well-off regions with structural problems. Such objective 2 (industrial conversion) regions were rather dispersed geographically. The CF targets regions in countries with an income below 90 per cent of the EU average. So the financial means of the funds have been attributed in such a way as to strongly favour low-income countries (two-thirds of the funds went to Spain, Portugal, Greece, Ireland and southern Italy).[20] Within these countries total aid per habitant was highest in the regions that showed the lowest income per head. So, here too, the principle of concentration has been put into practice.

Important funds have also been made available for more well-off regions. This reflects the effect of forces favouring an EU cohesion policy that goes beyond the defined objectives into other implicit objectives, such as the facilitating of moves into higher integration by giving hesitant partners so-called side payments.

Due to recent enlargement, it has emerged that a new set of 'convergence' regions in the NMSs are clearly all at a distance from the EU mean. So it is logical that these regions would receive the highest amount of aid. Pre-accession aid levels per head in these countries were lower than those in the countries of the EU 15. In order to prepare the accession countries for membership a pre-accession aid has been given of some €1–2 billion per annum. Over the years this has gradually increased. It has increased again on accession: from some €4 to some €12 billion a year between 2002 and 2006. However, there is a considerable increase for the current programming period and the aid per head figures in these countries will gradually align on those for the older member states.

The present distribution of the funds also shows a high degree of concentration, albeit now in terms of the EU 27. Indeed, for the period 2006–13 about four-fifths of the SCF are allocated to convergence regions; these regions count for only about a third of the total population of the EU 27. Most of the remaining funds are allocated to regions with a GDP/P between 75 and 90 per cent of the EU mean. Only a small part is devoted to regions with a GDP/P level around or above the EU mean.

7.5.3 How much redistribution: equity versus 'juste retour'?

The budgetary consequences of EU policies have always been the subject of very heated debates and major political struggles. In these struggles the member states were particularly keen to limit their contributions to the budget. As the sharing out of the EU expenditure is based on fairly simple rules (Molle, 2006) this meant that the rich member states were, generally, in favour of a low budget while the poor favoured a high budget. The second point of attention then became the receipts from the budget, as member states wanted to limit their net position to a certain amount. This gave rise to the famous expression of the 'juste retour' (in practice: getting back from the EU as much as you have paid to it). In this respect the restaurant bill example is often used; if I have to pay a certain sum of the total bill I want to be entitled to an extra glass of wine or so. Due to political trade-offs the EU has indeed accepted that rich countries that are net contributors to the budget have received quite important sums of money.

In order to know the combined redistributional effects of both allocations (A) from and payments (P) into the EU budget we have defined an A/P index. By the end of the 1990s the EU 15 member countries fell into three categories: A/P very high (>4: Ireland, Greece, Portugal); high (>1.5: Spain); medium (between 0.7 and 1.4: all other countries) and low (<0.5: Germany and Luxembourg). High A/P indices corresponded generally with low GDP/P indices and vice versa. This shows that the EU budget has been a mechanism for the redistribution of wealth across the member states. The total redistributional effect of the EU budget can be evaluated at less than 0.5 per cent of GDP.

Figure 7.1 gives an idea of the net position of the member states in 2004. One sees that the rich member states of the northwest are all net contributors. There is one exception: Ireland. On the other hand, the NMSs and the old cohesion countries in the EU 15 are all net beneficiaries. So far, the picture is more or less in agreement with the idea of redistribution.

7.5.4 National versus regional allocation

The EU is composed of member states that in turn are composed of regions. The question comes up whether the redistribution needs to take a national or a regional criterion as the basis. For both there are arguments:

- *National.* Allocation is based on the basis of relative wealth levels of the country. Rich member states are willing to pay for poor member states. They can be thought to be capable of handling internal regional problems themselves. Rich countries that have solved their internal problems do not consider it fair to have to put up resources to compensate for the effects of a lenient attitude of another rich country that has let internal regional problems persist.
- *Regional.* Allocation is based on the relative wealth levels of the regions. Regions that have been empowered to act (devolution) are in charge of

148 *Specifying objectives*

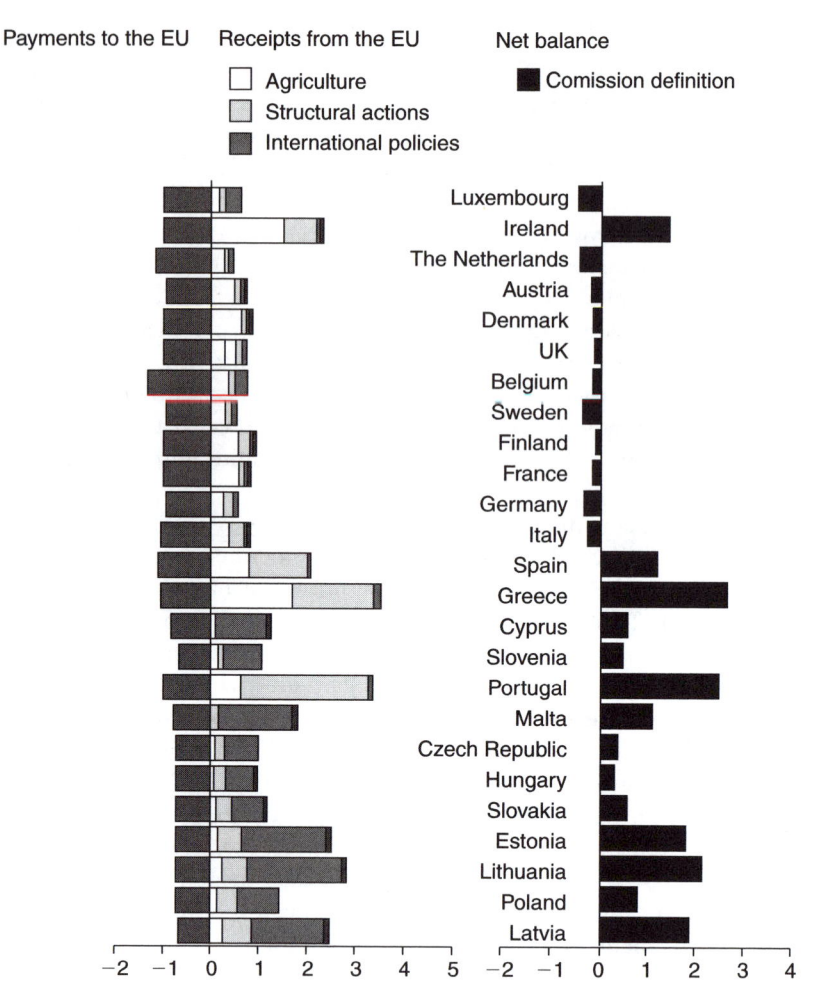

Figure 7.1 Net position of member states as to the EU budget (2004) in percentage of GDP with member states ranked by GDP/P (in PPP)

Source: ESPON 221
a) Structural Funds (EU 15, 1994–99), Phare and ISPA (1998–2000)

their own destiny. Moreover, the problems are often not so much related to national institutional and political conditions but rather on economic restructuring and geographical handicaps.

In the past the EU has hesitated between the two models. In the beginning the national model was used quite extensively. The rules were not very explicit, depended much on qualitative information and the result was largely based on political horse trading. In order to put more objectivity in the allocation rules the EU has decided during the latest reform (2005) to use a set of clear criteria that is clearly based on the regional model. They indicate how EU aid is stepped up in function of the increasing problems regions are confronted with. The passing from the national model to the regional one has been facilitated by the devolution trend of the last decades (see Chapter 6) and the increased strength of the EU delivery system (Chapters 8 and 9). The present rules are given in Box 7.4.

Box 7.4 Allocation methods for EU support

Objective: Convergence
Each member state's allocation is the sum of the allocations of its individual eligible regions. We recall that these are determined on the basis of their relative prosperity and unemployment level. The procedure consists of three steps:

1. Calculation of the absolute amount of aid (in euros). This amount is obtained by multiplying the population of the region concerned by the difference between that regions GDP/P (in PPPs) and the EU average GDP/P (in PPPs)
2. Application of a percentage to the absolute amount of step 1 to determine the regions' financial envelope; this percentage is graduated to take account of the relative prosperity (4.25 per cent for regions in member states whose national wealth level is below 82 per cent of the EU average; 3.4 per cent for regions where the national figure is between 82 and 99 per cent; and 2.7 per cent for regions in countries with a national level above 100 per cent).
3. Adding of a premium in regions that have an unemployment rate above the EU average, amounting to €700 per unemployed person; applied to the number of persons unemployed that exceeds the number that would be unemployed if the average EU rate had been applied.

Objective: Competitiveness and employment
Here, too, the share of each member state is the sum of the share of its eligible regions. The latter are defined according to the following criteria with their specific weight:

- total population (0.5);
- number of unemployed persons in regions with an unemployment rate above the rate of the relevant group (0.2);
- number of jobs needed to reach an employment rate of 70 per cent (0.15);
- number of employed people with a low education level (0.10);
- low population density (0.05).

Source: Reg. 1083/2006: Annex 1

150 *Specifying objectives*

7.5.5 Additionality: financial cooperation between EU, nation and region

The fundamental idea of EU support to cohesion is that it contributes to activities that would not have been done anyway. EU subsidies are meant to enhance the efforts already made by the member countries, not to replace them. This basic idea has been formalized in the principle of additionality. This serves two objectives. The first is that the member state maintains its level of expenditure for each objective on levels that they were at pre-EU aid times. There is evidence that this has not always been realized in practice: EU money has been 'crowding out' national money (Ederveen *et al.*, 2002). This is natural as it involves a budget saving to the member state in question that may be used for other priorities (both other expenses of tax cuts). The second objective is to maximize the contribution of public intervention. If EU money were allocated to projects that are not really felt as a priority by the most concerned beneficiaries it would not be efficiently spent.

How does this work in practice? This is given in a schematized form in Figure 7.2, that shows how the financial resources from the SF come together with funds from national states to fund the commonly agreed programmes.

The idea of additionality also finds expression in the co-financing levels that the EU demands. The EU principle is that its contribution is larger (in percentage terms) the higher the problems of the region in question. This leads to the following support percentages:

- Convergence (objective 1) regions; support percentages vary between 75 and 85 per cent of total eligible cost.
- Competitiveness (objective 2) regions; the maximum contribution of the EU is generally below 50 per cent of total eligible cost.

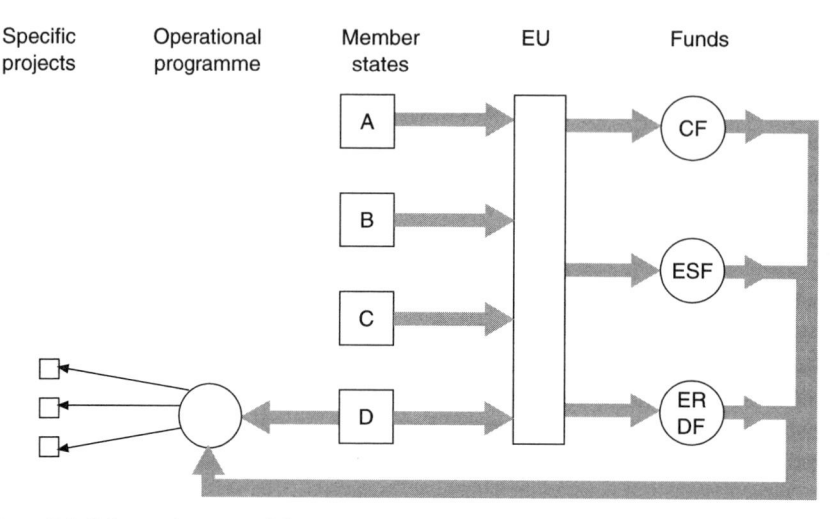

Figure 7.2 Schematic view of financial flows for structural support
Source: Author

The putting into practice of the principle of additionality has not been very easy. Actually there are mainly two problems:

1. *Interpretation.* As the principle implies the commitment of very scarce national resources, it is of vital importance for co-financing organizations to know exactly to what level such financing is needed in specific cases. More generally, it is necessary for long-term strategy making that the ideas about what resources can be shifted between various government programmes without infringing the principle. In practice many problems have arisen in the interpretation. The Commission has tried to resolve them in two ways. First, by reformulating the principle in terms of an obligation for member states to maintain its structural expenditure to the same level as in the previous period. Second, by regulating the share of EU support in the financing of projects. For instance in objective 1 regions the maximum support that can be given is 75 per cent of total cost; in other regions the cap on the EU shares is much lower.
2. *Verification.* It is not easy to check how far the principle has been respected. This is partly due to the vagueness of the definition. But it is also due to the intricacies of the public finance systems of the various member states. A clear illustration of the problem is given by the lack of adequate information that is given by the member states, even the richer ones, preventing a proper ex post evaluation (see Chapter 10). In order to limit the burden to all involved additionality is only verified for convergence regions. The rationale being, that EU support in these regions is large with respect to total expenditure while in other regions it is only a small part of the total.

7.5.6 Final equity effect

How far has the equity objective been maintained after all forces described have had their effect? In order to give an answer to this question we can look at the degree of concentration. Figure 7.3 gives the SF aid per head of population for the four main recipient countries (cohesion countries) of the EU 15 for several periods. The aid per head was significantly higher in the four countries than in the EU as a whole (situated around €40 per head). The position of the other member states is not given; all are situated in a small cluster below the EU average. So, in practice, the main objective has prevailed.[21]

There has been a mitigation of the concentration effect (Martin, 1998b) first, because of EU and national support to the productive sector in all regions (see Chapter 9) and second because of national support of rich countries to their regions. To safeguard the redistributional effect the EU has tightened its control on the latter, notably on state aid (see Chapter 8). The concentration of aid to the poorest countries and regions is moreover limited by the absorption capacity of the recipient countries. The EU has set a cap on the total share of its aid to the GDP of 4 per cent.

EU cohesion policy is only one element in the total set of redistribution mechanisms in the EU. First, other EU budget outlays also have a redistributional impact, notably agriculture (see Chapter 11). Second, national redistribution

152 *Specifying objectives*

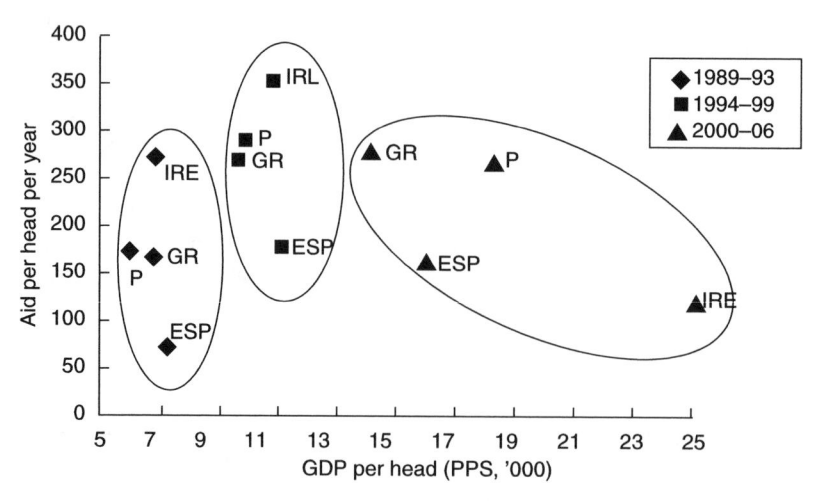

Figure 7.3 Structural aid per head of population in cohesion countries, 1989–93, 1994–99 and 2000–06

Sources: For first period Hall, Smith and Tsoukalis (2001: 321); for later periods own calculations

through the budgets of the different member states has a considerable weight in total GDP; on average some 50 per cent.[22]

The contribution of the EU cohesion policy to redistribution can be measured in another way: in the 1990s the SF aid amounted to an average 3 per cent of total GDP and some 8 per cent of total investment in the three poorest member states, Ireland, Greece and Portugal. Somewhat lower percentages obtained for other objective 1 regions. The figures can be augmented somewhat, due to the leverage effect that results from the application of the principle of additionality.

7.6 Eligibility of type of investments and the resources by objective[23]

7.6.1 General

The next question that comes up is about the distribution within these categories. This is notably relevant for objective 1 (regions <75 per cent of EU mean) as they receive the bulk of the resources. Here the main criterion is that regions with low GDP/P levels receive relatively more than regions that are already at a somewhat higher level. Most of the money (some 95 per cent) is distributed in this way. The second criterion is the level of unemployment. In the end the decision has been a political one.

The discussion for the objective 2 regions (competitiveness and restructuring) is not less important, as it is actually highly political.

The question about the distribution of resources can only be solved together with the distribution over eligible expenditure. Of course the type of project supported needs to match the type of problem the area is confronted with and the need to fit in an overall strategy for economic and social renewal.

An idea of the total distribution over different objectives and countries is given in Table 7.2. In terms of the geographical zones we distinguished earlier one sees that the East (coinciding largely with the NMSs) gets about half of the funds, whereas the South still obtains about a third. The still substantial flow of EU money to the North region is mainly explained by the large needs of eastern Germany.

Table 7.2 Allocation of SCF aid (2007–13) by objective and country (billion euro of 2004)

	Convergence			Competitiveness		Territorial cooperation	Total
	CF	Normal	Phasing out	Phasing in	Normal		
Germany		10.6	3.8		8.4	0.8	23.5
France		2.8			9.1	0.8	12.7
Italy		18.9	0.4	0.9	4.8	0.8	25.6
The Netherlands					1.5	0.2	1.7
Belgium			0.6		1.3	0.2	2.0
Luxembourg							–
UK		2.4	0.2	0.9	5.3	0.6	9.5
Denmark					0.5	0.1	0.5
Ireland				0.4	0.3	0.1	0.8
Spain	3.2	18.7	1.4	4.5	3.1	0.5	31.5
Portugal	2.3	15.2	0.3	0.4	0.4	0.1	19.1
Greece	3.3	8.4	5.8	0.6		0.2	18.2
Austria			0.2		0.9	0.2	1.3
Sweden					1.4	0.2	1.7
Finland				0.5	0.9	0.1	1.5
Poland	19.6	39.5				0.7	59.7
Czech Republic	7.8	15.1			0.4	0.4	23.7
Hungary	7.6	12.7		1.9		0.3	22.5
Slovakia	3.4	6.2			0.4	0.2	10.2
Slovenia	1.2	2.4				0.1	3.7
Lithuania	2.0	4.0				0.1	6.1
Cyprus	0.2			0.4			0.6
Latvia	1.4	2.6					4.1
Estonia	1.0	2.0					3.0
Malta	0.3	0.5					0.8
Romania	5.8	11.1				0.4	17.3
Bulgaria	2.0	3.9				0.2	6.0
Not alloc.						0.4	0.4
EU total	**61.6**	**177.1**	**12.5**	**10.4**	**38.7**	**7.8**	**308.0**
North	–	15.8	4.8	1.8	29.6	3.3	55.3
South	9.3	61.7	7.9	6.8	8.3	1.6	95.6
East	52.0	99.5	–	1.9	0.8	2.7	156.9

Note:
The figures in the column total may differ from the total of the figures in the columns due to rounding

Source: EC

154 *Specifying objectives*

7.6.2 *Main objective: convergence*

The present convergence objective, which is similar to the previous objective 1, aims to accelerate the convergence of the least developed member states and regions by improving their growth and employment conditions. The fields of action are physical and human capital, innovation, knowledge-based society (see for an example Box 7.5), adaptability to change, environmental sustainability and administrative effectiveness. Finances for objective convergence come from the ERDF, the ESF and the CF. The total resources allocated to this objective for the programming period 2007–13 are €251 billion, equivalent to 81 per cent of the total.

The *eligibility criteria* are as follows:

For the SFs (ERDF and ESF) are eligible regions where per capita GDP:

- is below 75 per cent of the EU average. They receive the lion's share of the funds allocated for this objective. The regions presently eligible under the convergence objective are given in Figure 7.4 in dark;
- would have been below 75 per cent of the EU average as calculated for the EU 15 (the so-called statistical effect of enlargement). They benefit from transitional, specific and decreasing financing. They are given in medium grey in Figure 7.4 (phasing out).

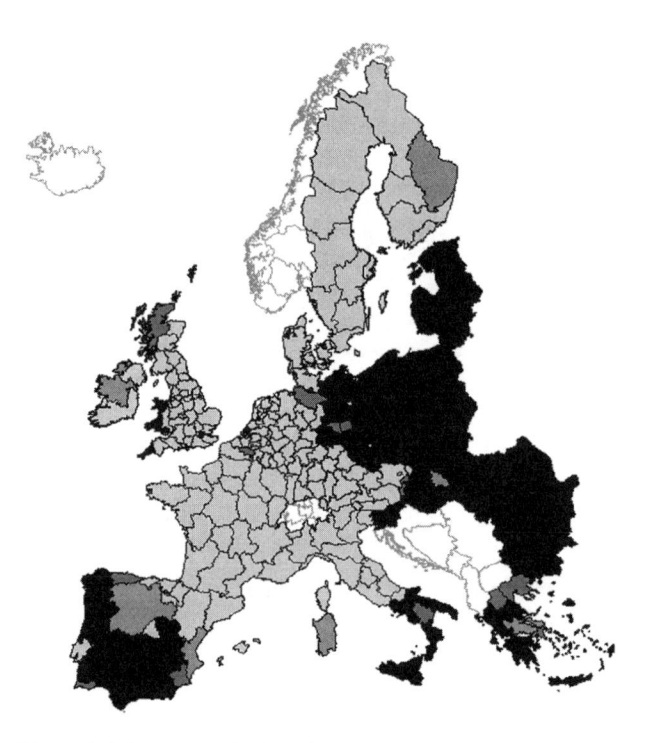

Figure 7.4 Regions eligible for support under the convergence and competitive objectives, 2007–13

The percentage aid the SF can contribute to total project cost is a minimum of 20 per cent. The maximum depends on the gravity of the problems, the degree of conformity with EU priorities, etc. However, there is always the condition of a minimum contribution (in practice some 15 per cent) of the member states (see additionality criterion). So in practice the EU contribution is 85 per cent for many projects in the NMSs and a maximum 75 per cent for most priority projects in the problem regions of the old member states.

For the CF: member states whose per capita GDP/P is below 90 per cent of the EU average and which are running economic convergence programmes. This fund will contribute to sustainable development, European priority transport axes and to improving administrative capacities and the effectiveness of public administrations.

Box 7.5 Creation of a R&D support centre in Basilicata (Italy)

Basilicata is developing a new industrial and manufacturing structure. The analysis of the region's strengths and weaknesses and the identification of the needs of companies in terms of research and innovation have incited the local authorities to orient their plan for the development of the regional economy towards innovative technologies. To support this plan the SINTER & NET project was launched in 1999. Central element of this project was the creation of a research and training centre aimed at maximizing the access to information and commercial and technical know-how by manufacturing companies at the start-up, development and growth stages. Total cost was €520,000 of which €475,000 was contributed by the EU SF.

The results achieved since (in terms of the advice and training provided) are testimony to the Basilicata Research Centre's strategic importance. Its problem-solving approach enables it to propose innovative and highly practical solutions, as a result of which companies can acquire a significant competitive potential on an increasingly demanding and sensitive market.

The principal factors in the project's success are both of a technological and a financial nature. A technology jump has been made possible by the good use of ICT and by close relations with the university and specialized research centres. Access to financing from various national and European support programmes has stimulated the spirit of initiative of many business managers, while at the same time placing the Basilicata Research Centre at the heart of an increasingly solid cooperative network.

The benefits of the initiative are not limited to Basilicata. Indeed, the whole of southern Italy benefits from the research results and technological breakthroughs achieved as a consequence of spillovers and extended networks of the various partners in the centre.

7.6.3 Second objective: regional competitiveness and employment

This objective aims to strengthen the competitiveness, employment and attractiveness of regions other than those which are the most disadvantaged. It must support efforts to anticipate economic and social changes and to promote innovation, business spirit, environmental protection, accessibility, adaptability and the development of inclusive labour markets. It is financed by the ERDF and the ESF.

With regard to the programmes financed by the ESF, the Commission proposes four priorities following the European Employment Strategy: to improve the adaptability of workers and businesses, to increase social inclusion, to improve access to employment and to implement reform in the fields of employment and inclusion (see, for a project example, Box 7.6).

The resources intended for this objective total €49 billion for the present programming period, equivalent to 16 per cent of the total and divided equally between the ERDF and the ESF. Of this total, some is earmarked for tapering transitional support to regions formerly falling under objective 1 but that due to the accession of the NMSs have seen their relative wealth increase above 75 per cent of the EU 25 average (the phasing in regions given in medium grey shading in Figure 7.4).

In the past the regions that were eligible under this objective were a very mixed bag. The archetype region for this objective is the one that had lost its industrial base due to technological change and international openness; a case in point is the northern region (around Lille) in France where the textile and heavy coal and steel industries had lost their competitiveness and where new activities had to be found. However, other regions soon emerged that had probably as many problems. Important among them were the city regions, where unemployment, notably among the immigrant population, was an issue. They housed too few competitive industries and services that could absorb this labour supply. So, urban regions became eligible for projects of the EU cohesion policy too (see Annex 7.1). Now the whole area of the EU that is not eligible for the convergence objective is eligible for the competitiveness objective (see Figure 7.4).

The new regulation concerning the competitiveness objective foresees intervention around a three-pronged menu of themes:

1. Innovation and the knowledge economy, which seeks to raise the quality of the regional economic structure.
2. Environment and risk prevention ensures the sustainability of these developments.
3. Accessibility to transport services and communication technologies ICTs, aimed at reducing regional isolation from transport and digital networks.

Under this objective, measures can be financed using up to 50 per cent public expenditure. The ceiling is raised to 85 per cent for the outermost regions not qualifying for objective 1 status.

Box 7.6 Ethnic Minority Business Support Network London (UK)

The project aimed at establishing an Ethnic Minority Business Support Network in Newham, London, to provide a range of specialist support services for both new and existing ethnic-minority-owned small- and medium-sized enterprises (SMEs) with a view to increasing the number of ethnic minority start-ups. The research surveys indicated that failures within the first year of operation were twice as high for ethnic-minority-owned businesses than for native-owned businesses. East London and Newham were especially interested in this project since they have over 90,000 ethnic-minority-owned fashion, retail and hospitality SMEs.

The specialist business counselling and support services offered by the network consist of the following: business planning, marketing, technology applications and innovation, exporting (including to the country of origin) as well as new learning opportunities such as start-up training, financial management, marketing and ICT business applications. The services offered were customized to SMEs needs and included the delivery of online business information and learning packages in the workplace.

The key outcomes of the project were: development of four local Business Advice Centres in key areas of Newham and of a series of workshops focused on business advice and development issues. The project supported 750 SMEs, over 400 jobs within SMEs were safeguarded and over 100 new jobs were created. Its total cost was €2 million, of which half was contributed by the EU SF.

Source: European Commission website Regional Policy, success stories

7.6.4 Third objective: European Territorial Cooperation

Apart from the two long-standing main objectives the EU has introduced a third objective that aims to strengthen territorial cohesion through cooperation. It will cover some €8 billion or 3 per cent of the total. It is based on the previous INTERREG Initiative. It is financed by the ERDF. To grasp the advantages of an EU-wide balanced area development the border problems (see Chapter 5) need to be overcome, which demands the strengthening of three types of cooperation:

1. *Cross border.* Cooperation is often advantageous as common solutions to common problems may exist. Part is to be taken into account by improvement of transport; however, a much more important part is to be taken by offering solutions to streamlining national administrative procedures.[24] Important in this respect is also the situation at the external borders. Linked to the new European Neighbourhood Instrument such cooperation is also facilitated by the EU.
2. *Transnational.* Cooperation between functionally related areas (e.g. a river basin) is advantageous to overcome cleavages due to national administrative

158 *Specifying objectives*

structures. The EU supports actions conducive to integrated territorial development linked to community priorities.

3   *Inter-regional.* In case the partners that can bring the solution to a specific problem are located in different regions cooperation over a wider area can take away bottlenecks to development.[25] The EU supports by establishing networks and exchange of experience at the appropriate territorial level.

In practice the EU actions aim at promoting common solutions in the fields of urban, rural and coastal development, the development of economic relations and the creation of networks of SMEs (see Box 7.7). Cooperation will be based around research, information technology, the environment, accessibility, natural and cultural resources and sustainable urban development (polycentric development). It does notably apply to networking and exchange of experience.

Regions eligible for funds are those situated along internal land borders, certain external land borders and certain regions situated along maritime borders separated by a maximum of 150 km.

In the case of networks of cooperation and exchange of experience, the entire territory of the Community is eligible. The ceiling for part-financing is 75 per cent of public expenditure.

Box 7.7 INTERREG project in central Europe: enlarging opportunities for SMEs

The 'Cross-border Business Cooperation for Central Europe' project focused on the exploitation of new business opportunities arising from the eastward enlargement of the EU.

Supported under the INTERREG IIA initiative, the aim of the project was to promote transnational economic activities and to assist small- and medium-sized companies to exploit opportunities in new markets. The central players in the project were the Austrian regions (federal states) of Vienna, Lower Austria and Burgenland and the adjacent regions in the Czech Republic, Slovakia and Hungary. There were also cooperation arrangements at the institutional level between the respective economic development agencies and regional management bodies, as well as directly at company level. The project activities included:

- networking with the relevant players and filling gaps in the existing range of services offered;
- support for companies, especially SMEs;
- improved marketing of Austria's 'competence for the East' in the international competition to attract business investment;
- initial and further training activities.

Total cost: €1.2 million of which half came from the EU SF.
Source: European Commission website Regional Policy, success stories

7.7 Summary and conclusions

- Cohesion policy is given substance in the third stage by defining objectives in concrete terms, by specifying the instruments available and by setting priorities as to eligible groups and regions. This framework is reviewed and adapted with a periodicity of some seven years.
- The EU has mobilized considerable financial resources that it devotes to cohesion. These are channelled through the so-called SF. They cover some 0.4 per cent of total EU GDP. The size of these funds is a balance between on the one side the needs and the capacity to absorb by the recipients and on the other side the willingness to pay for solidarity by the contributors.
- The main objective of cohesion policy is convergence that is a decrease in disparity. A considerable share (some 80 per cent) of EU SF's resources is devoted to this objective. In order to enhance effectiveness support is highly concentrated on the regions that are most in need of it (indicated by the lowest levels of wealth and the highest levels of social problems).
- The EU cohesion policy has two other major objectives. First, to prevent new problems arising and to increase competitiveness and employment in other regions than those covered by objective 1. Next, to improve territorial cooperation of regions negatively influenced by border situations. To these objectives smaller parts of the total package (some 20 per cent) are devoted.
- The three present objectives do not match very well the three dimensions of cohesion. Economic and social cohesion are very closely intertwined at the policy level in both the convergence and the competitiveness objective. Territorial cohesion finds its expression to some extent in the objective of territorial cooperation.

Annex 7.1 The urban issue[26]

Over the past decades there has been a growing recognition that urban areas were not by definition strong motors for growth of economic activity and social well-being. On the contrary, in many member states urban areas faced increasingly complex problems consisting of an accumulation in certain neighbourhoods of high unemployment and socio-economic deprivation, affecting, in particular, members of ethnic minority communities. Long-term unemployment tended to lead to social exclusion while the poor environment often enhanced problems associated with crime and lack of security. The disparities within individual cities were often greater than disparities between the regions of the EU. Solutions to the problems tended to be difficult as private and public investment in these areas did not come off the ground.

In the 1970s and 1980s one saw in the first instance a *national response* to the problems. Some member states experimented with area-based policies. They tended to have a sectoral focus; that means that they were attacking in special programmes either unemployment by job training schemes or security problems by interventions in the built environment. As these proved to lack effectiveness, notably the UK and the Netherlands introduced integrated approaches to urban regeneration. In many countries, however, little was done.

In the late 1980s the awareness grew that many member countries had to attack their urban problems and that without some experimenting and coordination the cost of coming to effective solutions could be very high. So an *EU involvement* became a real option. The architecture of EU cohesion policy had provided room for experimenting via the so-called CIs. Urban problems qualified as the problems were common to many member states while innovative action was needed. So, in 1994 the EU launched the URBAN I CI.

What type of action has the EU taken? URBAN I adopted an area-based approach.[27] It supported actions in clearly and narrowly delimited neighbourhoods with particular high concentrations of problems in cities of more than 100,000 population. URBAN I allocated almost a billion euro to some hundred target areas with a total population of some three million. It involved both ERDF and ESF funding. The projects were orientated towards several domains such as entrepreneurship and employment, physical and environmental regeneration and social inclusion. All member states participated with at least one programme. To enhance coherence of the total EU policy effort priority was given to urban areas in objective 1 and objective 2 regions. As with all EU actions URBAN required the application of the partnership principle; associating closely local actors to each of the projects.

The *evaluation* showed that URBAN I has been a success. Measures chosen were found to be largely appropriate and the programmes had in the large majority of cases made a significant contribution to targets. The evaluation made clear that one of the most sustainable impacts of URBAN was the lasting change in the approach to urban regeneration; all member states have now established urban regeneration policies that take an integrated and participative approach to the subject. However, on the score of efficiency the evaluation is less positive; cost of management, technical assistance and transaction were considered very high, although this is largely the price that has to be paid for the application of the partnership principle. Moreover, the effects of learning by international networking were found to be disappointing.

Given the success of URBAN I a follow up was agreed on for the period 1999–2006. URBAN II has devoted a similar amount of money to new programmes for the period 2000–06. A certain number of adaptations were made as to the selection of the areas; the type of projects to be supported and the mode of operation that took into account the lessons from URBAN I. For instance, to simplify procedures URBAN II is only funded by the ERDF (even if this implies social measures). Since 2006 URBAN-type measures have been 'mainstreamed' and fall under the heading of 'competitiveness and employment'.

8 Reaching objectives by regulation and coordination

8.1 Introduction

The EU has set its cohesion objectives and has now to put in place the systems and instruments to realize them. This is stage three of the policy cycle. In the previous chapter we have explained the first important part of this stage: the financial instruments designed to stimulate private and public actors to improve the conditions for growth and catch up. However, this is not enough to get the effect. The second important part consists of regulatory instruments that either forbid actions of private and public actors that may have a negative effect on cohesion or prescribe actions that may enhance cohesion. Lighter forms of such instruments are coordination and consultation. The present chapter will deal with these instruments.

In its structure[1] we will make a distinction between two aspects. In the first group of sections we deal with the *vertical aspect of coordination and regulation*, which means the way the EU actually constrains the actions of its member states. First, we discuss some general aspects trying to disentangle the intricacies of such coordination. Next, we deal subsequently with the three ways in which the EU does this:

1   coordination of efforts of national cohesion policies;
2   limits to national support to firms; and
3   setting of EU standards.

In the next group of sections we deal with *horizontal aspects*, that means the coordination of the various policies on the EU level. The objective is to make sure that the different policies of the EU reinforce each other, or at least are not contradictory. We deal subsequently with the ways this can be done and with the choices made by the EU.

A summary of the main findings will conclude the chapter.

162　*Specifying objectives*

8.2 Vertical: the intricacies of vertical coordination – some models

8.2.1 Vertical coordination

Economic systems are not likely to come by themselves to outcomes that are socially desirable. Hence, there is in all European countries substantial government intervention in the economy with the aims to enhance economic welfare (by correcting imperfections of markets) and to realize a number of political objectives (such as more cohesion). Traditionally the various member countries of the EU have made their own choices as to specific objectives and forms of policy (finances, regulation) based on their own preferences, traditions, institutions and so on. The coexistence of such national policies is not sufficient to come to efficient solutions of cohesion problems on the EU level. So a coordination of EU and national policies on cohesion has been set up.

The need for such vertical coordination has been recognized right from the start. The EU has been endowed with a series of instruments to give effect to this coordination (see Chapter 6). One of the major instruments is regulation. Regulation limits the freedom of policy design and policy making with the aim to frame policy competition. Policy competition is in principle a good phenomenon as it tends to keep public authorities alert, sort out best practices and stimulate adaptation to specific circumstances. But policy competition can have negative effects when it leads to subsidy wars (see section 8.4) or to a race to the bottom in terms of social standards (see section 8.5).

The EU has elaborated different forms of vertical coordination. We will detail in the two following sections the main ones. They tend to differ in the degree to which they combine the use of EU and national instruments to reach EU and national policy goals. Next we will illustrate the various EU forms of coordination with practical cases.

8.2.2 Light EU influence: the Open Method of Coordination

In some areas the EU involvement in cohesion is limited by the application of the principle of subsidiarity, which attributes the prime responsibility to the member states. However, in order to increase effectiveness on the EU level some sort of coordination of the efforts of the member states is to be realized. Over the years the EU has experimented with a series of methods for coordination. The one that has become the most relevant in matters of cohesion and related policies is the so-called 'Open Method of Coordination' (OMC).

The OMC uses an iterative approach that consists of various actions at each *stage of the policy cycle*. Its essential characteristics are that coordination is based on the acceptance of the problem as one of common concern, on the common setting of objectives, on the voluntary cooperation of national governments to coordinate their efforts, on national freedom of choice of instruments (hence the term open), and on peer review of the results. No formal sanctions will be taken against underperforming member states.[2]

The OMC necessitates a good interplay of the *various institutions* at each stage of the policy cycle. In practice the various stages of the OMC cycle run as follows:

- *Problem.* The Commission is charged with the study of the problem. Member states discuss the quantified assessment and the analytical diagnosis of the problems. They assess the need for action and agree on the type of action to cope with the problem.
- *Objectives.* The Commission is charged with the preparing of proposals for objectives. The Council defines and quantifies these EU objectives, deducts from them intermediary objectives for which quantified targets are also formulated and sets timetables for their realization.
- *Implementation.* The member states draw up National Action Plans (NAPs) in which they translate the EU objectives in national (and regional) objectives and specify the action (instruments) they are going to use and the indicators they are going to use to measure performance. In order to improve the effectiveness of this process the EU (Commission proposal, Council decision) sets guidelines as to the type of actions that need to be pursued.
- *Monitoring.* Member states put in regular reports on their performance on the indicators chosen and on the progress of their policy implementation. The Commission is charged with the critical study of these plans and with the monitoring of the progress. To that end it often integrates these in so-called scoreboards, observatories or monitors.
- *Evaluation.* The Commission and the Council regularly evaluate the situation and make an international comparison of the instruments that have been most successful with the objective of mutual learning through adoption of best practices.

The iterative character of the OMC process makes it conducive to constant improvement. In the beginning there is much fluidity as to the best indicators to choose for capturing the reality. Next, there is an effort to be made to set up comparable databases and to complete them progressively. Then, there is a learning process on policy measures and the institutional context that conditions their effectiveness. Finally, there is a choice to be made as to the key indicators that will guide policy targets as working with a multitude of indicators (some 30–50) proves to be distracting from essentials (Atkinson *et al.*, 2004).

The OMC is not only about coordination between the EU and the member states. Application of the *partnership principle* (see sections 6.6 and 9.4) has led the EU to urge the national states to include in the NAPs lower-level governments and social partners (and even non-governmental organizations). This is particularly relevant as the mobilization of all relevant actors is essential in the legitimization of the process, the appropriateness of the indicators and the effectiveness of the policies.

8.2.3 Strong EU influence: the Community Method

In other cases where the EU has strong powers and there is a big need for uniform application of common rules the so-called 'Community Method' is used. The elaboration of such EU legislation follows a certain sequence that has the following main steps:

- The European Commission has the initiative. It makes an assessment of the problems, proposes EU action and submits draft texts of the regulation.[3]
- The Council of Ministers decides by qualified majority voting on the proposal by the Commission.
- The European Parliament debates the proposal and gives its agreement, which implies democratic legitimization.

This shorthand description of the legislation process leaves out the political processes of bargaining between different actors. The two most important ones are the Commission and national governments. The latter ones negotiate bilaterally with the Commission on certain aspects of the proposals and multilaterally in the Council. In matters of cohesion policy the most important negotiations take place at the time when the SF regulations need to be changed (that is for every six-to-seven-years-long programming period). These negotiations are in effect the major point of vertical coordination between the EU on the one hand and the member states on the other hand. This can be more or less constraining for the member states (Mendez et al., 2006) as the illustration of the case in Box 8.1 shows.

Box 8.1 Negotiations on eligibility and area coverage

Critical in the regulation of the EU cohesion policy process is the determination of the *regions that qualify for support of the SF*. This mapping of eligibility is essentially the result of negotiations between the member states and the Commission, each trying to realize as much as possible their own preferences.

In the period between 1988 and 1999 the designation of objective 1 regions was fairly straightforward. However, the criteria for the other objectives were quite loose. Member states introduced a wide array of problem areas with the result that a very high percentage of the EU population lived in areas that were in one way or another entitled to aid.

At the start of the negotiations for the regulations for the period 2000–06 the Commission expressed its strong interest in concentration of EU aid on the regions with the highest problems. Member states accepted first, the principle of concentration and next, the Commission's proposal that only 40 per cent of the EU population would be entitled to EU (SCF) aid. As objective 1 regions counted for some 22 per cent of the EU population further negotiations concentrated on the criteria to designate the areas that would qualify for the remaining 18 per cent. The Commission (represented by DG Regio) entered into detailed bi-lateral negotiations with each member state on area designation. It sought to respect, as closely as possible, national and EU priorities. In this way an overall agreement could be reached. Remaining hesitations on the side of member states were taken away by the Commission accepting lengthy transition periods during which certain areas could be phased out in member states that had to make the most painful cut backs. Once the principle was accepted, the ceiling fixed and the objective 1 regions defined the Commission could be fairly lenient as to the final result, because its prime priorities were not affected.

Much more adaptation on the part of the member states to EU norms was required for the designation of areas exempted from the ban on state aid. In the 1990s the Commission (here represented by DG Competition) has taken an increasingly restrictive stand. It has imposed its views on the member states notwithstanding fierce resistance in three ways:

1. It set pressure on the member states by stipulating at the beginning of the period that all existing derogations would expire automatically at the end of the period. So, as of 2006, any possibility of allocating in an individual case state aid would depend on prior agreement of the Commission on the whole package.
2. It made the areas where the general derogation (Art. 87.3.a) applies, practically, identically with objective 1. Given the high problem status of this group of regions the argument was difficult to counter.
3. For other claims on derogations member states had to show why the derogation had such an importance for each of the areas they wanted to designate. Controlling aid in these well-to-do areas in order to prevent distortions in the competition process is the prime task of DG Competition. So it was very strict in the application of its criteria and accepted only very few derogations.

Many member states were very frustrated by the process and unhappy with the outcome. Germany even challenged the Commission's application of its conditions in the European Court of Justice. However, it was refused what it wanted in this legal dispute, just as it had been refused in the earlier political struggle.

For the present period 2006–13 the political situation is different. The main objective is convergence. These areas are clearly delimited and hence are the areas of the general derogation. For the remaining areas the Commission intends to tighten up considerably the rules on state aids.

Source: Mendez *et al.* (2006)

8.3 Vertical coordination: EU frameworks for joint use of EU and national instruments

8.3.1 Rationale for choice of a stronger coordination method

The EU has become involved in matters of cohesion because national actions did not suffice to solve the problem effectively. We have seen that the EU has elaborated the system of intervention and the rules of its application. These imply that the member states take the lead in specifying their objectives, elaborating their programmes and implementing their projects. The EU assesses quality, provides funds and checks results.

In the previous chapter we have seen that the EU has opted for a system where it intervenes not only in matters of convergence where it helps member states and regions to catch up, but also in countries that have GDP/P levels well above the EU average. The objective here is now mainly competitiveness. Had the EU opted for limiting itself to only one objective, it would have implied the so-called 'netting of the funds', where some countries are just contributors to the funds and do not benefit from them. These member countries also have internal problems of disparities. They might have been interested in discussing the solution for them in the EU framework with the help of the OMC.

However, now that the EU intervenes on three objectives it supports, in a sense, all member states to a certain extent. The OMC is thought to be too flexible to guarantee the effective use of EU funds to realize EU priorities. So in matters of cohesion a more stringent coordination method is used.

We recall here the results of the previous chapter where we have indicated how the EU has set up a system that determined the areas where the EU intervenes (objectives), set maximum levels for EU contributions in function of the gravity of the problems (intensity of support) and suggested the focus by apportioning some funds for special purposes (e.g. Urban or Equal). The system left it to the member states to respond to the EU priorities within the framework set. The EU coordinated these efforts. However, the member states did bend their choices in this coordination framework only in as far as the co-financing they had to put up for the subject was in their eyes justified given their own priorities.

In the past this system has worked relatively well because the stated objectives of the policy were fairly straightforward (limiting disparities) while offering sufficient flexibility to cope with local situations. Nevertheless, the system of programming, where the member states set the priorities and used their own (co-financing) and EU money for the funding of these programmes subject to limited coordination on the side of the EU, has on quite a number of occasions produced insufficient emphasis on the EU priorities (see Box 8.2).

In order to be sure that the EU money is well spent the EU, therefore, wants to have a clearer framework for SF interventions and make sure they meet the various EU priorities. This stronger influence is clearly justified for those cases where the EU is the largest contributor to programmes, which is in general the case in the areas that fall under the convergence objective. However, it has also

Box 8.2 The case of social inclusion

What problem? The EU member states are all among the wealthier ones if compared by world standards. Yet there are many EU citizens that do not have a fair part in this wealth and are stricken by poverty and social exclusion. There are various national systems in place to alleviate such problems. However, the main mechanisms for distributing opportunities and resources (the labour market, the tax and social security systems and those regarding public services such as health) do still leave some people out in the cold.

Why EU commitment? The member states have agreed that they were faced with a common problem and that they all had to work on its solution. Moreover, they agreed that they could learn from each others' experiences. They have said on several occasions that the EU should be involved in finding solutions. The EU has committed itself solemnly to reduce the risk of poverty and social exclusion (European Councils of Lisbon, Nice and Stockholm).

What activity? The overarching policy aims have been translated into the following four major objectives.[4]

1 Facilitate participation in employment and access for all to social security, housing, healthcare, education, justice and culture.
2 Prevent the risk of exclusion. This has been worked out in three points: promoting inclusion; preventing over-indebtedness; and preserving family solidarity.
3 Help the most vulnerable. Among them are people facing persistent poverty, disabilities, ethnic discrimination and children.
4 Promote equality between men and women.

What results? The EU has financed (in the framework of a number of national programmes) projects that were geared to reducing social exclusion. However, together these did not add up to a clear EU strategy on the subject. So the EU has introduced the coordination method to help. The iterative and evolutionary character of the method is clearly visible in the case of social exclusion. The first round of coordination has provided a variety of results. First, it has given a clearer view on the scope and structure of the problem and of the need to come to better and more comparable statistical indicators. Second, it brought the recognition of the considerable differences that exist between member states in the social policy systems in place. Third, it showed that the set up did not permit a good evaluation. The second round has produced net improvements on a number of these scores. However, the improvement of monitoring and the evaluation remain key points on which in future improvements need to be made.

Source: EC (2002b, 2006); Atkinson *et al.* (2004)

a justification in those cases where the EU contributes relatively less, for instance in the areas falling under the competitiveness objective. These are located in countries that are generally highly developed and can assume responsibility for all projects that do not fall under the EU priorities. For the ones for which they do ask for support, however, it is only logical that they do show their projects help the reaching of EU priorities.

One could in this respect even go as far as the adoption in cohesion matters of the system used for instance in EU science and technology policy where proposals are submitted to the EU and compete for available EU funds. The EU picks from these the ones that it thinks will contribute most to its objectives. In cohesion matters the EU has, however, not adopted that system, as it would have implied a quite radical difference in governance between the convergence objective that is subject to the programming method and the competitiveness objective that would be subject to a project-selection method. Moreover, it would have put the whole burden of ex-ante and ex-post evaluation on the EU Commission or on a specialized agency. With the subsidiarity principle in mind the EU has preferred to leave the member states in charge of much of the process (as described in the previous chapters and the next chapter) and keep the unity of the governance for the whole cohesion policy.

However, in matters of coordination the EU has chosen to bring its support more in line with its objectives and priorities by giving stricter guidelines to the member states as to the subjects it wants to see addressed in the programmes. This approach follows in principle the same sequence of the OMC as outlined in the first section of this chapter; however, it details further the targets, monitors better the split of financial support over specific objectives, controls stricter the fit of national programmes with EU priorities, etc. We detail hereafter two of the most salient features of this cohesion method of coordination by the major actor.

8.3.2 Need for and compliance with regulation

The operations of the SF have been subjected to a fairly strict EU regulation. Such regulation is not self-evident. As a matter of fact the 'constitutional' treaties of the EU demand also in this case the application of the proportionality principle. We can illustrate the need for strict EU rules to reach certain (non-cohesion) objectives with two examples:

1 *Monetary Union.* A common monetary policy leads to the recovery of the effectiveness of policy making. In order to make the common monetary policy work, the European System of Central Banks supervises the financial sector. This supervision can only be made operational by obliging the operators in the field, e.g. banks to observe very detailed and specific rules about administration, accounting and control.
2 *Internal Market.* The completion of the internal market increases efficiency and hence, wealth. The adoption of very detailed EU regulation on product specification and certification takes away the cost of compliance for com-

panies that operate internationally under a multitude of different national regulations.

In the case of the regulations that govern the operations of the EU cohesion policy such arguments are hardly relevant. Even the opposite is true; European regulation imposes very high compliance cost on all concerned. The justification for this choice resides essentially in the principle of accountability of the EU Commission for the effectiveness of its operations. It means that the Commission has to be able to show to the Council of Ministers, the European Parliament and beyond that to the European public at large that the money it has spent is well used. Given the large variety of national situations the EU wants to create the conditions that increase the inclination of the beneficiaries to comply with the objectives of the policy and their capacity to audit the operations.

In order to deal with these problems the EU has opted for the use of the legal form of the Regulation, as European regulations take immediate effect in all member states. The basic rules are common to all SF (the most recent one is Reg. 1083/2006). Others are fund specific (one for the ERDF, one for the ESF and one for the CF).

Notwithstanding the detailed character of the EU regulation it cannot cover all the aspects of the practical functioning of the complicated system that is needed to bring the EU cohesion policy to life. So many national governments feel the necessity to specify and regulate certain aspects even further. The EU gives leeway to the member states to do so; however, in order to safeguard consistency with the EU rules, these national rules need to be approved by the Commission before they can take effect.[5]

In many cases detailed rules are made to realize an objective but the organization lacks the means to make people and organizations observe them. Now compliance with the rules of the SF is not really a problem. The reason is that the EU has two types of weapon:

1. Specification of mutual obligations. During the negotiation stage of the programmes (see the next chapter) the Commission exerts influence that leads to sometimes significant changes in documents; these often include detailed specifications of the commitments and the obligations of the member state in question.
2. Withdraw its support. The use of this weapon is not merely a threat but a reality. Indeed the EU has in several cases obliged member states to repay subsidies because the member state had not strictly observed (part of) the rules (for instance on justification of certain expenditure items).

8.3.3 The role of the Commission

The Commission prepares and the Council adopts so-called Community Strategic Guidelines (CSGs) on economic, social and territorial cohesion. These CSGs define an indicative framework for the intervention of the funds, taking account of EU cohesion and other relevant EU objectives. The cohesion objectives are formulated as follows: 'to give effect to the priorities of the Community with a view to promote harmonious balanced and sustainable development' (Reg. 1083/2006, Art. 25). The other objectives have been specified by the different European councils and deal with broad economic subjects, such as employment or sustainability. We will discuss these later in this chapter.

The guidelines are not very strict. On the contrary, they provide quite a large menu from which the member states can actually choose to adopt the mix that is most appropriate in their case for developing national and regional programmes.

8.3.4 The role of the member states

The guidelines are the framework for the member states to prepare so-called National Strategic Reference Frameworks (NSRFs) (Reg. 1083/2006, Art. 27). They should identify the link between Community priorities on the one hand and national reform programmes on the other. They need to guide the choices made in the Operational Programmes (see next section) that are made by the various beneficiaries (regions, etc.).

NSRFs have to have a logical and internally consistent structure. They have to address the following aspects:

- analysis of the disparities, the weaknesses and the potential;
- strategy, chosen on the basis of this analysis, including thematic and territorial priorities;
- presentation of the concrete actions adopted;
- description of how the expenditure for the convergence and competitiveness objectives shall contribute to the EU priorities of promoting competitiveness and jobs;
- indication of the annual allocation of each fund to the various programmes.

We recall here that the elements contained in the list above can all be related to the first part of the policy cycle. The other parts of the cycle will not be forgotten in this set up. Indeed, the whole procedure is to be completed by monitoring and evaluation (to be put into effect by the Strategic Reporting by member states and the EU Commission). These can lead to adaptations of both the guidelines and the NSRFs.

8.3.5 The role of the regions

In matters of vertical coordination the EU cohesion policy sets a number of rules for the relation between EU, member state and region. The general framework for these rules has been given in Chapter 6. Their specification is a matter of negotiation between the Commission and the member states. Once adopted they can flexibly be put in practice by the member states in function of the specific arrangements that the constitution of the member state in question has made for the distribution of tasks among various layers of government.[6]

The main instrument through which this coordination occurs is in the establishment of the so-called operational programmes (OPs). These programmes cover the whole planning period and are specific for one of the three objectives. They are financed by only one fund. They are set up in partnership. OPs shall contain:

- analysis of the eligible area in terms of strengths and weaknesses and the strategy chosen in response;
- justification of the priorities chosen having regard to the CSGs, the NSRFs and the evaluation of previous programmes;
- information on the priority axes and the specific targets. These targets shall be quantified using a limited number of indicators for output and results, taking into account the proportionality principle. The indicators shall make it possible to measure progress in the realization of the targets;
- breakdown of the use of SCF and a financing plan with the contributions of other partners;
- information on the management structure and the competent bodies involved in the execution; the payment and auditing procedures, etc.

The Commission appraises the OPs to determine whether they contribute to the goals and priorities of the NSRFs and the CSGs. After discussion and revision the Commission will adopt the OP and it will thereby become the basis for concrete interventions and their accompanying financial transfers.

The establishment of these OPs is often the result of fierce battles between the national government and the regions. The former often reserve some competences for themselves and prefer to set up thematic operational programmes (often sectoral ones: SOPs). The regions claim more competences and the corresponding financial resources by favouring Regional Operational Programmes (ROPs).[7]

It is important to note that the procedure of coordination outlined assumes a hierarchical situation in multilevel government. Such a relation is quite adequate for the two main objectives of cohesion policy: convergence and competitiveness. However, it is not for the third objective: territorial cohesion. Here, new forms of vertical coordination are needed that are akin to networks and bypass the traditional hierarchy of multilevel government. In the EU these concern notably cross-border cooperation. The EU sponsors such forms and their institutionalization. Much experimentation has been done in the past (notably in the framework of INTERREG; see Chapter 7) that has given rise to a range of forms with different empowerment of the actors involved in these (Blatter, 2004; Perkmann, 1999). However, on many scores these proved to be inadequate so that a new institution was required.

In order to overcome the legal obstacles to territorial cooperation the EU has established a new legal form, the European Grouping of Territorial Cooperation (EGTC) (Reg. 1082/2006). To be effective the EGTC has in each member state the most extensive legal capacity under the national law. Members in the EGTC may be member states, regional and local authorities and bodies authorized to execute certain public tasks. Recourse to an EGTC is optional.

8.4 Vertical EU law limits national support to firms (state aid)

8.4.1 Some concepts, some theory

Economic systems are confronted with a number of rigidities. Some of these are of a behavioural nature, for instance the low inclination of labour to move. Others are of an institutional nature, for instance labour laws that prescribe firms to pay minimum wages. As a consequence firms may find it difficult to produce profitably in a region where the combination of factors needed for production are not very advantageous. Agglomeration and concentration tendencies (described in Chapter 3) may exacerbate such problems. The existence of significant unemployment in problem regions will lead to claims for support. Government intervention is then justified by both the efficiency and equity argument (see Chapter 6).

In the course of the past decades most countries have taken up forms of cohesion policy. They have developed a panoply of instruments (Yuill *et al.*, 1999), that can be divided into two groups that apply to:

- *Firms*. This group covers financial benefits (soft loans, investment grants, tax relief and so on) which is meant to attract industrial activity in view of alleviating unemployment in certain assisted areas, or to support existing industries that have come into difficulty. These instruments are generally called state aid.
- *Public sector or individual persons*. This group of instruments intends to improve the location conditions in certain regions (such as the improvements of roads, ports, industrial sites, adaptability of workers, public utilities, innovation and so on).

State aid has certain negative effects. The most important is that it distorts the fair competition by favouring certain firms in a sector over others. Moreover, it may lead to some rent-seeking behaviour of firms trying to justify continued support by poor performance which in reality is not only due to unfortunate external circumstance but internal factors such as poor utilization of management insufficiencies. Moreover, its very existence may bring a sort of subsidy race; firms in medium locations claiming support because they find themelves in difficulty because of the change in the competitive environment.

In the recent past there has been a shift of emphasis in the EU as to the type of instrument that is best deployed in matters of cohesion policy. This is based to a large extent on a change in paradigm; one puts more faith in market forces and less in specific government intervention. As a consequence one now puts less weight on financial interventions in the market (e.g. through state aid). The consequence is that more weight is put on the second type of intervention, that intends to increase the quality of the location factors in a region and thereby the competitiveness of all firms in such a region.

8.4.2 Regulation

Given the important distortions that state aid may produce, the EU has since its start applied strict rules and has even tightened them since. The application of the proportionality principle has in this case resulted in the abandonment of the instrument of coordination and in the application of the instrument of unified EU rules. First of all, they have been set on the constitutional level (Art. 87). The objective of these rules is to preserve the effectiveness of the main policy areas of the EU (see Chapter 6).

The EU rules forbid, in principle, all state aid. As state aid favours one firm over another it distorts the fair competition. The EU Commission is empowered to safeguard the good functioning of the CM and under that role it monitors competition and it controls state aid. It targets most directly aid that is specific to certain sectors of economic activity or to individual firms.

There are a few exceptions to this general ban. State aid that helps to attain EU objectives (called 'horizontal measures' in common EU parlance) such as the protection of the environment or the enhancement of innovation are accepted under certain conditions. Also under this category falls aid that promotes the economic development of areas where the standard of living is abnormally low or where there is serious unemployment.

In order to work out these constitutional principles in regulatory practice the EU has defined the conditions under which state aid can be allowed in so-called guidelines. Most important for cohesion policy are the guidelines that apply to regional aid. The main objective of these rules is to prevent governments from outbidding one another with subsidies, in other words to prevent the richer member states to propose aid packages that nullify the effect of aid packages allowed to the less well-off ones.[8] To that end the EU has set four types of conditions that constrains state aid:

1. *Where*. The EU has defined different categories of regions dependent on the seriousness of their cohesion problems. The broad categories correspond to the types of regions defined earlier (Chapter 7) but they detail further subcategories.
2. *How much*. The EU has put a ceiling on aid levels for each type of problem region: that is, the bigger the problem, the higher the ceiling.
3. *Who*. The basic EU rules (in terms of aid percentage ceilings) are set for large firms. They are less severe for medium (+10 per cent) and small (+20 per cent) firms. The rationale of this modulation is that aid to small firms is unlikely to affect in a serious way the competition conditions in the CM.[9]
4. *What*. The EU permits subsidies to relieve cost of a structural character – such as investment in plant and machinery – which is clearly inspired by the objective of economic cohesion. In view of the improvement of social cohesion the EU permits the support to the cost of training of people to adapt them to the new employment conditions. Finally, in terms of territorial cohesion the EU permits, as a special exception, subsidies to offset transport cost to firms located in the outermost regions, thereby improving their accessibility.

174 *Specifying objectives*

Table 8.1 Maximum allowed aid intensities (% to total cost) in different types of regions (wealth level in % of EU)

Policy category	GDP/P level	Aid level
Convergence	<60	40–50
	>60 <75	30
Intermediate	>75	30
	(formerly <75% of EU 15)	(after 2011: 20)
Competitiveness	>75	10–15

Source: EC.

Conditions 1 and 2 are detailed in Table 8.1. They give the situation that prevails in the present policy period for big firms. In the past, different categories and different (often more generous) aid levels prevailed.

8.4.3 Who is responsible?

In matters of state aid the EU Commission plays a different role than it does in matters of the SF. The control of state aid is entrusted to DG Competition (formerly DG IV) while cohesion matters are dealt with by DG Regio and DG Employment. The role of the Commission in matters of competition is very extensive. It proposes the relevant regulations (legislation); it monitors developments (execution); it investigates cases; it prosecutes infringements of the rules; and it judges these infringements. Depending on the seriousness of the infringement it imposes fines or orders firms to pay back the sums they have received from their national governments. Firms or member states that do not agree with the decisions of the Commission can turn to the European Court of Justice to have their case reviewed.

In matters of legislation the Commission coordinates with the member states as the Council has eventually to pass the legislation. This legislation (as far as it is relevant for cohesion), follows the same periodicity as the budgetary cycle that also determines the SF cycle (described in Chapter 7). So, the present set of rules applies to the period 2007–13.

With respect to the other activities (monitoring and adjudication) the Commission is very independent. Although it will weigh in its decision some political considerations it is solely responsible and will act independently of national government influences.

8.4.4 Size of state aid

The annual spending on state aid is very considerable: some €60 billion a year (figures for the years 2004–05). This means that this spending exceeds the spending of the SF, which amounts to some €50 billion a year for the planning period 2007–13.

The spending on state aid has gradually decreased over the past decades (see EC, 2000b). This decrease is due to two factors. First, the increasing strict control of the Commission. Second, the change in paradigm; direct aid to firms is now deemed less effective than indirect aid to competitiveness.

Notwithstanding this drop, state aid remains very important. A few cases may illustrate this. Aid to agriculture absorbs (apart from the EU support to the sector) some €14 billion. For manufacturing industry and services roughly the same amount is spent. Other important categories are environment and R&D. Finally, regional aid needs to be mentioned.

The biggest spenders (per head of population) in matters of regional state aid (RSA) are Germany (that has to cope with the problem of its new federal states) and Spain (that has increased the use of the instrument of RSA over the past decade). Two cases of state aid in Germany are given in Box 8.3. Most of the other countries in the West and South of the EU spend more or less the same sums per capita as the EU average. The countries in the East, however, show very low aid levels (some 30 per cent of the EU average). This East–West split is an illustration of the way in which the richer countries outbid the poorer ones for state aid. This has very significant anti-cohesion effects and is the justification for continuous vigilance of strong action by the EU Commission to curb such state aid.

Box 8.3 Authorized and unauthorized state aid

Schott Lithotec planned to build a plant in Hermsdorf (Thuringia, an assisted area in east Germany) for the production of calcium fluoride crystals for optic lithography used to produce wafer steppers. The proposed state aid amounted to €80 million out of a total of €230 million in eligible cost. The Commission has authorized the aid. It thereby gave three considerations to justify its decision:

1 The plant would create 560 direct jobs for highly educated and roughly 1,000 indirect jobs, so the project contributes to the employment and the knowledge society objectives.
2 The sector does not suffer from over capacity, so the risk of the project distorting the CM is small.
3 The support stays within the limit of 35 per cent set for aid to large firms in the area, so respects the caps set by the EU regulation on state aid.

The Treuhandanstalt was a German state holding, set up to privatize former state-owned companies in eastern Germany. IFA, a heavy truck producer, was sold by the Treuhandanstalt to Mercedes Benz. There was no open tender. The Commission wanted to know whether the price paid by Mercedes was justified. They asked an independent expert, who arrived at a higher value for the company. The Commission found that the difference between the two constituted effectively a state aid that could not be justified under the prevailing rules. They obliged Mercedes to pay the difference to the Treuhandanstalt.

Source: Official Journal J L5, 9–1–1997

---

176 *Specifying objectives*

Interesting in this respect is the comparison of the RSA with the support the various member states get from the SF. In the EU as a whole SF support far exceeds RSA. The ratio of the RSA to total regional support (RSA/(RSA+SF)) is very low in the East (the NMSs) as the level of state aid per capita is very low whereas, the SF support is very high. In the South (Spain, Portugal, Greece) the ratio is low, given the considerable sums these countries get from the SF. However, in the bigger member states of northwestern Europe the ratio is quite significant as these countries get little out of the SF and have the capacity to spend much on state aid. (In 2004 the ratio was about one-third for Italy, France and the UK and about half for Germany.)

EU rules about the limitation of state aid have been set in order to preserve the effectiveness of the instrument in the less-well-to-do countries of the EU. They do constrain considerably the possibilities of the richer member states to influence the situation in their problem regions with the instrument of support to mobile firms. Many of these countries are confronted with considerable internal disparities though. So they will have to find other instruments to cope with these problems.

8.5 Setting of EU standards

8.5.1 Social standards

The stipulations of the Treaty (Art. 137) offer the possibility to impose minimum EU standards. The use of such standards is, however, the subject of much debate. Many think[10] that standards should be an essential instrument to realize progress on the social dimension of European integration. This is a wide-ranging notion covering very heterogeneous policies regarding salary, working conditions, social security, trade unions, professional training, equal treatment of men and women, co-determination, etc. (EC, 1994b). Others are more cautious and say that the application of the two main principles of subsidiarity and proportionality do not produce clear-cut results that support going in that direction. This may be illustrated with the case of social standards (see Box 8.4).

Box 8.4 Social standards

In member states that have high social standards labour costs are higher than in states with low standards. This has given rise to the accusation of social dumping: employment will be lost in the former states and won in the latter because firms faced with losses in market shares due to high cost will relocate to low-cost, low-protection locations. National governments have few possibilities left to counter such tendencies. EU integration makes that they can neither use the instruments that apply to goods and service markets (hamper free movement), nor those of a macro economic nature (a devaluation is precluded by the monetary union). EU regulations setting for all member states minimum standards on wage levels, social provisions and health and safety could be a solution to the problems felt.

There has been much controversy on this issue. The arguments in the debate on EU-wide standards can be summarized as follows:

- *Advocates*, also called 'regulatory school', argue that EU standards prevent 'unfair' competition from countries that have low social standards to wipe out activities in the countries with highly developed welfare states. This would set in motion a downward spiral in social protection with considerable negative effects of two types. First, serious social problems may lower productivity. Second, labour market institutions may become less efficient as the positive external effects of regulation are forgone.[11]
- *Opponents*, also called 'competition school', argue that standards restrict the functioning of markets. This causes two problems. First, a regional problem as standards increase the cost level of the below average income member states, which restricts their chances of competing successfully on product markets, which in turn increases the chances that they will become demanders of cohesion policy support and hence become dependent on transfer payments.[12] Second, a social problem as EU standards increase the rigidity on labour markets, which is one of the major causes of unemployment; the unemployment in the less developed areas can also lead to mass out-migration with uncertain welfare effects both in emigration and immigration countries. To avoid such problems one should refrain from standards; the increase in wealth that will be engendered by the high competitiveness of the catch-up countries (regions) will then in turn lead to an increase in the level of social security and hence to convergence of the levels of protection in the EU.

A general conclusion as to which approach is the best is not possible; case-by-case solutions have to be found. The preference, thereby, is for EU standards formulated as a set of common objectives, one should be careful not to go into too much detail and into standard procedures.[13]

The regulatory activity of the EU has the big advantage that it does not involve any visible redistribution. However, regulation that imposes uniform standards does have a redistribution effect. It comes about because the costs of their implementation are borne by those who are subject to regulation. These costs can be different for different countries. For instance, countries that have already national rules in place (standards) that are grossly equivalent to the ones the EU wants to impose will not have any particular cost or drop in competitiveness. However, member states that have to come up to new standards can sometimes only do that at the cost of government expenses (e.g. minimum levels of old-age benefits) or to the companies (implementing equal standards of safety at the work place). The latter can lead to a drop in competitiveness and hence to a drop in wealth levels of the country in question. So one sees that there is an internal conflict in cohesion policy between the economic and territorial cohesion on the one hand (pleading for few and low standards) and social cohesion on the other hand (pleading for many and high standards).

The setting of high standards may actually trigger higher financial redistribution and transfer payments. This case will occur when a country, due to high standards, loses competitiveness, experiences a drop in wealth levels and becomes, thereby, eligible for support from the funds. A case in point is Germany who has integrated the new federal states (Bundeslaender) and immediately introduced western standards. In order to avoid such situations many countries are fiercely opposed to extending the realm of EU standards.

8.5.2 Services of general interest

Strong lobbies have pushed the idea of equal access to high-quality Services of General Interest (SGI) as the best means to promote territorial cohesion (see Chapter 5). The notion of services of general interest is already taken up in the treaties.[14] The term is not further defined in the treaties. In EU practice, however, it relates to services to which governments attach certain public service obligation. Under present EU conventions member states' governments are free to classify certain services to be of general interest in case they think it necessary to guarantee access to them at affordable prices for everyone, irrespective of the geographical situation of their residence or location. In practice it often concerns large network-related services such as transport, energy, postal services and (tele)communication. The determining on the EU level of certain rules or standards as to SGI has run into several difficulties. First, it did not prove to be easy to select the types of services, to define what is meant by quality, affordable prices, equal access, etc., nor to evaluate the consequences in terms of public budget expenditure and burden sharing. Second, the application of the subsidiarity principle (that is the determination of the role of the EU) did not prove to be easy at all in this case. After a wide-ranging consultation it was agreed that this field is one of a joint responsibility between member states and the Union. The EU has, however, not been given a very strong role; it has no power to set standards, or regulate other aspects. It has merely been asked to monitor developments. The main responsibility for guaranteeing access to the services of general interest is entrusted to the member states, taking into account the specific situation of service, time and place.

In view of these results the ideas about a framework Directive for all SGI has been abandoned; the Commission has decided to follow where appropriate a sectoral approach (e.g. specifically on electricity or telecom).

8.6 Horizontal: the systemic aspects of achieving consistency between EU policies

8.6.1 The EU between the national and the world model

Whatever the geographical level at which public authorities operate (regional, national, European or international), they all have to find organizational solutions to solve the problem of consistency between their various specialized policies (e.g. cohesion, competition, environment, trade). This is never easy. At all levels and in all fields there is a tendency to specialize further and to let the policy process evolve as much as possible within each specialization. So there is a big need for *horizontal coordination*. In the following sections we will discuss how this type of coordination has been given shape by the EU.

The EU has taken upon it to limit the risk of non-consistency among its policies by horizontal coordination. As we mentioned in Chapter 6 this has even become a constitutional obligation. The way in which this constitutional obligation was to be put into practice did, however, raise quite a few problems. Indeed, improvement of horizontal coordination is an uphill fight. The main opponents argue that it is complicating an already involved process with all the risks of slowing it down and making it more costly.

The EU has opted for some experimentation and has elaborated in a practical way an EU solution to this general problem.

In the beginning, the problem the EU had was limited in the sense that it had only a few policy fields for which it assumed responsibility. Later, with an increased number of fields and a deeper involvement of the EU through more funds and more constraining regulation the problem became much more important.

The solution has also evolved over time. The EU had to define its model as a supranational organization somewhere between the model of a national state and the model of an international organization in the classical sense. We will detail hereafter the latter two models and the specific features of the EU model.

8.6.2 *The national model*

Many countries show quite some disparity between their regions and social groups. They try to solve this problem of lack of cohesion with a number of policies. The most important are policies that deal in a specific way with each dimension of cohesion. For economic cohesion a regional policy is pursued using a battery of instruments often comprising support to investment, to infrastructure and to schooling. For social cohesion, welfare-state policies are pursued comprising elements such as social security and taxes. Finally, for territorial cohesion, spatial planning is done with specific instruments such as control on developments and transport infrastructure.

However, national governments also use quite an extended range of other policies to promote cohesion. Important, in this respect, is the support to infrastructure. The national priorities for major infrastructure works will take into account the needs of improved accessibility of the least-favoured regions of the country. In the past when railways were national companies under complete government control the tariff structure of the railways was often set in such a way that transport on links that were important for stimulating cohesion was less costly than the same traffic between major centres (in other words it comprised an implicit subsidy to firms in remote areas). Modern EU transport policy has done away with the latter type of practices but infrastructure provision is still an important instrument to foster internal cohesion of countries.

National states execute important tasks in other areas as well. We may cite the regulation of environmental quality, the setting of social standards, etc. Many of these policies have an intended positive impact on internal cohesion. For instance, national financing of public services such as health tends to be provided at the same price and the same quality in all regions irrespective of their tax contribution to the cost of the national health system.[15] Moreover, the social security system maintains income in high-employment regions.

The national institutional systems tend to be conducive to consistency of various policies. In other words the political institutions on the national level make that the chances are weak, that the effects on economic and territorial cohesion are not taken into consideration while elaborating such national policies without an explicit cohesion objective. We can explain this with a few examples. Countries that have a district system for representative democracy have a built-in coordination, as local politicians will be very keen to see that the national government supports projects that benefit their constituencies. Even in countries with proportional representation it is very likely that the political process will take the regional impact into account while hammering out new policies. Moreover, in matters of all three dimensions of cohesion, national political systems have built-in checks as pressure groups have no difficulty in getting the attention of policy makers (take for instance the case of trade unions in matters of social cohesion, industrialists of remote areas in matters of economic and territorial cohesion, etc.).

8.6.3 The global model

The world is confronted with large disparities between countries. There is a strong correlation between economic and social disparities on this level. A particularly problematic aspect of the global situation is the large number of people that live in absolute poverty; notably in the countries with the lowest incomes per head (e.g. Bangladesh). Poverty alleviation and the improvement of the catching up of poor countries with the developed countries is a stated policy goal of international organizations. On the international level there is not one organization that covers all policy fields such as the national state or the EU. On the contrary there is a multitude of specialized organizations each with its proper objectives and internal rules (Molle, 2003).[16]

One way to improve the global cohesion situation is via support to economic development; this task is notably entrusted to the World Bank (WB). Social cohesion matters are not very far developed on the global level; the WB does some work in this area, while the International Labour Organization (ILO) promotes social justice, human and labour rights and standards that take away some risks of exclusion. On the global level there is no organization that is specifically concerned with territorial cohesion.

The method for the improvement of the economic situation is bilateral and multilateral development aid (akin to the cohesion policy on the EU level). Some of this may be called social (e.g. food aid and aid to refugees) as it is specifically directed to disadvantaged groups. Moreover, some support is given to social development such as reform of institutions and education, but this is often in the perspective of creating the conditions for better growth. The impact of such policies on the diminishing of disparities has been limited. So, much attention has to be put on the harnessing of other policies with a potential positive effect on global cohesion.

The most obvious example of such a policy is trade; permitting access of the Less Developed Countries (LDCs) to the markets of developed countries. The World Trade Organization (WTO) has set very strict rules for the way in which trade has to be conducted (similar to the internal market of the EU). One basic principle is non-discrimination. However, in view of the barriers for LDCs in matters of market access the WTO permits exceptions to the principle in the form of Generalized Systems of Preferences that the developed countries can give to LDCs. Unfortunately this is not a very effective measure for several reasons. First, with the general decrease in tariff levels the preference is eroded. Second (and more important), developed countries have maintained other trade barriers for a large number of products that are of considerable importance to LDCs. Particularly relevant in this respect is the way in which the developed countries support their agriculture (up until now accepted by WTO). They block imports of LDCs into their countries and hinder LDCs exports to third countries. Many estimate that this annihilates the effects of development aid transfers.

Another example concerns the global monetary and financial institutions. In principle the International Monetary Fund (IMF) improves the stability of currencies and in so doing improves the macro economic environment that is generally conducive to growth. However, in practice the institutions do not always work out in such a positive way. In order to be able to benefit from financial support of the IMF, the latter gives detailed prescriptions as to the policy packages and institutional set up of LDCs. To many observers such conditions run counter to the long-term convergence of these countries. Unfortunately there exists no formal platform at the global level for safeguarding the consistency of policies.

A third example is in the field of the environment. The global policy measures taken to limit the negative effects of greenhouse gases (Kyoto Protocol) have adopted the principle of common but differentiated responsibilities. It implies that no targets have been set for the reduction of emissions by less developed countries. This is understandable from the point of view of their low contribution to overall pollution levels and their limited financial capacity to contribute to investments that are needed for abatement.

The three examples given here show clearly how large the differences may be of the effects on world cohesion of these different policies. Coordinating these policies remains, however, a very difficult exercise, given the fragmented structure of the global organizations and the political economy that determines the actions of the major national players. The results of some efforts constitute at best a very fragile equilibrium that is at a constant risk to be broken by new incidental developments.

8.6.4 The EU model

The EU occupies an intermediary position between the national and the global model of horizontal coordination (Molle, 2006). We recall here a few fundamentals that were described in Chapter 6.

In the first instance the EU model contains a number of policies that aim at optimizing the allocation function (e.g. internal market). In the second instance it provides for a number of policies that pursue goals such as stability (e.g. EMU). In the third instance it contains a policy to combat disparities by a cohesion policy. There is a need for a constant checking whether EU policies are designed in such a way that they corroborate each other or at least do not contradict each other.[17] We remind here the preponderance of the first instance policies over the others, including cohesion. This dominance is very visible in the increasingly strict application of the rules on state aids that are meant to preserve the good working of the CM (see also Chapter 11).

The specific cohesion policy is based on a set of measures that aim to stimulate the competitiveness of regions and the inclusion of social groups. These measures apply to the supply side of the economy; that is to the improvement of the conditions for convergence (catching up) such as infrastructure, institutions, etc. This is thought most appropriate because such expenditure can be geared towards specific needs (including compensation for negative integration effects).

However, many of these measures do also come in the framework of other EU policies. The most obvious examples are in the field of the environment (the cleaning up of polluted sites), transport (building of new infrastructures), employment (retraining of workers) and R&D (creation of innovation centres). So a close coordination between these (horizontal) policies and cohesion policies is warranted.[18]

However, the very organization of the EU (which has its foundations in some cases in the treaties, e.g. the special place for agriculture) makes that this coordination is difficult to put into practice. The internal organization of the various EU institutions is always according to the same specialist lines. To give an example: the specialist DG of the Commission (e.g. Agriculture) elaborates a proposal. It thereby consults the parties that represent the interest of the agricultural sector that voice their opinions through two channels: specialist advisory committees and lobby groups. The proposal of the Commission is then transmitted to the Council of Ministers that meets for the occasion in its composition of the 27 national ministers of agriculture. The European Parliament when it is asked to pronounce itself will do so via its specialist Committee on Agriculture. So, the whole process is organized in a way that tends to be a closed circle of partial interests.

Yet other interests have to be taken into account to avoid that one policy goes contrary to the objectives of another policy. Such cases are frequent. For example, a project that seems to be very good for cohesion (e.g. a new airport in a remote area that will enhance its attraction for tourism) may have a negative impact on the environment. On the other hand, a project that is good for the environment (e.g. the setting of environmental standards) may be bad for cohesion as it limits competitiveness. Such standards raise the cost of firms in, for example, the NMSs (that up until now had more lenient regulation), thereby putting in jeopardy many jobs in these countries that are already confronted with heavy unemployment.[19]

To make sure the objectives and workings of the various policies are consistent the EU has imposed that cross-policy impact analyses be made before a specialist policy is hammered out (e.g. the effect on cohesion of monetary union). It means that the different DGs of the Commission have to coordinate their proposals for legislation or budget spending and adapt them in function of the results of the possible impacts. (In Chapter 11 we will go further into this subject.)

8.7 Horizontal: the practical aspects of achieving consistency among EU policy areas

8.7.1 The main EU objectives and the key EU instruments

In the recent past the EU has on several occasions tried to define some overarching policy objectives. These have usually been set in meetings of the European Council, that is in meetings of the heads of government. The strategic decisions are often referred to by the name of the city where the meeting was held. In the past the Council has defined such strategic objectives as to cohesion, employment, competitiveness and sustainability. Now the objectives are not always matched by instruments. For cohesion the EU has the instrument of the SF. For the other objectives the financial resources available are much weaker. So the EU has set as an expressive objective to use the SF in such a way that they are also conducive to reach the objectives of its other major policies.[20] These objectives have been specified on several occasions.

The Lisbon Council of 2000 defined as the major objective of the EU *to become the most dynamic and competitive, knowledge-based economy in the world by 2010.* The Council of Nice of the same year has specified that this should go hand in hand with *poverty reduction and improved social inclusion.* The Gothenburg Council of 2001 agreed to a strategy that added an *environmental dimension* to the Lisbon strategy. The Council established, moreover, the principle that economic, social and environmental effects of all policies should be examined in a coordinated way and taken into account in decision making.

The EU cohesion policy overlaps with other policies; notably employment policy. So, vertical and horizontal coordination tend to overlap. The OMC is set up to deal with this combined cohesion, social and employment policy. Every two years the member states have to make a NAP on employment. Parallel to it they also make a NAP to combat poverty and social exclusion. As discussed in the previous sections they also have to make NSRFs for cohesion policy. The EU sets certain rules as to the structure of the NAPs; they need to give a description of the problems, the institutions and the instruments. The national policy measures used need to be geared to the causes of the problems and the EU policy priorities. These factors may seem self-evident but the practice has shown that in this respect much progress can still be realized.

The recent past has shown that it is impossible to reach this set of very ambitious objectives within the time set and with the instruments available. The instrument of the OMC (on which much of the implementation of these strategies depends) is indeed too weak to produce the desired effects.

The OMC has worked well in areas where realistic and clear policy goals have been set. It was ineffective in those areas where goals were broadly defined and the national instruments are insufficient for reaching those goals. A particular worrisome case is where national institutional factors inhibit the putting into effect of policies capable of reaching the set objectives. So, if member states do not put up the necessary resources or do fail to make the necessary institutional changes, the targets on the EU level will not be met. Moreover, the simultaneous reaching of a series of objectives through the coherent deployment of national and EU instruments proved a very difficult exercise in practice.

Improvements in the match between objectives and means have to be made by either the deployment of stronger instruments or by the setting of less ambitious objectives. The member states have done both:

- *Objectives* have been redefined to more realistic proportions. The EU has given up the ambition to reach, by 2010, the targets set by the Lisbon Council and to pursue them in a fully integrated way. For all practical purposes the overriding objective of the EU for the coming years has been reformulated as the enhancement of competitiveness for higher growth with more and better jobs leading to more cohesion. Moreover, the EU pursues the objective of improvement of the sustainable development (e.g. EU, 2004b).
- *Instruments* have been adapted. First, the OMC has been made more constraining than in the past by a stricter framing of national actions within EU priorities. Second, the SFs have been instrumentalized to foster jointly cohesion, employment, competitiveness and sustainability objectives. As a matter of fact 60 per cent of the amount of money earmarked for the convergence objective and 75 per cent of the money for the competitiveness objective has to be spent on programmes with the explicit objective to contribute to the 'Lisbon' goals.

8.7.2 Contribute to EU competitiveness

In a world that is increasingly globalizing, where economies are increasingly open to external trade challenges and where new economies are quickly developing their potential, the EU can only safeguard its level of wealth and employment by keeping abreast in terms of competitiveness.

In the framework of the Lisbon Council strategy for more competitiveness a whole series of policies are pursued, that can be captured under the following four headings:

1 *Industrial structure.* Promoting the renewal of the industrial structure, notably the competitiveness of enterprises in a fully integrated single market.

2   *Innovation.* Strengthening innovation by an increase in the European effort in research and technological development.
3   *Labour force.* Improving the quality of the labour force and adapt it to the knowledge society by adequate education and training programmes.
4   *Transport and telecommunications.* Connecting the various parts of the European spaces through EU-wide transport and telecommunication networks.

The first two are closely associated with economic cohesion, the third with social cohesion and the last with territorial cohesion.

The cohesion policy and competitiveness are not antagonistic entities; on the contrary they reinforce each other. As a matter of fact cohesion policy can make an important contribution to achieve the 'Lisbon' goals. The coherence of competitiveness policy and cohesion policy can be seen on two points:

1   *Objectives.* The main objective of cohesion is convergence; and the catch up of the backward regions and countries can only be achieved by enhanced growth that in turn is dependent on the improvement of the factors that shape competitiveness. The second objective of cohesion policy is the enhancement of the competitiveness and employment in the other regions and countries of the EU. This will have to be done by taking away a number of structural weaknesses. Progress on the competitiveness score will mean an enhanced capacity to deal with social problems such as exclusion.
2   *Instruments.* The policies that were mentioned under the four headings for the EU have their counterparts in the tasks that are carried out at regional level; they are the most important areas of activity of the SF.

8.7.3 Employment: more and better jobs

The second part of the stated objective is to arrive at more and better jobs and to a reduction in poverty and social exclusion. We have seen that the capacity to realize the former (that is to provide paid jobs to the active population) determines to a large extent the degree to which the latter objective (more inclusion) can be reached. For some time the greatest concern of European citizens, irrespective of their nationality, is the risk of unemployment. This has led to action by the EU to implement the European Employment Strategy. The reason for EU involvement (subsidiarity test) has been twofold:

1   The EU was partly responsible for the problems created[21] (in so far as open trade policies and globalization entailed heavy job losses) and thus had to take responsibility for the solution.
2   Member country policies are insufficiently effective.

The proportionality test (instruments) led towards the choice of a light form; the OMC of national policies coupled with financial support from the ESF.

The question about the type of EU involvement that is needed is thus mostly about the intensity of the EU instruments used. Given the persistence of unemployment there may be some question about the lack of effectiveness of the set-up chosen. However, there are reasons why a stronger regulatory involvement of the EU does not seem to be more effective. The main one is the uncertainty about cause–effect relations. So, the best solution cannot be prescribed but needs to be found by experimentation. Successful experiments are very much dependent on national societal choices and national institutional conditions. This involves decisions as to the level and the duration of the unemployment benefits, dismissal procedures, etc., that countries are unlikely to be subjected to EU norms and standards. So, simple adoption of policy recipes from other countries is not adequate and national governments are best placed to judge what adaptations would be most appropriate.

So, notwithstanding considerable pressures to set in motion more effective and more constraining EU instruments a continuation of the present policy set-up is likely. In that light it is good to note that the available cohesion policy instruments give significant support to the employment objective; the CSG, indeed, put a very strong accent on jobs and growth.

8.7.4 Innovation and knowledge

The notion of knowledge-based economy recognizes the structural changes that are going on in the modern economy. The EU's wealth during the past era was largely based on its qualification in matters of the material-based economy: that is manufacturing industries, such as cars, etc. Now the structure of the economy has gone into more immaterial things related to knowledge. Here we find activities such as R&D, but also software development and web-based services. The EU has in the past realized adaptation to the new challenges (e.g. in energy use from coal to oil-based energy) and intends to do the same now (e.g. from oil to durable energy). To that end a lot of innovation of products and production technology is needed.

8.7.5 Sustainability

The EU is confronted with difficult environmental problems. Some of these have to do with pollution; the abatement of pollution engenders considerable cost. Others have to do with preservation; these programmes too put a cost to society. However, a key element of the Gothenburg agenda is the recognition that the pursuit of environmental improvement does not only put a burden on society in general and certain activities in particular, but that sustainable development does also present significant economic opportunities. The development and wider use of environmentally friendly technologies in sectors such as energy and transport can unleash a wave of innovation and investment and thereby lead to new growth and higher levels of employment.[22]

The question is then how such a spur of innovation can be achieved. The EU policy framework is in this respect somewhat similar to that for cohesion.

First, there are the EU environmental programmes that take up about €2 billion a year (EU budget for the 2007–13 period). A comparison with the total funds available for cohesion (Table 7.1) shows that the specific funds for environment are fairly limited.

Second, there is the EU regulatory activity. This applies mainly to:

- *Environmental standards.* These define, for exmple, the quality of air and water in numerical values about the maximum accepted content of polluting elements. Another example is the maximum of content of pollutants in exhaust gases of motor cars. In order to comply with such standards often very large investments are needed to restrict emissions by industrial and private users and to treat existing resources (e.g. water basins).
- *Constraint on state aids.* DG Competition considers a restrictive policy is justified because aid to firms to reduce pollution risks making a mockery of the polluter pays principle and the related principle of internalization of all cost. Moreover, it considers that EU standards are a legal obligation and firms should not be subsidized to conform to such obligations. However, exceptions are allowed, for instance, to clean up contaminated land where the owner can no longer be traced or to develop new technologies for efficient or renewable energy use.

While carrying out explicit cohesion policies, such as regional policy (for example, with infrastructure projects), due account should be taken of such matters as environmental policy objectives. The SF regulation and the CSG do indeed make aid conditional on compliance with a number of such other policy objectives.

8.8 Summary and conclusions

- In the third stage of the policy cycle the instruments have to be specified. Next to the financial instrument (previous chapter) the EU uses the instruments of regulation and coordination to reach its objectives. Regulatory instruments forbid certain actions of private and public actors that may have a negative effect on cohesion or prescribe other actions that may enhance cohesion. Lighter forms of instruments that tend to improve the consistency of policy making by different actors are coordination and consultation.
- One distinguishes between *vertical* aspects, where the EU determines the framework for lower forms of government such as member states and regions and *horizontal* coordination where different services of the EU have to make sure that their policies are consistent.
- In the group of vertical instruments the lightest form is coordination, which leaves most freedom to the member states. The EU has developed in cohesion matters an *original form of coordination* that uses the setting of national goals as a function of EU objectives, and the regular reporting of results of the actions by the member states to foster the effectiveness of cohesion policy and the consistency of cohesion policies with other policies such as employment.
- However, there are quite a few cases where this is not sufficient to get

results. Here the EU uses the Community Method that regulates in detail the joint efforts of the EU and the national governments and defines targets, areas of intervention, intensity of support, etc.
- A very strong instrument used by the EU in vertical matters is the *limiting of state aid*. The general constitutional rule forbids such aid, but exceptions are allowed under certain conditions. The EU regulations specify these conditions: the locations (where), the type of projects (who), the type of investment (what) and the amount (how much).
- Another strong vertical instrument is the setting of *standards* that apply through the whole of the EU. Notably in the sphere of social protection a number of such standards have been set, but in general the EU has been very cautious in the use of this instrument. Some attempts have been made to use the instrument for territorial cohesion but these have not resulted in clear EU action.
- In matters of *horizontal coordination* the EU has a bigger problem than national governments. This is related to the fact that much of the decision making is done in specific pillars dominated by sectoral interest. However, overarching objectives have been defined and methods to foster consistency introduced.
- Consequently, there is in general no divergence between stated objectives of the different policies. Actually the support EU cohesion policy instruments give to reach other EU objectives is now well defined and to a certain extent integrated into the total EU policy system.
- The EU cohesion instruments are only a part of a battery of national and Community instruments. All of the former and much of the latter (through the choice of priorities) are actually in the hands of national governments. So much depends, therefore, on the member states to arrive at a balanced result in terms of the various objectives.

Stage IV
Implementing actions and delivering results

9 Implementation and delivery

9.1 Introduction

This chapter deals with the fourth stage of the EU cohesion policy cycle: the actual putting into effect of a policy by deploying financial and regulatory instruments. So this stage is very much about questions of governance. Getting governance right is not easy. Decades of practice with the operations of the SCF have shown that it is even more complicated in the multilevel framework of the EU cohesion policy. The architecture of the system does permit a lot of leeway to national and local actors. This entails the risk of loss of effectiveness due to a distortion of the policy as the agents responsible for the implementation are tempted to use the EU resources for national or local objectives.[1]

In the previous chapter we have described how the EU has tried to cope with some of these problems by elaborating an increasingly detailed regulation of the whole process of its cohesion policy. The member states and all other organizations involved in the SF operations have to comply with these rules. In this chapter we will see in detail how this EU system is elaborated for the implementation stage.[2]

The basis for the analysis in this chapter is different from the ones used in the previous chapters. Whereas the negotiation and regulation needed for the realization of the previous stages of the policy cycle have attracted much attention from both theoretical and empirical academic analysis, the literature on the implementation stage is very scanty. What is available is often specific on particular segments of implementation, in particular the fraud issue. So this chapter is largely based on experience; on the one hand, the experience gained by the EU instances (Commission and Court of Auditors (CoA)) and on the other hand, expertise gathered by practitioners (such as consultants and operators).[3]

The structure of this chapter is as follows.

We will start with the conceptual and theoretical foundations for organizing implementation. We will thereby use again the concept of the policy cycle but adapt it to the aspects that are essential for policy delivery. Next we will detail the conditions that need be fulfilled for institutions to have the capacity to implement effectively the EU cohesion policy.

The conceptual framework thus elaborated will be used as structure for the discussion in the rest of the chapter. This means that we will devote a separate section to each of the stages in the delivery cycle: namely, creating institutions, building partnership, programming actions, managing implementation, monitoring progress and auditing operations. Each of these sections will be structured according to the determinants of institutional capacity: structure, human resources, systems and tools and finally functioning.

The chapter will be rounded off with a short summary of the main findings.

9.2 Theory and concepts

9.2.1 Theory

The theory of implementation deals mainly with the incentives that organizations and individuals require in order to implement correctly the regulations and decisions bestowed upon them from a higher authority.[4] Often this will be in a *principal–agent relationship*. A principal–agent relationship exists between two parties when the latter acts on behalf of the former.

In the EU the relation between the Commission and the national governments has changed over time. In the beginning one got the impression that the policy was rather a bottom-up approach and that the Commission was the agent of the national governments. However, in the present day, the EU cohesion policy has been elaborated in very strict rules and targets. So, as far as implementation is concerned the member states act rather as the agents and the EC as the principal.

The problem in a principal–agent relationship is the agent being more mindful of his own interests than of the interests of his principal. So the question becomes what methods can be used to make sure that the agent executes the tasks delegated to him in a loyal way. In other words, once the SF money starts to flow in, what methods can be used to make sure that member states resist the temptation to use it for their own purposes instead of for the stated EU goals? The principal–agent literature proposes mainly four mechanisms to remedy this problem. An application to the EU cohesion policy (Blom-Hansen, 2005) of each of these methods gives the following results.

Careful choice of agent. By choosing the agent that is most likely to have parallel interest with his principal the risk of non-compliance is limited. Now there is a problem at the EU level in applying this method. As a matter of fact the EU cannot choose its agent. The member state is the natural partner. Other options (as the choice of the direct beneficiary as agent) are ruled out for two reasons. First, legal reasons: the treaties and regulations designate the member state in a central role for implementation. Second, efficiency reasons: opting for beneficiaries as agents would put a very heavy administrative burden on the principal as he would have to deal with a multitude of cases.

Designing the agent's contract. The agent will be inclined to pursue the interests of his principal in case he has himself an interest of doing so. So the contract between the two can be made in such a way as to give the agent incentives to comply. In the private sector, one often sees profit-sharing arrangements. In the public sector other incentives must be relied upon. The most potent ones are economic and administrative incentives.

- Economic incentives are often made in the form of grants. However, in matters of cohesion policy grants cannot be used at the discretion of the EU; the selection of the beneficiaries is part of a programming process in which multi-actor negotiations lead to final choices that leave no room for discretionary incentive grants.
- Administrative incentives operate in a different way. They use specifications of rules that guide the choices of projects and of the partners involved. The more the partners are likely to have similar interest with the principal the higher the chances of compliance. However, the EU is not the final decision maker; it is the member state and the region that decide on the choice of projects. There is no way for the EU to impose its preferred partners in preferred projects.

Monitoring the agent. There are two types of monitoring devices. The first one, colloquially called 'police patrol oversight' is characterized as centralized, ongoing, thorough and systematic. It consists mainly in reporting, evaluation and auditing. The costs of this type of monitoring are high. The second one is called 'fire alarm oversight'. It requires less involvement of the principal; it relies on third parties to signal deviations from the contract and even to challenge the agent's decisions. The EU uses both types of device. The main ones will be discussed in later sections of this chapter. They consist essentially of first-type measures such as the setting of detailed requirements on reporting, evaluation and audit and second-type measures such as empowering multiple stakeholders to participate in the programming and monitoring of the policy.

Sanctioning agency drift. The monitoring device induces compliance on the part of the agent because it makes the effects of his actions visible. It supposes that the fear for a loss of good reputation will bring compliance. However, in many cases stronger methods are needed to make an agent comply. The most common one is sanctions. Sanctions can take various forms. The most important one is the withdrawal of support. This is a road that is difficult to take in the case of the EU as allocations of money are made in the process of a multi-annual multinational bargaining. Renegotiations of this type are not likely to lead in time to an agreement that will compel the agent to change his behaviour. However, a more direct sanction exists in case there is a clear break of the rules (abuse of funds and/or sheer fraud). Here, the EU can withdraw the support promised (that is, not pay out the funds committed).

So the conclusion of these theoretical exercises is that the options of the EU are limited. The first one cannot be applied. Indeed the EU is not free to choose its agents. The second one is of limited value; there are no direct incentives that can be used by the EU to induce the agent to comply. However, the EC can exert quite some influence in the negotiation stage of the programming documents (see section 9.5.4). The other two instruments have serious drawbacks. Effectiveness of the in-course mechanism (the monitoring device) comes at a very high cost. The application of the ex-post mechanism (sanction device) is limited to a specific field (fraud) which reduces its effectiveness. So theory suggests that the EU has to use, to the maximum, the monitoring device notwithstanding its drawbacks.

9.2.2 The policy cycle

In Chapter 1 we have given the essential characteristics of each stage in the policy cycle from the systemic perspective. In the practical delivery of the policy another cycle can be identified. This delivery cycle is characterized by a shorter periodicity and a higher level of specification. The essential features of the delivery cycle were introduced during the 1988 reforms that revolutionized the EU cohesion policy and the operations of the SF (e.g. Bailey and de Propris, 2002). The delivery system has since gradually been improved, the relevant regulations have become increasingly specific. It shapes and sometimes constrains the day-to-day practice of all involved in the implementation of the EU cohesion policy.

The characteristics of the two cycles are given in Table 9.1 (stages in the rows; type of cycle in the column).

The 'implementation and delivery' cycle starts with the creation of institutions; the assignment of tasks to each of these institutions and the building up of the necessary capacity in these institutions. The next stage is the programming of actions, consisting of several tasks. First, it concerns a specification of the most pressing problems (including actions that correspond to the first stage of the systems cycle). Next, it concerns the (support to the) elaboration of a series of concrete projects that can remedy these problems. Moreover, it concerns the prioritization and approval of these projects. In practice the stages of programming and implementation often run parallel. The MA is appointed and starts programming; the intermediate bodies (IBs) are appointed and start work on the priority axes. In the following stage the projects are implemented. In the last stages of the implementation and delivery cycle, progress is monitored, beneficiaries are paid, results are evaluated and lessons are drawn from experience. These lessons are finally conveyed to those responsible for the design of new projects.

In the following sections we will detail the various stages. The list, as given in the right-hand column of Table 9.1, will thereby be adapted on several points. On the one hand, we have singled out two aspects from the general description of the stages. First, partnership, because it is an important EU principle (see Chapter 6). Next, financial management and control, because these are essential prerequisites for the correct spending of EU resources. On the other hand, we will not deal with evaluation in this chapter as it is the subject of the next chapter.

9.2.3 Institutional and administrative requirements

In the past the need for a cohesion policy has been increasingly felt. On the EU level there was little or no experience that could guide the putting into effect of the stated policy. So the management, implementation and delivery were factors

Table 9.1 Main characteristics of the stages of the policy cycle on the systemic and delivery level

Stage	System	Implementation and delivery
1 Identify problems	Measure tendencies in disparities	
2 Design intervention system	Define legal and financial instruments Assign responsibilities to layers of authority	*Create institutions* Define roles of administrations and project beneficiaries Adapt institutions and reinforce administrative, management and control systems *Build partnerships*
3 Select objectives and instruments	Define major priorities Designate eligible areas Limit levels of national support Prioritize other EU policy objectives Agree on CSG and NSRFs	*Programme actions* Identify strengths, weaknesses, opportunities, threats (SWOT) Define concrete targets in terms of improvement of accessibility, creation of number of jobs, etc. Agree on operational development programmes Detail these in terms of projects Prioritize these projects
4 Implement actions	Set delivery principles	*Manage implementation* Make calls for proposals, select best ones, contract projects (such as the building of roads, the creation of training centres), facilitate procedures, give technical and administrative support
5 Check (monitor) progress and (evaluate) effectiveness and consistency	Check appropriateness, effectiveness and efficiency Check synergies with other EU policies	*Monitor progress* Monitor inputs and outputs *Evaluate* outcomes and outputs Check consistency with other EU, national (e.g. sectoral), regional and urban policies *Manage and control finances* Make financial transfers and audit spending Pay contractors Audit payments made
6 Draw lessons	Identify flaws in the system Redefine objectives Adapt roles of different partners Go for more concentration	Identify what works in practice and what does not work Reorient interventions to better instruments Check adequacy for new targets
Dealt with in:	Other chapters	This chapter

Source: Own elaboration by author

that have not received very much attention. It has only been when specific problems occurred that the EU has started to think seriously about this subject.[5] Many of the deficiencies in the implementation system that became visible in the past have been remedied in the meantime. A few persist. Moreover, new problems have occurred as new member states with little experience and weak structures have now entered the SCF scene. The EU has defined, in an ever more elaborate way (and with stricter requirements as to quality), the main elements that it wants to see in place.

For many member states it has proved difficult to come up to these increased requirements. Yet they are obliged to because non-compliance means that allocated funds are not disbursed. So many member states have had to reinforce their institutions and administrative systems to make sure they do receive the money available. In EU jargon, they have to improve their administrative absorption capacity.

Absorption capacity can be defined as the extent to which a member state is able to fully spend the allocated financial resources from the SCF in an effective and efficient way.[6] *Administrative absorption capacity* can be defined as the ability and skills of central, regional and local authorities and the (potential) applicants and beneficiary organizations to work together to complete efficiently the whole cycle. This implies: to design policies; to prepare acceptable plans, programmes and projects in due time; to decide on programmes and projects; to arrange coordination among the various partners; to cope with the vast amount of administrative and reporting work required by the Commission; to finance and supervise implementation properly, administer all processes transparently and accountably (avoiding irregularities as far as possible); and finally to monitor and evaluate the performance.

The measurement of the absorption capacity in general and of administrative absorption capacity in particular is not easy.[7] The criteria on which one can base such measurement are implicit in the definition given above. We have made them more explicit by detailing the following three features (NEI/ECORYS, 2002):

1 *Structure.* Clear assignment of responsibilities and tasks to all agencies and institutions involved at all stages of the delivery cycle.
2 *Human resources (HR).* Securing the timely availability of experienced, skilled and motivated staff that is assigned to each task with a clear job description and getting an adequate remuneration. For the filling of vacancies a good recruitment system needs to be available.
3 *Systems and tools.* Functioning instruments, methods, guidelines, manuals, procedures, software, etc. These enable organizations to transform tacit and implicit knowledge into explicit knowledge that can be shared within and across organizations. They make organizations less vulnerable and reduce the risk of malfunctioning.

The elements specified here form together only the basis for a high administrative capacity. However, even the best people using the best tool in a state-of-the-art workshop will by itself not deliver quality results. On the contrary, the smooth functioning is dependent on the way the process is managed. Given the importance of this factor we will devote some attention to this aspect as well.

The determinants of the administrative absorption capacity (described in this section) can be detailed for each of the stages of the implementation and delivery cycle as described in the previous section. This will be done in the following sections.

9.3 Creating institutions

9.3.1 Structure: assigning responsibilities

In matters of implementation the EC has no direct involvement. It has delegated frontline implementation to national and local agencies. These have, in turn, charged final beneficiaries with the delivery of the results of projects. The EC supervises and controls the process through detailed regulations. The EU prescribes in these regulations the roles of a series of institutions at the different stages of the implementation and delivery policy cycle (see Table 9.2). The main institutions that have to exist (Reg. 1083/2006, Art. 59) are a Managing Authority (MA), a Certifying Authority (CA, formerly the Paying Authority) and an Audit Authority (AA).[8] The member states, in practice the MA, may designate one or more IBs to carry out some or all of the tasks of the MA and CA. MAs may also choose to fulfil all these tasks themselves. Managing authorities can exist at two levels, at the aggregate level (MA NSRF) and at the operational level (MA OP). The responsibilities of each of these organizations and their functioning will be discussed in detail in the following sections.

These organizations need to exist for each OP (see sections 8.3.4 and 9.5.3). The same authority may be designated for more than one OP. In case institutions exist that can assume one of these functions national governments can entrust them with the relevant responsibility; in case there are no institutions qualifying for this role they have to be created.

9.3.2 Human resources

In the more developed member states the mobilization of qualified staff for the implementation and delivery of the EU cohesion policy does not pose particular problems. However, the same is far from true in the NMSs. The main problem is the insufficiency of incentives for good staff to join and stay in the public sector. Pay is often low and career advancements are often based on length of service rather than on performance. The lack of a civil service offering a variety of careers and the increasing politicization of nominations of senior staff are also developments that tend to hamper the administrative capacity of countries, in particular the NMSs (World Bank, 2006).

In most countries capacity-building initiatives are underway. Moreover, there will be a learning effect, as in the course of the present programme period, new experience will be gained and confidence in internal capacity will be built up.

Table 9.2 Responsibilities and tasks of major institutions involved in the implementation*

	NSRF MA	OP MA	IB	MC	CA	AA
Creating institutions						
Appointing and organizing the IB	R	R				
Organize monitoring committees	R	R				
Setting up a management information system	R	R	x	R	R	R
Preparation of management guidelines/job aids	R	x	x	R	R	R
Training of staff	R	R	R	R	R	R
Building partnerships						
NSRF	R	x	R			
OP	R	R	R			
Programming actions						
NSRF	R	x				
OP	x	R	R			
Managing implementation						
Creation of a project pipeline		x	R			
Assistance and information to applicants	R		R			
Setting up a financial and statistical information system	R	R	R	R		x
Check on compliance with community policies	R	R	R	R	R	x
Ensure correctness of operations	R	R	R	R	R	R
Make adjustments to the programme	x	R	R	R		
Annual implementation report	x	R	R	R		
Monitoring progress						
Monitoring operations, reporting and corrective actions on operations		x	R	R		
Monitoring priority NSRFs, reporting and corrective actions	R	x	R	R	x	x
Monitoring measures/priorities OPs, reporting and corrective actions		x	R	R	x	x
Financial management and control						
Certification of expenditure and control		x	x		R	
Payments		R	R		R	
Internal audit	R	R	R		R	R
Full audit					R	R

Note:
R: responsible; x: contributing
* The table gives only an overview of the main responsibilities of the bodies at the central level. The table represents the most common situation. Slight deviations from this common division of tasks and responsibilities are possible for individual member states

Source: Updated, adapted and complemented from NEI/ECORYS (2002)

Several cases in the NMSs show that it is indeed possible to improve significantly the HR capacity over a relatively short period.

In many of the NMSs, capacity deficiencies are addressed by a systematic recourse to external technical assistance (TA). TA teams are often led by experts from the old member states. This approach has the obvious advantage to solve in the short term the capacity problem. However, only in those cases where a real transfer of expertise has been realized does the TA also provide a long-term solution.

9.3.3 Systems and tools

Organizations need reliable systems of management and control. Each member state has developed in its history such systems on the national and regional level. These do, in general, also organize relations with third parties such as agencies and contractors.

However, the practice has shown that the national systems do not always provide adequate tools for the smooth delivery of policy in general and of the policies supported by the SCFs in particular. In the NMSs policy management systems are new and vulnerable and innovations (such as the e-government system in Estonia) have still to prove their effectiveness. Weaknesses exist as to legal provisions for such basic things as public procurement, expropriation of land and the issuing of construction permits (e.g. for a transport infrastructure project). Relevant national legislation has only been established recently and the staff of the organizations involved lack proficiency with the new rules and systems. The same is true for the judicial system to adjudicate disputes.

9.3.4 Functioning: the need for institutional strengthening

The importance of creating an institutional environment for the catching-up countries cannot be underestimated. Indeed, the efficiency and integrity of the public administration and the quality of the governance structures are essential prerequisites for growth.[9] This also holds for the institutions that have to deliver the cohesion policy and administer the SCF.[10]

The regulatory framework of the EU puts a very heavy burden on all concerned. The old member states have been able to adapt relatively smoothly to the EU exigencies due to the versatility of their highly developed administrative systems. For the NMSs the situation is radically different. They were all (and many still are) confronted with very large problems of economic, social and territorial cohesion. The policies that used to be applied in the past are completely inadequate under the present circumstances and so are the legal regulations and administrative practices that supported them. After the demise of communist governments of the NMSs there has been hesitation as to the choice of the type of policies and administration (e.g. Gorzelak and Kuklinski, 1992; Keune, 1998). Much of this hesitation has been taken away by the decision to join the EU.

Indeed, the EU has set as a criterion for accepting new members to the club that they adopt the whole 'acquis communautaire', including all the regulations that apply to the SCF. For the NMSs this provided a clear framework for the devising of new cohesion policies in their countries. However, given on the one hand, the starting point of the NMSs (transition) and on the other hand the intricacies of the EU system, the building up of the necessary institutional and administrative capacity has been a heroic task to accomplish. In the recent past much progress has been made but the administrative capacity to deal with the SCF is still a matter of concern as it may impede the absorption capacity of the countries in question and thereby the speed of their catching up with the EU average.

Evaluations of the different national situations[11] show on the one hand that the administrative absorption capacity of the NMSs has much improved; and on the other hand that further improvement is very much needed in order to come up to the EU requirements. In order to support this improvement, the new regulations have created a facility to strengthen administrative capacity. This should provide the NMSs with an incentive to invest in the professionalization and modernization of public management systems.

The public institutions mentioned here are not the only ones involved. The end user (or final beneficiary) is often a semi-public or private body. In many of the NMSs such organizations are non-existent; in all member states they are often weak. This implies very high demands on central public bodies. They have either to do the work themselves or in the case of poorly performing final beneficiaries have to put up extra effort in terms of support to their staff, of ironing out the effects of misunderstandings and the improvement of documentation and reporting.

9.4 Building partnerships

9.4.1 Structure: assignment of responsibilities

The good functioning of the economy is dependent on the quality of its institutions. We recall (see Chapter 6) that in matters of cohesion the EU shares responsibility with member states and with local authorities. The EU has worked out the notion of multilevel governance in the *principle of partnership*.[12]

Partnership is a set of rules and procedures that prescribe that civil servants of the EC, national governments and regional authorities together with representatives of private and third sector (among them local business, labour unions and social action groups) collaborate closely and continuously in the design, implementation and evaluation of EU-funded programmes.[13]

The advantages of the application of the partnership principle are that it mobilizes the available expertise and the various forces and interests around a common programme. By creating ownership of the programme by those directly concerned, conditions are created that are conducive to the best possible use of public money and hence effectiveness.

The partnership approach does not imply that everybody involved does have the same type of responsibility. There is a certain division of tasks with differences in responsibility for the various actors. We may describe the various responsibilities along each stage of the cycle as follows (see also Chapters 6 and 8):

- *EC.* In the programming stage the Commission puts forward its Strategic Guidelines (SG). She then negotiates and approves the development programmes proposed by the member states. She participates in the intergovernmental negotiations for the framework; she proposes solutions and compromises in case there are stalemates between different government levels; she allocates the credits, etc. The Commission also has a role of expert; she proposes changes and improvements in the institutional set up and delivery systems of the member states and the various beneficiaries. During the implementation stage she studies the monitoring and evaluation made, pays the expenditures that have been authorized, verifies the quality of the control and auditing systems in place and finally proposes changes on the basis of the evaluation of the results obtained.
- *Member states and regions* have the responsibility to propose the programmes, to set up the institutions to implement them, to select and prioritize projects, to evaluate results, etc. This is to be done in cooperation with third parties and with the responsible project managers (final beneficiaries). Every country has within the broad framework of the EU regulations a considerable degree of freedom to give form and substance to this responsibility. This applies notably to a delegation to regional and urban authorities.
- *Direct addressees of the policy.* In the implementation and delivery cycle the final beneficiaries (often the organization that carries out the project) have a critical role; they propose concrete projects, execute them, receive the funds made available and provide the information for monitoring and control. These beneficiary organizations are as varied as there are detailed targets.

The actors listed above can be regrouped in two functionally and compositionally different communities:

1. *Programming and managing community*, which includes the governmental institutions at different levels. They prepare and negotiate the programmes in collaboration with the EC. They carry out the programming and mobilization of national and EU funds and do the monitoring and auditing of expenses. This group of agents deals mainly with implementation.
2. *Development community*, which includes the local and regional actors in development (the final beneficiaries of the financial support). They identify needs and priorities, prepare a project pipeline and implement the approved projects. This group of agents deals mainly with delivery.

The different roles of these communities are given in Figure 9.1. It shows the relation between these communities and the programme and project levels (described in section 6.8), the partners involved and the role in the implementation and delivery process (described in the later sections of this chapter).

The EU does not impose a particular model; it leaves the member state considerable leeway to make the appropriate institutional arrangements that fit best into its total institutional architecture and to choose the type of organizations in the public, semi-public and private sectors with which it wants to conclude

```
    Programmes                    Projects
┌──────────────────┐         ┌──────────────────┐
│  Programming and │         │                  │
│     managing     │  ═════▶ │   Development    │
│    community     │         │    community     │
└──────────────────┘         └──────────────────┘
   Implementation                   Delivery
```

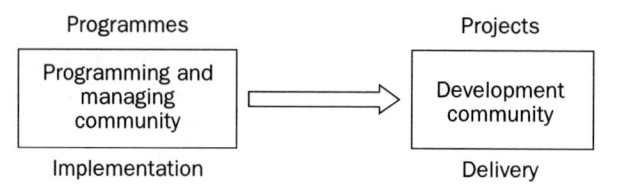

Figure 9.1 Role of the different actors in the absorption of the SCF
Source: Adapted from: UNDP (2004)

partnerships. However, using the leverage of the SF the Commission has had quite some influence on national institutional choices. Indeed, in countries where subsidiarity had not been much of an issue and where many decisions were taken by central government EU cohesion policy has been a factor for stimulating devolution. Countries with very weak sub-national government structures (such as Italy) have been induced to empower the latter better (Lion et al., 2004).[14] For the NMSs the situation has been confused for some time. Initially the EU has put some pressure on the accession countries to come to formal regionalization but after some time has accepted, for efficiency reasons, more flexible solutions with a strong involvement of the central government (Hughes et al., 2004). So, in all member states, old and new, specific institutional forms have been adopted that meet the objectives of the EU cohesion policy,[15] respect the EU demands as to the organization of the delivery system and make optimal use of the national situation (Heinelt and Smith, 1996; Artner, 2005).

9.4.2 Human resources involved

The deliberate choice for partnering combined with the strict EU regulations about functioning makes the EU cohesion policy very demanding in terms of human resources. We will give some examples in later sections but we will try here to make a rough estimation as to the overall picture.

- *EC.* Several DGs share the responsibility for the EU cohesion policy: DG Regio, DG Employment and (in the accession stage) DG Enlargement. To evaluate total human resources involved we cannot just add up their total number of staff. On the one hand, we need to deduct some as not all their staff is deployed for dealing with the devising and implementation of the policy in a full time way. On the other hand, we need to add to this number staff Commissioning work in the delegations in the different national capitals and who deal with the various aspects of the implementation of the cohesion policy. One might also add part of the staff that is involved in the coordination of cohesion policy with other policies. The total EC staff involved can be roughly estimated at some 2,000 persons.
- *National, regional and local governments.* In each of them a certain number of persons are directly occupied with the various stages of the cohesion policy cycle. To the ones that work in the country itself we have to add those that are involved in the representation of the countries and regions in Brussels.

Indeed, all national administrations traditionally have their permanent representatives in Brussels, who deal with cohesion during the stages of negotiation in the Council of Ministers. Moreover, many regions and even local authorities have established offices in Brussels that act as embassies.[16] They lobby with the Commission and Parliament; they gather information about possible policy changes and relate with other networks. Much of this activity is actually focused on the obtaining or maintaining of entitlements for funding from the SF. In the following sections we give an idea of the number of persons involved in typical member countries in the cohesion policy cycle. On the basis of a grossing up of the figures contained there, we may estimate the number involved at least at 10,000 persons.[17]

- *Private and third sector.* Each programme is composed of projects for which organizations take responsibility; they have to prepare the applications, implement the project and report on progress and results. Of course given the multitude and diversity of projects any estimate would be very inaccurate.

9.4.3 Systems and tools

The creation and functioning of partnerships is not facilitated by a specific set of tools and systems. There exists a very large diversity of forms. Indeed, each country uses its own legal and administrative framework. Even within a member country much diversity exists as different ministries tend to have different sets of procedures.

Relations between partners of the public sector are governed by public law and administrative procedures. Contracts between partners are therefore often of the type of any public finance agreement. Contracts between the private partners (often the final beneficiary) and public partners are governed by the public procurement laws of the country in question; these are in turn subject to EU regulation (e.g. on public tenders).

9.4.4 Functioning

The minimum form of partnership is that of consultation: asking stakeholders for their opinion on draft programmes. However, consultation alone is not very likely to yield real ownership among the relevant stakeholders, especially if there is no strong tradition of policy development on a partnership basis. So real cooperation is needed, which involves the active participation of stakeholders in identifying problems, in defining solutions and in setting priorities.

The application of the partnership principle has many advantages. The most important one is the commitment of parties to the end result, which is bound to improve the effectiveness of the efforts of all concerned. However, the enumeration of the variety of organizations and the number of people involved makes clear that this set up has in practice much difficulty of functioning efficiently. This cumbersome functioning of the EU cohesion policy engenders three types of disadvantages:

1 The lack of clarity in the division of roles, responsibilities and decision taking power engenders high cost of coordination: both vertically (e.g. between regions, country and EU) and also horizontally (e.g. bilateral cross-border coordination of regions). Many discussions tend to be long wielding in the absence of a clear decision maker (formerly the national state) and the emergence of rival arbitrators (national state and Commission).
2 The partnership principle may be felt as a top-down, normative and bureaucratic requirement rather than a system that needs to take care of the complexity of roles in the mobilization of potential. Moreover, it may lead to the establishment of parallel structures that compete rather than cooperate with existing structures.
3 The involvement of many local actors makes the set up vulnerable to clientelism and corruption.

9.5 Programming actions

9.5.1 Structure: assignment of responsibilities

As we have seen in the previous chapters the EU cohesion policy addresses major structural problems. The actions thus need to be put into a long-term policy perspective. As a consequence the EU has adopted a multi-annual programming approach. It imposes this approach on all those who want to benefit from the SCF.

The responsibility for programming is entrusted to a MA. Although created principally for the implementation stage, it is only logical that the MA is also made primarily responsible for the programming stage, given the strong interrelations between the two functions. Most of the principal beneficiary countries of the EU cohesion policy have indeed chosen this option. However, depending on the national situation, a number of other organizations take (part of) the responsibility too. This involves on the one side IBs, that provide essential information on the projects that have sufficiently matured for inclusion in the programming. It involves on the other side national ministries that often take a coordinating role.[18]

9.5.2 Human resources

The whole process of programming is very labour intensive. It can take up to a year and a half to draft a programme, depending on the number and type of partners involved. A rough estimate from Germany is that some six people are on average involved in programming in each MA. In Spain, at least two people in each MA and IB were involved in the programming activities. It is the experience that programming is a task that should be started in time; especially, the preparations for the higher level plans tend to take a lot of time. This of course adds to the total number of man hours involved in this stage of the cycle.

9.5.3 Systems and tools

We recall here the standard instruments created by the EU (introduced already in sections 8.3.2–4) for the programming of the EU and national efforts in matters of cohesion policy (and synergy with other policies):

- The *CSG* has to transpose the priorities of the Community into actions to be supported by the SF.
- The *NSRF* presents the priorities of the member state for cohesion policy for the period 2007–13. (It replaces a series of instruments; see Annex 9.1.) It ensures that assistance from the SCF is consistent with the CSG and identifies the link between Community priorities on the one hand and the national reform programme[19] on the other.
- The *OP* set out the development strategy with a coherent set of priorities to be carried out with the aid of the SCF. Each programme is concerned with one objective only and receives financing from only one of the SFs.[20]

The EU regulations require that a programme shall contain: a statement of the strategy and priorities for joint Community and national action, a summary of the measures (fields of intervention in the new EU jargon) for the implementation of the priorities (priority axis in the new EU jargon), the types of final beneficiary (groups of operations), a description of the involvement of social and regional partners, a financing plan for each measure (the financial resources and the forms of assistance), the results of an ex ante evaluation, a plan to make the programme public and finally, arrangements made to make electronic data exchange with the Commission possible. The major components of this process are detailed further in Box 9.1.

The general notions for programming as defined by the EU (and concretized in an EU manual for negotiation and implementing programmes) are often refined in national guidelines and manuals for those involved in programming. They help to smooth the process by limiting the uncertainties among partners and by facilitating the transmission of good practices from one person to another.

Box 9.1 Major components of the programming process

A good programming contains the following stages:

Analysis of the socio-economic and environmental situation. This is often in the form of a SWOT analysis of the strengths (S) weaknesses (W) of the area in question and the opportunities (O) and threats (T) it is confronted with. One of the most difficult exercises is to reconcile the outcomes of a socio-economic or SWOT analysis with (sometimes politically pre-fixed) programming partners' ideas, wishes and shopping lists.[21]

Reliable indicators. Specifying the objectives by the formulation of usable, measurable and meaningful indicators, their subsequent quantification and their mutual consistency in the overall framework has proven to be hard work. Yet, it is essential to the proper fixing of priorities and eventually for the measurement of the output and the confrontation of realized with expected results during the ex post evaluation.

Project proposals. Organizations thinking of proposing a project often find it difficult both to judge whether their idea would qualify for support and to meet the administrative and financial requirements.[22] In countries that have a long-standing experience with the SF support structures have been created that help to mobilize good ideas for projects and to format correctly their application for support. In the NMSs an effort is still needed to make improvements on these scores.

Project selection. The selection is done on the basis of published criteria. Some of these criteria are valid for all OPs, the rest is determined specifically for individual OPs. They are in general derived from general principles, such as effectiveness, relevance, efficiency and utility or from the principles of other EU policies such as equal opportunities and sustainability. The concrete procedure for the selection of projects is generally laid down in the guidelines. For specific types of projects (e.g. infrastructure) special steering committees exist with members from the responsible departments of both MAs and IBs deciding about project proposals. There are sometimes working groups on the level of the ministries and subordinated bodies who pre-select projects (e.g. infrastructure). A trend can be discerned towards introducing a larger degree of competition between project applications. The selection criteria play an important role in this respect. The queue-based grant approval systems are gradually being replaced by processes in which potential projects compete on the basis of clear criteria.

Financial cost estimates and financing plans. The programme budget on each priority axis needs to contain an estimate of the total cost. The way these costs will be covered is a matter of negotiation between different partners. We recall (see section 7.5.5) that the EU principle of additionality implies the need for co-financing. In countries with a high degree of fiscal decentralization the regional and local authorities can mobilize such funds from their regular budgets. In countries where these structures are weak such co-financing has to come from the national budget. In some countries (e.g. Bulgaria) a Fund has been created to facilitate such co-financing.

Ex ante evaluation. The likely effects of the programme (and if possible of its constituent parts) need to be established before deciding on the final content of the programme. During the last programming round (for the 2000–06 programmes), each of the member states has built up experience with an interactive ex ante evaluation. This meant that in some cases there were two (groups of) external parties working with the public programming partners: one (assisting) in the drafting of the programme itself and one in the ex ante evaluation. The ex ante evaluation is supposed to assess the connection between analysis and strategy, the quantification of indicators, the estimation of the impact the programme can be expected to

> have, as well as the arrangements made for management and implementation. Due to the fact that the evaluation is interactive, meaning that the evaluator's feedback is received continuously and can be used to steer the programming process, it takes more time and effort than previously. Generally, the experience with interactive evaluation is positive, provided that it is not regarded as just another official requirement without any practical use.

9.5.4 Functioning

There are in theory two ways to organize the programming process:

1   *Bottom-up*. It has the advantage that true partnership is organized in an early stage and that the programme is more likely to reflect the real needs of the sector, region or country.
2   *Top-down*. The advantages are a better overall coherence of the programme and the adequacy of the measures and priorities to reach the programme's global objective.

In practice the process is very much embedded in the constitutional (FED or not), legal and administrative organization of the member country. The predecessors of the NSRFs were normally top-down exercises, beginning with the heavy and tough work of preparing a National Development Plan (NDP). Under the supervision and coordination of one ministry all technical staff of the ministries and of the regions have been usually involved in preparing these documents. Drafting the documents (including many OPs) has been carried out under the direct supervision of top-level staff.

The programming process has often been hampered by lack of timely elaboration of strategic documents, lack of specificity of policy goals, uncertainty about eligible partners, etc. A particular difficult problem is the attitude of the staff to be active development agents rather than passive administrators. However, as experience is gathered with the practice of the programming process, most of these problems tend to be overcome.

Negotiations with the Commission involved principally top-level managers of the OPs and political representatives of each ministry associated to each OP, always with the strong involvement of the coordinating ministry. These negotiations over the final content of the programme are one of the essential devices the EC uses to safeguard conformity of the concrete projects with EU priorities and to avoid any drift on the part of the beneficiaries to use the EU funds for purposes that have only a strong national or local relevance. In practice the EC exerts a strong influence at this stage by requiring adaptations on the details of both strategic and operational elements of the programme. The second device that plays an equally important role is the ex ante checking by the EC of the application of the principle of additionality for actions under the convergence objective. It has to safeguard that EU money is not merely used for substituting national money but will really be used as an additional resource devoted to speed up the required processes and to realize projects of larger scale or better quality.

External institutes and consultants were often invited to draft or organize the drafting of the strategic part of the programmes. In some cases, this only concerned the execution of a socio-economic or SWOT analysis. In other cases, even the elaboration of the whole document has been contracted out. Intensive discussions among relevant institutions within and outside the responsible ministries are therefore a necessary step in writing an OP. Nevertheless, the final drafting of the OP is the core competence of the public sector itself, in practice of the ministries.

9.6 Managing implementation

9.6.1 Structure: the role of the MA

The administrative structure of implementing the actions (co-)financed by the SF is very complicated. In general the authorities of the member states and the regions ensure the implementation of the programmes. This is very concrete work that involves making sure roads are built, people are trained, etc. Member states appoint a MA for each operational programme. We have seen in the previous section that they are often also made responsible for programming. However, their main task (Reg. 1083/2006, Art. 60) is (as their name suggests) the management of the programme, which means making things happen.

In particular these responsibilities (functions) refer to:

- selection of projects; development of a project pipeline;
- ensuring that the co-financed products and services are delivered;
- establishing proper computerized systems and procedures for recording each operation (project) permitting to deliver reliable data necessary for financial management, monitoring, verifications, audits and evaluation;
- guiding the work of the Monitoring Committee (MC) and providing it with the documents and the information it requires to execute effectively its tasks;
- evaluation and checking the effectiveness of the programme (including collection of statistical and financial data);
- ensuring that the CA receives all necessary information on the procedures and verifications carried out in relation to expenditure (permitting to check the correctness of operations financed under the assistance);
- preparing and transmitting to the Commission of annual and final reports on implementation and of information to appraise major projects.

These responsibilities are shared between the MA of the NSRF, the MAs of the OPs and related bodies. The MA responsible for the NSRF MA keeps the final responsibility. The responsible MA has to ensure that only those operations are selected for funding that are in accordance with the criteria applicable to the

OP and that they comply with applicable EU and national rules for the whole of the implementation period (Reg. 1083/2006, Art. 60).

9.6.2 Structure: delegation to IBs

The organization of the implementation of SF operations is firmly rooted in national, regional or local administrative structures and planning traditions. The organization is, moreover, shaped by the balance of power and the size of the country. So, every country has set up a tailor-made structure and no uniform concept regarding the delegation of tasks by MAs has as yet emerged.

However, in most countries the larger part of the implementation process is delegated to IBs. The number of IBs per OP can exceed ten and there can be hundreds of IBs in the (larger) member states. However, in many cases the number of IBs is more limited; in the smaller countries there is just one or a few IBs per OP. Implementation of the SF is in many cases only a part of the daily tasks of these IBs. In addition to various agencies and bodies, ministries can also be involved as intermediate bodies. The existence of implementing ministries or departments often coincides with a 'multi-tier' implementation system in which tasks are delegated further by such a 'first level' IB to 'second level' IB. In many cases staff members of the IBs are also involved in other duties, and there is not always a specific separation of EU-specific tasks. This has the disadvantage that it tends to blur responsibilities. However, it has the advantage that by integrating the SF practice in everyday regular work and tasks at the level of IBs, the project pipeline will be more easily started up.

The lower-level IBs are the first recipients of applications and the first level at which compliance with eligibility rules is analysed and improved. They are in charge of defining the content of measures and of developing project pipelines, since they are closer to the final beneficiaries and are supposed to know best the main problems and needs to be solved. They are also responsible for the different tasks ranging from selection, contracting, monitoring and evaluation of co-financed projects to the production of certifications of expenditure and six-monthly and annual performance reports.

The IBs are often not purpose built but are established as a special unit within an existing organization. The type of organization chosen depends much on the administrative tradition and policy structure of the recipient country (see Box 9.2).

Box 9.2 What type of organizations act as IBs?

One of the most difficult discussions in programming concerns the co-existence and reconciliation of regional and sectoral angles. The guiding rule should be that those issues that are priorities from a national development point of view be dealt with in Sectoral Development Programmes (SDPs) and those that are sub-national in nature (e.g. those that are a priority only for certain regions) in Regional Development Programmes (RDPs).

RDPs play a more important role in some larger member states with established competences at the regional level, such as Germany and Spain.

> These regional competences are also required for identifying co-financing from regional budgets. In smaller member states and in countries with weak or young regional governments (such as Ireland, Portugal and Bulgaria) finding regional co-financing has been more burdensome. Here the role of the RPDs is less and the role of SDPs more important.
>
> For SDPs, the choice of IBs falls often on national development agencies, foreign investment agencies, tourism agencies and development banks. RDPs can have as IBs: municipalities, associations of municipalities and civil society organizations such as regional development agencies, development associations and other non-profit organizations. In some cases a special unit within (or associated to) a regional self-governing body assumes this role.

9.6.3 HR

The staffing of MAs is perhaps one of the most central issues in the Management of the funds. Numbers of staff vary widely from one MA to the other, depending on the type of programmes and the delegation of tasks. A minimum of some five and a maximum of some 13 dedicated staff are commonly required for carrying out the key tasks of OPs. However, numbers of MAs involved in the implementation of programmes can be considerably higher (up to almost 100 staff for the Portuguese OP on Education for the previous programming period), especially when it concerns labour-intensive operations (e.g. ESF-supported projects). Due to its nature, the management of the CF tends to be less laborious.

Analysing projects and candidatures is a time consuming task, making a large claim on resources. For example, a little under 100 people work for the ESF-pipeline in just one of the German federal states. But the actual number of human resources needed to implement projects co-financed by SF depends much on the type of projects they manage. Across the board, one IB staff member manages €4 million SF every year. However, at a more detailed level, large variation exists among the types of measures concerned. Staffing requirements are relatively modest in the fields of infrastructure (roughly €15 million per staff member), moderate in the case of business support (about €4 million per staff member), and high in human resource development or small-scale forms of support (up to €0.1 million per staff member for the latter). Bodies responsible for the implementation of activities related to SME support schemes, vocational training or agricultural grants need the highest level of human resources. This means that not only the funding level but also the number of projects appears to be determining staffing requirements.

9.6.4 Systems and tools: the project

The building stones of the SF structure are the individual projects. Projects come in very different forms and are proposed, implemented and delivered by a large variety of organizations. Here, we give some examples of objectives and of typical projects to realize that objective and of the responsible organizations (final beneficiaries).

- Improve *transport*. The project involves, for example, the building of a road or a bridge. The project can come under the responsibility of a public organization in charge of the transport infrastructure. In case the projects are small the final beneficiary may be a local community, for major projects the central government may assume a strong involvement (see Box 9.3).
- Enhance the *innovative capacity* of the regional industry. The organization responsible for it may be a special-purpose (semi-public) agency that organizes the interest of the private sector (sometimes represented by business organizations or chambers of commerce), semi-public bodies like universities and R&D centres and other bodies, such as specialized consultants (see, for example, Box 7.5).
- Create *jobs* through the renewal of the industrial base of a backward or a restructuring region. Private firms may be responsible for a project to realize certain capital investments (see, for example, Boxes 7.6 and 7.7).
- Promote *social inclusion*. Here charity organizations can take the lead to improve the chances of finding jobs for deprived groups, for instance, through the training of basic (social) skills (see, for example, Box 8.1).
- Promote *professional skills* for employees, unemployed and entrepreneurs to be ready for the challenges of new competitive activities (see Box 9.4).

Box 9.3 The improvement of the River Danube as a main transport axis

The NMSs are likely to show a fast economic growth in the near future. That will entail an even faster growth in transport. The EU wants this growth to be channelled, as much as possible, to environment-friendly modes, such as inland waterway transport. However, the development of this type of transport in the NMSs is hampered by a deficient infrastructure. This is even the case for the most obvious natural waterway: the Danube. Its navigability is poor due to factors of a very different character: natural (sand banks, water supply), political (Serbia) and institutional (Danube Commission[23]).

The EU has decided that the improvement of the Danube should be part of the priority TEN (see Chapter 11). The government of Romania is planning to make (in coordination with the other riparian country Bulgaria) considerable investments to enhance navigability. An ex ante evaluation of the project showed that it is advisable to adopt a staged approach whereby the least available depth of the river will be gradually increased so as to be able to accommodate larger ships and ensure accessibility and reliability during the dry season.

Moreover, this infrastructural improvement will not lead to increased internal waterway transport if not combined with a substantial (approximately €200 millions) investment programme in the Danube fleet and some investment in upgrading of river ports.

212 *Implementing actions and delivering results*

Given the importance of the infrastructural part of the project the Romanian government is the prime recipient of the EU funds (in practice the Ministry of Transport, Construction and Tourism).

We mention that the total Danube river fairway project has, up until now, functioned under a secretariat to facilitate cross-border cooperation. The possibility created by the latest reform (Reg. 1082/2006) to establish an EGTC can help to make this cooperation more efficient.

Source: ECORYS *et al.* (2006a)

Box 9.4 Combating unemployment in the Gdansk region of Poland

Poland is among the member countries with the highest unemployment problems. These are most acute in regions that have gone through a considerable restructuring of their economic base (see section 4.3). One such region is Pomorskie, of which the capital is Gdansk, once famous for its shipyards and port-related activities. So, combating unemployment is one of the prime objectives of the country in general and the Pomorskie region in particular.

Since 1999, Poland has had a well-elaborated multilevel system of government, consisting of four tiers. Labour and social (including employment) policy is designed and implemented through the three highest tiers: the national Ministry of Economy and Labour, the Voivod (region) Labour Offices and the Poviat (county) Labour Offices. On the national and voivodship level Strategies are elaborated. Within these frameworks the Poviat Labour Offices can choose the measures deemed most effective for achieving their specific objectives.

In 2003–05 a programme co-financed by the pre-accession funds was carried out in the Pomorskie region (financed 75 per cent by the EU[24] and 25 per cent by the Polish government). The different projects in this programme aimed at:

- training and counselling the unemployed in vocational and entrepreneurial skills;
- encouraging entrepreneurship among those unemployed or threatened by unemployment;
- enhancing competitiveness of the local SME sector through training and advisory services in EU requirements, standards and norms;
- strengthening local capacities to tackle unemployment, initiating local partnerships – mainly in the field of upgrading vocational training and SME support;
- strengthening (administrative) capacities of authorities and other relevant agencies.

The implementation structure was complex. The final beneficiaries (providers of the services essential for the implementation of each project)

> were a much diversified set. They comprised commercial consulting and vocational training companies, NGOs dealing with training and awareness creation, the university, a regional department of a semi-public vocational training institute, etc. The general coordination of the implementation of all these projects was done by ECORYS, given the lack of administrative capacity that prevailed in the region at the moment of execution it acted in practice as the IB.
>
> The monitoring and evaluation of the results showed that the interventions were successful. This can be seen in looking at the impact on the ultimate beneficiaries of the policy (the target groups): most of the thousands of unemployed that had completed vocational training found a job; 30 per cent of the hundreds of people trained in the entrepreneurial component established a firm; over 1,000 SME saw their competitiveness strengthened. Finally, the institutional capacity of the public, semi-public and private organizations involved was strengthened.
>
> Source: ECORYS et al. (2005)

The success of a programme depends on the appropriateness and quality of its projects. The first depends in turn on the degree to which the projects contribute to the reaching of specific objectives of the programme. The quality depends on factors such as strength of the organization that delivers the project, on the expertise of its staff, etc.

The 'projects market' is subject to the same rules as any market where supply is ample (resources in the form of programmes and measures) but demand (appropriate projects) is weak. This is what makes project formulation capacity a crucial factor for SCF absorption.

9.6.5 Functioning

In practice the implementation of SF operations is firmly rooted in national, regional or local organizations dealing with socio-economic development and environmental protection. In principle, these mainstream organizations are most capable of identifying the right problems, the right projects, the right ideas and ultimately the right people, provided they are functioning according to common expectations.

The way *project pipelines* are organized depends largely on the type of assistance and the size of the projects. These tend to be either:

- *Top down.* This is the case for infrastructure measures where the NDP/NSRF can be seen as the umbrella document, supported by multi-annual national strategies for roads, public transport, telecommunications, etc. The same can hold true for environmental projects that involve heavy investment, which can be prioritized on the basis of national environmental policies or action plans. In these situations, the project pipeline is already being shaped at the time of programming. The respective OPs can reflect

the outcomes of such a programming exercise by referring to individual (large-scale) projects.
- *Bottom up.* For smaller-scale measures, however, project pipelines tend to be derived rather bottom up. Sometimes ideas for (grant) schemes are mentioned in programmes. But usually there is much more work to do in order to mobilize project ideas. Publicity and promotion actions are then crucial. The IBs have a pivotal role in this respect. The 'regular' contacts of personnel in IB outside the scope of the SF are an important source of information and influence. By integrating the SF practice in everyday regular work and tasks at the IB level, the project pipeline will be more easily started.

9.7 Monitoring progress

9.7.1 Structure: the role of MCs

In order to make sure that the agreed programmes and projects are implemented according to agreed specifications and time schedules, monitoring is needed. The responsibility for this monitoring is with the member states; they have to report annually on the progress.[25] In practice it is entrusted to the MC. The MC is the highest decision-making body in each OP. These Committees have the following tasks (SF Reg. 1083/2006, Art. 65):

- consider and approve criteria for selecting the operations;
- review periodically progress made towards achieving objectives;
- examine results of implementation, particularly achievement of targets for the mid-term evaluation (MTE);
- consider and approve reports before these are sent to the EC;
- propose adjustments to the programme likely to help the attainment of the objectives;
- consider and approve any proposal to amend the content of Commission's decision as to the contribution of the SF.

In practice the MAs and the IBs carry out a lot of the more practical tasks for monitoring. They rely very heavily on the information provided by the final beneficiaries on the progress in terms of inputs and outputs of their projects. They are also responsible for proposing corrective actions that have to be approved by the MC.

9.7.2 HR

The total number of MCs ranged during the 2000–06 programming period from seven (in Ireland) and ten (in the new German federal states) to 20 (in Portugal) and 25 (in Spain). Normally there is one MC per OP. A large number of OPs calls for a larger administrative capacity to report and hence to monitor the programmes.

The monitoring task is executed in a way that is consistent with the principle of partnership. The membership structure is fairly similar in all countries; MCs include MAs as a Chair, other ministries, implementing bodies, social partners, non-governmental organizations and regional partners, representatives of the Commission (as observer) and of the CA. The number of members per MC can vary considerably. Overall, NSRF (formerly CSF) MCs are larger with up to 80–100 members. The MCs for individual OPs tend to be much smaller, with an average of 20–30 members.

In addition to the general staff needed for collecting and processing the data, a specialized monitoring staff is in charge of the development, maintenance and upgrading of the management and monitoring information system. IT staff is in particular necessary for the development and programming of the system.

9.7.3 Systems and tools

Monitoring of complex programmes cannot be done without a well-functioning IT-based monitoring information system. Comprehensive monitoring systems are needed in order to fulfil, for example, the reporting tasks on inputs, outputs and results in the annual implementation reports. IT-based monitoring systems have gradually developed and evolved in EU member states, particularly over the past decade. They have, by now, in some cases reached high standards and are able to provide overviews of financial and physical progress at any moment during the implementation of a programme from the level of individual projects up to the level of a programme as a whole. However, in many cases the system in use is rather embryonic, implying much manual work.

EU cohesion policy programmes usually have complex organizational structures. Indeed, the total number of bodies involved with the implementation of individual measures and priorities within an important operational programme can amount to 30–40 organizations. Usually the numbers will be more modest, however. They all play a role in collecting and processing data and feeding it into a monitoring system. They are also users of the system, requiring data on the progress of the projects that are being implemented.

This poses a big challenge to the designers of the system. In practice it comes to the dilemma to impose a central (top-down) model upon each OP and IB; or to adopt a bottom-up model starting from the operational level. The latter option often results in several monitoring systems, which are, however, more adjusted to the particular operational needs. Given the strict claims of the EU regulations some type of centralized monitoring system has been developed in most countries.

The primary focus of the monitoring function is often financial. The systems generate overviews of financial data at all required levels of the programme. The common practice in most EU member states is that strategic decisions about changes in a programme's financial table are in the first place taken on the basis of financial information and the absorption rate of the measures. This stems largely from the fact that EU funds that have not been spent within two years after their commitment will be lost to the OP.

Nonetheless, the past decade has seen a trend of using increasingly advanced systems for recording the physical progress of programmes. The EC working papers and the standardization of output, result and impact indicators in the 2000–06 period have provided an extra impetus to this trend. The extent to which physical progress data can be monitored through the monitoring system depends partly on the nature and scope of the programme. In general, output indicators for specific measures lend themselves best for monitoring purposes. Notwithstanding this, many monitoring systems do contain, also impact or even context indicators.

9.7.4 Functioning

MCs draw up their own rules of procedures within the institutional, legal and financial framework of the member state concerned and in agreement with the MA. Therefore they have a certain degree of autonomy in deciding upon, for example, the frequency of their meetings and the issues that are discussed during the meetings. The number of monitoring committee meetings is usually linked to the publication and reporting sequence. During one of the meetings the annual implementation report is approved; the second meeting is used for discussing the six-monthly report.

MCs are often seen as negotiation bodies rather than follow-up entities. As a result monitoring committees are often very formal and political (in some countries politicians do chair them) where an open debate does not exist about the findings of the programme and the strategy to be followed to optimize effectiveness and efficiency. The size of the MCs does not provide the best conditions to have a frank debate. As decisions, generally, have to be taken by consensus the usual approach is the following: the technical discussions and decisions are prepared during the preparatory work before the meeting and the meetings are indeed more formal gatherings.

Mainly, as part of the preparatory work, but formally also during the actual MC meetings, the MCs also have an important function as a platform for coordination between the various ministries involved with the implementation of an OP, either as managing authority or as implementing departments.

9.8 Financial management and control

9.8.1 Structure: the role of the CA

The various EU SFs do only disburse their financial contribution after proof of conformity with a set of rules and criteria. There is an important function involved here: authorization. This involves the process of approval for competent bodies to access funds that have been allocated to the programme headings. It assumes that the selection of the projects and the contracting of operators have been made and that the latter have (in part) delivered their expected outputs. This role is given to CAs. In practice, they are national, regional or local authorities or bodies designated by the member states for the purposes of drawing up and submitting payment applications, receiving payments from the

Commission, certifying the payments of individual projects and making payments to those projects.

Their predecessors (with a somewhat different role) were called Payment Authorities (PAs). Most member countries had established a PA for each of the SFs. These PAs tended to be located within the ministries responsible for the programme (e.g. ESF in the Ministry of Social Affairs).

The precise assignment and division of responsibilities in the field of financial management requires much attention. Main tasks of the CA include (Reg. 1083/2006, Art. 61):

- submitting certified statements of expenditure and applications for payment to the Commission;
- certifying that the statements of expenditure are accurate, that expenditure has been made for SF-relevant projects and that expenditure complies with applicable EU and national rules;
- maintaining computerized accounting records of all expenditure that can be submitted to verifications and audit;
- recovering sums due to the funds; keep a record of recovery orders and amounts withdrawn following cancellation of all, or part, of an operation and repay recoveries to the Commission.

9.8.2 Structure: the role of the AA

The system of multi-layer government brings many advantages but also many disadvantages. One of them is the limited capacity of the higher layers (in particular the Commission) to verify the legitimacy and regularity of the expenditure. This problem stems notably from the wide differences in national administrative traditions and the limited administrative capacity prevailing in some member states. The European CoA, the institution that is charged with the task of checking the regularity of the expenditure, has on many occasions complained about the persistence of the problems.[26] The Commission (the institution accountable for the correct spending of the EU resources) has taken many steps to improve the situation. In general these meant the stricter regulation of the whole process of programming and management and the setting of specific rules for the quality of the systems and the independence of the controlling organizations. The requirements of this regulation in the field of financial management and control have resulted in a sharp rise in the demand for auditing. In the past, member states tended to reply to this requirement by establishing Internal Audit Units, staffed by regular civil servants, who have received auditing training. The result of this way of handling audits has not been very satisfactory. To remedy these persistent inefficiencies the EU has sharpened its requirements as to the institutional set up and the quality and independence of the auditors.

The new regulation requires the member states to establish for each OP an AA. These AAs need to be independent of the MA, the CA or any IBs. Its audits have to be conducted according to internationally accepted auditing standards. The AA is responsible for (Reg. 1083/2006, Art. 62):

- ensuring that audits are carried out to verify the effective functioning of the management and control systems;
- ensuring that audits are carried out on the operations on the basis of an appropriate sample to verify expenditure declared;
- presenting to the Commission an audit strategy covering the bodies which will perform the audits, the method to be used for auditing and sampling in order to make sure that the main organizations involved are audited and that these audits are spread evenly over the programming period;
- reporting to the Commission on the results of the audits – this includes an answer to the question whether the management and control systems function effectively. The aim is to provide a reasonable assurance that transactions made under the SF support are legal and regular.

On the level of the individual projects all expenditure needs to be audited. This auditing function tends to be contracted out to private firms. The attention that project managers have to give to these functions has increased very considerably. Actually audit costs are now a significant part of the total project cost.

9.8.3 HR

The resources needed are rather important. In the past the predecessors of the CA and AA (the PA) had a staff of some four to seven persons. However, much more resources are used as the audit is a costly exercise. To give an example: in the year 2000 Ireland (in addition to the staff of the MA) employed some 25 staff members specifically working on the financial management of the SCF, either within Internal Audit Units or Financial Control Units. The exercise is particularly costly and cumbersome for smaller projects that have a very diversified cost base. Such projects are very common notably in the field of the ESF. For instance, under a programme aiming at stimulating equal opportunities in the Netherlands, during the 2001–06 period, some 220 projects were approved for a total of some €209 million. Some 28 of these were in the Amsterdam region; they aimed at activating socially vulnerable groups preparing them for participation in the labour market. An estimate of the cost reveals that on average some 10 per cent needs to be spent on administration and control and that for the smaller projects the audit cost can easily amount to 15 per cent.

That is not all. Audits are made at many levels. On the one hand, we find certain specialist services of the Commission, the CoA and the member states. Assuming that the tasks of the CoA are proportionally spread over the various budget items this means that at the EU level alone some 400 people are involved in auditing cohesion expenditure.

9.8.4 Systems and tools

The importance of financial management and control has increased significantly over the previous programming periods. The enforced EU requirements (lastly Reg. 1828/2006) for financial management and control have resulted in the strong development of systems, tools, manuals and procedures. These are generally designed in close cooperation with stakeholders, and sometimes accompanied by awareness-raising activities.

9.8.5 Functioning: payment flows and budget commitments

Payments from the SF are being transferred from the Commission to the member states. The latter pay the final beneficiaries, supported by receipted invoices or accounting documents of equivalent probative value.

Commitments are effected annually. Administrative rules exist that stimulate effective and timely implementation. One such rule is commonly referred to as the automatic de-commitment or $N+2$ rule. It says that delays on delivery can trigger a loss of support of the EU to an operational programme. In technical terms: the Commission automatically de-commits the part of a commitment which has not been settled by the end of the second year following the year of commitment. The contribution from the funds to that assistance shall be reduced by that amount.

In the past a certain number of programmes were financed in part by the ERDF, the ESF and sometimes even other sources. Each of these funds operated according to different modes. This brought extra compliance cost to the authorities and to many other actors involved in the operations of the SCF. In order to do away with the losses due to these complications it has been decided to simplify the procedures and henceforth each operational programme shall be financed by only one of the funds (ERDF, ESF and CF). This may even imply the financing by the ERDF of social projects and vice versa.

9.9 Summary and conclusions

- The fourth stage of the policy cycle concerns the implementation and delivery of the EU cohesion policy.
- The theoretical basis for the implementation suggests that the EU needs to strengthen notably the monitoring devices in order to safeguard compliance of the member states and the other partners involved with its objectives.
- Over the years *practical experience* has identified the aspects that determine the quality of the delivery system: basic principles, institutional structures, general rules and detailed administrative procedures. Member states and other actors involved have to observe these while implementing the EU cohesion policy.
- Essential determinant in the effectiveness of the policy is the administrative capacity to comply with the EU rules. It depends in turn on the quality of the structures, human resources, systems and management.
- The EU wants to be able to oversee the delivery of the policy. To that end it requires that member states *create a number of institutions*. They are entrusted with very specifically described responsibilities. The major ones are MAs, MCs, CAs and AAs.
- One of the basic principles is *partnership*. Partnership implies that civil

220   *Implementing actions and delivering results*

servants of the EC, national governments and regional authorities together with representatives of private and third sector (among them local business, labour unions and social action groups) collaborate closely and continuously in the design, implementation and evaluation of EU-funded programmes. It has the advantage to increase effectiveness by involving all concerned; it has the disadvantage of a loss of efficiency due to uncertainties in the division of responsibilities and the high input of human resources that it requires.

- A second principle is that of *programming*. It involves the definition and adoption of a multi-annual framework that sets out the problems to be attacked, the instruments put in place, the priorities set, the EU and other funds to be deployed and, the most important, implementation provisions. It takes account of the EU strategic guidelines and is made concrete in sets of clearly defined operations.
- The *implementation* of these programmes is entrusted to the national governments. They have delegated this task to MAs, in turn supported by IBs. The latter are the first recipients of the project applications and select the ones that have the highest contribution to the realization of the objectives. The actual delivery of the results of the various projects is done by a multitude of final beneficiaries of the financing. Of course the ultimate beneficiaries are the target groups; for instance, unemployed that are brought back into employment.
- In order to make sure that the agreed programmes and projects are implemented according to agreed specifications and time schedules, *monitoring* is needed. The responsibility for this monitoring is with the member states that have entrusted this to MCs. They have to report annually on the progress.
- The SFs disburse very high amounts of money. *Financial management and control systems* need to be in place to make sure that this money is rightly spent on the agreed projects and on authorized expenditure. Internal and external audit complements the delivery system by testifying to all involved the justification of the expenditure.

Annex 9.1 Systems and tools used in the previous programming periods

In the past each member state prepared a strategic national policy framework (NDP) document that had to be agreed with the Commission. Next, the member states submitted programming documents to the Commission following its general guidelines. Programming documents[27] could take the form of:

- *CSFs* translated into OPs: documents approved by the Commission in agreement with the member state concerned, which contain both the member state's and the fund's strategy and priorities for action, their specific objectives, the contribution from the funds and the other financial resources;
- *SPDs*: comprising a single document, approved by the Commission and combining the data contained in a CSF and OP.

These documents are abolished for the present programming period 2007–13.

Stage V
Checking effectiveness and consistency

10 Evaluation

10.1 Introduction

After a long period of experience with EU cohesion policies the question of how far the policies have been able to reach their objectives, of course, arises. In other words, in how far the considerable amounts of taxpayers' money devoted to cohesion policy have been well spent. The answer to this question has to be given at the fifth stage of the policy cycle, which is evaluation. The results of this evaluation can be used to reshape policies so that they better respond to the demands put on them.

The chapter is based upon a survey of the theoretical foundations and of the empirical evidence of the past performance of cohesion policies. This survey covers both studies commissioned by organizations involved in the policy process and academic studies.

The present chapter will break down this fifth stage into several parts.

First, we will discuss the theoretical frameworks that have been elaborated for making proper policy evaluations.

Second, we will make a structured survey of the studies that have been made to evaluate EU cohesion policy.

We devote separate sections to each of the three major groups of stated objectives that up until 2005 characterized the EU cohesion policies (see Chapter 7): objective 1, formerly backward areas, now convergence; objective 2, formerly restructuring areas, now competitiveness and the former objectives 3 and 4 (employment/social; now mainstreamed in objective 2). We will also survey the evaluation studies made into the special objectives of enlargement (pre-accession aid to the NMSs) and cushion the effects of enlargement (support to Mediterranean countries from the CF).

After this survey by objective we will discuss some overarching aspects. One is the evaluation of the adequacy of the management and implementation aspects. Another one, the extra impulse that the EU has been able to give to cohesion (beyond what would have been done had cohesion been a national policy); an impulse that is often termed the 'Community added value'.

Now the objectives of the EU cohesion policy are broader than the stated objectives of decreasing disparities. As we have indicated in Chapter 7, these wider objectives concern, notably, the facilitating of package deals which permit the move into higher forms of integration. We will shortly deal with the past record of the EU on this score. We will not deal with the present ambitions of the EU in this matter, such as the contribution of the EU cohesion policy to the knowledge society and employment. The EU has only recently put its cohesion policy instruments at the service of these other policies, which means that the empirical evidence of the effect is not yet available.

The practice of evaluation as it has evolved over time is itself subject to improvement. In a final section we will indicate some of the present (in)adequacies and indicate avenues of improvement.

We will as usual give the main insights from this chapter in the summary and conclusions section.

10.2 Theory and methods

10.2.1 Developing a sound and practical model

Theoretical and empirical analyses indicate that integration may unleash forces that tend to lead to an increase in economic, social and territorial disparities (see Chapters 2 to 5). In order to stem divergence forces and to stimulate convergence forces the EU cohesion policy was devised and gradually elaborated (see Chapters 6 to 9). It devotes substantial amounts of money to improve cohesion. This is money that has been taken from the EU taxpayer to whom the European authorities are accountable and to whom they have to show that all this money is well spent.

How can the EU demonstrate that the resources spent on its cohesion policy are justified? The first way is to show that the policy has reached its objectives; in other words that has it been effective. The second way is to show that no money has been wasted; in other words that the policy has been efficient.[1] The demonstration of effectiveness and efficiency can be done by *evaluation*.

Apart from accountability (or legitimacy) evaluation can serve other purposes. In practice this is the improvement of the other parts of the policy cycle; that is planning, programming and implementation and hence performance (effectiveness and efficiency). Implied in all this is learning.

Evaluation of projects, programmes and policies has been only gradually elaborated in theoretical and practical terms (see, for example, Just *et al.*, 2005). Up until fairly recently there was quite some controversy as to the best approaches. The different DGs of the EC, with their specific traditions, working environments and requirements, have initially developed evaluation methods for their own purposes.

The DGs that are mainly responsible for SF spending (DG Regio and DG Employment) were the first to feel the need to come to sound and practical evaluation methods.[2] They have adopted some practical methods, given the inadequacies of the academic literature (e.g. Patton, 1986, 2001; Schmid *et al.*, 1996). After a period of experimentation it became clear that a more standard approach was needed. Only in this way could a considerable risk of misunderstanding due to the use of different concepts and definitions be removed and could one be sure that results would be comparable between the different projects and programmes. A considerable effort to come to a set of standard practices has been made in the framework of the so-called 'MEANS' programme. This acronym stands for Methods for Evaluating Actions of a Structural Nature. These ideas have later been elaborated and concretized in a detailed practical 'Guide'.[3] The framework had the advantage of taking into account multiple stakeholders and partners involved in the programming, design and implementation.[4]

10.2.2 The basic features of the EU/SF evaluation model

The EU imposes fairly strict standardized systems for evaluation to the beneficiaries of its SF support. The adoption of such standardized approaches is essential, in order to be able to compare and sum up the impact of all interventions.

The SF evaluation model reflects a number of the basic design principles of the EU cohesion policy.

First, it corresponds to the EU programming principle by requiring that impact assessments have to be made at each of its three stages (EC, 2002e):

1 *Ex ante*, also called appraisal. Before a programme or project is started an analysis should be made about its likely effects. This needs to be as specific as possible; so the type of result that one wants to obtain needs to be defined in a quantitative way.
2 *In course*. A first point concerns monitoring. It controls on a regular basis whether the programme runs according to schedule; whether the means that are foreseen are indeed committed to the activities specified; and whether they are spent in function of the aims that are pursued and in conformity with the administrative rules set. The main aspect is, however, intermediate (mid-term) evaluation (MTE); that is to see whether and why ongoing interventions do really produce the intended effects.
3 *Ex post*. This involves the check of whether the initially specified objectives have indeed been achieved; the assessment of the type of difference that occurred; the tracing of the causes of such discrepancies and the suggestions for improvement for subsequent programmes.

The advantages of this three-stage evaluation process can be seen at two different levels:

1 *Direct and instrumental*. Findings are directly fed back and lead on both the project and programme levels onto adaptations of the targets set and instruments deployed. There is, however, a problem in this respect with ex post evaluation that is difficult to solve. Ex post can only start once the programme is finished. As the new programmes, in general, start immediately after the end of the preceding one there is no time to feed into the preparation of the new programme the lessons of the evaluation. A good intermediate evaluation has to remediate this problem.

2 *Cumulative and process.* The process of experimentation, challenge and argumentation leads to improved policy making and implementation by clarifying issues, specifying objectives, developing frameworks and testing instruments.

Moreover, the EU/SF method responds to subsidiarity and partnership principles by involving local and national government and stakeholders not only at the design stage but also at the evaluation stage. This is a fragile equilibrium. Of course the evaluation as such has to be made by independent organizations. However, the involvement of stakeholders and administrators alongside evaluators is an essential prerequisite for success as it builds up commitment, not only to the programme, but also to its successful implementation.

The EU/SF approach (compulsory for all SF aid) has introduced a culture of evaluation in all member states of the EU. Before, many national programmes tended to be vaguely specified and were only rarely properly evaluated (see e.g. Gualini, 2004). Under the impetus of the EU many member states have designed administrative rules and created the administrative capacity to make sure that their policy cycle is well structured and correctly evaluated. This does of course entail extra cost. But these costs have been kept limited as the EU standard specifications have taken away the need to develop own methods and the uncertainty as to the best method to adopt.

10.2.3 The logic and structure of evaluation approaches

The first step in each evaluation is to get a good understanding of the intervention logic, which explains what is to be achieved and how it is to be achieved. The key elements in the intervention logic are inputs, activities, outputs, results (initial impact) and outcomes (longer-term impact) or objectives (see Table 10.1 and Figure 10.1). Often a SWOT analysis is associated to this set up.

These elements differ depending on whether they are applied to a policy, a programme or a project. A policy is the most general and is concretized in

Table 10.1 Elements of the intervention logic

Elements	Project level	Programme level
Inputs	Human resources, finance, goods	Individual projects' design and execution
Activities or projects	Building infrastructure Setting up an institution	Different projects, combined in a programme
Outputs	Goods and services produced by the project	Results of the different projects
Results (initial impact)	Purpose of the project	Outcomes of the different projects (changes effected in different sectors of the economy/society)
Outcomes (longer-term impact)	Sustainable change effected by project	Change effected in the entire national economy/society

programmes, the latter again in projects. On the policy level, objectives and ways and means are mostly defined in fairly general terms; while on the programme and project level they become much more concrete. As a consequence most of the evaluation work is done at the programme and project level. The specifics of these two levels are given in Table 10.1.

The understanding of each of these elements is important for evaluation and so is the understanding of the direct and/or indirect relation (causal links) between these elements (see Figure 10.1).

Once these elements are in place the key questions can be addressed: (relevance or) appropriateness,[5] effectiveness and efficiency (see Figure 10.1). In the following sections we will systematically address these aspects in the evaluation of each of the objectives.[6]

In order to make the whole set up operational one needs to select and measure for each stage in the sequence Objectively Verifiable Indicators (OVIs). In general OVIs for concrete projects are easier to formulate and measure than OVIs at the programme level, let alone at the policy (or strategy) level. The use of similar criteria for the evaluation of comparable programmes (e.g. in different countries or regions) allows comparison.

Measurement of effects is not a straightforward exercise either. It is easiest in terms of OVIs on the project level; for instance the number of unemployed trained for new jobs. The effects on the objective of the programme (for instance decrease of regional unemployment) and further on the objective of the policy (decrease in disparity) are much more difficult to capture. Indeed, the observed change in the OVIs can only partly be attributed to project or programme: the rest is imputable to external factors (among them the quality of the institutional environment) and to other projects and policies. What needs to be measured is the difference between the 'without intervention' and 'with intervention' situation. So, there still exists many inefficiencies in our ability to calculate effects; in other words to relate in an unequivocal manner objectives and means.

10.2.4 Actors involved in the process

All partners in the cohesion policy are to some extent involved in the evaluation exercise. However, they have quite different roles. Thus, the ex ante evaluation is the responsibility of the competent authorities in the member states, whereas the

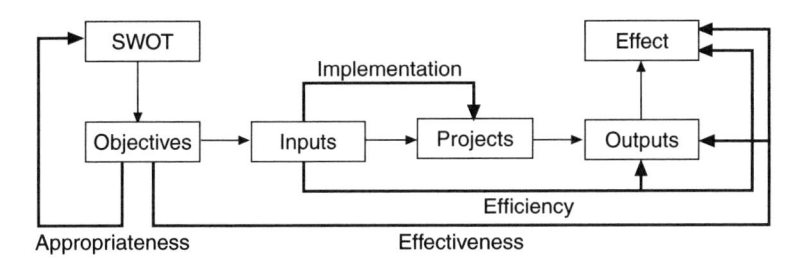

Figure 10.1 Key elements in the evaluation of SCF programmes

MTE must be carried out by the authority managing the programme in collaboration with the Commission. The ex post evaluation is the responsibility of the Commission, in collaboration with the member state and the managing authority.

The various partners work according to the so-called 'cascade' model, which ensures that the responsibility of evaluation is cascaded down the whole institutional (politico-administrative) hierarchy.

- *EC:* analyses evaluation methodology and practices and, on the basis of the results, provides both regulations on what tasks to perform and guidelines for evaluators on how to perform them. It assesses ex ante and MTEs, carries (or contracts out) ex post evaluation of groups of programmes and makes thematic evaluations on subjects such as partnership, transport and innovation.[7] The Commission has created specialist evaluation units in each of the DGs that share responsibility for cohesion policy. Moreover, Commission civil servants can participate in the Evaluation Steering Groups.
- *Member states and regional authorities:* they carry out or contract out ex ante and MTE and monitoring studies. Often the MA[8] awards the contract to the independent evaluator (a consultant, university or independent scholar), monitors the work of the latter and coordinates the work of the Evaluation Steering Committee. The findings of the evaluator will be discussed in the relevant Monitoring Committee and then submitted to the Commission. The evaluation reports must be made available to the public.

Within this general framework evaluation is highly differentiated among countries and even more so among regions. This is a reflection of long-standing differences in administrative traditions and in evaluation experience and capacity.

10.3 How did the EU perform?[9]

10.3.1 Are EU interventions appropriate?

The question about the appropriateness of policy interventions can be answered by checking whether the policy set up and the measures it uses are relevant for the solving of the problems. At the level of the cohesion policy as a whole the problems have been defined in general terms as the persistence of economic, social and territorial disparities. At the level of the instruments one considers mainly the SF and the CF. Let us recall here that the SFs are called that because they intend to improve the structural conditions that determine disparities. So, the actions of the SCF concentrate on the taking away of deficiencies on the supply side, in other words on the growth potential (competitiveness) of the backward countries and regions and of disfavoured social groups (see Chapter 6). In practice this means that most of the support has been given to infrastructure and manpower. Moreover, the SCF have contributed to the quality of institutions in many poor regions and hence on the quality of the regional investment conditions (i.e. Lion *et al.*, 2004). Finally, the EU system takes due account of aspects of policy consistency (see next chapter).

In the past, the SFs have targeted their actions to decrease the economic and social disparities. The new dimension of territorial cohesion could not yet benefit from such explicit actions. However, in looking at the daily practice of the SFs one sees that they have also (albeit coincidentally) contributed to territorial cohesion. This effect has increased over time. First, because the SF actions are now more oriented towards the regions that have the highest needs; and these tend to be the regions that score highest on indicators such as peripherality and lack of urban services. Second, because the method of delivery of the SF favours the integration of local actors in the process and supports the capacity of the regions outside the core to deal with problems and mobilize support.

The positive aspects cited here do not give the whole picture, however. There are also negative aspects to the working of the SF. We cite in the final section of this chapter a few of them. The negative aspects are in general considered to be much less important than the positive ones. So, the critical evaluation of the EU system of support to cohesion as it has evolved over time does not suggest that there is a major problem with respect to the appropriateness of its policy packages.

10.3.2 Are EU interventions effective?

Interventions can be considered effective in case the ex ante expected effects of the policy have been obtained and that objectives have been achieved. The effectiveness of interventions is not easy to establish. In principle one calculates this by relating an indicator of output (result or impact) to a quantified objective. In practice one has started by answering the following two questions:

1. Did the SF support reach the right regional target groups? In principle the design of the system foresees a concentration on low-income regions. This, indeed, proves to be the case: the poorer a region the more support it gets.
2. Has SF money been spent on the programmes and projects that do contribute to reaching the policy objectives? Evaluation studies of individual projects and programmes suggest that transfers were indeed carefully aimed at meeting the objectives[10] and specific policy targets.

However, these questions do not reach the heart of the matter. We have seen that the basic objective of the cohesion policy is to reduce disparities. In Chapters 2 to 5 we have seen that disparities on many scores have actually decreased over the past decades. Now the real question to which research needs to give an answer is whether the SCFs have contributed to a reduction of these disparities. Or would the observed reduction have occurred anyway? Empirical studies have not led to unequivocal answers to these questions; on the contrary they have produced a considerable controversy between the following two camps:

1. *Positive.* A first group considers that the evaluation made of the policy shows largely positive results. We find on this side not unexpectedly the Commission.

In matters of objective 1 regions she states: 'The SCF do not only stimulate demand by increasing income in the regions assisted. By supporting investment in infrastructure and human capital they also increase their competitiveness and productivity and so help to expand income over the long term' (EC, 2001: xxi). In matters of objective 2 regions she finds that cohesion policies have had a cushioning effect on the regions that lost out in this game and have permitted them to catch up (EC, 2004a). This view is supported by many academics that have found empirical evidence for the relation cohesion policy decrease in disparity.[11]

- *Negative*. Some claim on the basis of empirical studies that the EU policy has no effect on convergence (Dall'erba and Le Gallo, 2003). Others consider that it is at best neutral in the sense that the transfers from the rich to the poor do contribute only that amount to the wealth levels of the beneficiary regions. However, they suspect that the welfare effect is actually negative due to the ensuing distortions of taxation and bureaucracy and sub-optimal location of activities.[12] These authors (e.g. Boldrin and Canova, 2001, 2003) doubt any long-term growth effects of the present EU cohesion policy. To give one citation: 'current (EU) policies are ineffective, based on incorrect or at least unsubstantiated economic theory, badly designed, poorly carried out, a source of wrong incentives and in some cases of corruption' (Boldrin and Canova, 2003: 35–36).[13]

How can different authors analysing the same reality come to such controversial conclusions? Could this be a consequence of deficiencies in the methods that are used to capture the complicated nature of the cause–effect relation?[14] Let us concentrate on the more sophisticated methods that use a model intended to isolate the effects of cohesion policy from 'normal' development.[15]

The first question to which we will draw our attention concerns the policy objective of decreasing disparities in regional incomes. The empirical studies made on this relation can be split into two types:[16]

1. *Demand-side effects* are mostly traced with macro economic models. Studies that look at the effect of increased spending by the SF in target regions[17] tend to show significant positive effects. For the whole of the cohesion countries the extra growth of GDP induced by the SF has been estimated at some 0.5 per cent per annum (EC, 1996a).
2. *Supply-side effects* are mostly traced by models that relate regional growth figures to factors determining growth such as infrastructure, HR, R&D, etc. SF support is then also included as a policy variable in these models. They show that SF support has had a significant positive impact on the growth performance of European lagging regions.[18] The effect of the SCF seems to be larger in regions that are well endowed with factors of growth; and lower in regions with poor endowment (industrial structure and R&D) and also lower in regions that are much less receptive to change. Regional spillover effects did not seem to play a role in peripheral areas and only a limited one in central areas (e.g. Dall'erba and Le Gallo, 2003).

The next question regards the second major policy objective of the EU: the reduction of unemployment. This question has not got as much attention in the literature as the question about wealth disparities. Neither is there much controversy among researchers.

There are various ways to attack the problem of assessing the effectiveness of the cohesion policy in matters of reduction of unemployment (disparities). One is in the analysis of the combined effect of the economic and the social parts of cohesion policy. In its simplest form this would consist of the adding up of the figures on employment created in activities that have been supported by the multitude of programmes and projects of the EU cohesion policy. But the question is how much of that employment would have been created anyhow, without support. Another way is to use macro models that relate (un)employment to SF support. Measured in this way the SFs have decreased unemployment (e.g. Bradley *et al.*, 2004). But the question is how much of that employment would have been created anyhow, without support.[19]

So, the conclusion of this section is that there is much evidence to justify the EU cohesion policy; however, there is also quite some concern as to the effectiveness of the policy package that the EU has put in place. We will go deeper into this problem by specifying the results for the various objectives that the EU policy distinguishes.

At this stage one should, however, point at a fundamental difficulty that cannot be overcome even with the best methods and with the most detailed investigations. It is related to the uncertainty that is brought up by the controversial outcomes of the theoretical models for the development of economic, social and territorial disparities (see Chapters 2 to 5). One will never be able to establish what would have happened without the EU interventions. Take two examples. If one observes convergence, is this due to policy or is it due to the autonomous development of the system? If one observes a weak tendency towards divergence, is this the net effect of on the one hand considerable divergence had the system been left to its own and on the other hand some convergence produced by policy? Therefore, conclusions as to effectiveness need always be made with some caution and rather in terms of plausibility instead of proofs.

10.3.3 Are EU interventions efficient?

Answering the efficiency question involves the checking of whether the EU has attained its policy results using as little resources as possible.[20] In operational terms this means that one defines an efficiency indicator, for instance by dividing the results obtained (e.g. jobs created) by budgetary inputs (outlays in euro). Many observers state that the EU cohesion policy suffers from a lack of efficiency. They tend to blame the high organizational and administrative costs of operating the system. This problem has two aspects: a general one and a specific one:

- *General.* The EU has opted for the allotment of its aid in the form of specific-purpose grants (see Chapters 6 and 7). The rationale for this is of a political nature; the EU is accountable to those who have provided the money and has to demonstrate to them that the money is well spent. This would not have been possible with general-purpose grants, as they would have tended to be amalgamated with other budget items of the recipient countries and regions. The implication is, however, a costly administrative system of delivery, monitoring and evaluation. The total cost consists of the inputs of the many actors involved: public authorities (such as local authorities, national ministries, various DGs of the EU), non-governmental parties (private firms) and increasingly intermediate organizations (such as trade unions, chambers of commerce, etc). This involvement occurs at all stages of the policy process (planning, implementation and financial justification) and at all levels of detail (programmes, but also detailed projects). The various reforms that occurred at some seven-year intervals (see Chapter 7) have improved the procedures and hence the efficiency of the workings of the system. However, the key to real success on the score of increased efficiency may lie in a stricter application of the subsidiarity principle, leading to a change in the distribution of responsibilities, with the EU limiting itself more to a banker's role, that is to critically evaluate the planning and implementation and leaving the more operational aspects to lower bodies (see Chapter 12).

- *Specific.* The EU spends in absolute terms large amounts of aid in the rich member states. So these countries get back part of the money they have contributed to the EU budget via the SFs.[21] The pumping around of money between member states and Brussels is inefficient and entails a welfare loss. Other welfare losses result from the distorted allocation of public funds because the richer member states spend money on projects that happen to be eligible for EU funding, but that they would often not have financed if they had followed their own priorities. A solution to this problem could lie in a trimming of the flows to and from the richer member states.[22] In practice this would boil down to a netting of parts of the EU budget: rich member states would pay less to the EU budget and would get no support from the EU funds. Such a policy would be in line with sound economics but is opposed by many regional, national and European political circles.

10.4 Objective 1 regions

10.4.1 Appropriateness

We now turn our attention to the specific objectives of the EU cohesion policy. Most important is of course objective 1, formerly backward areas now convergence. The evaluation of the objective 1 support has been the subject of a range of studies.[23] The most recent one available (ECOTEC, 2003a) covers the period 1994–99, a period in which some €210 billion has been spent on the backward areas. The problem of economic backwardness is reflected in a concentration on low-value-added economic activities, a lack of infrastructure and inadequate labour qualifications.

Evaluation 233

The programmes of the objective 1 regions have set priorities that are in general in line with their needs. They came broadly under four headings (in brackets the approximate distribution of resources in the period 1994–99):

1 Infrastructure, transport and environment (50 per cent).
2 Business and tourism (some 25 per cent).
3 Education and human capital (some 15 per cent).
4 Agriculture and rural promotion (10 per cent).

The programme balance of the 2000–06 period was somewhat different from the one at the end of the 1990s. Infrastructure was still an important item. The accent has shifted to growth, to competitiveness and job creation (economic cohesion), to education and training (social cohesion) and to a better distribution of specific social services over cities in the region (territorial cohesion).

10.4.2 Effectiveness

The effectiveness of the policy can be measured at different levels and with the help of different indicators. The highest level indicators refer to the two major targets: decrease in disparity in wealth and in (un)employment.

The prime target is the decrease in the disparity in GDP per head. The GDP per head gap between objective 1 regions and the rest of the EU with regard to GDP per head (in Purchasing Power Standard) has narrowed from 64 per cent of the EU average in 1993 to 69 per cent in 2000. Indeed the objective 1 regions' rate of growth has been significantly higher than the EU average. Moreover, among the objective 1 regions one observes a positive correlation between GDP growth and the intensity of SF intervention (see Figure 10.2). So, although the causal relation has not been established, it is at least likely that the policy has contributed to overall cohesion. However, this general evidence of convergence and hence of effectiveness of the policy masks the persistence of significant problems. One is territorial cohesion. Indeed, disparities among objective 1 regions have increased; in many countries growth has been concentrated in the core areas of these regions. This has been stimulated by the distribution of the available funds. So, territorial cohesion has apparently not got overriding priority.

Decrease in unemployment is the second indicator of the success of EU cohesion policy. We recall that this indicator is closely related to the objective of social cohesion. With respect to this indicator the record of success for objective 1 regions is less positive than for GDP/P. Indeed, the unemployment rate in this group of regions stayed almost stable at 16 per cent during the evaluation period; considerably above the EU average of 9 per cent (ECOTEC, 2003a).

Following the method of Table 10.1 one can check the effectiveness of objective 1 interventions by relating the outputs in terms of the priority measures (e.g. infrastructure construction) to the efforts made to realize them. The measurement of the efforts is fairly straightforward; normally this is done in terms of public investment. In the past their size has been very impressive, for example, investments in human and physical capital have amounted to 8 per cent of total capital accumulation in the four countries that were the major

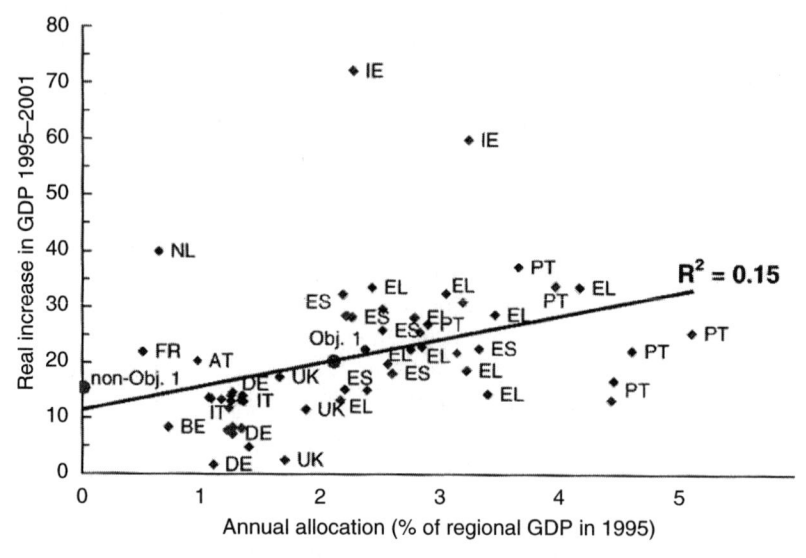

Figure 10.2 Structural Fund allocation and GDP growth

Note:
AT = Austria; BE = Belgium; DE = Germany; EL = Greece; ES = Spain; FR = France; IE = Ireland; IT = Italy; NL = Netherlands; PT = Portugal; UK = United Kingdom

Source: EC (2004a), Graph 4.4

beneficiaries of the cohesion efforts over the period 1994–99 (Spain, Portugal, Greece and Ireland). However, the expected output is much less easy to quantify. There are many factors that inhibit quantification. The list of problems starts with the non-comparability and questionable reliability of OVIs. Even when some of these are available performance is difficult to judge as one has often omitted to define, at the start of the cycle, clear and quantified objectives and targets. Given these constraints it has not been possible to evaluate correctly the effectiveness in the programming period 1993–99 (ECOTEC, 2003a).

Hence, the effects of inter-regional transfers on the growth and performance of the backward regions is a matter of considerable controversy. As objective 1 regions have a very heavy weight in the overall cohesion policy, this is in line with the discussion we reported on in the first section of this chapter. We give here the contrasting results of some analyses specifically done for objective 1 regions.

- *Supportive*. The aid packages have important demand, supply and other effects as mentioned in the endogenous growth literature. The effects were found to be positive for both GDP and employment growth in objective 1 regions. The real long-term effects are higher the better the region responds to opportunities arising in the rest of the country and the rest of the EU single market (Bradley et al., 2004). Next to this modelling approach positive employment effects have been captured by subtracting from the observed development (partly dependent on aid) the likely autonomous development (without aid) (Martin and Tyler, 2006).

- *Critical.* Each of the components (given in the previous section) of the aid package has a different effect. Infrastructure and business support notwithstanding the huge sums involved have had only a negligible impact. Support to agriculture has short-term positive effects but these wane quickly. Only investment in education and human capital (representing only 8 per cent of outlays) were found to have significant positive returns in the medium term (Rodriguez-Pose and Fratesi, 2004).

In view of the difficulties with an overall assessment we try to see how in far more detailed studies we can shed light on the subject of effectiveness. To that end we give here the results of evaluation studies that are made for the different countries eligible for objective 1 aid.

Spain. SF spending on public infrastructure and education in backward regions of Spain has accelerated the growth of these regions by up to two percentage points, and had diminished the disparity in productivity between Spanish regions by some 5 per cent, which represents one-third of the observed decrease (de la Fuente and Vives, 1995).[24] But grant programmes seem to have been ineffective at stimulating private investment or improving the overall economies of the poorest regions (Garcia-Mila and MacGuire, 2001).

Portugal. The funds transferred in the period 1996–2006 add 3.4 per cent to the level of GDP and 0.15 percentage points to long-term GDP growth (Gaspar and Pereira, 1995).

Greece. For Greece aid is supposed to have increased long-term annual growth by half a percentage point (Lolos, 2001). A more detailed ex ante analysis of the effects of the last CSF (Christodoulakis and Kalyritis, 2000) found no lasting demand side effects. However, the authors found a significant contribution of the SCF spending to growth under the condition that the supply improvements were done in such a way that they could be immediately used by producers (e.g. training labour for jobs for which a real demand exists).

Ireland. European aid has resulted in an initial acceleration of the growth of GDP/P of 1 per cent per year; after some years, the growth bonus has become much higher, because the supply-side effects did take some time to materialize. The extra percentage point to the growth has contributed to the decrease of the difference in wealth levels between Ireland and the EU (Bradley et al., 1995). The role of the SF has been essential but could only come to fruition in a supportive policy and institutional environment (see Box 10.1).

So, on the basis of these studies on the national level we can conclude that SF aid has decreased GDP/P disparities.

10.5 Objective 2: from restructuring to competitiveness and employment

10.5.1 Appropriateness

Many regions that are confronted with the problem of industrial restructuring have been the beneficiaries of a significant amount of European money (some

€3 billion a year over the 1994–99 and 1999–2006 programming periods). It has taken some time before the effectiveness of this aid was properly evaluated. The first study consisted of reviews of the programming documents for the periods 1989–93 and 1994–96 (Bachtler and Taylor, 1996). It showed that there was a wide diversity in economic structures, problems and hence in specific objectives, approaches and types of projects. This considerable heterogeneity presented a considerable barrier to come to generally applicable conclusions in the ex-post evaluation study (CSES, 2003).

The programmes evaluated appear to address the major problems objective 2 regions are confronted with. Unlike objective 1 regions, these are not so much related to lack of infrastructure (transport) and of human capital, but to some inadequacies of these endowments for modern economic activities. Major problems are the lack of innovativeness and the heritage of derelict (and often heavily polluted) industrial sites. The allocation of funds was broadly in line with these priorities:

- infrastructure: mainly industrial sites (27 per cent);
- support for business: access to services, promotion of trade (25 per cent);
- training and developing skills of work force (20 per cent);
- innovation, R&D, ICT (10 per cent).

Box 10.1 Catching up: the case of Ireland

Catching up can be step by step or incremental: but at least in small member states it can, under right conditions, be quantum. Within the EU, Ireland affords a clear example of this in that its GDP and active work force has more than doubled in less than ten years, its unemployment rate has dropped from nearly 20 per cent at the start of the 1990s to just 4 per cent in 2005, while its macro economic situation, from being among the worst in Europe, has converged to that of the best. From watching its young people emigrate for one and a half centuries, the country now requires the young people of other countries to meet its labour market requirements.

What were the determinant factors for this success? The answer lies in a complex interplay of factors among which the following formal and organizational features stand out.

- Government action on the basis of long-term policy objectives, which did not even change in difficult circumstances and after changes in government. These objectives commanded widespread understanding and support and were anchored in broad social consensus. They have been developed on the basis of hard-learned experience (including multiple mistakes). Policy and resources (investment capacity) were integrated over a long period.
- Constant drive towards improvement of the quality of policy making and to a lesser extent implementation, based on evaluation of

previous experiences. Delivery and implementation structures (such as State development agencies, the Employment Service, tourism promotion agency, Roads Authority) have always been substantial and relatively professional bodies, and have been constantly urged to become more efficient.
- Organization of the State's finances on a long-term logic, whereby the parameters of EMU have been fully reconciled with the demands of further public investment in policy-priority areas. This has demanded, among other things, a full review of taxation policy, and more recently tax-gathering mechanisms and practices. No country in the Europe of 15 has undergone such a thorough and radical change in this respect.
- Sticking to strict prioritization. For example, all secondary infrastructures have had to await investment while preference has been given to human resource development, entrepreneurship, business development and primary (telecom) infrastructure.
- Stable, independent and relatively efficient public service, an increasing climate of transparency, a quasi non-existent level of corruption among public officials, the growing confidence of a relatively youthful population and their consequent demands for change and access to new opportunities.

So, the Irish success factors go well beyond the support of the SCF. When at the time the public debt was over 100 per cent of GDP, the government deficit was 12 per cent of GDP and unemployment was 18 per cent (the situation in 1988–91), the SF allowed Ireland to continue to give expression to ambitious policy objectives which otherwise could not have sustained public and political support. Over time as support from the SFs have become less important in relative terms, they have transferred to Irish investment planning, programming and evaluation a discipline that has reinforced the historic strengths of policy and policy implementation and helped to address many of their weaknesses. By allowing policy makers to continue to invest in key endowment levels of long-term growth and competitiveness despite the strong sense of crisis of the late 1980s and early 1990s, SFs were, at a critical time, a major factor in Ireland's longer-term success.

Source: Adapted from ECORYS (2004b)

The heterogeneity of the programmes and the highly fragmented character of the eligible areas make it difficult to check the overall appropriateness of the policy as to the three dimensions of cohesion. But some general observations can be made. Stemming economic decline by stimulating the introduction of new economic activities does make a contribution to economic cohesion. Preventing unemployment to increase in areas that are often concentrations of deprivation does contribute to social cohesion. And although many of the interventions are in central areas and hence do not contribute to territorial cohesion in the EU as a whole, some do improve territorial cohesion on a lower level in the sense that they prevent certain cities loosing out with respect of the more central cities in the country or region.

10.5.2 Effectiveness

The major objectives of the policy are the renewal of the industrial base and the decrease of unemployment. A secondary objective is preventing decreases in income.[25] Many programmes cite other objectives as well, such as environmental improvement, etc. The objectives have seldom been translated in clear targets. It means that the evaluation of the effectiveness of the objective 2 interventions cannot be assessed properly. One is therefore limited to a quantification of the change in some policy variables without being able to indicate the causal relation between these changes and the SF support. The results of two exercises[26] are:

- *Restructuring.* In each period some 700,000 to 800,000 jobs have been created in new industrial and service activities (some 500,000 if one takes account of the displacement effect of existing jobs). Some 300,000 SME have received assistance in adapting themselves to new market conditions. They have been essential for employment growth. In the second period some three million people received training to get qualified for new jobs.
- *Unemployment.* Over the 1994–99 planning period unemployment decreased by some 3 per cent against a decline of some 2 per cent in the rest of the EU and only 1 per cent in the regions of the EU excluding objective 1.
- *Income.* Growth in GDP/P was marginally below the average of the EU as a whole. As a consequence the index of the average GDP/P in objective 2, with respect to the EU average, decreased marginally.

Effectiveness seems finally to have been negatively influenced by two important factors (EC, 2004a):

1. The small size of the eligible areas. As a corollary to small size of the regions the size of the interventions is rather small which makes it difficult to measure the effects. Moreover, the effects tend to spill over into neighbouring areas.
2. The limited time period for which support is available. This favours short-term projects at the expense of strategic ones for which results become visible later.

The MTE of the 2000–06 period provides evidence of important learning effects. The quality of the implementation, monitoring and evaluation have much improved (Basle, 2006).

10.6 Social problem areas (former objectives 3 and 4)

10.6.1 Appropriateness

The main problems of social deprivation are related to unemployment and access to education (see Chapter 4). Specific categories such as long-term unemployed and youth were particularly vulnerable. Under objective 3 the EU set as main policy targets the combating of long-term unemployment, and the integration into working life of young people and other persons excluded from the labour market. Next to this the EU also wants to contribute to the adaptation of workers of either sex to industrial change and changes in production systems.

We consider that there is a major problem with appropriateness in the sense that cohesion policy instruments do not apply to one of the main root causes of unemployment, namely ill-adapted national labour market institutions (see Chapter 4). These are only addressed by measures of the EU programme on employment and the Lisbon strategy. The instrument available here is the OMC (see Chapter 8). But national states are sovereign in choosing whether they adapt their structures or not and if so in which way.[27]

The ex post evaluation of the 1994–99 programming period (EC, 2004d) and the MTE of the 2000–06 period (EC, 2005) considered that the actions of the ESF were nevertheless appropriate as they did reach the target groups, while the distribution over target groups followed the policy priorities set by the programmes. The measures supported were very wide ranging; they covered the set up of public employment services, intensive counselling and job search activities, life-long learning, training and education, employment subsidies and incentives for start-ups. Much of these were deployed in the framework of active labour market policies. The ESF has supported the spread of good practices to those countries that lacked experience with such policies.

10.6.2 Effectiveness

The effectiveness of the policy measures that attack social deprivation cannot easily be evaluated in general terms due to a range of factors. These include: (1) the multitude and wide variety of ESF support schemes; (2) the lack of clear specification of targets; (3) the poor design of the programmes; (4) the small contribution of ESF funds with respect to national funds; and (5) the difficulty of measuring outcomes instead of outputs.

So it is difficult to generalize the effects of specific measures of European social policy and the evaluations of the EC (EC, 2004d, 2005) have practically no reference to effectiveness. Some have tried to get to results notwithstanding the difficulties. Examiners of the programmes of the early decades of the policy have mostly come up with unfavourable critiques. They argue that, at best, the ESF has served the redistribution of European money, but failed to attain any specific social objectives (e.g. Laffan, 1983; Steinle, 1988). Examiners of the more recent policy have concentrated on the effects of Active Labour Market Policies (ALMP), as most of the EU/SF interventions fall into the category of

240 *Checking effectiveness and consistency*

ALMP. ALMP try to stimulate the moving out of unemployment into employment and to prevent the move in the opposite direction (see previous section). The effectiveness of ALMP to reduce unemployment was found to be rather ambiguous and at best a small positive effect could be found. The analysis of a series of EU countries suggested that the effectiveness may be enhanced in case projects are geared to local situations.[28]

10.7 The new member countries of central Europe (from Phare to objective 1)

10.7.1 Appropriateness

The accession countries face a large number of problems. As evidenced in Chapters 2 to 5 their productive structure is weak; their infrastructure deficient and the qualification of their labour force inadequate. Moreover, they have institutional weaknesses. The eastern enlargement of the EU has been very different from all previous ones for a set of reasons.

First of all, the difficulties for the accession countries were much larger. Indeed, all countries that joined the EU in the previous century had a market economy. Admittedly, some of them, notably those in the Mediterranean basin, had to make the adaptation from an economy very heavily influenced by national government regulation and dominated by state enterprises to one with more competition and efficient institutions. However, they had all the essential prerequisites for accession to the EU. In contrast the countries from central Europe that recently acceded have had only a short period to make a (very painful) transition from a protected, state-planned economy to a market economy that is open to the world.

Second, the objective is set much higher. In the past countries entered into a CM; now they integrate in a union that has progressed to the stage of an EMU.

Third, the institutional environment has changed as well. The instruments the EU uses are now considerably more refined compared to the previous situation. Moreover, the density of regulation has much increased.

Finally, the 'quality' of the EU institutions has much changed. This puts more demands on national governments for efficient cooperation with the EU. The NMSs have had a long way to go to build up institutions that are able to deal with the sheer size, with the complexity and with the intensity of the interference of the EU and the national domains. Moreover, they came from further afield than the previous accession countries, even if the latter had often to adapt their structures inherited from fascist types of government.

In view of these circumstances, pre-accession assistance has been given to the candidate countries. These started in the early 1990s, which provided know how (including policy advice and training), invested directly in infrastructure and acted as an accelerator for other donors by guarantee lines (EC, 1996a). These programmes amounted to some €1 billion a year.

From 2000 up to 2006 the support to the new member countries has come

Evaluation 241

from three sources that correspond to the major problem that the accession countries have faced:

1 ISPA: support to investment in transport infrastructure and the improvement of the environment (some €3.2 billion).
2 SAPARD: support (some €0.5 billion a year) to rural areas and adaptation to the Common Agricultural Policy (CAP).
3 Phare: some €1.6 billion a year for institution building, investment in regulatory infrastructure to comply with the 'acquis communautaire'.

Given the problems of the candidate countries the choice of the priorities seems obvious and hence we can consider the policies as fully appropriate.

10.7.2 Effectiveness

There are huge needs in the NMSs and in the accession states and these justify that huge sums are devoted to the solving of those problems. However, the recipient countries have considerable difficulties to absorb this amount of money. We have seen these problems while discussing the delivery and implementation aspects in the previous chapters. These problems have, however, been gradually eased under the influence of two factors: previous efforts and a cap on the ratio of support.

Previous efforts have prepared the ground. Indeed, the EU redistribution has not started with formal accession: considerable sums in pre-accession aid have been spent in the new member countries. In this way the NMSs have gained experience. However, the adoption of the EU framework for programming, partnership, monitoring and evaluation has not been without difficulties. Unfortunately the EU has contributed to such difficulties as the governance aspects of the Phare funds were different from those of the SF. So the accession countries had to adapt institutions, train people and adjust administrative and political habits, once to meet Phare and next to meet SF requirements. In order to limit the cost and keep the process going one has often opted for a simplified set up notably in the refocusing of the projects to a limited set of targets. The improvement of the administrative and absorption capacity has often been explicitly taken up as a major development goal. In this sense the very existence of the EU framework has contributed to the effectiveness of the SF efforts (Blazek and Vozab, 2006).

A cap has been set. The absorption capacity of the NMSs is relatively limited. The EU has set a cap (ceiling) on its support; total funds flowing to a certain beneficiary country should not exceed 4 per cent of that country's GDP. The amounts available within this 4 per cent cap have up until now been sufficient for covering the needs of the recipient countries. A general 4 per cent cap has, however, the perverse effect that support grows as the beneficiary country catches up. This effect can be illustrated with Figure 10.3. The assumptions are that receipts from the SF per capita increase up to a level of €10,000 to reach €400, remain stable at that point up to a level of €15,000 and decrease to cease

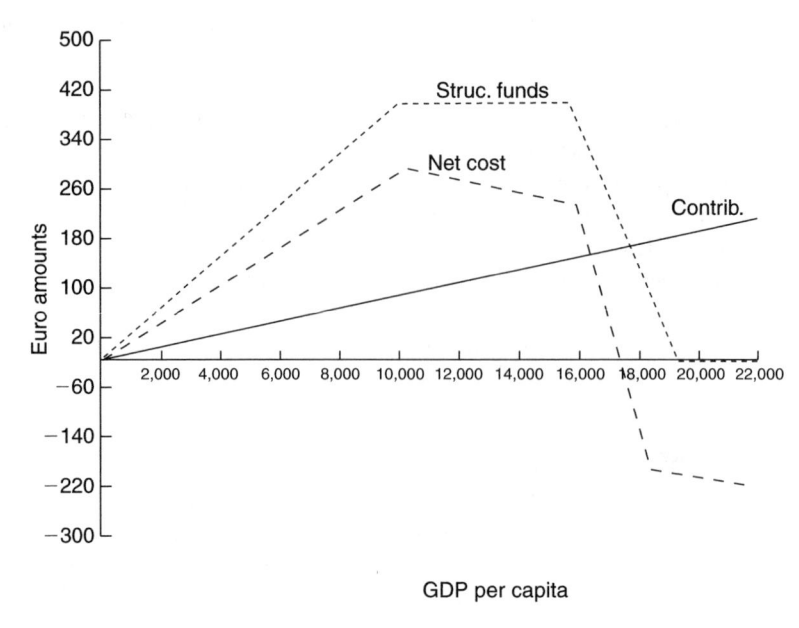

Figure 10.3 Effect of the 4 per cent cap on SCF receipts for the NMS
Source: Gros and Steinherr (2004: 286)

completely at €20,000. For completeness we assumed that contributions to the budget remain 1 per cent of GDP at all levels of wealth. So the net receipts can be obtained by subtracting the two lines.

The effects of this rule are clearly at odds with equity considerations as the amount of aid per head of population is actually higher the higher the wealth level. For that reason the EU has differentiated the cap by the level of development of the recipient country. The cap is 3.8 per cent for countries with a GDP/P below 40 per cent of the EU average; 3.2 per cent for countries around 75 per cent of the EU mean; the 3.2 per cent figure is decreased by 0.09 percentage points of GDP for each increment of 5 percentage points of the ratio of the country GDP/P to that of the EU.

10.8 The CF

10.8.1 Appropriateness

We recall that the CF was established in 1993 to support the least prosperous member states to prepare for participation in the EMU. The support is targeted in two fields: environment and transport. The total available sums have been some €16 billion for the 1993–99 period and €18 billion for the 2000–06 period. The level of assistance is high (80–85 per cent of eligible cost); by implication the degree of co-financing required is low. The latter came mostly from the national budgets; co-financing from the private sector was found to be almost negligible. Recently the ex post evaluation has been made (ECORYS, 2004b).

The projects carried out in the field of environment were mostly very relevant for reaching the policy priorities of both the national and the EU. However, they were not always clearly part of a well-established strategy. In the course of the operation of the CF this integration has been improved. A point of concern in the appropriateness assessment has been that many projects were designed to solve environmental problems that had been caused by specific actors. Now the CF support means that one of the basic principles of the EU environmental policy, namely, the 'polluter pays', has not been respected. The EU has identified the problem without solving it (EC, 2000c). In practice the solution found is that a charging system should be put in place that covers at least the operating and maintenance cost.

Transport projects are appropriate from an EU point of view as they take away serious bottlenecks in the infrastructure of the beneficiary countries. This applies to both road and other projects (rail, port). They were included in national plans and found relevant.

Project priorities have been selected jointly by the Commission and the member states. There has been an inherent tension between the national and EU priorities. Some of the projects selected were not top priorities from a national point of view.

A particularly important aspect to be seen in the case of CF projects is that many of them might also have qualified under the SF, as they were located in objective 1 or objective 2 regions. The allocation of the various projects over the SF and CF has in all cases been done in a rather pragmatic way; the larger projects clearly contributing to EU objectives and priorities tended to go for CF support, others for SF support.

The final appreciation as to the appropriateness of the CF interventions is very difficult. The type of projects selected is not specific for the CF. The chosen types are certainly relevant for the improvement of the conditions for competitiveness of these countries (e.g. infrastructure) and contribute to EU objectives (sustainability). However, other types of interventions could be justified with these arguments as well.

10.8.2 Effectiveness

Generally the projects reviewed have achieved their outputs, results and goals. This can be seen in simple indicators such as the doubling of the motorway network in Greece, Ireland and Portugal. Also, in the majority of cases, the utilization of the infrastructure and the beneficiary population was largely in line with the ex ante expectations. In the case of individual projects the evaluation was hampered by the lack of quantified information and suitable indicators. It has also been hampered by the blurring of concepts; in many cases objectives, outputs and results were mixed up despite the prescriptions of the MEANS standard (see earlier section on methods).

The impact in terms of return of the projects has been in general positive, although the quality of the Cost Benefit Analysis carried out has been on many instances insufficient. The impact of the CF projects on a number of points (such as employment, additional value added and investments generated by business) has overall been impressive (LSE, 1999).

10.9 Some overarching aspects

10.9.1 The bright side: EU added value

Overlooking the results in the previous sections we see that the EU has contributed to a number of improvements as to cohesion that can be termed the value added of the EU. It is good to recall in this respect the reasons why policies should be moved to a higher level of jurisdiction (see Chapter 6). The principle motive for an EU cohesion policy as compared to national ones is economies of scale. It implies that things would not have been achieved or would have been achieved in a less complete or less efficient way had the EU cohesion policy not existed. In other words: value resulting from EU assistance that is additional to that which would have been secured by national and regional authorities and the private sector. The EU involvement has both a financial and a regulatory dimension. Specifying value added according to the financial dimension we should find that spending of money via the SF has had better effects than it would have had if it were spent via national budgets. Specifying value added along the regulatory dimension implies the identification of positive effects on cohesion that would not have existed without EU rules and institutions.

The EU has created value added[29] in matters of cohesion on each of the stages of the cycle:

- *Analysis of the problems.* In quite a number of cases countries failed to recognize the gravity of certain problems. The EU has contributed to a good assessment by making pan EU surveys based on uniform definitions and leading to comparable figures.
- *Selecting the right intervention system.* The EU cohesion policy favours competitiveness and thus growth. Concentration of resources on investment in the improvement of the stock of physical capital and human capital has taken away clear barriers to growth.
- *Mobilizing substantial resources.* The EU funds are much larger than the cohesion countries would have been able to mobilize had they been on their own; there is a clear and substantial redistribution within the EU. Moreover, the EU requires co-financing for investing in projects. In this way extra finances from public and private sources have been mobilized (and often secured in times of budgetary restraints) so that total levels of investment have been enhanced.
- *Regulation and coordination.* The EU has prevented subsidy wars and a race to the bottom in terms of social and environmental standards.
- *Improving the quality of the implementation and delivery system.*[30] The EU wants

partnership and good governance generally applied. As a consequence many countries have improved their administrative structures and procedures, notably those that deal with the programming cycle as depicted in Figure 7.1. The multi-annual programming approach of the EU has introduced predictability as to the availability of funds permitting beneficiaries to go ahead with projects that under the uncertainty of single year budgetary allotments would not have come off the ground. The EU regulations have contributed to strategic thinking and planning both on the national and regional level. The ownership of projects on low levels of organization has improved the adequacy of the projects with the real needs of the region or group. The strict rules about good governance have decreased the degree of fraud and corruption. An example of the influence of the EU on a national delivery system is given in Box 10.2.

- *Enhancing learning effects.* The EU obligation to regularly evaluate interventions has made it possible to regularly adapt the system to new demands. It has also had important positive effects on the quality of the programmes and projects carried out. Moreover, the EU has fostered exchange of knowledge about the understanding of the problems and about the best ways to attack them. The EU experience has clearly influenced changes in national policy regimes that are now more geared to competitiveness and less to simple redistribution.
- *Realizing synergies between EU policies.* There are two sides to this:

    1 There is, on balance, a positive influence of the EU institutions and of EU integration. The EU regimes about such diverse matters as internal market, EMU, product safety, competition, etc., have stimulated growth in the countries that earlier had problems in terms of volatility of exchange rates, inflation, lack of trust in the legal system, etc.
    2 The SF devote considerable amounts in the least-favoured areas in the EU to meet EU standards and reach EU policy objectives in matters of transport, innovation, information society, environment and energy. The resources earmarked for cohesion and spent on these items are often more important in financial terms than those devoted to the respective sectoral EU policies. However, the impact goes further in the sense that the EU cohesion programmes have stimulated national governments to develop strategic views on other policies and improve their impact. A clear case in point is environmental policy under the impetus of the CF support.

> *Box 10.2* Italy's institutional restructuring to reach conformity with EU norms
>
> With the 1988 reforms of the SF a set of new rules was introduced. The mid-1990s evaluation of the Italian implementation of the SF under these new rules showed the persistence of rather low levels of aggregate policy effectiveness. It showed also the very large differences that existed between Italian regions in the quality of their institutions and hence in the quality of the implementation of the SF. The Commission then threatened to reallocate funds earmarked for badly performing regions to other Italian regions and even to other countries. After negotiations Italy obtained some more time to comply with the new rules under the condition of a clear commitment to a rationalization of its administrative structures and procedures.
>
> In practice this restructuring implied two elements:
>
> 1. At the regional level the designation of single centres responsible for programme management, technical coordination of administrative structures, implementation procedures, monitoring and the provision of co-funding. These centres are accountable to the regional political authority.
> 2. At the national level a new structure (steering cabin later taken over by the Ministry of Finance) with several responsibilities. First, to act as technical reference for the regions. Second, to exert central control over the implementation of EU-funded programmes. Lastly, to develop monitoring and evaluation capacities and apply systematically, monitoring and evaluation to all Italian programmes.
>
> These exigencies of the EC offered the national administration the opportunity to develop a sense of common national mission for making the best use of Community resources, and to force regional administrations to adopt cooperative attitudes, good administrative practices, clear performance criteria and a sense of accountability. The ensuing changes have contributed to the reaching of better levels of efficiency and effectiveness.
>
> *Based on:* Gualini (2004: 146–61)

10.9.2 The shady side: EU added cost

The value added items listed in the previous section do not represent the net effect of EU involvement. There is indeed a cost to it that should be deducted. For each of the stages in the cycle there are the following negative points:

- *Right intervention system.* The improvement of the governance of cohesion has in many member states come at a considerable cost; while the decentral-

ized system is subject to fraud and corruption. This is notably so in some of the NMSs.
- *Money mobilized* leads to two problems:
  1 Aid dependency of the beneficiaries. Member countries are inclined to regard the aid as a major source of income and have difficulty to develop new resources for investment in productive and competitive activities. Where support by the SCF leads to higher than normal factor prices this support constitutes a barrier rather than a stimulus for innovation and productivity. That mechanism seems to have had a negative influence on the performance of Greece, for instance.
  2 Welfare loss. The money transferred to the EU might have been more efficiently used had it stayed at the disposal of the member state. The present system of mobilizing funds first and next to redistribute them via EU funds could be simplified which would have two advantages. It would do away with the administrative costs involved, that are quite significant (see next point). It would, moreover, do away with the distortion of preferences that ensues because the EU imposes its criteria on aid eligibility of projects, which does not always match the priorities of the country.
- *Regulation and coordination.* Some of the instruments of the EU are too constraining; for instance, investment subsidies in problem areas may be a necessary complement for attracting new jobs there. On the other hand, the OMC is not capable of realizing the side objectives of the EU cohesion policy; such as quickly realizing innovative dynamism and job growth.
- *Implementation and delivery system.* The EU system leads also to two problems:
  1 Unclear division of responsibilities leads to lengthy and costly procedures for having projects prepared, the expenses justified and the process monitored. There does not seem to be much difference between the various funds in total administrative burden, which is estimated at €0.35 per €100 investment (ECORYS, 2004b). The disadvantage of the cumbersome and time-consuming coordination, decision making on strategy and priorities, monitoring and evaluation is notably negative for small projects that have intangible targets or where the contribution of the EU to total project cost is relatively small.[31]
  2 Predictability has created, on some scores, a lack of flexibility.[32] Once the priorities and the measures are decided it can appear that the character of the problem is different and that the approach adopted is no longer adequate. Adaptation to such new facts is then very difficult. In some cases this problem is exacerbated by the development of a risk-aversive culture among partners (notably administrators).
- *Learning effects.* One of the objectives of evaluation is learning. However, this is a problematic aim in the sense that it may lead to an attitude of irresponsibility on the part of those involved; as they may impute running cost

of mismanagement and mistakes on the (virtual) capital account of learning. Another point that needs to be mentioned, in this respect, is the penalty the EU puts on bad performance; in EU jargon the so-called 'performance reserve'. Although the idea is quite right to stimulate good performance and to discourage bad performance, it may have a perverse effect on evaluation. Indeed, the risk of losing money due to poor performance may lead to undue pressure on evaluation to come up with results.
- *Synergies between EU policies.* This is a blurring of responsibilities. Sectoral policies that can use adequate finances and instruments for their proper functioning tend to be most effective.

The problems listed here can be grouped under the heading of 'lack of efficiency'. Some funds and programmes suffer more from this problem than others. In general, one can say that those geared to infrastructure (e.g. the CF and the ERDF) perform rather well as there is a clear idea about cost of inputs and the measurement of outputs. Indeed, infrastructure projects that involve considerable outlays require only fairly small cost of preparation, administration and audit. On the other hand, funds and programmes that are geared to social targets (e.g. the ESF) such as education, training and social inclusion have often to be split up in a multitude of smaller projects that demand very high manpower inputs for relatively limited financial outlays. Moreover, the outputs and outcomes of such programmes are in general much more difficult to establish than for infrastructure.

However, even with infra projects there are some problems with efficiency. Time and cost overruns are the main weakness of the projects, which is due to: (1) ill-preparation; (2) external factors such as unexpected archeological of ecological findings; (3) the involvement of the local community; and (4) lack of managerial capabilities.

10.10 The other objectives

10.10.1 Indications for trade offs

The previous sections have dealt with the evaluation of the cohesion policy on its stated objectives; that is the reduction of the disparities and the improvement of the competitiveness and employment situation in the EU. We recall here (see Chapters 7 (section 7.4.3) and 8) that cohesion policy has also served a number of other purposes. On the one hand, to facilitate the construction of political compromises that permitted the passing into higher stages of integration, on the other hand the reaching of goals such as competitiveness and sustainable development. The question then becomes, even if the cohesion policy would not be justified because it failed to have reached its own objectives, would it be justified because it has contributed to reach these other objectives? The answering of this question is fraught with difficulties.

First, it is difficult to pinpoint in practice the existence of a relation between increased integration and increased cohesion efforts. Second, it is difficult to pinpoint the effects of increased integration. To that end we have to detail deepening (the passing into higher stages of integration) and widening (enlargement of the EU). We will deal with them separately. In a last section we will go into the question of the effect of the instrumentalization of cohesion policy for other EU policy objectives.

10.10.2 Widening

The economic benefits of the various rounds of the enlargement of the EU have in general been positive in welfare terms.

The effects of the *first enlargement* in the 1970s (with notably the UK) has had positive effects on trade and welfare, although less so than those of the creation of the EU 6.[33] Of course the period differs from the preceding one in many respects. At the start of the EU 9 most tariffs were lower than at the time of creation of the EU 6; besides, a profound need for economic restructuring was recognized, energy prices were on a steep increase, trade balances were adversely affected and new protectionism was becoming generally accepted.

The effects of the *second enlargement* in the 1980s (the accession of the Mediterranean countries) are not well known as they cannot very well be dissociated from other changes in the same period, notably the completion of the internal market.

The accession of the central and eastern European countries to the EU has been estimated to be marginally beneficial for the old member states and very beneficial for the NMSs.[34]

A particularly poisonous effect has been the compensation of the distortion created by the CAP. This can be explained as follows. The very high protection levels in the EU 6 created high prices for consumers. On accession, countries such as the UK and Portugal were used to import these agricultural products from the world market at low prices. Accession thus meant, henceforth, an increase of local price level to the one in the EU 6 and a transfer of money from accession country consumers to agricultural producers in the EU 6. Notably, in the latter case, it was overtly anti-cohesive as a poor country had to transfer resources to rich countries. As the CAP could not be renegotiated the cohesion policy also had the task to compensate for these transfers. The welfare effects of this operation are very negative as they created a costly cohesion system to perpetuate a very costly CAP. It is only recently that the cutback in price support has taken away this negative distortion effect (see Chapter 11 and Molle, 2006).

10.10.3 Deepening

In terms of the effects of deepening (new stages of integration), we have to look notably at two major events: the completion of the internal market in the 1980s and the creation in steps of the EMU in the 1990s.

The total welfare gains resulting from the completion of the internal market of the EU were rather optimistically estimated at some 6 per cent of GDP; provided the right macro economic policies were carried out (Checcini report). In the mid-1990s, the Commission made an ex post evaluation of the effects of the completion of the internal market (EC, 1996b). The effects on GDP were found to be considerably less than those calculated in the ex ante study. Including the effects of the liberalization of the so-called network activities (e.g. telecom) the total effects were estimated to amount to some 1 to 2 per cent of GDP. However, as some of the medium-term (dynamic) effects may not have been fully captured, the growth bonus may be significantly higher. The efficiency gains have anyway more than compensated for the initial losses due to restructuring.[35]

The creation of the EMU has been done in two stages: first, the EMS and next the EMU.

- The EMS was meant to bring medium-term stability in exchange rates. It permitted, however, daily variations of the exchange rates. By combining stability (central rates) and flexibility (daily rates) it has stimulated intra-Union trade and capital movements.[36] Such increases in allocational efficiency bring higher welfare.
- The EMU is of fairly recent origin. As a consequence there is, as yet, not much evidence to claim that the adoption of the euro has actually delivered the expected enhancing effect on trade.[37] However, some effects are visible. The reduced exchange rate volatility and the higher quality of the institutions seem to have had a weak effect on growth (Bagella *et al.*, 2004). In any case the introduction of the euro has had a positive effect on investment by firms from countries that had weak currencies before (Bris *et al.*, 2006).

10.10.4 Other objectives

As we have indicated in Chapter 8 the EU cohesion instruments are also used to reach the objectives of other policies. This concerns first the Lisbon strategy, which aims at increases in competitiveness, more and better jobs and quicker innovation. It concerns next the Gothenburg strategy that aims particularly at improvements of environmental sustainability. The EU has come to integrate much of its actions for these objectives in coherent policy frameworks and it has instrumentalized the SCF to contribute to the realization of these goals.

The evaluation of these policies has in the past been done in a segmented way. They fall outside the scope of this book. The integration of policies has only just started. The same is true for the use of the SF in this framework. The evaluation of integrated policies with a diversified set of instruments adds an extra set of difficulties to the evaluator, the solving of which would be far beyond the ambitions of this book. For those reasons we will not go further into this matter.

10.11 Evaluating the evaluation: ways to improvement

10.11.1 Systemic aspects

The model that the EU has developed in matters of evaluation seems in general adequate for the goals it serves and the tasks it has to perform. We recall that this is first and foremost to provide accountability; second, it has to deliver improvements in the carrying out of the tasks in the whole policy cycle and lead to learning effects. In broad outline the EU evaluation system is well adjusted to the systemic aspects of the whole policy system and (provided it is well applied) produces answers to the relevant questions.

This is not to say that all elements of the system are perfect. On the contrary, many points can be identified where the system could be refined and could be better adapted to needs. The question is, however, whether it is a task for the EU to identify these points, prescribe more detailed regulation and control its application. We have seen that the present system already puts a heavy burden on efficiency. Further refining and compulsory application of those refinements would aggravate the efficiency problem. Moreover, it would go against the application of another principle for the design of EU systems, which is subsidiarity. The Commission is committed to apply this principle more strictly than in the past and has consequently decided that it would henceforth only deal with the more strategic questions and leave more of the implementation in the hands of the member states.

10.11.2 Operational aspects: improving the evaluation culture of practitioners

Although the system itself does not need much strengthening and improvement its application does. Much is to be gained by the fair implementation of the existing rules where this is still insufficiently the case. Examples are in the NMSs where the application is often hindered by a deficient institutional and administrative capacity. The same is the case for the older member states where it is rather a question of a feeling of discomfort with the rules than lack of capacity. Indeed, although the evaluation has made considerable headway in the past it cannot be denied that many consider its application as inconvenient to the political game and as threatening to individual and institutional reputations.

Evaluation is not an easy exercise. All sorts of practical problems have to be solved to achieve a satisfactory result. One has to prepare the ground by correctly specifying the problems, selecting priorities and quantifying policy targets. Next databases need to be established, records need to be made of the resources deployed, etc. Finally, output and outcome need to be highlighted. Lack of enthusiasm with these processes can produce insufficiencies that make the evaluators' task difficult and the results of the exercise dubious. However, these failures can be described and improved.

A much more problematic point in this respect is the (lack of) independence of the evaluator. In this chapter we have said that the application of the partnership principle made for a fragile equilibrium in matters of evaluation. It means that a variety of interests are involved in the policy and hence in the results of the evaluation. The independent contractor of the evaluation tends to be subject to a variety of more or less subtle pressures to limit criticism. The techniques applied consist, in general, in giving the contractor as little leeway as possible in terms of restrictions as to the calendar time, the amount of money available for the analysis and the scope of the investigation. As a consequence current budgets and study timetables often allow only a superficial approach.

In order to improve on this point and to limit the dead hand influence of vested interest it may be good to consider the procurement, funding and oversight of evaluations by genuinely independent units.

The accent put on thorough evaluation practices also has a shady side. Indeed, the evaluation practice imposed on all beneficiaries of the SCF puts a heavy burden on resources. Ex ante, in course and ex post have to be made at very brief intervals, sometimes before effects become visible. In the case of ex post evaluation of a programme that is rounded off and therefore discontinued the effort is even without any visible benefit for the parties involved. So, it need not be a surprise to find a certain fatigue among them. What remedy to these illnesses? A simplification seems possible in those cases where the involvement of the EU is limited (in terms of percentage contribution to financing) here one might envisage the use of less demanding practices so as to improve the efficiency of the operation.

10.11.3 Methodological aspects: improving the tools of the research community

In the previous sections we have seen that many inadequacies of evaluation exercises were related to the supply side. In other words to the incapacity of the research community to come up with clear answers to the basic questions raised by evaluation. Essentially these questions concern effectiveness: Have the instruments deployed led to an increase in the target variable? And if so, by how much?

We have seen that the cause–effect relation is very difficult to establish. To give a few examples:

- Modelling approaches risk rediscovering in their conclusions the assumptions that have been fed into them.
- Micro-level approaches suffer from a lack of possibilities to generalization.

Better approaches, notably experimental and quasi experimental methods, longitudinal studies, etc., could mean an improvement but these are often costly and cannot be accommodated within the present atomized structure of programme evaluation studies.

10.12 Summary and conclusions

- The EU evaluates systematically its cohesion efforts in the fifth stage of the policy cycle. It has devised standard methods for doing so. These evaluations serve two main goals. First, accountability; they provide evidence to all stakeholders that money is well spent. Second, learning; evaluation provides lessons that make that policy, programmes and projects in the future will respond better to the stated goals than those of the past.
- However, the effectiveness of the EU cohesion policy is still not easy to establish due to lack of specification of targets and numerous methodological and data problems. Notwithstanding these weaknesses the analysis permits a few general conclusions:

  - First, that the *appropriateness* of the policy measures is satisfactory. This means that the type of measures that have been taken in the pursuit of cohesion policy have in general been well geared to the objectives of the policy.
  - Second, that the *effectiveness* of the policy is a matter of considerable controversy. Although there is a majority of studies that find positive effects, quite a few find only very limited or even negative effects. This controversy is partly due to inefficiencies in the methods.[38] So it is plausible that the policy is effective although there is not yet firm proof.

- As to *efficiency* there is almost unanimity of views. Most studies find that the delivery of the policy entails high cost. (This appears to be in particular the case for programmes and projects in the social field.) The reasons are to be found in the need of the EU to constantly check eligibility and performance, given its accountability for the expenditure.[39]
- The evaluation of the cohesion policy on its *side objectives* is positive. The cohesion policy has permitted the EU to pass into higher stages of integration, which has had positive welfare effects.
- There is little need for improvements as to the evaluation system as such. Yet there is still a lot to be gained by the better implementation of the present system and the improvement of the independence of the individual evaluation exercises.

11 Consistency with other EU policies

11.1 Introduction

As we described in the previous chapters, the EU pursues an active policy to promote economic, social and territorial cohesion. It checks through constant evaluation its effectiveness. However, cohesion is not only influenced by policies that have cohesion as their specific target. Many EU policies have side-effects on cohesion. So, in order to maximize the effects of its efforts the EU has to make sure that the effects of these other EU policies are consistent with the objective of cohesion. To that end the EU assesses, during the fifth stage of the policy cycle, whether the impacts of its policies are positive or negative and in the latter case tries to bend them in such a way that the negative effects are minimized and positive effects maximized.[1]

The objective of the present chapter is to make an overall assessment of the consistency of the various EU policies with the policy on cohesion. A drawback is that the issue of policy coherence is a relative newcomer in the academic debate. There is no well-established practice or methodology for evaluating it, compared to conventional topics such as evaluation. Moreover, many programmes that are part of other EU policies lack explicitly formulated objectives or criteria for the effectiveness of policy instruments, so checks on coherence are difficult. Notwithstanding this drawback we will make an assessment on the basis of a review of the evidence from the most relevant theoretical and empirical studies that are available.[2]

The structure is as follows. First, we select the most relevant EU policies. Next, we describe for each of these policies their impact on cohesion. For each of the selected policies we will specify the objectives, describe the channels of transmission and make an attempt to quantify the impacts. In a third part of this chapter we will combine the results for the past and present situation into a total picture. Finally, we will summarize the main results of the discussion in this chapter.

We will as much as possible try to specify the economic, the social and the territorial aspect of cohesion. However, as in most cases, the studies on which we draw focused on the regional aspect so we cannot avoid a certain bias in that direction.

Contrary to previous chapters we will not be able to devote a fair share of attention to the NMSs, as there is very little available evidence.

11.2 General aspects

11.2.1 Selection of policies, methods and level of analysis

The EU pursues a whole array of policies. In the limited framework of this chapter we can only see a small part of them.[3] We have selected for further scrutiny those EU policies that have the biggest presumed impact. There are two main channels through which these policies impact on cohesion: the budget and regulation. As far as the former is concerned, it is clear that we have to look at the biggest spender which is agriculture. With respect to the latter we anyway address the policies that refer to the essentials of the EU (internal market, macro and monetary, trade, transport, environment and innovation).

If the policies to analyse are easy to identify, the same is not the case for their effects. Unfortunately the empirical analysis of the effects of these policies on cohesion is very difficult as it is sometimes impossible to dissociate these effects from those of simultaneous developments (like accession of new member countries) and of the support by the SF. We found for each subject only a limited number of studies that have looked in depth at the problem. Only very few do actually give a quantification of the impact; and unfortunately those that do are not comparable among each other in terms of units of measurement and category of impact. As most do give a qualitative assessment we will put the accent here on the direction of the impact.

11.2.2 A major channel for transmission: the budget

One of the major ways in which EU policies affect cohesion is by the distribution of the expenditure over the different member states, regions and social groups (see Chapters 6 and 7). The size of the budget devoted to different policies varies considerably.

Most important is the CAP. In the 1980s this category used to absorb some two-thirds of the total budget, mainly through the outlays for guaranteed prices. A series of decisions have been taken to change the structure of the CAP and as a consequence its share in the budget has been much decreased (to some two-fifths). The other budget lines of the EU for horizontal policies are all of limited size. Together the outlays for policies such as energy, manufacturing industry, transport, research and environment add up to less than 10 per cent.

These budget lines have a distribution over countries, regions and social groups that may favour cohesion, but may also run contrary to this objective by favouring presently strong areas and groups.

The way in which cohesion can be influenced through the budget can be illustrated with a policy field that we will elaborate on somewhat further hereafter. The EU stimulates innovation by financing certain R&D programmes that would not have been realized by the member countries due to lack of scale, etc. In order to maximize the effect of these programmes the EU wants to select those that are of outstanding quality. The top quality R&D organizations tend to be located in the most developed member states. So, most of the funding of the EU research policy tends to go to the richer member countries. Although the logic of the programme is undeniable, it is most likely not supportive of cohesion.

11.2.3 Another channel of transmission: regulation

Another major way in which EU policies have effects on cohesion is by regulation (see also Chapters 6 and 8). We can cite as an illustration a policy with a potentially negative and policy with a potentially positive effect.

On the negative side, the internal market policies tend to favour the regions that are very competitive for the location of high-value-added economic activities. Liberalization leads to fiercer competition and the regions that are best equipped will tend to become winners in this game. In practice this will lead to a strengthening of already rich regions (we come back to this in more detail later in the chapter).

On the positive side, the EMU tends to create stable conditions for poor countries that shield them from the negative effects of instability. So, the EMU may favour actually all the regions of these poor countries (we come back also to this in more detail later in the chapter).

We recall that the EU uses several models to put its policies into effect through regulation. The examples provided are specimens of the Community Method. It consists of binding rules, fairly centralized policies and harmonization based on common decisions. Much of the agricultural policy is actually pursued in this way. For a number of policy fields the EU increasingly uses an alternative method, the OMC. This method (see Chapter 8) is, for instance, applied in matters of employment policy. Intermediate forms combining rather non-binding instruments with constraints and sanctions are applied in matters of economic and monetary policy.

11.3 Agriculture

11.3.1 Objectives

The first objective of the CAP is to stabilize markets. The second, is to reinforce the production structures, notably in backward areas. Considerable financial resources have been and still are devoted to the CAP. In the past the CAP (which consumed the lion's share of the EU budget and involved the largest redistribution of income among European citizens) mainly benefited the 'rich' regions (Henry, 1981; Franzmeyer et al., 1991). They led to overproduction, to distortion of world markets and to very high welfare costs for the EU consumer and taxpayer. In view of these problems the CAP has been gradually reformed.

In the framework of the 1992 reform and later of the Agenda 2000, a switchover has been made from price support to direct income support. This has made it possible to cut back many of the very high guarantee prices that led to overproduction. The introduction of a policy of direct payments (per ha or per farm) made it possible to make the payments dependent on the contribution of the farmer to the objectives of other EU policies, for example, in matters of the environment.

11.3.2 Transmission

The major channel by which the agricultural policy transmits its effects on cohesion is through the direct payments that flow from the EU budget outlays. This is evidenced in Box 11.1.

Box 11.1 Cohesion impact of CAP budget outlays

The effect on cohesion of budget outlays can be measured by checking the part that goes to the least prosperous regions. If this is large one may infer that the effect is positive; if it is low one may assume that the effect is negative.

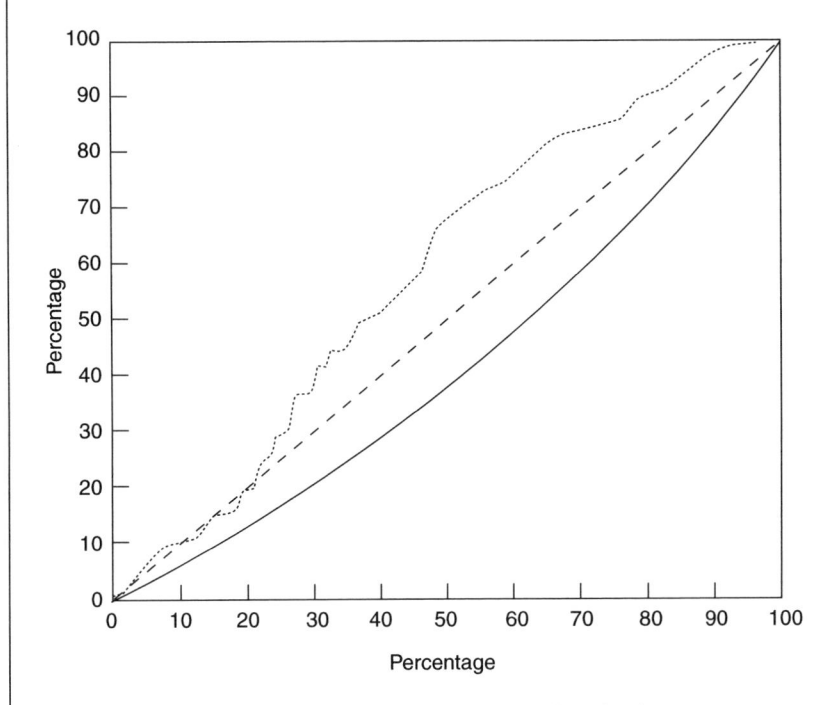

Figure 11.1 Cohesion impact of EU agricultural policy funding
Sources: ECORYS NEI (2001)
Curves: Lower continuous line: Income; upper dotted line: CAP

This approach has been formalized in the Lorenz curve, that is the graphical counterpart of the Gini coefficient, a measure of disparity. Both are constructed as follows. All EU regions are arranged in ascending order according to their GDP/P. Next, the cumulative shares of the regions in the total EU figures are calculated, starting with the regions with the lowest GDP/P. The graphical representation gives in the bottom curve the cumulative share of total GDP (left-hand axis) and the cumulative share of the total population (horizontal axis).[4] The lower the Lorenz curve with respect to the diagonal (where shares in GDP and in population are equal) the higher is the disparity and the lesser cohesion. The figure that is of interest here is not the GDP/P but the agricultural spending of the CAP. We have approximated the CAP outlays with the help of the Producer Support Estimates for 1997. The CAP line (upper left) shows a mixed picture. A slight negative effect on cohesion can be noticed; indeed for the poorest 20 per cent of the regions (left-hand part of horizontal axis) the curve runs below the equity line. After that point the contribution of CAP to cohesion is positive (more so for the regions in the 20–60 per cent brackets) as the curve runs above the equity line. In other words, as support to producers is higher in the backward regions and lower in the most prosperous regions, the CAP seems to have a positive impact on cohesion.[5]

A point that should not be forgotten in this respect is that apart from this direct effect there is also an indirect effect. The consumer prices have been high as a consequence of CAP support. This has had a perverse redistribution effect as (generally poor) regions characterized by Mediterranean products tend to pay high prices for their food bill, income that might have been spent on other items had the agricultural policy not imposed these high prices. This transfer from net consumption regions to net production regions is not picked up in the figures of the distribution of expenditure. Unfortunately, the studies we found that acknowledge this effect do not quantify it.

11.3.3 Impacts

The impact of the agricultural policy on cohesion must be seen by its three dimensions (Labour Asociados, 2003).

The impact on *economic cohesion* has generally been judged as negative. The reason is that the high prices for agricultural products have hindered the competitiveness of industries that use these products as primary inputs. Moreover, the system is supposed to have put a brake on the modernization of economic structures. Finally, the deadweight burden to taxpayers has caused important inefficiencies.

The effect on the *social dimension* of cohesion is, in the first instance, positive as it supports vulnerable groups in rural areas. However, in the second instance the effect is, among other factors, negative because the price support system has worked as a degressive income tax (Tarditi and Zanias, 2001).

As far as *territorial impact* is concerned, the influence seems at a first glance to be positive as the CAP transfers income from rich urban and industrial regions to poorer agricultural regions. There is evidence of this positive effect (College of Europe, 1997). This finding is corroborated by the study reported in Box 10.1 (the richer the region the lower the total support). Seen in a different way, however, the conclusion may be different. The total support per Agricultural Working Unit was found to be higher in the richer regions and lower in the poorer regions (ESPON, 2004a). Direct income payments are providing a positive impulse on cohesion, but even here some problems occur as the support was found to be highest in the more accessible areas of the periphery. The ESPON study concludes that on aggregate the CAP works against the objectives of balanced territorial development.

11.4 Internal market

11.4.1 Objectives

The essence of the EU is the internal market. It is the clearest example of the EU regulatory model. It has been put in place right from the start of the integration process. The prime objective of the internal market policy is to optimize welfare creation by improving the allocation function. Internal market policies, intensified in the 1980s and 1990s, have consisted of mainly three parts:[6]

1. Taking away of the remaining barriers between countries.
2. Introducing the market mechanism in a number of sectors that up until that moment were sheltered (such as many services, in particular, network services, such as transport and electricity).
3. Tightening a number of policies aimed at improving the working of markets (institutional reform such as the competition policy and tax harmonization).

Progress has been substantial on all three scores mentioned. There are still some barriers, notably in service markets.

11.4.2 Transmission

The effects of market integration on cohesion have been the subject of quite some theoretical and empirical research. From a theoretical point of view the results are inconclusive (Braunerhjelm *et al.*, 2000). So it is a matter of empirical studies to show the real effects. A point of major concern has been the effect on the regional level. In order to take away the doubts as to the effects on regions several approaches have been tried out:

- *Sectoral change.* The impact of the completion of the internal market is estimated by identifying first, the sectors that might be influenced, either positively (through the seizing of new opportunities due to increased market access or exploitation of economies of scale) or negatively (by increased competitive pressure on less competitive firms). Second, by applying these

effects on the structure of the regions where these sectors are or may become located. This approach has in the past not been very successful[7] (Molle, 1990). It supposes uniform reactions which in practice do not occur. Some industries face the challenge and develop competitive activities; others in similar positions fail to find new opportunities and have to leave the market. The net effect is uncertain.
- *Location tendencies.* New (including foreign direct) investment did not strengthen the concentration in central areas. In the early period of the EU the tendency was rather to de-concentrate, favouring notably intermediate areas. The more recent tendencies go in the same direction (e.g. Mold, 2003). However, there is one exception; the process of mergers has often entailed a relocation of functions, with the management and R&D functions being concentrated in central areas and the other functions being spread more evenly.
- *Regional specificities.* Case studies show that regions respond differently to the increased pressures to restructure and to improve competitiveness and that the effect on cohesion cannot be ex ante determined. Whether positive or negative is the end effect of a large number of contradictory pressures.[8]

The end effect is reason for concern. Take for instance the case of the NMSs where growth tends to concentrate in the areas that are most capable of receiving modern market-oriented industries and services, and this enhances the concentration in central urban areas and in the regions bordering the present EU. Another important aspect is risk. Peripheral regions tend to depend more on non-market services and have a more risky specialization (Stirboeck, 2002).

For many sectors of activity the internal market has, for a long time, already imposed its logic. However, for some this is new and it is notably for these that the cohesion concern can be made effective. So, we will, in particular, look more into the effect on cohesion of the *liberalization of network industries*.[9] Network economies influence location. Networks are most efficient in densely populated and highly developed areas and least efficient in sparsely populated areas. So the price of these services may be highest in problem areas and lowest in developed areas. This would create an extra hurdle for cohesion countries and regions. So network activities have become the subject of the EU policy on SGI. Maintaining, in remote areas, minimum levels of such services at a price comparable to those in central areas is the main aim of this policy. In order to get a licence network service operators have to accept to provide these minimum levels of services to all clients in their area.[10] The impact of the liberalization of network industries can be studied by taking the example of telecommunications. The net direct impact on economic cohesion is positive; while the impact on social and territorial cohesion is assumed to be negative (Young et al., 2001) as small users and remote area customers have higher access charges. On the other hand, distance costs have fallen dramatically so this could be a positive aspect for territorial cohesion. Unfortunately the empirical basis for such statements is still very weak (ESPON, 2004b).

In matters of *competition policy* the situation differs as to specific policy fields. We will detail here three of these fields.

The strong EU *competition rules for enterprises* curtail cartels and forbid the abuse of dominant positions. These are applied irrespective of the type of industry and type of location. In the short term the effect of competition rules on cohesion can be negative as firms in problem areas that had been sheltered from competition by restrictive practices can thus come into difficulties. However, in the long term they will help to raise competitiveness (by taking away distortion) and hence favour cohesion. A case in point is the financial sector in Italy, where distortions in competition led to high cost to firms and constituted a serious handicap for the development of many firms in the distressed regions of the Mezzogiorno (Faini *et al.*, 1992).

The EU rules on *state aid* (see Chapters 6 and 8) say that this is only conditionally permitted. These conditions take into account both industry and regional characteristics. We recall the ratio of this negative stand. If aids are given on a sectoral basis they tend to benefit mostly firms in the developed regions. Some figures may give an indication of the magnitude of this effect. The expenditure on state aid is some 1 per cent of the GDP whereas the total size of the SF is only 0.45 per cent of GDP. This means that state aid given for sectoral reasons and benefiting richer regions can completely overwhelm the aid given in the framework of cohesion policy.

We recall here that already at its creation the EU has set rules to stem this potentially negative effect for cohesion (see Chapter 6). These rules have since been sharpened. They consist of:

- Allowance of state aid (under conditions) in problem regions.
- Limits (ceiling) on state aid in developed regions in order to prevent such aid to annihilate the effect of aids in problem regions.

The ceilings have recently been reduced and in step therewith the overall expenditure on aid has decreased significantly as well. Aid in regions that are authorized under the rules has also been significantly reduced in the member states that are not benefiting from objective 1 status. Whether these policy measures have done much good to cohesion remains a matter of debate; some find that national state aid has had little effect, either to good or to ill.

11.4.3 Impacts

Most studies cited suggest that the effects of the internal market have been increasingly positive in general terms. However, the picture becomes more shaded if we detail by dimension.

- As far as *economic cohesion* is concerned the profound restructuring of the economies of all cohesion countries (disposing of ailing sectors and leading in general to a better situation in terms of competitiveness) implies that in the long run effects have been positive.

- However, the same is not true for *social cohesion*. Restructuring often entails an increase in unemployment, including its most severe form, long-term unemployment. In the past the problem has been very acute in the older industrial areas that had difficulties in restructuring. Nowadays, the problem is notably severe in the NMSs. The positive growth effects tend to take some time to work themselves through the economy and alleviate the problems of those out of work.
- In matters of *territorial cohesion* the completion of the internal market has indeed favoured growth in the cohesion countries (Spain, Portugal, Greece and Ireland); the GDP of this group was in 1993 some 10 per cent higher than it would have been had the pre-1987 growth trends continued (EC, 1996a, b).

11.5 Macro and monetary

11.5.1 Objectives

Over time the EU has gradually developed its macro and monetary policies. Initially they were limited to the mere coordination of exchange rate and budgetary policies. However, with the growing interdependence of its member countries the EU has narrowed the scope for independent policies. As a consequence the EU first set up the EMS and then a full EMU. The objective of the EMU is to do away with the negative effects of macro economic instability, including exchange rate uncertainty.

11.5.2 Transmission

The initial stages of the EU macro and monetary policy did not have any marked influence on cohesion. Even then, however, there was some concern as one thought that the deficiencies in the structure of the financial sector in cohesion countries might make them less capable of drawing advantages of the increased integration.

The introduction of the EMU is thought to have a number of effects on cohesion (Molle *et al.*, 1993; Ardy *et al.*, 2002). Some of them are of a transitional nature; others are more permanent.[11]

The first effect of EMU is on allocation. The introduction of the euro increases confidence and decreases a large number of cost items on international transactions, which will lead to substantial higher internal trade and investment. The size of this effect is a matter of controversy. The results of a worldwide analysis showed a very large impact indeed (Rose, 2001; Rose and Stanley, 2005). An analysis specifically done for the euro area (Rose, 2000; Rose and van Wincoop, 2001) showed that intra-euro zone trade will expand by some 50 per cent due to the EMU. Others came at lower estimates ranging around 10 per cent.[12] The EMU does also influence positively internal FDI flows.[13] As we have discussed in the previous section (internal market) this is growth enhancing; so it has a positive effect on economic cohesion.

The second effect of EMU is the elimination of the need for adjustment to problems coming from bilateral exchange rate shocks from partner countries. The effects of this decrease in macro economic vulnerability are supposed to be particularly beneficial for cohesion countries that are most exposed to this type of problem. This positive effect, however, comes at a cost. The single currency eliminates the possibility to adjust via the exchange rate (in other words to improve competitiveness by devaluation), so other mechanisms such as wages and price flexibility will have to do more of the job. Cohesion countries are not well equipped with institutions that efficiently operate these mechanisms.

The third effect of EMU is the decrease in the interest rate that follows on from low inflation, the elimination of exchange rate risks, the higher credibility of the debtors and the more efficient capital markets. This again is particularly interesting for cohesion countries, traditionally confronted with high interest rates. The lowering of the cost of capital stimulates private investment and frees resources from the public budget (less debt servicing) that can be spent on programmes that improve productivity or that can lower the tax burden. The low inflation target (2 per cent) is found to have beneficial effects on growth (Tsonias and Christopoulos, 2003), in particular, on growth in the formerly high inflation countries, many of them characterized by below EU average income levels. So, the effect on cohesion might actually be positive.

We should keep in mind that these benefits are gained by surrendering to two EU regimes (Ardy et al., 2002). First, to the Stability and Growth Pact (SGP), that limits budget deficits and, thereby, the possibility of independent macro policies. Second, to the European Central Bank's (ECB) monetary policy, that sets targets for the whole Union that may not correspond to national preferences. Both may have a negative effect on cohesion countries; the first, as it limits public spending in times a particular effort for cohesion purposes would be required. The second, because it may lead the ECB to setting interest rates high to curb inflationary tendencies stemming from overheating in some countries where the cohesion countries might have been better of with lower rates.

11.5.3 Impacts

In order to catch up backward countries have to realize above average growth. The question is whether the three effects of EMU mentioned would stimulate such growth. The answer is not very clear-cut. A comprehensive review of the historical evidence (Eichengreen and Leblang, 2003) would suggest that flexibility is better for growth than fixed exchange rates. However, this study only looked at stability of exchange rates and does not take into account the specific features of a full EMU. In principle the effect on cohesion can be positive. One is inclined to think that this has also to be the case in practice. Indeed, in the early stage of EMU the cohesion countries have shown much more dynamism (that is higher growth rates) than the richer member countries of the euro zone. More rigorous empirical work on the real effects of monetary policy is scarce. The available studies (e.g. Huchet, 2003) do not find clear patterns as to effects on cohesion. The effects of entry into the EMU of the NMSs are also, as yet, very ambiguous (Devereux, 2003).

These analyses on the national level are only a first step in the sequence of our analysis. We need to move to the regional level. Policies that benefit national territories (such as macro and monetary) may work against regional convergence if all the benefits are gained by a limited number of strong regions. There is some reason for concern here as in the recent past regional divergence has occurred together with national convergence. There is also some evidence that this is related to EMU. For instance in Spain the relatively large and more diversified regions were best prepared for EMU (Costa-i-Font and Tremosa-i-Bacells, 2003). An important factor in this respect is the higher instability in the pattern of credit availability for some peripheral regions (Rodriguez-Fuentes and Dow, 2003).

11.6 External trade

11.6.1 Objectives

Over the whole period of its existence the EU has cooperated with its major trade partners to realize a more open global trade system. In the framework of the various WTO trade rounds it has agreed to lower its external tariffs and to abolish non-tariff barriers on industrial goods. This policy has not been carried out across the board; important parts of the EU economy have for a long time been sheltered from external competition (part of this has been done with cohesion objectives in mind, for instance, the protection against textile and clothing imports). At the moment almost all sectors are exposed to external competition. The objective of EU policy is not free trade but free and fair trade. To that end a certain number of instruments such as anti-dumping can be put in place.

11.6.2 Transmission

The question is in how far EU trade policies have negative effects. In the public debate one can hear alarming statements. The allegations are that the participation of the EU in the globalization tendency by liberalizing trade creates unemployment, reduces wages, notably of the lower-skilled workers, and finally wipes out institutions that have been created to safeguard social cohesion. There is a particular fear that the less diversified and hence often less developed regions will suffer most as they are less resilient to change than the central diversified regions. So the general presumption is that liberalization of external trade may be positive for economic cohesion and negative for both social and territorial cohesion.

To avoid such effects protectionist policies have been pursued, concerning notably so-called 'sensitive goods'. These related to productions that were of particular interest to cohesion countries and problem regions. Cases in point were the textile regions that have for a long time been sheltered against competition with the help of a whole battery of protectionist measures. An even more important case concerned agricultural goods; for many products the EU market was actually completely cut off from the world market in order to protect EU production, some of it in backward areas. These measures have mitigated a downward pressure on employment and wage levels of notably the lower skilled in the EU. So they are supposed to have worked out positively for social cohesion. However, this is only one side of the problem; the other side is that protection has worked out negatively for social cohesion as it involved a transfer from the consumers (often the low paid) to producers and because it has hindered the transformation of the economy (Hine and Padoan, 2001).

The products subject to high protection are particularly relevant to developing countries. So, after much hesitation the EU has given in to the pressure to liberalize these markets too, in order to be consistent on the world level and to help effectively the developing countries. It means that the long-term promotion of cohesion on the world level has to get priority over short-term concerns for social cohesion at the EU level.

11.6.3 Impacts

A review of the theoretical and empirical studies (Molle, 2002) of openness to external trade on labour markets shows that most fears with respect to negative impacts are not justified. However, there is quite some uncertainty of the direction and magnitude of the effects. This is notably the case for the regional effects.

Most of the effects seem very similar to the effects of the internal market. For many activities it is indeed irrelevant whether the competition comes from other EU countries or from countries in the rest of the world. So, it seems right to stick to openness as it is found to have beneficial effects on growth. It means that presently the support to the European problem regions and social groups can no longer come from trade instruments but has to come from cohesion instruments.

11.7 Transport[14]

11.7.1 Objectives

The objectives of the CTP have developed gradually over time. In the first decades of the EU the policy did not really come off the ground. Most of the basis for the CTP has actually been laid only by the 1992 programme on the completion of the internal market. That comprised the liberalization of transport services and the necessary harmonization of elements of transport policy like road and vehicle safety, etc. Since then the situation has further evolved. The EU has defined the objectives of the CTP as the promotion of effective and sustainable transport systems that respond to the needs of the CM. Moreover, the CTP should contribute to the reaching of the goals of other policies, such as environment, employment and cohesion. To that end the EU has put more emphasis on the way tariffs are set. It is indeed good economics that the prices for transport services reflect well the total (internal and external) cost.

Another important aspect that in the 1990s became integrated in the CTP is the optimization of the European transport infrastructure. Particularly important here is the EU financial support to the TENs. TENs cover the whole EU (including the NMSs) and are meant to take away bottlenecks and fill in the missing links. Cohesion has not been a major concern of the CTP. Only at the end of the 1990s has the subject got some attention (EC, 1998).

11.7.2 Transmission

In matters of transport both the financial channel and the regulatory channel of transmission of effects of the EU transport policy on cohesion are important.

Transmission through the budget can be followed by detailing the relevant EU budget items according to the type of region in which the transport investment is actually made. The more there is in objective 1 regions the more likely there is a positive impact. However, this is only a direct investment effect. There are a few other effects to be seen. The most important one is the change that the improved transport infrastructure makes to the relative accessibility of regions. These in turn change competitiveness and thus growth rates.

The effects of this increased accessibility on GDP per region (ESPON, 2004c) are rather diverse. The improvement of the accessibility of remote areas does not open only new opportunities for activities in the remote areas but also exposes the latter to increased competition from firms in the more central areas. In the end, extra investments in the highly developed core regions tend to have small growth effects while the opposite is true for investments in the periphery of the enlarged EU.

The second channel is regulation. Here we detail two mechanisms:

1 The impact of *liberalization* of the market for transport services can be illustrated with the case of air transport. In the 1990s the number of cities (also in cohesion countries) with international connections has almost doubled while economy fares have significantly decreased (budget airlines). This has had a positive effect on their economic, social and territorial cohesion. For the other modes the impact is less well documented, but a safety net of *public services* has been put in place.
2 The effects of a *better tariff structure* (pricing of the use of infrastructure) depend on two factors. On the one hand, the change in relative cost, which tends to make transport in congestion areas more expensive. On the other hand, it can add cost to remote areas. The net cohesion effect is thus unclear. Indeed, the model results show a very mixed pattern; it is positive for some but detrimental to many peripheral regions (ESPON, 2004c).

11.7.3 Impacts

The major impact is thus via the EU expenditure on infrastructure. This investment by the CTP concerns mostly roads and motorways, railways, airports, etc. Total EU expenditure on transport is to a large extent financed by the SF and the CF.[15] The part that is financed directly via a separate budget line concerns the priority projects on an EU scale which are defined in the TENs. To put things into perspective we have given in Box 11.2 the contribution to cohesion of the expenditure coming from the various financial sources.

Box 11.2 Impacts of EU expenditure in transport infrastructure

For measuring the effect on cohesion of the European budget outlays for transport infrastructure we will use the same approach as the one that has been followed for agriculture (Box 10.1). In the graph below we give the Lorenz curves for a series of outlays. From left to right above the equity line we have given the curve: (1) transport outlays financed by the CF; (2) transport outlays financed by the SF; and (3) transport outlays of the previous two taken together. Below the equity line we give from the left to the right the outlays for the TEN financed as a regular EU budget item and finally to the extreme right for comparison purposes the Income (GDP) line.

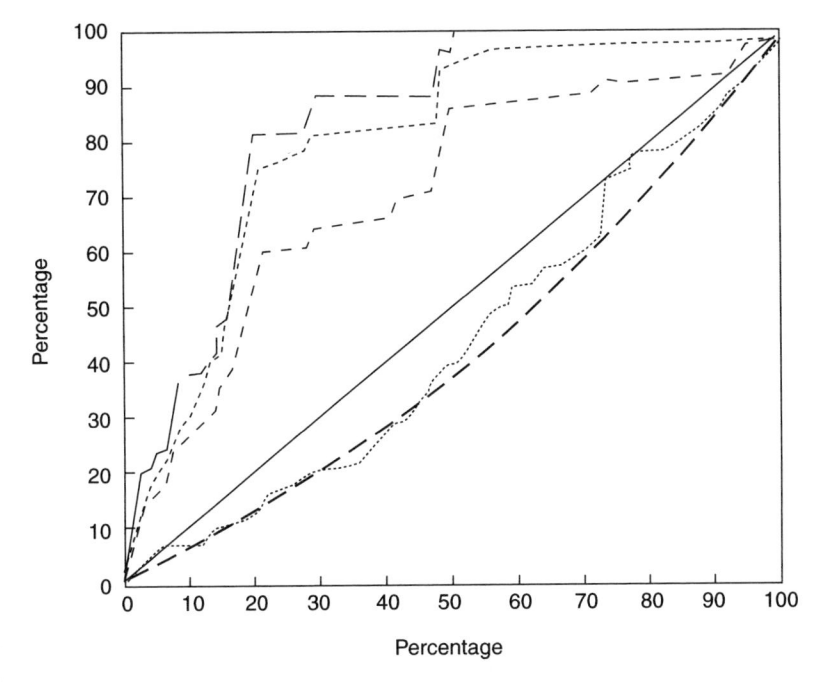

Figure 11.2 Cohesion impact of EU transport policy funding
Source: ECORYS/NEI (2001)

As one would expect the expenditure on the parts of the policy that come from the SCF (lines 1, 2 and 3) is strongly contributing to cohesion.[16] On the other hand, the expenditure on the TENs does not contribute to the three dimensions of cohesion; the reason is that expenditure on the TEN budget line is very much concentrated on the missing

> links in the developed part of the EU (in other words TEN expenditure has a bias towards areas that are not eligible for the SCF). Here the efficiency criterion internal to the transport sector has clearly overtaken the equity criterion oriented towards cohesion.

It appears that as far as TEN-related investment is concerned EU transport policy is largely cohesion neutral (see the line in Figure 11.2 that runs largely parallel with the GDP line). However, the EU budget item is not very large in comparison to other sources of expenditure on transport infrastructure (see Box 11.2). In total, transport investments have a positive impact on cohesion, although there are significant differences between countries. On the one hand, we find that the effects are very high in regions with a large deficit in accessibility, particularly so in the NMSs. On the other hand, the effects of more investment in developed regions are fairly low. Territorial cohesion is hardly affected by more transport investment as all regions of a country seem to benefit from the increased accessibility (ECORYS et al., 2006b). The same effect seems to predominate in matters of EU support to telecommunication infrastructure investment (ESPON, 2003, 2004c).

So we may conclude that this part of EU policy does not seem to have contributed much to the three dimensions of cohesion (ECORYS/NEI, 2001).

11.8 Environment

11.8.1 Objectives

The EU environmental policy is of relative recent origin.[17] The EU environmental policy *aims at preserving, protecting and improving the quality of the environment at a high level*, protecting human health, prudent and rational utilization of natural resources and promoting measures at the international level to deal with regional or worldwide environmental problems. The Sixth Environmental Action Programme (EU, 2002) has set four areas for priority action: climate change; nature and bio-diversity; environment and health; and natural resources and waste.

11.8.2 Transmission

Most of the policy is elaborated in terms of regulation, very little has to do with big spending (Karl and Ranne, 1997). Regulation implies the setting of targets and hence programmes to attain these targets. Compliance with such regulation adds to cost, which might reduce competitiveness. The EU water quality directives are cases in point. They oblige the poor member countries to make costly investments.[18] On the other hand, it stimulates innovation, which actually can enhance growth. If the former effect dominates, regions with heavily polluting industries would suffer; if the latter dominates, the regional impact may actually be positive.

A number of measures have been taken to account for improved cohesion while elaborating environmental policy. These can very well be illustrated by the Kyoto Protocol, which aims at limiting the emission of greenhouse gases. The EU has defined the national targets to implement its commitment to the Kyoto Protocol in line with the principle of 'common but differentiated responsibilities'. The EU has agreed to decrease its emissions by 8 per cent. Cohesion countries that do not have very high industrial pollution levels but do want to have the possibility to increase transport with the ensuing rise in emissions (transport is one of the big polluters) have been given the possibility actually to let their emissions increase by 15–27 per cent. On the other hand, highly developed countries such as Germany and the UK have accepted cuts between 13 and 21 per cent (EU, 2002).

Much of the greenhouse gases actually come from thermal power stations. Cohesion countries and regions tend to be dependent on secondary energy, most of which is produced in the central regions. So the peripheral regions tend to have higher energy costs than central ones. This has a negative impact on their economic growth. The limitation of emissions by energy plants pushes into the direction of renewable energy sources. This may be positive for cohesion, as access to renewable energy is important for cohesion regions. The EU policy to stimulate renewable sources (e.g. in terms of investment support) is thus in principle conducive to cohesion.

11.8.3 Impacts

We have not found any study allowing a quantified estimate of the impact of environmental policy on cohesion. Even information about the impact in qualitative terms is patchy. But some studies lead to the following conclusions by dimension of cohesion:

- *Economic cohesion.* A review of case studies (Hitchens, 1997) shows that on balance environmental regulation has negligible effects on changes in competitiveness.
- *Social cohesion.* The number of jobs created by the directives (Labour Asociados, 2003) per unit of expenditure is inversely related to GDP per capita. It would suggest a positive relation to social cohesion. This effect comes about as labour costs are generally higher in the richer member states.
- *Territorial cohesion.* The cost of environmental policies as per cent of GDP tends to decrease with increasing income levels (Labour Asociados, 2003). This indicates that the effort to implement the environmental policy is higher the lower the income. This would seem to run counter to cohesion. We can illustrate this as follows. The high targets set on many scores imply that most of the adaptation burden comes on the areas that have most problems of pollution. Cases in point are the NMSs in central and eastern Europe; here the distance between targets and reality is still very large on most scores.[19]

11.9 Innovation

11.9.1 Objectives

The EU has set itself the objective to become the most competitive and dynamic knowledge-based economy in the world, capable of sustainable economic growth with more and better jobs and greater social cohesion. To realize this objective several policies are pursued. One is the enhancement of innovation. Innovation is often equated with technical change and with R&D. The EU has already, from its very beginnings, been involved in R&D policy. Its scope has been gradually widened. Nowadays the EU considers that many other forms of innovation (e.g. in organization) are complementary and determine the ultimate success in the marketplace. The EU considers that improvements on all scores are objectives of its innovation policy (EC, 2003b).

11.9.2 Transmission

The main channel of transmission of the innovation and R&D policies to cohesion is through the EU budget. For some time the EU spends relatively significant amounts for reaching its objectives on this score. This has actually been increased in function of the objective of the Lisbon strategy (see Chapter 8) that puts a very heavy accent on innovativeness to improve competitiveness. For large segments of the innovation policy the instruments are in the hands of other players than the EU. There is one exception to this; that is research. The EU spends significant amounts on support to R&D in the form of programmes that come up for public tendering. Important in this respect are the EU framework programmes (e.g. on information technology).

Regulation is much less important. Of course, there is some influence in the sense that much EU regulation that is intended for instance to improve the quality of the environment leads to innovation in terms of the technologies used both for products and for production. For the quality of air standards, set by the EU, could preclude the location of industries that do pollute relatively heavily in regions that are already under heavy pressure. This may trigger new technologies that may actually lead to a stronger position of these regions in the competitive game. Unfortunately these ramifications of the effects of policy are so diverse and so uncertain that they do not justify efforts of quantification.

11.9.3 Impacts

The allocation of EU financial support to innovation is made on criteria that are internal to innovation policy. That means that programmes are entrusted to the organizations that are best qualified to make them successful. These are often located in the wealthy core areas of the EU. Existing regional strengths are thus a key factor in determining a region's propensity to benefit from this type of funding (ECOTEC, 2004). So, the direct impact of the EU support to R&D does not seem to improve economic and may actually be detrimental to territorial cohesion.

However, some form of attenuation of this anti-cohesion tendency comes from the introduction in the allotment criteria of the obligation on the winning contractor to cooperate with organizations in less developed regions. This seems to have been effective as the share of objective 1 regions in funding was higher than their share in R&D capabilities (ECOTEC, 2004; Sharp and Pereira, 2001). However, the more central regions of the cohesion countries mainly realized this effect, which means that all other areas were left pretty much in the cold (EC, 2004a).[20]

11.10 The total picture

11.10.1 How to come to an overall assessment

The different EU policies (such as agriculture, trade, energy and monetary) have had different and often contradictory effects. Certain objectives were contradictory and policy and institutional interests did diverge. In the worst cases, the achievement of goals in one field had actually neutralized or even hampered the achievement of goals in a different domain. A case in point is agricultural policy; it was found to actually have increased the regional disparities in the EU. At the end of the 1980s, the combined effects of the major EU policies tended to be more positive for the non-assisted areas and more negative for problem regions of long standing in southern Europe (Molle and Cappellin, 1988).

So, it became clear that the policy objective of consistency, let alone mutual reinforcement, was not met. As a result the coordination of EU policies with a cohesion impact was strengthened. It did, however, take quite some effort to bring all EU policies in line with the cohesion objective.[21] Over the years the task has become more involved with the constant increase in the coverage and intensity of many EU policies.

The studies reviewed show a very large variety in terms of methods and concepts used, the specification of the various subjects covered per policy area, the quantification of the impacts and the coverage of the three dimensions of cohesion. In order to make nevertheless a total picture we have had to see how far the mixed bag of results of these studies could be fitted into a standard format.

11.10.2 Evolution by type of area and by sector

The approach described in the previous section has been applied to the available data. The results of the exercise are given in the Table 11.1.[22] The various dimensions of this table merit some further explanation.

- *Regions*. The diversified regional impact categories used in the studies could only be brought on to a common denominator at a very high level of abstraction. We distinguish between Central, Intermediate and Peripheral regions. This distinction is based on its policy relevance for most of the period.[23]
- *Periods*. We have distilled the regional impact of a set of EU policies first for

Table 11.1 Schematic view of the impacts of EU policies by policy area and type of region, 1985–2000

Effect on	Central		Intermediate		Peripheral	
In period from:	1985	2000	1985	2000	1985	2000
Agriculture	0	0	+	+	−	0+
Internal market	−	0	+	0	0	−+
Macro/monetary	+	~	0	~	−	0+
Transport	+	+	0+	0+	−0	−+
Environment	0	~	0	0	+	+
Innovation	n.a.	+	n.a.	0	n.a.	−

the year 1985 on the basis of our earlier study (Molle and Cappellin, 1988). Next we have done the same for a recent year on the basis of the studies reviewed in the previous sections.[24]

- *Industries.* The industries in the rows follow, as closely as possible, the ones that we have described in the previous sections.
- *Effects.* After careful comparison it appeared that the maximum we can achieve is an indication of the direction of the effects on total disparity. So we have translated the results of this review of studies for each policy domain in one out of four possible scores: − negative, 0 neutral, + positive or ~ indeterminate. In case we found different impacts for different dimensions of a policy area we have introduced several scores next to each other. We did the same in case the impacts seemed to be contradictory on several levels (for instance, positive for the national level and negative for the regional level).[25]

With the necessary precaution the table makes it possible to draw the following conclusions:

- In the 1980s EU policies tended to aggravate the cohesion problem. Indeed, Central and Intermediate regions tended to accumulate more positive scores while the long-standing problem in the Periphery tended to show more negative scores. So, the urgency attached by the EU to bend the policy to become more positive for regional equilibrium was warranted.
- Around the year 2000 we see that there are few policies that have actually a net negative impact on any of the regional categories. However, there is still reason for concern in view of the contradictory effects on the peripheral regions of a series of policies. However, the total effect seems on balance rather neutral.

In comparing the situation in the two benchmark years we see that the impact of the policies reviewed tends to become more positive for the periphery. This is good news for cohesion as it says that on balance the horizontal EU policies have become less detrimental to the cohesion countries and regions.

11.10.3 Impact by dimension of cohesion

Presently the general notion of cohesion seems insufficient to serve well the more sophisticated policy set up of the EU. So, increasing efforts are made to detail three dimensions of cohesion; viz. economic, social and territorial. Although the studies reviewed in the previous sections do not all specify their results by these three dimensions it has nevertheless been possible to infer from their results indications about the direction of their effects. We give an overview of the scores we have given to these impacts in Table 11.2. It shows again a very diversified and on many points an indeterminate pattern.

The table shows that the EU policies have had very differentiated and at times even contradictory effects. With much prudence we can draw the conclusion that on balance EU policies do not seem to be detrimental to any of the three dimensions of cohesion (un-weighed average of the scores). We see moreover that the total impact on economic cohesion is probably positive, while it is indeterminate for social and territorial cohesion.

11.11 Summary and conclusions

- The EU pursues many policies (such as agriculture, monetary, etc.) that can have a positive, a neutral or a negative effect on cohesion. In the fifth stage of the cycle one has to check whether the influence has been positive and if not what can be done to make it positive or to attenuate the negative effects.
- In the past some of them (such as agriculture) had indeed a clear negative impact on cohesion. At that time even the total set of policies seemed to have had on balance a negative impact on cohesion. In the course of the past decades most of these policies have been redesigned so as to minimize their possible negative effects. At present the effects seem on balance neutral.
- In view of the limited beneficial effects of other EU policies on cohesion, one cannot count on these policies to bring about sufficient improvement on cohesion so a proper cohesion policy needs to be pursued.

Table 11.2 Schematic view of the impacts of EU policies by dimension of cohesion (2000)

Effect on:	Economic	Social	Territorial
From policy area:			
Agriculture; price support	−	−	~+
Agriculture; income support	0	~+	+
Internal market; liberalization	+	−	~
Internal market; competition	+	~	~
Macro and monetary	+	~	~
Transport	0+	0+	−+
Environment	−	+	~
Innovation (research)	0	0	−

- The impacts of the non-cohesion policies that work out mainly through the financial channel seem to be rather negative (CAP, CTP, R&D). However, it need not be forgotten that considerable amounts of money for these purposes (such as transport and R&D) are not spent under the heading of these policies but are spent in the framework of cohesion policies (SCF). The latter tend to be conducive to cohesion (see previous chapter).
- Although our analysis is fraught with difficulties it does permit to give a short answer to the main question of this chapter: 'Are EU policies good or bad for convergence?' The answer is: 'In the past they tended to be bad; at present they tend to be neutral.'

Stage VI
Drawing lessons

12 Conclusions and outlook

12.1 Introduction

In the previous parts of this book we have gone into the different stages of the policy cycle. We have started by analysing in the first stage the cohesion problems of the EU, detailing its economic, social and territorial dimensions. Next we have turned our attention to the intricacies of the policy that the EU pursues to improve cohesion. We have described in detail the various stages of the policy. We have gone successively into the design of its intervention system, and into the definition of its objectives and the provision of financial and regulatory means. We have continued our trajectory through the cycle by evaluating the effectiveness of the policy and by checking its consistency with other policies. Coming now to the close of the cycle we have to draw some lessons from this wealth of analyses and to suggest some improvements for the future.

This chapter is structured as follows. In the first section we will sketch the main challenges that are likely to confront the EU cohesion policy in the future. These concern both the restructuring of its economy and the integration of the candidate countries.

Next, we will draw the main lessons from this analysis of the past performance of the EU on all stages of the cohesion policy cycle discussed in the previous chapters. We will put these lessons in the light of the new demands that will be put on each of these stages in the future.[1]

Finally, we will draw attention to the fact that the experience of the EU in matters of cohesion policy may be of help to other countries in the world that are confronted with similar problems.

12.2 Challenges in the future: prepare for higher EU integration

12.2.1 Prepare for EMU participation of all member states

The setting up of an EMU brings the need to help member countries deal with problems resulting from external shocks. The most adequate solution is a Union redistribution policy. Its aid can be a combination of specific and of general-purpose grants. The latter may take the form of block payments from the Union to a member country. These payments are automatically triggered in case certain deficiencies occur. The disadvantage of this system is that the Union has no control over the actual use of the funds transferred, which thus risk being used in a way that is not expedient to structural improvement and may erode the solidarity on which it is based.

The question is whether the EU should not have a more far-reaching system of redistribution in order to improve cohesion. The answer depends on the balance between theoretical and the empirical arguments.

From a theoretical point of view there are strong arguments for an EU fiscal system with redistribution over member states and citizens via automatic transfers (see, for example, Persson and Tabellini, 1996). Indeed systems with intergovernmental transfers based on bargaining provide under-insurance. However, the system would not go as far as to set up a centralized social security system as this is likely to lead to over-insurance against risks of unequal development. The EU has now entered the stage of the EMU that would justify such a set up (see Table 6.1). However, in the case of the EU, the premise of the above-mentioned theory does not obtain. The EU is characterized by (1) important areas where the EU has no competence at all (national governments are indeed not willing to give up autonomy in tax matters); (2) a complicated decision-making process where the EU has powers. So, the EU may very well have chosen the right set up given its institutional constraints (see, for example, Alesina and Perotti, 1998).

The empirical evidence leads to two views:

1 *Inadequate.* There is a real need for an additional redistribution mechanism. First, idiosyncratic shocks do occur and tend to have very persistent negative effects in Europe (Breuss, 1998). Second, redistribution mechanisms as used in federations such as the USA and Canada are very effective in coping with the effects (see, for example, Sachs and Sala-I-Martin (1992) and Bayoumi and Masson (1998).
2 *Adequate.* The present set up is able to function in a satisfactory way. First, because the frequency and the severity of asymmetric shocks are much smaller than suggested by some alarmists (for example, Vinals (1998)). Second, because the effectiveness of the centralized systems is often exaggerated; the potential of an EU fiscal federation under the present circumstances is too small to compensate for the many problems of design and implementation (e.g. von Hagen, 1992; Fatas, 1998).

So, it seems as if there is no clear-cut conclusion as to the need for a fiscal federalism type redistribution mechanism under EMU.

12.2.2 Prepare for the Full Union

In Chapter 6 we gave different forms in which the redistribution could be cast. Given the present stage of integration the EU has (in conformity with our theoretical scheme) opted for a redistribution policy that is based on transfers between governments benefiting the most vulnerable groups and regions. In that scheme we gave also the variant of direct income taxes coupled with social security payments as an alternative. The higher forms of federation do indeed use this option. Now the EU has over the past moved into higher stages and the question thus comes up whether the EU should not prepare for a set up that is in line with this next stage.

Indeed, at the stage of the Full Union (federation), solidarity among member states is likely to have grown sufficiently to justify more extensive union redistribution via the budget. On the receipts side one would leave the present system of contributions that are proportional with income by member states and adopt progressive income taxes dealing directly with the individual EU citizen. On the expenditure side one might add direct transfers to low-income individuals as elderly persons, unemployed persons, etc. These are more effective in redistribution terms the stronger the federal powers over income taxes and social security and the higher the portion of the federal budget of GDP. As problem groups are often concentrated in specific countries or regions, inter-personal income transfer policies work out as inter-national and inter-regional transfer policies. From an economic development viewpoint these policies have a drawback however, as they have only a very indirect influence on the improvement of the productive capacity of the recipient country or region.

The introduction of such a system might take different forms. Key will be the bringing into focus of the various European social security policies and the adoption of a pan-EU coverage of certain risks.

However, the introduction of such a system increases the political uncertainty (Alesina *et al.*, 1995); citizens are less clear about the use of the tax involved. This is indeed the result from surveys among the general public, that show that 55 per cent of European citizens prefer to stick to national solutions (in many of the smaller northern countries a much larger majority does indeed prefer this option). That is not so surprising if one takes into account that social security rights have all been conquered in a national context and that the form they take are the result of complicated arbitrages between different segments of the national society.

So we may conclude that the adoption of a fiscal union involving international interpersonal redistribution of the social security type is not a likely outcome.

12.2.3 Make a success of the upcoming enlargements

In the past the EU has been able to integrate successfully new members. Some of them had particularly strong cohesion problems. In this way the EU has gradually covered the west of Europe and has recently made an historical step of the reunification of the subcontinent. In matters of widening the challenge is to integrate the present and potential candidate countries.

At the moment of writing (2006) there are two official candidate countries. First, Croatia, that fulfils in the meantime the political criteria for accession;

negotiations started in 2005. Next, Turkey, that is a special case for several reasons; its long-term relation with the EU dating back to the 1960s; its mere size (in terms of population it would become the biggest member country by 2020); its economic problems (macro economic weaknesses, very low GDP/P); its geography (largely outside the European subcontinent); its internal disparities (very considerable between West and East) and finally, its culture (predominantly Muslim). For these reasons the EU reckons that the negotiations with Turkey may take a very long time to complete and has made the special proviso that they may also lead to other solutions than full membership.

Countries on the western Balkans are potential candidates. The EU has said that it considers, as such, Albania, Bosnia-Herzegovina, Serbia-Montenegro and Macedonia. The situation in these countries can in a very simplified manner be characterized in economic terms by their GDP/P position that is (often considerably) below the EU average and in political terms by their social instability due to ethnic tensions. The EU is fostering the economic growth of these countries by its external development policy and their political stability by its security policy. Bringing these countries into the EU zone of prosperity democracy and security is a very important task ahead.

The accession of the candidate and potential candidate countries will come at different moments. If we take the time that has elapsed between the start of the negotiations and the accession of the CEECs as an indication, the accession of Croatia may come by the end of the present programming period of the SFs. For the potential candidates (the countries on the western Balkans) it is very unlikely that they will be able to speed up their reform processes. So their accession will come at the earliest in the post-2013 programming period.

The geographical notion of Europe is well delimited in the West, North and South but becomes elusive in the East. For that reason the EU has set the frontiers of its potential members in political terms. Excluded from membership are the countries of the former Union of Soviet Socialist Republics (USSR), including Belarus and the Ukraine. With respect to these countries the EU has concluded a neighbourhood policy. In the framework of this policy it has developed cooperation and partnership agreements. The EU supports this cooperation with a specific financial instrument (Reg. 1638/2006).

The EU has to gear itself up to the challenge of increased pre-accession aid to the countries on the western Balkans and to Turkey in order to help them to adopt the 'acquis communautaire' and to speed up their economic restructuring and catching up with the EU average.

12.2.4 What cohesion policy in future?: elements of continuity and flexibility

The question can now be asked whether the combination of the challenges discussed in the previous sections would call for a different type of cohesion policy. Actually the answering of that question implies an effort to identify already at this stage the adaptations that may be necessary to make the policy fit for the next programming period (that is likely to cover 2013–20). This is a daunting task. However, two approaches can be followed to develop and formulate an answer.

In a first approach we try to find the hard core of the future shape of the EU policy by interpreting and extrapolating the long-term trends that we have depicted in the previous chapters (both in terms of analysis of the problems and the adequacy of the solutions). These trends indicate continuity on the following points:

- *Objectives.* In future the EU is likely to be confronted with cohesion problems that are in essence similar to the ones it faces now. The analysis in Table 2.4 makes clear that the catch-up time of most of the present convergence regions will by far exceed the seven years of the present programming period. Moreover, new convergence regions will come to the fore in the low-income countries that will join the EU in the future. So, the major objective of the cohesion policy, convergence (that has been a constant over the past decades), is likely to remain a constant in the coming decades.
- *Resources.* These serious convergence problems cannot be solved without a major intra-EU redistribution of financial resources. As in future the size of the problems does not seem to decrease, a decrease in the level of funding does not seem likely either. On the contrary, a few factors suggest that an increased effort will be needed. One need but think for the present convergence regions of the long-standing character of their present problems, the occurrence of new problems (EMU) and the increase in their absorption capacity. Moreover, the severity of the problems in new convergence regions in accession countries asks for a stepping up of the efforts as well. An increase in the size of funds would be a continuation of the trend of four decades (1973–2013).
- *Instruments and methods.* The fundamental idea of specific purpose grants going hand in hand with the application of the major principles (such as partnership, programming and evaluation) has shown its adequacy in the past decades. The problems in the future will not be fundamentally different from the ones in the past. So, it is very likely that these basic elements will be maintained, albeit with some adaptations as to modalities.

Given the arguments presented in the previous sections about the challenges we do not expect that a need will emerge in future for new instruments (such as redistribution by a social security type system). And, in case it would come up, we do not think that a political agreement will be reached to put it in place.

So we can conclude that the hard core of the EU cohesion policy post-2013 is likely to be characterized by the same features that have marked it in the past.

Next, we can try to identify the points where in future flexibility is likely to dominate. This approach implies looking at the elements where in the past most changes have occurred. We mention here a few salient ones under the same headings as we used for continuity.

- *Objectives.* In the past the stated objectives other than convergence have changed frequently. The same is true for the criteria for designation of the regions and social groups that fall under these objectives.

- *Resources.* Now that the whole of the EU outside convergence regions is falling under one objective (accommodating a wide variety of specific problems and objectives) it is easy to change priorities within this general framework. This could apply to a switch of resources but also to a dwindling of the total resources as the richer nation states may take over most of the responsibility for coping with such problems.
- *Instruments and methods.* The main factor of change here is likely to be the drive for further efficiency in the delivery of the policy outside the convergence regions. In this respect alternatives as the OMC have been suggested. Most of the concrete changes will depend on the priorities of the EU in other areas than cohesion and the best support cohesion policy instruments can give to such measures.

In the next sections we will further detail the possible changes that can be made in future as we draw the lessons from the experience in the past.

12.3 Lessons from the past in the light of future change

12.3.1 Assessing the problems and their long-term evolution (Stage I: Chapters 2 to 5)

The EU is confronted with huge cohesion problems. These have been considerably aggravated with the recent enlargement of the EU. For the EU 15 cohesion seems to have improved over the past decades; this is evidenced from a decrease in disparities in GDP/P levels. This has been notably favoured by an increase in economic cohesion. However, the evolution of the other two dimensions of cohesion is less clear due to the paucity of a series of comparable data. We give an overview of the main aspects of this long-time development in Table 12.1.

As one sees, very important disparities remain and new ones always tend to emerge. The major lesson is that there is a need for continuity in the efforts and of vigilance as to the type of problems that emerge and for flexibility as to response.

12.3.2 Optimize the institutional framework (Stage II: Chapter 6)

The considerable economic, social and territorial disparities that the EU is faced with have negative influences on the welfare of the EU. Not only are they economically inefficient, they are also felt to be morally unjust and this is politically unacceptable. A policy to alleviate them is therefore in order. The national governments are not capable of providing an efficient solution so the EU has stepped in. Cohesion policy is a fundamental choice and it therefore has become a constitutional obligation.

Constitutional economics, political science and related strands of thinking show that cohesion policy should be a matter of shared responsibility between the EU and its member states. However, they do not define precisely what the specific roles should be for the two levels of authority. The treaties (in line therewith) define some principles and leave the exact demarcation to the EU

Table 12.1 Main characteristics of the various dimensions of cohesion

	General	Economic	Social	Territorial
Definition: cohesion prevails when:	Disparities in social and economic welfare between the different regions or groups are politically and socially tolerable	All segments (notably regions) of the socio-economic system are inserted in the total European economic fabric in a balanced way	Disparities on a number of social indicators are politically sustainable	People and firms are not unduly handicapped by spatial differences in access to basic services
Objectives	Improve convergence Decrease in disparity in wealth levels between member countries, social groups and regions	Increase competitiveness in all regions Stimulate notably lesser developed areas	Improve access to jobs Social integration	More balanced spatial development
Indicators	Wealth (GDP/P) levels	Industrial structure Spatial concentration Attractiveness for FDI Industrial migration	Unemployment Education Personal migration and segregation Social exclusion Social protection	Market access (connectivity) Knowledge and innovation Border-related barriers
Evolution	*National level:* Convergence; Consistent decrease in disparities *Regional level:* Initial convergence followed by quite some divergence	Tendencies towards spatial deconcentration. FDI and industrial migration have contributed to convergence	Disparities: persistence as to unemployment Increase as to social segregation Decrease as to education (slight) and social protection	Disparities: decrease in accessibility to markets Strong in access to innovation Persistence of border problems
Remaining problems	Big disparities continue to exist New may emerge with globalization and enlargement	Ranking of regions has not changed much Constantly new threats to existing economic base	Poor member states' unemployment; Urban segregation	Peripherality; Institutional barriers

Source: Chapters 2–5

legislator and to actual practice of politicians. This distribution of roles is not stable but changes under the influence of diverse factors. In the past the power has shifted from national states to the Commission. As a result the Commission now stands out as the most important actor. It is involved in the day-to-day preparation, delivery and evaluation of the policy, whereas the other institutions are involved in one part only (advice and decision on new legislation and on financial frameworks; preparation and execution of specific programmes). The Commission has a formidable advantage over the other institutions in the sense that it controls much of the information flows. This pivotal role of the Commission has changed the role of the central governments of the member states. Nowadays, their role is rather one of negotiation in the legislation stage while their role of coordination, facilitation and arbitration in the implementation stages is shared with others. The pivotal role of the Commission is likely to be reinforced with the new Community strategic guidelines.

To most observers the set up described is justified for countries that are the main beneficiaries of the SCF, in practice now, the NMSs of central and eastern Europe. However, many observers think that the correct application of the subsidiarity principle should lead to less centralization than has evolved, in practice, for all other member countries. These voices plead for a partial or complete repatriation of the cohesion policy for the latter group. For instance, the UK government suggests[2] that the current EU cohesion policies are often too centralized to effectively incorporate the locally determined and delivered policies. They explicitly plead for a locally led and devolved cohesion policy, which allows for sufficient flexibility to meet the increasingly diverse needs of regions in an (enlarged) EU. In practice, this would mean that many countries would net their contribution to the EU budget with their entitlement to EU SCF. The advantage would stem first from a gain in efficiency by saving on transaction costs (no pumping around of money; no cumbersome procedures[3]), next from welfare gains (because the prioritization of projects would not have been distorted by EU considerations[4]) and finally from gains in effectiveness (as countries would naturally use methods that work in their institutional environment). The alternative would be to give to these countries general-purpose grants that they can spend to ease for instance inner-city social problems related to migration.

One might even think of doing the same for the 'convergence' countries. However, here there is much concern as to the lack of adaptation of national programmes to the main problems of these countries and as to the risk of corruption and fraud. If one let the arguments for specific-purpose grants for convergence countries prevail and one does the same for the arguments about general-purpose grants for competitiveness regions it would mean a split regime for both. Many have been frightened by the risks of stigmatization that such a dual system would create and for political reasons the EU has not gone along that road. So, there is a political trade off between the lack of efficiency and the need for equal treatment.

So, the drawing of a lesson here is not straightforward in terms of the form of adaptation needed. However, it is clear as to the need for a constant checking whether the system put in place is still adequate.

12.3.3 Match the objectives and means (finances) (Stage III: Chapter 7)

The increased demands of cohesion and other policies require financial resources at the EU level. The first question we can ask in this respect is whether adequate resources will be mobilized and made available. The answer to this question is shaped by three factors:

1 The willingness to pay of the member states.
2 The assessment of the needs in terms of cohesion.
3 The prioritizing of cohesion in comparison with other objectives.

In the past, the interplay of these three factors has led to a regular increase in the expenditure for cohesion. Cohesion is now the second policy area of the EU in financial terms. Whether the amounts that have become available are sufficient to tackle the problems remains essentially a political question. Why increased amounts have come available is, however, an interesting research question. The answer to that question lies not in cohesion-specific characteristics but in the dynamics of modern public institutions.

Indeed, it is often observed that representative democracies show a long-term tendency towards a *growing share in government expenditure* as a percentage of GDP. This is caused by interest groups that form cartels and bargain their political support in elections against subsidies. The central government subsequently acts as a cartel enforcer (e.g. Blankart, 2000). However, there are also reasons why this tendency may be checked. In a multi-layered structure voters tend to strategically delegate power to representatives who are averse to public spending and prefer decentralized solutions (Lorz and Willmann, 2005). Empirical research shows that there is no such general tendency, probably because in the long term better knowledge exists as to effectiveness and efficiency of government involvement (Breuss and Eller, 2004). We may expect that this is indeed the case in the EU and that by and large the available resources are adequate to respond to the challenges.

A problem with the discussion about the level of spending for cohesion is the *blurring of objectives* in the present set up. Much of the spending that is accepted under the label of cohesion and paid for by one of the SFs could actually fall under another heading: that of competitiveness and employment. The criteria for eligibility for support for projects in areas exceeding the 75 per cent GDP/P threshold in fact are similar to the criteria for horizontal programmes aiming at objectives such as R&D. This tendency has been formalized recently with the instrumentalization of the SF for other EU objectives than cohesion. This channelling of the effort for integrated policies through the SF has, however, an important side effect. It implies that all projects proposed have to comply with the very demanding rules for implementation of the SF inclusive of the programming and partnership approaches. Other rules might here be more appropriate (see section on delivery and efficiency)

Regulation is an important determinant of the level of the finances needed for cohesion. This is the case on several scores.

- Assume that *social cohesion* is enhanced by the setting of high labour standards in all EU countries. It will imply that the presently poorer countries loose their competitiveness and become dependent on redistribution from the rich core. Important lessons need to be learnt here from the cases of the Mezzogiorno of Italy and the integration of the former DDR in the FRG (Belke and Hebler, 2002) that have made both dependent (addict) on structural redistribution.
- Assume that *economic cohesion* is impaired by the competition rules that restrict the use of state aids. Other instruments of the cohesion battery need then be called to the rescue.

The next question we can ask is about the distribution of the available money. In the past and present the actual distribution over the various objectives of cohesion policy has followed the concentration principle; which means that the bulk of the available resources is spent on the convergence objective and hence that actions are concentrated in the weaker member states. However, a fairly substantial expenditure is still going to the relatively rich member states under the competitiveness objective. There are several arguments for this but the arguments of a netting of this expenditure with contributions and leaving the member states to deal with these problems is still a valid one, notably in view of the inefficiencies involved in the present set up (see section 12.3.1 and the next section).

So, the lesson is to verify constantly whether the measures are still in line with the objectives; the risk should be avoided that policies pursue objectives with instruments that are designed for other purposes; the welfare losses created by the distortions introduced by the CAP should in this respect serve as a warning signal.

12.3.4 Regulation and coordination of other EU and national policies (Stage III: Chapter 8)

Next to the financial instrument the EU uses the instruments of regulation and coordination to reach its cohesion objectives. Regulatory instruments forbid certain actions of private and public actors that may have a negative effect on cohesion or prescribe other actions that may enhance cohesion. Lighter forms of instruments that tend to improve the consistency of policy making by different actors are coordination and consultation.

In matters of vertical coordination the EU has gradually moved towards the stronger methods; the recent regulations define more subjects and give more details than those of the past. Moreover, the Commission plays a stronger role in the coordination than it did previously. The bigger the problem and the more EU money involved the stronger the role of EU legislation and the EU administration. Yet this does not mean a strong centralization. On the contrary, the Commission has realized that it would be rapidly overburdened if it would assume direct responsibility for implementation. So it has reserved for itself the strategic aspects of the policy (in terms of design and prioritization of objectives) leaving the practical aspects to the national governments. This seems to be the right choice.

In matters of horizontal coordination the present practice is far from ideal. The EU has the ambition to pursue in an integrated way a set of policies to enhance competitiveness and employment, to reduce social exclusion and to improve sustainability and cohesion. The existence of the large funds for cohesion purposes and the relatively modest financial resources for the other objectives has led the EU to make the SF instrumental to these other objectives. All areas such as competitiveness, employment, sustainability, infrastructure and innovation are also targeted by cohesion policy. This puts a considerable challenge to policy makers. On the one hand, much of the coordination is to be done with the help of the OMC; and the recent past has shown the weaknesses of this method to achieve results. On the other hand, most of the financial instruments are subject to the mechanics of the cohesion policy delivery system.

The lesson to learn here is that the present coordination mechanisms are in need of a review and that more adequate mechanisms are to be found to produce lasting and balanced results.

12.3.5 Efficiency of the delivery system (Stage IV: Chapter 9)

Over the years the EU has identified a number of conditions that need to be fulfilled in order to come up to the efficiency requirement. One of these is a high-quality delivery system. All the aspects that determine the quality have been identified and translated in basic principles, general rules, detailed administrative procedures and institutional structures that the member states have to observe while implementing the EU cohesion policy.

The SCF transfers very substantial amounts of money. The EU is accountable to the European taxpayer who wants to be sure that the substantial amounts of money that it transfers are well spent. So the EU has developed an elaborate system regulating the access to and the spending of this money. This comes at a cost of some loss of efficiency, as programming, monitoring, evaluation and auditing are all fairly voracious in terms of human resources.

The past has shown that the EU programming and delivery system has improved the practices of many member states in matters of policy design, implementation and control. It seems thus fully justified that the rules as have been elaborated in the past as to implementation be followed for the major beneficiaries. The EU has incorporated these rules in the 'acquis communautaire' that new member countries have had to accept to apply in full.

Many of the NMSs have learned in the meantime how to deal with it. However, there is still quite some progress to be made. For one, many countries have still considerable problems in correctly implementing the rules. For another, some have difficulties in producing sufficiently good projects that come up to all the criteria for eligibility. The reason is limitations in administrative capacity that has to do with both institutional weaknesses but also with the lack of experienced staff.

So, the main lesson is that the administrative capacity of the NMSs and the accession countries has to be improved consistently. A number of *concrete recommendations* that are based on experience can thereby be made:

- Have the courage to make clear choices as to the priorities to support and the definition of clear targets. Avoid concentrated support on infrastructure even if this is the easiest aspect to handle in institutional and human resource terms and even if political pressure is often on these programmes. Keep in mind that institutional development is as important a condition for growth.
- Integrate better the financial support of the SF and the national outlays for established priorities. Avoid the SF to become isolated items following their own logic and procedures.
- Make an up-front effort with the adaptation of administrative structures that improve the absorption capacity. Resist the lure of using ill-adapted existing administrative structures for operating the SF; it has the perverse effect of maintaining the wrong and preventing the putting in place of well-adapted structures.
- Build up the human resources needed for the successful implementation; this means, notably, skills in terms of all the stages, namely, programming, monitoring, evaluation and control.
- Use the demands of the EU delivery system to fight endemic corruption; in the short term it helps to improve the effectiveness of the policy; in the long term it maintains the willingness of the net contributors to the EU cohesion policy to continue to provide the funds.

Some of the most developed member states benefit from the SF. The question can be asked whether this support is still adequate. In case their access to SF money would be skipped (see previous section) the SF standard model need no longer be applied. These member states would then participate in the cohesion policy through a variant of the OMC. Even, in case some access to SF money is possible, one could ask the question whether for such limited amounts the same heavy procedure would be justified. Some headway along this road has been made (no more additionality proof for these countries).

The main lesson for a change of the delivery system for this group of beneficiaries is that the test on the *proportionality principle* has to be done rigorously in order to see what advantages can be had by reducing the complexities of the delivery system.

12.3.6 Enhance effectiveness (Stage V: Chapter 10)

The EU evaluates systematically its cohesion efforts. It has devised standard methods for doing so. These evaluations serve two main goals. First, accountability; they provided evidence to all stakeholders that money was well spent. Second, learning; evaluation has contributed greatly to improve the various parts of the delivery due to which policy, programmes and projects correspond better to the stated goals.

The EU cohesion policy has as its main objective the decrease of the disparities between the countries and regions by facilitating the catching-up process of the less well to do. We have concluded in Chapter 10 that by and large the policy has indeed helped to bring the EU closer to this objective. The brightest example is Ireland. Moreover, the relatively poor NMSs all tend to be much more dynamic than the rich old member states; a tendency that also contributes to the decrease in disparity. There are two shady sides, however.

Making a success of the convergence of the new member states is the big challenge of the convergence policy. Much remains to be done in terms of economic, social and territorial cohesion. How to decrease the dependency of firms in the NMSs on the decision centres in the heartland of northwest Europe? What additional action is needed to create, in each of the NMSs, efficient, transparent institutions that are resistant to fraud and corruption? What to do to make, for example, Czech or Polish universities rank among the top league of Europe? What extra input is needed to enhance productivity of the labour force and the capabilities of private and public sector managers?

Moreover, a new challenge is to check the tendency of disparities within countries to grow during the catching-up process (see Chapter 2). How to find the resources to stem these tendencies?

So, the lesson here is to step up the effort to improve the evaluation of the effectiveness of projects, programmes and the policy as a whole.

Apart from the formally stated objectives, the EU cohesion policy has also served the side objective to compensate member states for (perceived) losses due to the passing into higher stages of integration or due to the enlargement of the EU with NMSs. Such major political trade offs are not very likely to occur in the future. For one, the further deepening will notably concern matters such as justice and home affairs that do not seem to have a strong bearing on cohesion in the present beneficiaries. For another the further enlargements (for instance Croatia) do not fundamentally change the present balance.

So, the lesson is that in future the policy makers should forget about side objectives and concentrate on stated and transparent objectives.

12.3.7 Secure consistency with other EU policies (Stage V: Chapter 11)

The EU pursues many policies (such as agriculture, monetary, etc.) that can have a positive, a neutral or a negative effect on cohesion. In the past the impact was in some instances rather negative; but policy changes have made that the impacts are now predominantly neutral. In future the EU will change and so will its policies. There are a number of reasons why we may expect that there is only a small risk that these present an additional threat to cohesion.

- *Budget outlays.* Expenditure on horizontal policies, although supposed to increase, is unlikely to change very much the structure and magnitude of their impact. There are two exceptions. The first is competitiveness. The increase in spending on this objective may have a stronger potential negative bearing on economic cohesion than in the past. However, this potential effect is likely to be neutralized as the package of horizontal policy measures is matched to a large extent by items in the catalogue of support that can be obtained from the new mainstream cohesion packages. The second exception to this is agriculture. Here, one may make a suggestion to study more in detail the possibility to differentiate the level of farm(er) direct income support according to various spatial criteria in order to safeguard territorial cohesion.

- *Economic regulation and coordination.* The Commission in its recent work programme has taken the view that for the good functioning of the EMU there is no need for significant new blocks of regulation. So the future of the EU will be characterized by other domains of policy. Its programme for work is oriented towards the following priorities: health (contagious diseases), security (terrorism), external relations (incl. development aid) and internal governance (corruption). Only one of these seems to have a potentially profound impact on cohesion, which is the external dimension. One need but think here of the further liberalization of the trade in agricultural products. However, the measures to cope with these potential effects can be integrated with the aspects of agriculture cited in the section on the budget. Another aspect that has received increased attention is security and governance. Notably, in the accession states economic growth has been severely affected by problems of organized crime and corruption. The EU has now fully acknowledged this problem (see EC, 2004a: 171) and reinforces its actions to combat the causes.

A recurrent point of critique is that of the inadequacy of the EU monetary policy with its cohesion policy. The finances of many EU countries will be under pressure due to increased competition. This is supposed to imply severe constraints on national policy action as the SGP obliges member states to squeeze expenditure in order to match income. This is supposed to lead to a lack of financial means to attack serious problems. But is this the whole truth? What has Germany shown us after the War? They have had a very strict budget and monetary policy and have recovered from a complete disaster. A country that was devastated has grown quickly into one of the richest countries of Europe.

So, the lesson is to continue to check systematically the consistency of the other policies with those on cohesion, even if the chances of major problems occurring on this score seem to be limited.[5]

There is another dimension in consistency that needs to be seen. It is the effect that cohesion policy has on other EU policies. The most important element in this respect is the consistency with the overarching EU policy on competitiveness (Lisbon strategy). It has been decided that the financial resources of the SF should be better geared to enhance the capacity of the EU to deliver cohesion and competitiveness at the same time. We recall that the same holds for other EU policy objectives; support from the SCF is given to projects that favour employment, equal opportunities or sustainability (EC, 2004e).

So, the lesson to be drawn here rejoins the one we drew earlier: improve the mechanisms for making sure that EU polices are mutually consistent.

12.4 Draw lessons for other countries and integration areas

12.4.1 Selection of countries and redistribution systems

Many of the fast-developing countries have been favouring efficiency over equity. Part of this has been stimulated by policies of openness to the outside world stimulating competitiveness. Worldwide openness has often been complemented by regional openness; through participation in regional integration areas. In many countries this has given rise to considerable inequalities, both interpersonal and inter-regional. Social forces are at work which show the need for a more balanced development of the country. National governments, NGOs and international organizations ask themselves how this could be given substance. And they ask themselves in how far money should be explicitly attributed to cohesion. These questions are essentially political and each country has to make its own choices.

In this section we will illustrate the cohesion problem and the reaction of the public authorities to it for two areas outside the EU: Brazil and China.[6] We will use only the overall indicator of disparity (an approximation of GDP/P per head figures) as data for more detailed disparity indicators are generally not available.

Brazil and China differ in many ways. For the sake of the illustration we highlight here three aspects:

1. *Internal devolution.* Both countries differ as to the extent to which and the way in which they have decentralized power and finances in their 'federal' system. Each of them has developed its legal, political and administrative system in the course of history. In that framework they have both made decisions as to the responsibility of the federal and the state authorities in matters of taxation and spending (e.g. on infrastructure, education and social security) and thereby explicitly or implicitly taken decisions as to the redistribution system.
2. *External cooperation.* Brazil has been one of the initiators of the regional integration area in South America; China has kept aloof for a long time and has only just associated itself to a regional integration area.
3. *Institutional history.* China comes from a centralized planned system. Brazil has mostly known a market economy. It is good to recall in this respect that many of the mechanisms that are working towards either convergence or divergence in the market-oriented models do not work in a socialist command economy. For instance, in China internal migration was controlled by government, investment spending was done over regions on the basis of political and security reasons, market returns were a very far-off concern. Moreover, technologies did not easily diffuse as much was controlled for military or bureaucratic reasons.

12.4.2 Brazil

Brazil is a federal state. Its 25 states are often grouped into five geographical regions. The distribution of income and population among these regions and states is very uneven (Azzoni, 2001). The highest incomes are in the south-eastern (SE) region; the lowest incomes in the northern and northeastern (NE) regions (see Table 12.2). The richest state Sao Paolo in the SE region has an income that is six times higher than the poorest states Maranhao and Piaui in the NE region. Population is rather concentrated in the southeast where over 40 per cent of the total Brazilian population lives. Most of them live in Sao Paolo, where 22 per cent of the population realize 35 per cent of the country's GDP. This concentration has been decreasing slightly over the past decades; to the benefit of the adjacent states.

The huge north–south disparity does not seem to have much decreased over the period 1950–95. However the disparities between the states have oscillated over time but overall have shown a tendency to decrease. This was notably due to the de-concentration from Sao Paolo we described before.

Over the past half a century Brazil has shown a remarkable growth in the national economy. One might assume that in this country one might see an example of the consecutive divergence–convergence model that says that in early stages of development divergence will prevail whereas in later stages convergence tendencies dominate. However, this could not be demonstrated.

12.4.3 MERCOSUR

Brazil has concluded with three of its neighbouring countries (Argentina, Uruguay and Paraguay) the MERCOSUR, which aims at creating a CM among the member countries. In the past decade internal customs tariffs have been lowered, FDI has been liberalized and the movement of workers has been regulated. MERCOSUR is now probably the most advanced regional integration area (in terms of stages of integration) in the world after the EU. The progress in integration has been hampered by considerable tensions between the member countries in matters of macro economic and monetary policy and in growth performance. Notably the two smaller partners had the impression they were losing out in the integration game. Apart from these member states a number of regions do not seem to have benefited from the integration. That has increased the existing tensions due to the very large differences in wealth between the members and a fortiori between the regions of the MERCOSUR. Table 12.2 gives an idea of these differences. However, the figures for the regions[7] given do hide important differences between the various provinces in Argentina and federal states in Brazil; differences that may imply a factor of six to eight between the highest and the lowest cases in both countries. Other indicators such as analphabetism and mortality (see Table 12.2) but also poverty and access to schooling confirm the picture of these disparities.

The development of the disparities over time is difficult to make for the whole of MERCOSUR due to the very high exchange rate volatility over the

Table 12.2 Regional disparities in MERCOSUR (around 2000)

Region	GDP/P (index)	Analphabetism (%)	Mortality (%)
Cuyo	104	3	1.6
Noreste	52	6	2.2
Noroeste	62	4	1.9
Pampeana	168	2	1.4
Patagonia	175	2	1.3
Argentina	*116*	*3*	*1.5*
Centro-Oeste	110	9	2.6
Nordeste	43	24	7.0
Norte	57	11	4.2
Sudeste	122	8	2.7
Sur	114	6	1.9
Brasil	*98*	n.a.	n.a.
Uruguay	*116*	n.a.	*1.3*
Paraguay	*36*	n.a.	*3.7*
MERCOSUR	100	n.a.	n.a.

Sources: Various national statistics

past period. However, calculations for the two big member countries show that over the period 1985–2000 disparities have tended to decrease in Argentina and to increase in Brazil (Blyde, 2005).

In recent years the conviction has grown that further integration would require a form of support to cohesion. The MERCOSUR Secretariat did prepare studies about specific aspects and operational modalities for the establishment of a fund, some of which had references to the European experience. In 2005 negotiations led to the creation of this Fondo para la Convergencia Structural del MERCOSUR (FOCEM),[8] in 2006 the ratification process of the regulations was finalized and in 2007 operations started.

FOCEM finances programmes in four fields: (1) structural convergence; (2) competitiveness; (3) social cohesion (in particular in the smaller and less developed economies and regions); and (4) institutional capacity (structure) (Art. 1/2). The fund amounts to $100 million a year. The fund is mainly financed by Brazil (70 per cent) while Paraguay (48 per cent) and to a lesser extent Uruguay (32 per cent) are the major beneficiaries.

12.4.4 China

The situation in China is characterized by the existence of a double split. First, between three geographical areas: the Coast, the Central area and the West. The next important split is between urban and rural areas. There are very large differences in income. On the level of areas there is an east–west gradient; the Coast is rich, the West is poor. Inside each of the three areas there is an urban–rural split; the former have high and the latter have low incomes. The highest incomes are recorded in the coastal urban agglomerations.[9] The lowest incomes are recorded in rural areas in the far west. The differences are very large: in 2001 the richest city, Shanghai, had an income per head some 14 times larger than the poorest western province of Guizhou.

There is considerable controversy both to the magnitude of the differences and to their evolution (Wu, 2002; Zhao and Tong, 2000; Lin and Liu, 2005). However, most studies tend to state that these differences are large in international comparison and that since 1985 they tend to grow significantly. This applies both to the differences between the three geographical areas and between the urban and rural population.

There is also much controversy as to the causes of this evolution.[10] However, most studies agree on the preponderant influence of changes in government policy. The period up to the early 1970s (and the 'Leap Forward' strategy) was characterized by massive investment in regions (many of them inland regions) that did not use the resources properly. So, contrary to expectations this policy has neither boosted national growth nor decreased regional disparities. The market-oriented reforms (and the 'Get rich first' strategy) have resulted in very high growth figures for the country as a whole but this growth has been concentrated in the regions of the Coast as these were best placed to grasp the advantages of internal and external liberalization. Indeed they have improved their access to FDI and hence their factor productivity (e.g. Liu and Li, 2006).

The disparities depicted lead to growing social, territorial and ethnic tensions. Gains in reduction of poverty have come from provincial and local spending, not central government programmes. However, even the subcentral public programmes have not been able to reduce disparity (Ravallion and Chen, 2006). The central government has decided to give more attention to the objective of a balanced development (see Ninth Five Year Plan and 2010 Long Term Development Plan). Yet adequate policies in this respect have not yet been developed.

12.4.5 ASEAN

China has for a long time tried to be as self-sufficient as possible. In that light it need not surprise that it has not taken part in early initiatives for regional or worldwide integration. Other countries have, however, seized such opportunities; in Asia some ten countries have created the Association of Southeast Asian Nations (ASEAN). ASEAN is an organization of ten countries that aims at a free trade zone and further integration. Together its member countries have half a billion inhabitants. However, their size and level of development are very different. We see on the one hand small and very rich countries such as Singapore and on the other hand poor medium-sized countries such as Myanmar. The per capita income of the former is 100 times that of the latter. We see also large countries such as Indonesia that take a middle position. Recently (2002) China has concluded with its southern Asian neighbours a FTA, the ASEAN–China Free Trade Area (ACFTA). The association has not increased disparities very much as China has an income per head that is about equal to that of the average of that of ASEAN.

Given the huge disparities and the very many differences that exist in culture and institutions the integration aims of ASEAN are very modest. They are mainly limited to trade. In this restricted field the results are very good. The same holds for the FTA with China; trade among ACFTA partners has developed very quickly.

The ASEAN region has worked on plans that go beyond trade, notably plans for monetary cooperation. The need for this had become apparent with the crises of the late 1990s. There are no plans for a major set up for cohesion. Some efforts in this direction are made on a bilateral basis: some of the richer countries provide Official Development Assistance to the poorer partners. Moreover, the Asian Development Bank provides loans. However, there is no fund-type redistribution; the reasons for this absence are the weakness of the institutions of ASEAN and the enormous differences between cultures and systems of its member countries that make political cooperation still limited. Given the specific and embryonic relation between China and ASEAN there is even less reason for a cohesion effort on that level.

12.4.6 Lessons?

The experience of the EU is unique. Such an experience cannot be transplanted one to one into a completely different set of conditions. So the EU model cannot serve as a blueprint for other regions and countries. They have to devise their institutions and policies to fit their own priorities and possibilities. However, within these limitations a few lessons can be drawn from the EU experience which seem to be pertinent for other regions and countries. We will enumerate them by stage of the policy cycle.

1. *Assessment of the problems.* Do not rely on the GDP/P disparity alone but go deeper into the aspects of economic structure, (un)employment, poverty, accessibility, etc. Select those indicators that reflect policy priorities.
2. *Designing the intervention system.* Do not embark upon a Union (or regional group) solidarity-based set of cohesion policies (involving financial redistribution) unless the political ground is well prepared and a minimum institutional strength has been acquired.
3. *Specifying objectives and matching with instruments.* Designate clearly the areas that are eligible for support. Concentrate effort on these areas. Orient redistribution on structural policies that aim at the improvement of the conditions for higher competitiveness for the regions.
4. *Implementing actions and delivering results*[11]
    - *Programming.* Avoid making attributions dependent on annual budget negotiations. Cohesion problems are long-standing ones. Their solution requires the long-term orientation to clear objectives; the earmarking of resources and the commitment to their spending in a multi-annual framework.
    - *Partnership.* Involve partners in the various stages of the policy. Effectiveness of the effort is much enhanced when partners become co-owners of

296   *Drawing lessons*

> the problems and the solutions. Devote a part of the resources to improve the (administrative) absorption capacity of the recipients.
> - *Implementation.* Establish a clear and consistent system of preparation and selection of proposals, of monitoring implementation and of financial management and control. Mind that the risk of corruption and of deviation of funds to other uses is endemic and make sure systems contribute to their eradication rather than their further spreading. Make sure these systems are simple and avoid high compliance costs (deadweight).

5. *Checking effectiveness and coherence*
   - *Evaluation.* Introduce a system of evaluation of the results of the policy. The EU experience has shown that this approach, notwithstanding its clear limits, helps to improve the effectiveness of the interventions. Anyway it forces both net beneficiaries and net contributors to reflect on the purposes and the impacts of the policy measures. It thus limits the negative effects of clientelism. (Mind that many government programmes are rather the result of political lobbying and rent seeking by interest groups than geared towards clear social economic objectives.)
   - *Coherence.* Check constantly whether other policies (such as transport infrastructure, support to innovation, etc.) can be designed and implemented in a way that is consistent with the objectives of cohesion.

12.5 Summary

- The EU cohesion policy has a sixth stage which is the drawing of lessons for the future from the experiences of the past. The importance of this stage is clear from the fact that in the past decades the cohesion policy has regularly been thoroughly overhauled. Yet there is still a need to improve further the effectiveness of its battery of instruments and the efficiency of its delivery system.
- The development of the EU has always been along two axes: higher stages of integration (deepening) and larger membership (widening). EU cohesion is in future challenged on both axes. First, by the possible negative effects of the EMU and second, by the integration of the accession countries into the EU system.
- The assessment of the future problems calls for a continuation of the cohesion policy on the following elements. First, maintaining its major objective: convergence. Second, keeping its main instrument: aid in the form of specific purpose grants from SF. Third, continued delivery according to principles, such as partnership, programming and evaluation.
- The overarching policy objective of the EU is to increase its competitiveness in a global system (Lisbon strategy). Cohesion policy can make an important contribution to reaching that objective as it puts the considerable resources it has available and the long-term experience acquired in delivering results at the service of the Lisbon strategy.

- On many points the EU policy can be amended so as to take into account the lessons from the past and to enhance its effectiveness and efficiency.
- The experience of the EU can be helpful for individual countries elsewhere in the world such as China, Russia or Brazil that are confronted with very big disparities and have up until now devoted limited attention to cohesion. The experience can also be relevant for other regional integration areas as they develop into higher stages.
- The lessons are not so much in terms of the large political decisions as to what areas are to be designated and how much money is to be devoted to policy. They refer more to the adequacy of delivery and control system such as programming and evaluation.

Notes

1 Introduction

1 Many books tend to be somewhat under the spell of the newest developments, disregarding the contributions from classic authors. As some of these 'new' approaches may turn out to be hypes rather than fundamentals we will present, in a balanced way, both the classic and the contemporary contributions.
2 The wealth of references are the result of several mutually reinforcing factors; my life-long professional experience in cohesion matters, my voracious appetite for new insights (an article a day keeps the doctor away) and my network of colleagues who signal matters of interest.
3 The original treaties spoke about the European Community. The term EU has become common only recently both in constitutional and colloquial situations. We will not go into the legal refinements on this point and designate for all practical purposes the present union and its legal predecessors as European Union.
4 The EU was formed in the early 1950s from a fairly small basis of originally six countries (France, Germany, Italy and the Benelux countries). In the early 1970s the UK, Denmark and Ireland left the EFTA (European Free Trade Area) to join the EU. In the first part of the 1980s, three Mediterranean countries (Greece, Spain and Portugal) who had overturned their totalitarian regimes and had become democracies were accepted as new members. In the early 1990s Sweden, Finland and Austria joined to take part in the economic benefits of the EU. During the 1990s, the central and eastern European countries became candidates after having gone through a process of transition from a centrally planned economy to a market economy and from a totalitarian regime to a democracy. The former Deutsche Demokratische Republik (DDR) was taken up in the EU as part of the Federal Republic of Germany (FRG) in 1990. Eight other Central European countries (Estonia, Latvia, Lithuania, Poland, Hungary, the Czech Republic, Slovakia and Slovenia) joined the EU in 2004 together with Cyprus and Malta. Romania and Bulgaria entered in 2007.
5 For describing the disparities and the policy interventions we will often refer to individual countries. As some of them reveal common characteristics we will also use some groups. The countries of the EU tend to fall into three groups, characterized by their relative level of development. These are the North, the South and the East. Into the North we group all countries in the north and north west of the EU; the South consists of the Mediterranean countries (Portugal, Spain, Italy, Greece, Malta and Cyprus). To the East we group the ten new member states of Central and Eastern Europe. In interpreting the data one has to bear in mind that these groups are of different sizes, the North has some 260 million inhabitants, the South some 120 and the East about 110.
6 In the jargon of the EC, this is also called 'real convergence' as opposed to 'nominal convergence'. The latter applies to macro economic indicators like inflation and is relevant in the context of the criteria for joining the EMU.

7 Mind that the cycle can be seen at two levels: first, on the level of the whole policy as is done here and second, on the level of programmes, which is explained in Chapters 6 and following.
8 GDP/P can be broken down into three components that help to understand the issue of cohesion better.

$$\frac{GDP}{Population} = \frac{GDP}{Employment} \times \frac{Employment}{Working\ population} \times \frac{Working\ population}{Population}$$

These are: GDP per person employed (approximately equivalent to labour productivity), the total number of persons employed relative to the working-age population (i.e. the employment rate) and the working population per head of population (activity rate). Each of them can be further decomposed and related to the dimensions of cohesion. The first term (labour productivity) is the main determinant of economic cohesion and the employment terms are the major determinants of social cohesion.
9 This is the third level in the regulatory hierarchy: (1) constitutions (Chapter 6); (2) laws (Chapters 7 and 8); and (3) daily practice (Chapter 9).
10 The disadvantages stem first from the time-consuming procedures. Second, they stem from the lack of clarity of the criteria for selecting partners. This leads often to the selection of partners that have little concern for the long-term strategic interests of the programme and more concern for the promotion of their own short-term interest by the planned interventions.

2 Disparities: general

1 The words convergence and divergence are used with many different meanings. The EU jargon uses two concepts. Real convergence is the decrease of disparities in income; the notion we use in this book. It is opposed to nominal convergence used in monetary matters to denote the adaptation to the Maastricht criteria on public finances.
2 One now distinguishes often between two basic notions (Sala-I-Martin, 1996):
  Beta convergence is based on the study of the type of mobility pattern of units within a group. Beta convergence obtains in case low-income units grow fast and high-income units grow slowly.
  Sigma convergence is much more a statistical measure giving, in one figure, the dispersion of income per head levels in a set (groups of national or regional economies).
3 The most common are the coefficient of variation and the Theil entropy index.
4 See subsequent chapters.
5 This choice is made notwithstanding the fact that this indicator suffers from some serious weaknesses. For one GDP is based on the local production whereas population is measured by residence which does not need to coincide with work place. At the regional level, GDP/head is not only determined by firm activity, but also by regional transfers and non-market gross value added (GVA). The latter are of importance especially so in poorer regions. Regional transfers include alternative income possibilities, such as the income of commuters, the sale of assets to foreign residents, public transfers (pensions, unemployment benefits) and private transfers (remittances from emigrants). Non-market GVA includes public sector activities; they can be very important, especially in (peripheral and rural) regions with only limited other economic activities. Moreover, for comparing the real value of GDP as a proxy of the spending capacity of income one needs to take into account differences in price levels. The prominence of the GDP/P indicator is based on the lack of statistics for other indicators.
6 The theory of *economic integration* highlights the forces that determine convergence. Indeed integration opens up markets, increases the mobility of products and

production factors, so in general can be assumed to lead to a better allocation and hence to increase convergence (Molle, 2006).
7 Many of the theories are well known and we refer the reader to standard textbooks where he can find the relevant references to classic and modern contributions.
8 See for instance: Borts (1960) and for a review, among others: Chipman (1965a and b, 1966).
9 Following the original work of Solow (1956).
10 The continuous process is set by a technical change inspiring the development of a new product. At the first stage of its development this product will need close contact with existing customers, located in developed countries. At the second stage, it will still require special skills to produce and a strong market potential to sell; this means that the production will be located in developed areas where it generates a high value added and sustains high wages. At the maturity stage, margins will fall and, to cut costs, the production will be relocated to areas where wages are lower. The richer countries will change over to new products that are still at an earlier stage of development.
11 In this respect one can distinguish between absolute and conditional beta convergence. Absolute beta convergence exists in case there is a negative correlation in a univariate regression between initial income and growth; conditional beta convergence exists in case the partial regression coefficient of the initial income is negative, given the values for the other influencing factors such as education (Barro and Sala-I-Martin, 1995).
12 The liberalization of European goods and factor markets was feared to have such an agglomeration effect (Giersch, 1949; Seers *et al.*, 1979, 1980; Keeble *et al.*, 1982). An analysis of the (changes in the) economic potential of the regions of the EU between 1965 and 1977 'lend further weight to the concern over widening regional economic disparities, now being expressed in official and academic circles' (Keeble *et al.*, 1982: 430). The same can be said about the effects of increased global openness (e.g. Seers *et al.*, 1979, 1980).
13 Scale economies refer to the possibility to distribute fixed cost over a larger number of sales. Scope economies refer to the possibility of using knowledge developed for a specific purpose in a different setting creating positive externalities of investment in innovation and human resources.
14 There is also a more *short-term* view of the alternation of convergence and divergence (Barro and Sala-I-Martin, 1991). It emphasizes the possibility of periods of divergent growth due to asymmetric regional shocks. Once these shocks are absorbed, the system returns to a basically neo-classical convergence model with poor regions catching up on the rich ones.
15 Integration enhances competition and hence tends to strengthen polarization in the early stages. That positive effect between integration and spatial disparity has indeed been observed in Europe through the past centuries (Bairoch, 1976, 1981). However, in recent years integration does not seem to have worsened the situation (see further sections of this chapter).
16 From Williamson's test of the hypothesis for non-socialist economies, the empirical evidence appeared to be well in line with the expected pattern (Robinson, 1976; Smolensky, 1961; Perin and Semple, 1976).
17 *Economic integration* has a clear effect on many factors of this indeterminate system. This is the case of market access, R&D and even education and public infrastructure.
18 See, for example, Boltho and Holtham (1992) and Mankiw *et al.* (1992). There has been much attention from both academia and politics for the capacity of policy to influence the factors mentioned above. By devising intelligent combinations of policies some poor countries succeed in accelerating their development, while others, failing to find such solutions, stay behind.
19 Some suggest that there is a pattern in that multitude of individual country processes. Countries are supposed to belong to clubs; within clubs there is convergence (for

instance among the Organisation for Economic Cooperation and Development (OECD) countries); between clubs divergence is observed. However, it has not been possible to identify the decisive factors of development from the common characteristics of the members of these clubs. See, for instance, Baumol (1986), Baumol and Wolff (1988) and Chatterji (1992).
20 See, for instance, Martin and Sunley, 1998 for a critical review of models of endogenous growth.
21 See, among others, Puga (1999) and Faini (1996).
22 *Economic historians* too, find convergence and divergence to co-exist (e.g. Rokkan, 1979; Pollard, 1981). Prevailing patterns stem from long-standing, highly complex interrelations among ethnic, religious, economic and political forces. They refute the idea of a direct relation between a region being economically backward culturally dominated and politically powerless, nor do they believe in an underdevelopment trap from which regions, once caught, cannot escape.
23 See, among others, Williamson (1976), Vanhove and Klaassen (1987: chap. 6), Vanhove (1999), Molle (1995) and Vickerman and Armstrong (1995).
24 Some pockets of relatively high development did exist; however, examples are Czechoslovakia, that had a rich industrial base and Romania, that prospered due to its highly developed agriculture.
25 This will be largely limited to western Europe as no information could be found for the predecessor states of the countries of central and eastern Europe (apart from some indications for the Austro-Hungarian Empire).
26 This result did not stand alone. Actually at the international level, convergence has also been observed through prolonged time periods (Baumol, 1986).
27 Particularly interesting is the case of Ireland. The growth of this country has been so substantial that it is no longer eligible for objective 1 status because its GDP/P is now higher than 75 per cent of the EU average (see Chapter 7 of this book).
28 See Kaldor (1966), Hudson and Williams (1986) and Boltho (1982).
29 From the beginning of the EU, the Commission has reported on the regional situation and regional developments in the Community (EC, 1961, 1964, 1971, 1973, 1981a, 1984, 1987, 1991a). In the middle of the 1990s it has broadened its scope and reports regularly on cohesion (EC, 1995a, 1996a, 1999a, 2001). The most recent report covers the enlarged EU (EC, 2004a).
30 Now the problem of empirical analysis in this domain was the serious lack of data. We have assembled all available evidence from a large variety of sources to palliate this deficiency. In our study (Molle *et al.*, 1980) we have shown convincingly that, actually, convergence dominated in the early decades of the existence of the EU. This result has been confirmed later for the larger area of the EU 12 and EU 15 (Molle and Boeckhout, 1995).
31 There has been a strong interest in the matter; in the past many studies have been made. This trend was sparked-off by studies such as Barro and Sala-I-Martin (1991, 1995). As illustrations of a long list of studies we cite here but a few, such as, Neven and Gouyotte (1995), Evans (1997), Fingleton (1997), Paci (1997), Persson (1997) and Badinger *et al.* (2004). Similar studies have been made for other countries. They showed convergence tendencies for the regions of other developed economies (see, among others, Barro and Sala-I-Martin, 1991 for the USA and Sala-I-Martin, 1996 for a whole series of countries). See, for further details about the time and regional patterns of convergence in the EU, the various contributions in Vickerman and Armstrong (1995).
32 This point was already highlighted in Molle *et al.* (1980) and has since been underlined in Rodriguez-Pose (1999) and Ezcurra *et al.* (2005). Regions do indeed show a clustering behaviour along national lines.
33 Evidence from: Hofer and Woergoetter (1997), Suarez-Villa and Cuadrado Roura (1993), Cuadrado *et al.* (1999), Persson, (1997), Kangasharju and Pekkala (2004) and Terrasi (1999). For Greece the evidence is contradictory as far as the first period is concerned (Petrakos and Saratsis, 2000; Tsonias, 2002).

34 Evidence in, for example, Kozak (2003), Tondl and Vuksic (2003), Ehrlich and Szigetvari (2003), Resmini (2003), Roemisch (2003) and Petrakos et al. (2004).
35 The challenges to the East are very big and they have limited resources. So, the EU supports them with funds (see Chapters 6 to 8).
36 Interesting in this respect is also Cornut (1963).

3 Economic disparities

1 This subject is, at the moment, of particular importance given the policy choices of the EU (Lisbon agenda) that we will discuss in later chapters. Mind that we will come back to the aspect of access to knowledge and innovation in Chapter 5 under territorial cohesion.
2 Molle (1997a) found indeed a close relation between the differences in growth of GDP/P and the differences in the sectoral composition of the economy. The improvement of the composition of the industrial base is important for explaining convergence (e.g. Cuadrado-Roura et al., 1999) and stagnation in the change for divergence (Kangasharju and Pekkala, 2004).
3 'An unfavourable sectoral structure together with a lack of innovative capacity seems to be among the most important factors underlying lagging competitiveness...' (EC, 1999a: 9).
4 Esteban (2000) and Ezcurra et al. (2005) demonstrate that the productivity differences are not so much attributable to differences in the sectoral composition but rather to across-the-board differences in regional productivity. The catch up would be more related to general measures of productivity increases and not so much to the sectoral composition.
5 See, for example, Aldcroft and Morewood (1995), Dobrinsky (2003), Resmini (2003) and Gacs (2003).
6 The speed of these two trends is different for each country. The growth of output performance (productivity) is not correlated with the profoundness of the restructuring; smoother adaptations tend to be positive for growth (e.g. Gacs, 2003).
7 See, for a more elaborate treatment, for example, van Marrewijk (2002).
8 Forward linkages are defined as relations with clients; backward linkages are defined as relations with providers of intermediary goods.
9 Empirical evidence from a wide range of countries shows that a nation's globally competitive industries tend invariably to exhibit geographical clustering in particular regions (Porter, 1990, 1998). In other words we observe strong tendencies of concentration of industries in such regions and hence of specialization of certain regions on specific clusters. In this view a region's relative competitiveness depends on the existence and degree of development of, and interaction between, the four key subsystems of his diamond. Weaknesses in any of the elements that make up these four subsystems reduce a region's competitiveness. In particular, the absence of functioning clusters in a region means, first, that the subsystems themselves will be poorly developed and next, that the interactions between them – vital for the generation of external increasing returns – will be hindered. The message for governments is that they have to stimulate this dynamic interaction and the quality of each of the four parts of the diamond to improve competitiveness. There are some problems with this view (Martin and Sunley, 2003). The assumption that the same basic notion can be applied to industries, nations and regions gives rise to problems of empirical testing. The definition of clusters is extraordinarily elastic, so that different authors after Porter use the notion in different ways. And added to this, the empirical delineation of the geographical boundaries clusters is vague (ranging from an inner-city neighbourhood, to county level, to regions, even to international level), and does not appear to be linked to the processes that are supposed to cause clustering.
10 See, for reviews, Amiti (1998) and Aiginger (1999).

11 See, for another application of the Gini coefficient, Chapter 11.
12 Specialization rose in six out of ten EU countries for which data were available. In an earlier study Amiti (1998) using data on five countries and 65 manufactured industries found that a 1 per cent increase in scale economies lead to a 0.5 percentage point increase in industrial concentration,
13 See Molle (1997a). The tendency towards de-specialization had already been observed earlier (Molle, 1983: 20) for the three ten-year periods between 1950 and 1980.
14 See Molle (1997a). The same conclusion, branch structure of the regions of the EU, has become much similar over time as was drawn by Paci (1997). In the same vein, specialization for the majority of regions decreased in the period 1980–95 (Hallet, 2000). Much in line herewith there was a very general trend of de-specialization of almost all European regions. Over time the economic structures of all EU regions have become very similar. The latter appeared to be largely due to the pervasiveness of the trends of declining agriculture and rising services. For the manufacturing sector the results were less clear-cut.
15 The description that follows is largely taken from UNCTAD (2000).
16 See EC (1996a and b). An effect of European integration on FDI has also been found by de Menil (1999); his model showed intra-EU FDI to be far higher than could be expected on the basis of the influence of the usual variables of a model of intra-OECD FDI.
17 The regional split up used in this section does not correspond to the standard ones used in this book. In order to get comparability we have recalculated the figures for the last two periods with the standard classification of member countries in broad geographical areas used in other parts of this book. The main difference is that a large part of the intermediate and periphery zones used in the table would be classified in North. For the three standard areas the concentration is even more marked than for the ones used in Table 3.3. Indeed internal North counts for 83 per cent of the flows; North to South for 8 per cent and North to East for 3 per cent.
18 The underlying material shows that these are often made up of two-way flows of comparable size, indicating a considerable interpenetration.
19 Recall that these countries were considered as the periphery of the EU 15.
20 See Petrochilos (1989), Buckley and Artisien (1987), Durán-Herrera (1992) and Simões (1992).
21 This was implied by the results of a simulation model reported in Baldwin et al. (1996).
22 A first exercise in Morsink and Molle (1991a and b) has been elaborated by Morsink (1998). The results on the various variables of the model used are confirmed by Mortensen (1992) for the rate of return on capital, by Devereux and Freeman (1995) for the real rate of interest and the tax wedge between the home and host country and by the studies summarized in the EC (1996a) for the ownership advantage and the trade variable. The results for most variables are also confirmed by de Menil (1999) but for the influence of the exchange rate. Pain and Young (1996) found that differences in taxation had a significant influence on the direction of intra-EU DI from British and German firms. Other studies suggest that the level of real wages (unit labour cost) is a very significant variable, low wages tend to attract incoming FDI and high wages tend to stimulate outgoing FDI (Hatzius, 2000).
23 See also Mariotti and Piscitello (1995).
24 FDI apparently concentrated initially in countries that went fastest along the road of preparing for membership (Bocconi, 1997).
25 See Brenton et al. (1999), Martin and Turrion (2003) and Carstensen and Toubal (2004).
26 To our knowledge, no comprehensive studies have been carried out on the welfare effects of DI in the EU.
27 For instance studies in Italy referred to by Roberto (2004).
28 Thereby raising profits of source country firms at the expense of host country firms.

304 Notes

The extent of cross ownership of firms and the relative supply of skilled labour alter the impact of FDI on welfare (Glass and Saggi, 1999).
29 This special focus should not forget that the existing firms account in most countries and regions for the lion's share of the development; so the attention on the factors that shape competitiveness is warranted.
30 See for a survey: Belessiotis et al. (2006).

4 Social disparities

1 The indicators mentioned are of course related among each other and with the economic indicator. Employment, wage level and job characteristics are important determinants of social inclusion and (lack of) poverty. The level of education is a determinant of productivity and income.
2 This is made possible by the fact that the urban audit has come off the ground; however, not for previous years, nor for CEECs.
3 See for instance Modigliani (1996), Bean (1994), Layard et al. (1991), Heylen and van Poeck (1995) and OECD (1994a).
4 For an overview see Nickell and Layard (1999); see also Blanchard and Wolfers (2000). The distortions on the labour market in terms of regulation were less harmful for growth than distortions on product markets. In terms of distortions due to taxes the opposite seems to be the case (see Molle, 2006: chap. 14).
5 Standard deviation decreased by half from 4.5 to 2.2.
6 Unemployment problems tend to cluster in regions across national boundaries; Overman and Puga (2002).
7 In periods of upturn the disparity tends to decrease and downturn to increase. This was notably so at the end of the 1980s and the beginning of the 1990s (EC, 1996a).
8 We have taken the data for cities used in this chapter from the Urban Audit 2006 website; we have included here all cities with a population higher than 400,000.
9 See the contributions of the new growth and endogenous theories cited in Chapter 2, in particular Barro (1991), Mankiw et al. (1992) and Romer (1990). Other contributions come from labour market research. See for an overview of the effects of social capital on growth: Temple (2001).
10 These correspond in general to objective 1 regions that are distinguished for policy purposes: see Chapter 6.
11 See Eurobarometer of various years that report that a majority of EU citizens are in favour of a policy of severely restricting immigration. The economics of such a policy are discussed in Böhning (1993), OECD (1993) and Siebert (1994).
12 The typical policy now is to stimulate integration into society for migrants already residing in the country and to restrict new immigration to persons who can fill in positions on the labour market that otherwise would not have been profitable. See, in this respect, notably Lahav and Guiraudon (2006).
13 See for a short overview of the major theories and the references to main authors, Gachet and le Gallo (2005: Introduction) and Skifter Andersen (2002).
14 See, for example, the case studies in O'Loughlin and Friedrichs (1996).
15 In the past there has been a growing reluctance to use the word poverty to denote certain degrees of disadvantage and many other terms have been proposed. However, we will use the indicator here as it is very revealing for exclusion.
16 These results are in line with those of other studies such as Eurostat (1994). Studies about the subjective poverty (Gallie and Paugam, 2002) find that the inter-country differences are more marked than objective indicators. For instance 66 per cent of Portuguese judged they were poor (compared to 23 per cent in Table 4.4) while 6 per cent of Danes judged themselves as poor compared to 13 peer cent in Table 4.4.
17 As social exclusion and deprivation are relative notions they have been defined with respect to national, not European, mean values.
18 These were complemented by regulation of the labour market (e.g. minimum

wages, dismissal, etc.) to limit the risks of becoming dependent on social security. For instance, legislation protects workers against safety and health hazards at their workplaces.
19 See Esping-Andersen (1990, 1999), Ferrera (1996) and CPB/SCP (2004). Note that there is also a certain degree of correspondence with the classifications we made on social exclusion.
20 This corresponds only to a limited extent to the three large areas we distinguished in other parts of the book.
21 The borderline between the private and public domains in matters of social security is in flux in all EU member countries (Ferrera, 2006). National systems have to adapt to increasing pressure from the forces in the EU that want to extend the liberalization of the internal market for services also to this domain.
22 See, for an early analysis of these effects, Molle (1986). We do not follow this subject up any further here as the following chapters will indicate that these policy domains are essentially national so that they are not the subject of the EU cohesion policy.

5 Territorial disparities

1 See for an analysis of the origins of the concept Faludi (2004). The meaning is still very diffuse; different strands of thought and different interest groups give their own, at times contradictory interpretations.
2 The Treaty of Amsterdam that amended earlier 'constitutional treaties' refers to territorial cohesion in the context of the objective of fostering harmonious development. The term was introduced in a similar succinct way in the Draft Constitution. However, there its status seems to have been enhanced, as in the Draft Constitution territorial cohesion has been placed on the same footing as economic and social cohesion (see Chapter 1)
3 So it need not surprise that studies about territorial cohesion give much attention to the spatial aspects of such policies. We will turn to that subject in Chapter 9.
4 The Council of Europe is an international organization that is actually older than the EU. It encompasses more countries in Europe than the 27 EU member countries. It deals with non-economic aspects such as culture, environment, migration, human rights, etc. (see for more information their website www.coe.int).
5 Text in EC (1999b); see for its genesis also Faludi and Waterhout (2002).
6 Attempts to come to such a comprehensive European Territorial Cohesion Index have run into many practical problems as to its realization (such as choice of relevant base indicators, statistical measurement and weighing of components) and into many interpretation problems that limit their use in policy terms. See for a short review Grasland and Hamez (2005).
7 The theory of polarization (e.g. Perroux, 1955) teaches that regions characterized by strong urban centres continue to grow by attracting new dynamic activities; while regions characterized by a lack of urban infrastructure decline as they loose people and economic activities which eventually leads to desertification.
8 However, the situation is not that simple. Economic studies have gone some way in defining the negative effects of concentration (congestion cost), but they have balanced these with the positive effects (such as lower transaction cost). So it is difficult to make, on economic grounds, a clear case for either more concentration or more de-concentration. There is one exception; regions with a clear lack of urban infrastructure do benefit from the strengthening of urban services.
9 Mind that these indicators (better accessibility to markets and to innovation) are determinants of the competitiveness of regions and could as such have been taken up in the analysis of Chapter 3. Other competitiveness determinants are entrepreneurship and quality of the labour force (the latter is analysed in Chapter 4).
10 This, indeed, is true for basic transport infrastructure as it is essential for decreasing transport cost of goods. It is also true for telecom infrastructure that it is of utmost

importance for growth of the service and information-related parts of the economy (e.g. Martin, 2003; Cieslik and Kawiewsk, 2004).
11 In the literature the latter notions have been extensively used. The EU-wide analysis of this type has been initiated by Clark et al. (1969), who used the notion of potential to illustrate the effect of the enlargement of the EU 6 with the three NMSs (notably the UK). Their analysis has been elaborated by Keeble et al. (1982, 1988). More recently there has been a revival of the attention for this type of study. We mention here Copus (1999), IRPUD (2000) and Lopez-Rodriguez (2002). The results tend to differ due to differences in choice as to regional division, distance matrices, market indicator, decay function parameter, etc. However, they all concord in putting the gravity centre of the EU in northwestern continental Europe and the lowest values in the southeast of the enlarged EU.
12 Although their main disadvantage is their distance to the centre of the EU they have other problems in common such as a small internal market and natural constraints such as mountainous landscape. Due to these specific problems they benefit from a specific EU regime in terms of regional aid (EC, 2000a).
13 Compared to the 'core' category of the previous section the grouping in the present section distinguishes between core group 1: major city regions such as Paris, the Randstad and the Ruhr and core group 2: areas between these cities. Compared to the former 'ring' the present grouping distinguishes group 3, the area directly around the core in northwestern Europe and group 4 consisting of areas farther from the core such as the other regions of England and those of central Italy.
14 See Hollanders and Rundel (2004) and also trendchart.cordis.lu/scoreboards/scoreboard2003/pdf/eis_2003_tp1_indicators_definitions.pdf.
15 See Cooke (2003) and Leydesdorff and Meyer (2006) and the articles referred to in the latter publication.
16 See, for a general introduction, for example, Camagni (1991) and Aydalot and Keeble (1988) and for special cases, Johannisson (1998) for Sweden and Ritsilä (1999) for Finland.
17 For example, assume that the lowest and observed values for business R&D are 0.5 per cent and 2.5 per cent and that country x has a score of 1.5 per cent. The rescaled score for country x is 50, which is equal to its position halfway between the lowest and highest observed values. Each rescaled score for an individual indicator is then multiplied by the weight assigned to that indicator to come to the Summary Innovation Index.
18 These approaches to the problem have been labelled the Triple Helix Model (Etzkowitz and Leydesdorff, 1997).
19 The picture given here is similar to the one provided by a recent map published on the ESPON website (www.espon.eu early 2007) on the 'Readiness for the Information Society'. This map depicts the performance of all EU 27 regions on a composite indicator in which similar elements as the ones in Table 5.4 are taken up.
20 This picture has also been found by studies for one specific indicator; for instance Paci and Usai (2000) showed that patent production is concentrated in the regions that have the highest scores on centrality as depicted in Figure 5.1.
21 These figures are corroborated by the analysis for Spain. Here the regional distribution of innovation activity, measured by the generation of patent applications, was particularly concentrated on the traditionally more dynamic regions (Guerrero and Seró, 1997). The public funding for supporting innovation was also concentrated in the provinces with these concentrations of applications. So the authors concluded that: 'The search for efficiency through technological policy brings about a vicious circle which goes against technological convergence.'
22 An example is the need for cooperation of a company specializing in a high-tech innovative activity with researchers from a university in a second country and a specialized consultancy in yet a third country.
23 In the recent past, floods have happened frequently in this area, making flood-risk management a particularly important transnational issue.

6 Policy fundamentals

 1 Various strands of thought define this in different but similar ways. Some speak about the constitutional level (Buchanan, 1991), others about the institutional framework (Hooghe and Marks, 2001). Yet others (economic institutionalists such as Williamson, 1998) speak about the interface between social embeddedness and principles (values, ideology, norms, functions leading to the distribution of roles among various actors involved, etc.).
 2 Other aspects are the concern for environmental sustainability, for international solidarity, etc.
 3 The foundations for and the basic structure of this European policy edifice were laid by the Padoa-Schioppa *et al.* (1987) report. See, for a structured view of the development of the EU on these three scores, Molle (2006).
 4 This factor becomes more important the higher the movement of capital (Arachi and D'Antoni, 2004).
 5 See, for instance, Vandamme (1986) and EC (1988).
 6 See EC (1992, 2002c). The results of these studies are corroborated by those of an international study that encompasses also the NMSs (Luebker, 2004). There is considerable support (50–90 per cent) for national redistribution; such support is notably strong in the NMSs and the cohesion countries and less so in the richest member states. The support for international redistribution drops in all countries (for most by some 25 to 30 percentage points).
 7 This definition is from the draft constitution (Art III.16, second par.); it takes up the essentials of the text of earlier documents.
 8 This is the main stated objective. Mind that there are also other objectives that we will come across in the next chapters. First, to reach political compromises that permitted the passing into higher stages of integration. Second, to reach other policy goals, such as competitiveness, employment, sustainability.
 9 For that reason we will not go into this further; the assessment of EU policies in terms of cohesion (see Chapter 9) will thus be made largely in terms of economic and social aspects.
10 Such an approach has been followed in the framework of the European Spatial Planning Observation Network (ESPON) project (BBR&P, 2003).
11 Concrete examples of such linkages exist, for instance, cooperation between cities is facilitated by the EU SF in the so-called INTERREG programme.
12 The fundamental ideas of different schools of thought on redistribution have been used for the setting up of international union redistribution schemes (Findlay, 1982).
13 The consequence of such limiting of claims to a well-delimited sub-set of the world, be it the nation or the union, is that international transfers to third countries have more in common with acts of charity than with distributional justice. For that reason development policies are ordered under external policies (Molle, 2006: chap. 17). The case of the aid to potential member countries is on the borderline between the two.
14 See, for the dynamics of the EU case, notably MacDougall *et al.* (1977), Padoa-Schioppa *et al.* (1987) and EC (1993a); see, for the specific aspects of the EMU case, for example, EC (1993b) and Bayoumi and Masson (1995); for a more ample discussion about the systemic aspects see Molle (2006) and Sapir *et al.* (2004).
15 Each of the stages indicated here is a theoretical construct; in practice a wide variety of organizational forms exist that correspond more or less to one of these concepts. So the comments made further on in the text on each of these stages do not need to apply to concrete examples (e.g. the USA as an example of a federation).
16 These theoretical insights have been developed at an early stage for market integration (Giersch, 1949) and also for monetary integration (see also Chapter 2).
17 Art. 159 of the present Treaty. The obligation to coordinate EU policies with an impact on cohesion has been there right from the start of the EU. Indeed, the Rome

308 *Notes*

Treaty (Art. 39.a) instructed the EU to take account, while working out the Common Agricultural Policy, of 'structural and natural disparities between the various agricultural regions'. Art. 80 stipulated that the Commission in examining rates and conditions of transport shall take account of the 'requirements of an appropriate regional economic policy, the needs of underdeveloped areas and the problems of areas seriously affected by political circumstance'. The draft EU Constitution uses almost the same wordings in its Art. III.117.

18 Of course the mirror picture is relevant as well: in implementing cohesion policies (e.g. giving support to infrastructure projects) it should be checked how far they are consistent with other policy objectives such as the preservation of the environment.
19 Indeed, the treaty has been amended and now obliges the EU to elaborate the environmental policy in line with the balanced development of its regions (Art. 174.3). The EU has also the obligation to check the consistency of all its policies with the objectives of its environment policy. The information about the consistency on this score is relatively scarce (see Lenschow, 2002).
20 This has been introduced by the Treaty of Amsterdam (Arts 125–30). This treaty specifies that the task of the EU to support the actions of the member states while respecting the national competences in the field.
21 This EU application of basic principles has forced member states into major adaptations of their national social security systems with respect to their institutional setting, organizing principles and administrative practices. See Sindbjerg Martinsen (2005).
22 See Hooghe (1996) and in particular Hooghe and Marks (2001) for further details on multilevel governance and cohesion policy.
23 See Molle (2006: chap. 2 for the fundamentals and chap. 18 for the effects).
24 See, in this respect, the study made for the NMSs by Brusis (2002) and for Italy by Fabbrini and Brunazzo (2003).
25 This is a real risk with considerable welfare consequences. The risk is illustrated by the Common Agricultural Policy that has fallen victim to sectoral interests with huge negative consequences for consumers, taxpayers and third countries (e.g. Molle, 2006).
26 Partly, it is close to moral hazard; interested parties have indeed tried to bend the use of indicators and the measurement of their problems to create a more or less artificial eligibility for aid (see next chapter).
27 There is a limited participation of regional representatives in the work of the Council (made possible by Art. 203). The UK has for instance given certain powers to the Scottish parliament and government. If matters concerning these powers come up in the EU then Scottish government representatives will come to the EU Council meetings. Regions of other countries have tried to obtain similar powers but up until now with very little effect.
28 Apart from these types of organizations we can distinguish other types of groupings. The first are the so-called 'general umbrella' organizations. Among these we find such organizations as the Council of European Municipalities and Regions (founded 1951) and the Assembly of European Regions (founded 1985). These organizations try to group very diverse interest and have lost a good deal of the limited influence they had in the 1970s and 1980s to the other groupings given here. The next are lobby organizations of strong regions that cannot hope to obtain much funding because their economic structure is strong and their level of development high, they have regrouped themselves also to show a certain quality label to investors and they exchange information and best practices to optimize their policies for regeneration and innovation. They lobby the EU for participation in cohesion programmes that are applicable to restructuring or to social problems (urban deprivation). Much of their lobbying is, however, for the horizontal programmes of the EU, such as Research and Development. To that end they team up with other interested parties (such as firms and research institutes).

29 The need for a social policy to complement economic integration had already been recognized by other international organizations (ILO, 1956).
30 The treaty articles were rather a mixed bag. For a long time the situation has been characterized by a dichotomy between aims and means. Indeed the aims set are broad and ambitious (Arts 136 and 137): 'the member states agree upon the need to promote improved working conditions and an improved standard of living for workers, so as to make possible their harmonization, while the improvement is being maintained'. However, the instruments provided are not very specific; the 'improvement is largely to be achieved through the beneficial effects of the Common Market'.
31 See, for the evolution of the European Social Policy, for example, Holloway (1981) and Hantrais (1995).
32 It was indeed only at the adhesion of the UK that the goal of *economic (regional) cohesion* was translated into concrete policy action.

7 Reaching objectives by financial support

1 This framework is laid down in detail in four regulations: the most important one gives the general provisions on the ERDF, the ESF and the CF (Reg. 1083/2006); three others give more detailed provisions for each fund separately (Reg. 1080/2006 for the ERDF; 1081/2006 for the ESF; 1084/2006 for the CF).
2 These comprise the overseas departments of France (e.g. the Caribbean islands of Martinique and Guadeloupe) and islands off the African coast such as Madeira (P) or the Canary Islands (Sp).
3 Mind that these do not correspond to the three dimensions of the disparity problem as detailed in Chapters 2–5. In each of the three objectives occur elements of economic, social and territorial cohesion.
4 Examples of such common problems have been given in the last section of Chapter 5.
5 This phenomenon is not very well documented but is referred to often in the literature. See, for instance, Bache (1998), Wallace (1983) and Vaneecloo (2005). See also Box 7.2.
6 For the period 2004–06 the ten new member states have received in total €24 billion, of which €15 billion has gone to the objective 1 regions of the NMSs and some €8 billion is from the CF.
7 The latter was even divided; some programmes were supported by the Guidance section of the EAGGF, others that dealt with rural development were financed through the Guarantee section. The number of instruments is even higher if one takes the instruments for the accession countries (Phare and Sapard) into account.
8 A good review of the philosophy behind the budgetary mechanisms of the EU is given in EC, 1993a.
9 Note that the UK contribution is particularly low both in terms of its relative wealth and in terms of GDP; this is due to the exceptional arrangement the UK has negotiated with the EU in the early 1980s, permitting it to pay only little more to than it gets from the EU. This has been a bone of contention ever since.
10 In order to limit the expenditure for agriculture and open up the possibility to use resources for other tasks of the EU the total amounts of spending on agriculture have been fixed. This has no economic foundation either; economists argue in favour of a much more drastic cut in EU agricultural outlays. Actually on the basis of the subsidiarity test a good case could be made for the total re-nationalization of the agricultural policy which would free considerable amounts of money on the EU level and would take away a mortgage on cohesion as claims for compensation of distortions stemming from agricultural policy no longer need to be honoured.
11 One can thus say that the implicit objective of the EU cohesion policy has been to facilitate major progress in integration. Hence, the evaluation of its effects that we

will make in Chapter 10 will be done both on the basis of its stated and of the implicit objectives.
12 This has formed the main justification for the significant increase of the resources devoted to cohesion policy. Compare, for example, the Delors report (Delors et al., 1989): 'Historical experience suggests that in the absence of countervailing policies, the overall impact (of more economic integration) on peripheral regions could be negative.' See also EC (1993c).
13 See, among others, Wallace (1983), Carrubba (1997), Laffan (2000), Hooghe and Marks (2001), Deltas and Van der Beek (2003) and Vaneecloo (2005).
14 Most of the other budget items have no explicit redistribution objectives. They do, however, have some redistribution effects; an aspect we will deal with in Chapter 11.
15 For a description of the proposals for the ERDF see EC (1969); for the creation of the fund see Talbot (1977); for the first restructuring see EC (1981b); for a description of the changes in its tasks see EC (1977, 1985b, 1990a); and for a review of its performance in the first ten years see the EU brochure EC (1985a).
16 See, for a study of the early development of the ESF, Collins (1983); for later years see Degimbe (1999) and EC website.
17 Improving the urban structure (polycentrism, see Chapter 5) has not been translated in the priority objectives of cohesion policy. It tends to be taken seriously (that means get financial support) only in as far as it corresponds to other priorities.

Stimulating polycentrism implies strong urban development in regions with weak urban structures. The ESDP (see Chapter 5) wants to apply this recipe at three geographical levels:

1 European. The aim here is to pass from the Pentagon (see Chapter 5) as the only EU centre of global importance to several centres that can all assume also global importance.
2 National. The aim is to go from a situation where one or some cities dominate the scene (such as London or Paris) to a more balanced situation where more centres assume important roles. This rejoins the older concepts of Metropoles d'équilibre in France and the Polos de Desarrollo in Spain
3 Regional. The aim here is to move from a single dominant centre to a situation where many small- and medium-size towns exist that provide essential services.

Mind that it is notably the NMSs who have a very strategic choice to make concerning the division of their efforts and available resources over space; either concentration of efforts on growth poles or growth corridors (favouring efficiency) or dispersion of resources over the remaining areas of the country (favouring equity).
18 See Chapter 10 (notably Figure 10.3) for the effects of the application in the EU of this rule and Chapter 9 for a discussion about the improvement of the administrative absorption capacity.
19 See, for example, Kandogan (2000), or for a refinement that accounts for coalitions such as the Franco-German tandem Kauppi and Widgren (2004). These results cannot be considered as conclusive, however, as the distribution of votes (after enlargement with a large number of small states) is strongly biased in favour of countries with considerable needs. And anyway the degree of redistribution is largely dependent on political horse trading and not on sound economics (Bayoumi and Masson, 1995).
20 These figures have been borrowed from the ESPON projects 2.2.1 and 2.2.2. See ESPON (2005: 50).
21 We will come back in Chapter 10 on the negative welfare effects of the pumping around of finances that is the consequence of this 'juste retour'.
22 On each side of these national budgets some categories (e.g. taxation on the income side and welfare on the expenditure side) have a very large redistributive power.
23 Much of the text of this section has been borrowed from the website of the EU.
24 This subject is notably important in the NMSs. For an illustration of the potential and difficulties of realizing this potential we refer to Scott (2006).

25 In Chapter 5 we gave the example of the cooperation of a company specializing in a high-tech innovative activity with researchers from a university in the second region and a specialized consultancy in yet a third region.
26 See EC (2002d), GHK (2003) and EC website.
27 See for the effectiveness of this method, for instance, Parkinson (1998).

8 Reaching objectives by regulation and coordination

1 The structure of the present, previous and following chapter is not straightforward. Some of the elements placed now fairly late in one of these three chapters might have been introduced earlier. An example is the third section of this chapter that could also have been placed before Chapter 7. Other elements might have been analysed later. An example of this category concerns sections 8.4 and 8.5 that could have been placed at the end of Chapter 9. Such alternative rearrangements have been tried but presented disadvantages that were as important as the disadvantages of the present structure.
2 But influencing of decision makers through 'naming and shaming' is possible.
3 It thereby takes account of the subsidiarity and proportionality principles (see Chapter 6).
4 These aims have since been reformulated but have in essence remained the same (EC, 2006).
5 Many of those who have to comply with these rules complain about the severe constraints they put on their operations. This complaint was voiced as follows by one project leader: 'In matters of regulation the EU makes a horse; national governments transform it into a camel and auditors into a monster.'
6 A more detailed idea of the implementation of these general rules is given in the next chapter.
7 See also, in this respect, the next chapter.
8 This did indeed happen in practice as shown by reports of the Commission (e.g. Vanhalewijn and Simon, 1999) and independent analyses (i.e. Martin, 1998b).
9 In this respect one might mention the so-called "De Minimis" rule that exempts aid to SMEs under a certain ceiling (smaller than €200,000 for three years).
10 There was not very much variation among member countries on this point; in fact there was a clear-cut majority in all countries (EC, 1992, 1994a). See also OECD (1994b).
11 A representative of this school is Vaughan-Whitehead (2003). There has been much popular support for this. Indeed, two-thirds of the European population (EU 12) thought that the social dimension of Europe, including a charter with fundamental social rights, is a good thing.
12 See, for example, Molina and Perea (1992) and Sinn and Ochel (2003). The example that is often cited in this respect is that of the German unification where standards have been set nationally notwithstanding the fact that the productivity level in the new German Bundeslaender was very much lower than in the old ones. Hence, economic development in the former has stagnated and transfer payments to them have stayed at very high levels. This should be a lesson for the EU not to apply similar things to the NMSs.
13 See, in this respect, Bean *et al.* (1990), Addison and Siebert (1994) and Brown *et al.* (1996).
14 See Arts 16 and 86 of the EC Treaty and Arts III 6 and III 35 of the draft constitutional treaty.
15 See Molle (1986). In this respect it is interesting to cite the Public Service Agreement target adopted by the UK government: 'Make sustainable improvements in the economic performance of all English regions and over the long term reduce the persistent gap re in growth rates between the regions' (HM Treasury, 2002).
16 Further information about the tasks, competences and governance systems of these

international organizations can be obtained from their websites (e.g. www.ILO.org, www.IMF.org, etc.).
17 Given the discontent over the (perceived lack of) effectiveness of the cohesion policy (see Chapter 10) one tries to limit the need for a cohesion policy by making sure that other EU policies have a beneficial or at least neutral effect on cohesion. This holds also for the external effects of other policies than cohesion; for instance, the case of environment, see Lenschow (2002).
18 Let us recall here that there is also a strong need for vertical coordination. Indeed, the EU role in many of these policies (e.g. transport) is limited and national governments continue to play a major role.
19 In some cases such a negative impact is considered to be part of the restructuring process that is needed for competitiveness. We recall that the EU has instruments to cope with this sort of impact. For example, the CF is set up for facilitating the adaptation of the Mediterranean countries to cope with the effects of the introduction of EMU (see Chapter 6)
20 The *instrumentalization* of the SF for other objectives has been codified at different levels. First of all on the constitutional level, the Treaty of Amsterdam of 1997 provided: 'The Union's financial instruments should work, simultaneously and in the long-term interest towards economic growth, social cohesion and the protection of the environment.' Next on the level of regulation, Council Regulation 1260/1999 that governed the SF programmes says that while making its 'efforts to strengthen economic and social cohesion in the Community shall also seek to promote the harmonious, balanced and sustainable development of economic activities, ... a high level of protection and improvement of the environment'.
21 The blame for this unemployment is not put on the EU (max. of 5 per cent), however, but on various other causes, like a poor economic situation, and notably inadequate government policies (EC, 1993b).
22 Empirical support for this thesis can be found in Jaffe and Palmer (1997) and for the USA in Brunnermeier and Cohen (2003).

9 Implementation and delivery

1 For an example of conflicts in implementation of the EU cohesion policy (due to the lack of specification of objectives, the blurring of responsibilities and complexity of administrative procedures) see the situation of the UK in the 1980s as described by Rhodes (1986) and Coats and Wallace (1984).
2 The level we discuss here is the same as the one in the previous chapters. The constitutional provisions and the fundamentals of the EU cohesion policy discussed in Chapter 6 are here translated into principles and practical rules for the design of its system of delivery. Mind that in Chapter 6 we have not mentioned the constitutional provisions on implementation. The ones of major importance are those that bestow powers on the Commission for implementation of policies (Arts 202, 211 and 226–8) and for budget outlays (Art. 274).
3 We cite in this respect the introduction in Levy (2000):

> The operational character of policy management does not connect with the discursive focus of the academic market for EU texts and monographs. The knowledge about implementation and management has been held and transmitted by an entirely different process. It is held by practitioners at all levels and has been disseminated through training workshops, reports and manuals in thousands of locations throughout the member states, mostly inaccessible to the academic world.

So, for information one has to turn to the work of practitioners. Now that work is mostly on specific subjects. There are very few papers of a general nature. I have drawn first on my own experience, gained over my whole professional career as associate and later director of NEI/ECORYS (see, for more information, www.ecorys.com). Next I

have drawn on the work that my colleagues at NEI/ECORYS have done over the past decades to support European, national, regional and local authorities in improving the implementation of the SF (such as ECORYS, 2004a). In particular I have borrowed largely from one of the reports that have been made in this respect: NEI/ECORYS, 2002. I am indebted to my colleagues in general for their support and to the authors of the report in particular because they have permitted me to use almost literally large parts of their text.
4 The relevant theoretical literature on the subject of this chapter is even scarcer than the empirical literature. Some early attempts have tried to draw general features from a study of the EU practice (e.g. Wallace, 1984). However, this avenue has not been pursued. Much of the theory has instead been worked out in highly mathematical exercises about game theory (Corchon, 1996; Palfrey, 1998). Only very few authors have attempted to close the gap between this latter type of celestial theories and the mundane EU practice. One such attempt is by Levy (2000) who focuses on the issue of performance during the different stages of the policy cycle.
5 See for instance with respect to the Social Fund: Laffan (1983).
6 Absorption capacity has two other dimensions:

1 Macro economic absorption capacity can be measured in terms of the capacity of an economy to absorb large amounts of income without creating significant distortions and/or inflationary pressures. The EU has made a provision for this as it has set a cap on the share of EU aid to the GDP of the recipient country (see Chapter 7).
2 Financial absorption capacity can be defined as the ability to co-finance EU-supported programmes and projects, to plan and guarantee these national contributions in multi-annual budgets, and to collect these contributions from several partners interested in a programme or project. This requires a strong discipline of the member state in matters of public finance.

7 See, for a first attempt, Herve and Holzman (1998); for the time being this constitutes an insufficient conceptual and theoretical basis. So, one needs to base oneself on practical experience (e.g. NEI/ECORYS, 2002).
8 Mind that this is auditing in the strict sense of checking the regularity of expenses. The term audit is increasingly used in a much wider sense encompassing the comparison of the outcome of projects with the objectives of the programme. In our terminology this is the task of evaluators; a role that we will detail in Chapter 10.
9 See Chapter 10 on evaluation. Most NMSs have taken the challenge very seriously. See for example Artner (2005) and ECORYS (ABCap) (2004a).
10 In the field of SF these requirements can be largely deduced from the relevant regulations (notably 1260/99, 438/2001 and 1083/2006).
11 See Papadopoulos (2003), Horvat (2005) and World Bank (2006).
12 The principle of partnership is closely related to the principle of *subsidiarity* (see Chapter 6). The lowest level of government that can efficiently deal with a subject has to be empowered to do so but in cooperation with the governments at other levels that deal with aspects they are best equipped for.
13 See, for the origin and basics of the principle, EC (1979, 1984) and the EU website. The complicated set up that is thus created is defined by some as a policy network (e.g. Heinelt and Smith, 1996) or network governance (e.g. Kohler-Koch and Eising, 1998) by others as multi-level governance (notably Hooghe, 1996; Hooghe and Marks, 2001) or cooperative federalism (e.g. Casella and Frey, 1992).
14 A similar development can be seen in Poland.
15 For instance in terms of (1) the involvement of representatives of the private sector in planning, and (2) the use of modern monitoring and evaluation techniques, etc.
16 Among the regions that have adopted this course we find without exception all those who have a very strong constitutional position such as Scotland, the German federal states and the Spanish autonomous regions.

314 *Notes*

17 This is likely to be a low estimate as only in the Czech Republic the number of staff working in SCF management and implementation structures (exclusive of final beneficiaries) amounts to some 1,200 people.
18 In Germany the whole programming process has been developed within a working group in close cooperation with the federal states. External assistance by a research institute has been used for the drafting of the Regional Development Plans. According to the MA this was a necessary step since capacities in the ministry for such an extensive task were limited. Although parts of drafting were sourced out, the whole process is assessed as very labour intensive.
19 These documents are in a sense national versions of the EU Lisbon strategy (see Chapters 11 and 12) with the central objective to enhance competitiveness, in particular, in the field of the knowledge economy.
20 Except for cases of transport and environment, which are jointly financed by the ERDF and the CF.
21 Because this is what happens: all kinds of sectoral and regional stakeholders will try to fund as much as possible from their wish-list from EU support.
22 In order to support project sponsors in preparing projects the Commission, together with the European Bank for Reconstruction and Development (EBRD) and the European Investment Bank (EIB), has set up JASPERS (Joint Assistance in Supporting Projects in European Regions). The contribution of the EIB and the EBRD is particularly useful for projects that need co-financing from the private sector (e.g. toll roads). JASPERS gives the do's and don'ts for the process but also suggestions for tools such as contract forms (e.g. for concessions). (See: japsers.europa.eu.)
23 See, for more information about the legal status and functions of this international agreement, www.danubecom-intern.org.
24 This finance came from the Phare programme but the objective was to mainstream financing and implementation after accession according to the ESF.
25 From 2009, the Commission will itself produce a report at the beginning of each year on the progress achieved with regard to the strategic priorities of the Union. This report will be sent to the Council, which will adopt conclusions on the implementation of the strategic guidelines; the Commission is responsible for monitoring their application.
26 Many such instances are reported in Levy (2000).
27 The programming documents for the former objective 1 (backward regions) were generally CSFs translated into OPs, although SPDs could be used to programme amounts of less than €1 billion. All the programming documents for former objective 2 (restructuring regions) were SPDs. By contrast, the choice of the form of programming documents for the former objective 3 (social and employment) was left to the regions and member states.

10 Evaluation

1 This concept of efficiency applies to the cost involved in the whole policy cycle (from conceptualization via delivery to monitoring and adaptation). It should not be confused with the concept of allocational efficiency as a motive for regional policy (by stimulating the putting to work of idle resources which enhances total production).
2 Another important one is the group around external policy to which the candidate countries had to report (Phare programmes). See in this respect the study Williams *et al.* (2002).
3 See CEEE (1995), EC (1999d) and Tavistock *et al.* (2003). The Guide is available directly at www.evalsed.info.
4 For those interested in further information about the EU methods and practices we refer to: europa.eu.int/comm/regional_policy/sources/docgener/evaluation/rado_en.htm.
5 In the literature, one tends to make a distinction between relevance and appropriate-

ness. The former puts the accent on orientation of the interventions to the objectives, the latter on the type of intervention and the choice of instruments. For our purpose the distinction between the two terms is not essential so we will use both for designating the same stage in the evaluation process. This is more justified because the different DGs of the Commission have not yet agreed on a common terminology in evaluation matters.

6 Due to lack of sufficient empirical evidence we are not able to specify the efficiency aspect for each of the objectives distinguished. So we will make an overall estimate of efficiency in the last sections of this chapter.
7 Working papers, evaluation reports and other related documents can be directly downloaded from the Commission's website europa.eu.int/comm/regional_policy/ sources/docgener/evaluation/evaluation_en.htm.
8 Commonly, the CSF MA provides the Terms of Reference and the evaluation method to be used, while OP MAs contract out the work.
9 Each programme consists of a multitude of projects (several hundreds per programming period); much too wide a variety and much too large the specificity to be dealt with in this chapter. So we will limit ourselves to studies that have drawn the main conclusions of this wealth of detailed studies.
10 See, for instance, Bachtler and Michie (1995) and EC (1996a); see also the subsequent sections that give the results by objective.
11 See, for example, Bradley et al. (1995), Bornschier et al. (2004), Martin and Saenz (2003) and Beugelsdijk and Eijffinger (2005).
12 The EU SF support has been at a cost to welfare because it tended to force R&D-intensive industries into regions not well endowed to make them competitive (Midelfart-Kvarnik and Overman, 2002).
13 They prescribe a cocktail of EU and national policies that tend to optimize the allocation function and that should lead to the rapid catching up of the backward areas. They tend, thereby, to put much confidence in the beneficial effects of further liberalization of markets. For the influence of market policies on cohesion see Chapter 11.
14 One can distinguish three main types of methods: case studies, simulations and econometric models. The former have the huge disadvantage of using very heterogeneous approaches so that their results are very difficult to generalize. The middle group is often used in ex ante evaluations, has the advantage of a systemic approach to reality, but can only produce the likelihood of change due to a policy on a number of assumptions. They tend to come to positive conclusions. The latter (often used in ex post evaluations) finally try to relate the observed development of target variables to those of policy variables. See, for example, EC (1996a; 2004a).
15 Many studies have been made along these lines that use different time periods, different data and different dependent and independent variables. An early attempt at such modelling has been made by Molle (1983), relating sectoral growth of employment for the regions of the EU 9 to a number of variables (location factors), among them regional policy. The effect of the latter variable could not be identified. Other models exist that explains well the significant part of the decrease in disparity by the usual growth factors, such as Crespo–Cuaresma et al. (2003) but do not include a policy variable.
16 Other models that combine both the supply side and demand side have also been made. See, for critical review of all three types of models, Mairate and Hall (2001).
17 An overview of these models is given in EC (1999a).
18 See Gaspar (1995), Cappellen et al. (2003) and Beugelsdijk and Eijffinger (2005).
19 See Martin and Tyler (2006) for an approach based on a variant of shift share analysis.
20 This definition of policy efficiency is different from the one of allocational efficiency used elsewhere in this book. The latter refers to the working of markets; it is higher the lower the cost of distribution of production factors to different productions and of goods and services to customers. Allocational efficiency can be improved by taking away barriers to movement and distortions of markets (e.g. competition). See Molle (2006: chap. 14) for an application in terms of EU integration.

21 One should also take account the fact that the SF outlays, in regions that are net recipients, have a number of positive effects in the regions that are net contributors to the funds. These come about because the former import many capital goods from the latter. This effect is estimated at some one-third of the total.
22 See the advantages of decentralization proclaimed by the fiscal federalism school signalled in Chapter 6.
23 See, for an early comprehensive one, Nanetti (1992).
24 Later confirmed by the results of de la Fuente (2003).
25 Growth is not a prime objective, as many of these regions have done well in the past and have traditionally relatively high incomes per head.
26 Programming period 1989–93 by Ernst and Young (1997) and programming period 1994–99 by CSES (2003).
27 A similar problem exists with another indicator of social disparities, the differences in access to social security. This is also the almost exclusive domain of the national state and the EU has only a very limited role to play here (see Chapter 6).
28 See, for a general analysis, OECD (1993) and Layard *et al.* (1991) and for an analysis of five EU countries, de Koning and Mosley (2001).
29 See, among others, Mairate (2006).
30 See in this respect the evidence for old member countries, for exampole, Gualini (2004) for Italy and Basle (2006) for France and for the new member states, for example, Blazek and Vozab (2006) and Paraskevopoulos *et al.* (2006).
31 A related problem (notably for the former objective 2 (restructuring)) has been the definition of small very precisely delimited areas. They were unsuited for the formulation of clear targets and for the definition of relevant policies for a balanced development of the whole region.
32 On the more general level of EU institutions and policies we mention that EMU takes away the possibility to use the exchange rate to adapt situations that otherwise could not be changed. Too high levels of EU social and environmental standards have sometimes put a break on development.
33 See Marques-Mendes (1986a, b), Petith (1977), Johnson (1958) and Miller and Spencer (1977).
34 See, for instance, Baldwin *et al.* (1997), Breuss (2002) and the literature cited in the latter article.
35 See Allen *et al.* (1996, 1998), Bottasso and Sembenelli (2001) and EC (2004f).
36 In the past, exchange rate uncertainty had negatively influenced direct investment flows between EU countries (Morsink and Molle, 1991a, b; Morsink, 1998). The same applied to foreign transactions in loans and stock (NIESR, 1996). These results are in line with those of a more general study (Rose, 2000) that shows that the decrease of exchange rate volatility and in particular the creation of a monetary union lead to large increases in trade among the participant countries.
37 See in this respect the discussion in economic policy where Rose (2000) predicted very high results, which were challenged by Persson (2001) followed by Micco *et al.* (2003) who did, as yet, find little effect.
38 One might expect academic studies to be more critical than studies made in the course of the EU policy process. However, this is not the case for two reasons. First, many studies from the former strand find their way into the academic literature. Second, some of the more critical academic studies are used by the Commission to improve the quality of the policy.
39 Accountability of the principal for the actions of the agent necessitates all sorts of control and monitoring mechanisms (see Chapter 9).

11 Consistency with other EU policies

1 We have given the constitutional basis for this horizontal coordination in Chapter 6.
2 We will of course mention those studies that refer to other relevant research.

3 In the subsequent sections we have used for the older period the overview study of Molle and Cappellin (1988) and the recent one of Hall et al. (2001). We also made use of the EC studies on the subject, notably EC (2001).
4 Of course the Gini coefficient reflects a static situation. In case a certain policy impacts favourably on poor regions we will assume that it is positive for cohesion.
5 Although the *effectiveness* of the contribution of the CAP to cohesion seems satisfactory there is room for questioning the *efficiency*: €54 billion spending on CAP produces a Gini coefficient of 0.16; while €22 billion spending on regional policy produces a Gini coefficient of 0.48.
6 Much of this policy now comes under the heading of competitiveness. The importance of the factors that drive competitiveness for cohesion is very well documented (see, for example, the special issue of Regional Studies (Vol. 38.9 of 2004) or CE/ECORYS (2004). However, as most of the documents we use speak about the internal market we will follow that mainstream.
7 The impact of market integration on regions has been studied notably in the framework of the completion of the internal market. Most studies have emphasized the diversity of the sectoral and regional effects (Molle, 1990; Bachtler and Clement, 1992; EC, 1996a; Rodriguez-Pose, 1999).
8 This result is both drawn from studies that analyse historical examples (Molle and Boeckhout, 1995) and more modern cases (i.e. Paluzie et al., 2001).
9 Network industries are a group of sectors based on infrastructural networks, such as railways, telecommunication, electric energy, etc.
10 Preserving the availability of services of general interest in problem areas refers both to the economic (firms in industry and services), to the social (individual citizens) and, in particular, to the territorial dimension of cohesion (e.g. with respect to accessibility to centres). See also, in this respect, Chapter 5.
11 As the EMU has been implemented only recently, there are as yet not many studies available that have well grasped the impact. So, provisionally, we must do with studies that are based on economic reasoning.
12 See Barr et al. (2003), Micco et al. (2003), de Nardis and Vicarelli (2003) and Persson (2001).
13 See Morsink and Molle (1991a, b), Morsink (1998) and Pain and van Welsum (2003).
14 This section draws on Agence Europeenne Territoires Synergies et al. (2001), Chapter 3. Note that similar results are obtained for telecommunications, a network industry that bears resemblance to transport (ESPON, 2004c).
15 The other proposition is also true: a very high proportion of the SF was actually spent on transport infrastructure projects.
16 The strong discontinuities in the graph are due to the fact that much (51 per cent) of the expenditure of the period of analysis was actually concentrated in only seven regions.
17 The EU has been given competences in the field first, with the Single European Act and second (in 1992), by the Treaty of Maastricht.
18 Mind that cohesion policy compensates for these effects; its catalogue of eligible projects includes projects that help countries to come up to EU environmental standards.
19 As the resources of these countries to tackle the problem (both in regulatory and in financial terms) are very limited the SF have moved in. Environment is a key priority in all the NMSs.
20 This impact is attenuated by the spending on innovation that comes from other sources such as the SF and national funds.
21 See Hall et al. (2001). They give the results of the renewed effort of the EC to gauge the impact of its other policies on cohesion.
22 We have not taken up the effects of external policy here because the basis for scoring appeared too scanty.

23 Indeed, peripheral regions belong mostly to the objective 1 category, while intermediate regions often were only eligible for the other objectives. Finally, the central regions did in general not qualify for SF aid (apart from projects such as URBAN). Mind that the data apply only to the EU 15.

24 Note that for the year 1985 we have assessed the situation before the Mediterranean enlargement, while the 2000 situation reflects the situation before the latest enlargement. This could have given some problems in case we had wanted to compare specific regions. Now we circumvent this by working with categories that keep their policy relevance whatever the specific composition of regions.

25 In order to limit as much as possible arbitrariness we have asked several persons to check the scoring. Of course there remains some arbitrariness in the translation of these considerations into scores. However, as all studies on which we base ourselves are published anybody can verify their plausibility.

12 Conclusions and outlook

1 The recent overhaul of the systemic aspects of the EU cohesion policy has incited many to bring forward proposals for change (see, for example, Sapir et al., 2004). The Commission has also made a series of proposals after consultation of experts and practitioners. Some of these have been accepted and are now part of the new regulations. Others, that have not been accepted, merit to be kept in mind. We will therefore mention a few of them in the coming sections.

2 A modern regional policy for the United Kingdom, DTI, March 2003.

3 Some of this has already been implemented, for instance the rule that additionality is only checked for objective 1 regions.

4 This argument is a difficult one as in a number of cases the application of EU considerations is supposed to provide welfare gains to the EU as a whole that may offset the presumed welfare losses of the country in question. Anyway the measurement of these effects is very difficult.

5 To make sure that the newest dimension of cohesion policy, viz. territorial cohesion, is taken seriously the suggestion has been made to introduce a Territorial Impact Assessment for other relevant common policies, particularly with regards to state aid (see ECOTEC, 2003b).

6 Other countries such as India, Russia, etc., could also have been taken. Integration areas such as NAFTA (USA, Canada, Mexico) would, however, require a much more in-depth analysis that would go far beyond the capacities of the present study.

7 Different statistical sources combine in a different way the provinces of Argentina in regions. The choice does not hamper our analysis though as the picture actually remains the same. A similar problem exists as to the comparison of the levels of the major countries. In some comparisons Brazil is supposed to have a much lower GDP/P level. It would only aggravate the disparity but would not affect the major conclusions.

8 The Council of Ministers' decision MERCOSUR/CMC/DEC Nos 18/05 and 24/05.

9 Mind that there is a statistical effect of the type that also produces very high figures for urban areas like Paris or Hamburg.

10 As to differences, see Wu (2002). As to causes some put the accent on conditional convergence theories, for example, Demurger (2001) who finds a very strong relation between the infrastructure development in China and the relative growth figures of the provinces, next to geographical location and openness to reforms.

11 Notably in this area the EU experience seems to be of much relevance for other countries. Mind that the EU in its recent experience with the introduction of the system in the accession countries, most of who have gone through a very difficult transition period and did show weaknesses as to their absorption capacity.

References

Addison, J.T. and Siebert, W.S. (1994) Recent developments in social policy in the new European Union, *Industrial and Labour Relations Review*, 48.1: 5–27.

Agence Europeenne Territoires et Synergies *et al.* (2001) *Spatial impacts of Community policies and cost of coordination*, Study for the European Commission (ERDF 99.00.27.156), Brussels.

Aghion, P., Caroli, E. and Garcia Penalosa, C. (1999) Inequality and economic growth the perspective of the new growth theories, *Journal of Economic Literature*, 37: 1615–60.

Ahmad, E. (1997) Intergovernmental transfers; an international perspective, in: Ahmad, E. (ed.), *Financing Decentralized Expenditures*, Edward Elgar, Cheltenham, 1–17.

Aiginger, K. (1999) Do industrial structures converge? A survey of the empirical literature on specialisation and concentration of industries, *WIFO Working Paper* no. 116.

Aldcroft, D.H. and Morewood, S. (1995) *Economic Change in Eastern Europe Since 1918*, Edward Elgar, Aldershot.

Alesina, A. and Perotti, R. (1998) Economic risk and political risk in fiscal unions, *The Economic Journal*, 108: 989–1008.

Alesina, A., Perotti, R. and Spolaore, E. (1995) Together or separately? Issues on the costs and benefits of political and fiscal unions, *European Economic Review*, 39.3/4: 751–8.

Allen, C.B., Gasiorek, M. and Smith, A. (1996) *Competitiveness, impact, and the quantification of trade creation and trade diversion due to the MSP* (background study to EC, 1996b), Brussels.

Allen, C.B., Gasiorek, M. and Smith, A. (1998) The competition effects of the Single Market in Europe, *Economic Policy: A European Forum*, pp. 441–86.

Amiti, M. (1998) New trade theories and industrial location in the EU, a survey of the evidence, *Oxford Review of Economic Policy*, 14.2: 45–53.

Amiti, M. (1999) Specialisation patterns in Europe, *Weltwirtschaftliches Archiv*, 135.4: 573–93.

Amos, O. (1988) Unbalanced regional growth and regional income inequality in the latter stages of development, *Regional Science and Urban Economics*, 18: 549-66.

Andersson, R. and Brama, A. (2004) Selective migration in Swedish distressed neighbourhoods; can area based urban policies counteract segregation processes? *Housing Studies*, 19.4: 517–39.

Arachi, G. and D'Antoni, M. (2004) Redistribution as social insurance and capital market integration, *International Tax and Public Finance*, 11.4: 531–47.

Ardy, B., Begg, I., Schelke, W. and Torres, F. (2002) *EMU and Cohesion: Policy Challenges*, South Bank University, London.

Armstrong, H. and Taylor, J. (2000) *Regional Economics and Policy*, 3rd edn, Blackwell Publishers, Hemel Hempstead.

Arndt, O. and Sternberg, R. (2000) Do manufacturing firms profit from intraregional innovation linkages? An empirical based answer, *European Planning Studies*, 8.4: 465–85.

Artner, A.-M. (2005) New modes of governance and EU structural and cohesion policy in Estonia, Latvia, and Lithuania, *Working Papers* no. 165, IWE/HAS, Budapest.

Atkinson, A.B., Marlier, E. and Nolan, B. (2004) Indicators and targets for social inclusion in the EU, *Journal of Common Market Studies*, 42.1: 47–75.

Aydalot, P. (1985) *Economie Regionale et Urbaine*, Economica, Paris.

Aydalot, P. and Keeble, D. (1988) High technology industry and innovative environments, *The European Experience*, Routledge, London.

Azzoni, C.R. (2001) Economic growth and regional economic inequality in Brazil, *The Annals of Regional Science*, 35: 133–52.

Bache, I. (1988) The Politics of EU regional policy: Multi-level governance of flexible gatekeeping?, *Contemporary European Studies Series*, Sheffield Academic Press, Sheffield.

Bachtler, J. and Clement, K. (eds) (1992) 1992 and regional development, *Regional Studies*, Special issue, 26.4: 305–419.

Bachtler, J. and Michie, R. (1995) A new era in EU regional policy evaluation: the appraisal of the Structural funds, *Regional Studies*, 29.8: 745–52.

Bachtler, J. and Taylor, S. (1996) Regional development strategies in Objective 2 regions: a comparative assessment, *Regional Studies*, 30.8: 723–32.

Bachtler, J. and Yuill, D. (2001) Policies and strategies for regional development: a shift in paradigm, *European Policy Research Papers*, no. 46, Glasgow.

Badinger, H., Mueller, W.G. and Tondl, G. (2004) Regional convergence in the European Union 1985–1999: a spatial dynamic panel analysis, *Regional Studies*, 38.3: 241–53.

Bagella, M., Becchetti, L. and Hasan, I. (2004) The anticipated and concurring effects of the EMU: exchange rate volatility, institutions and growth, *Journal of International Money and Finance*, 23.7/8: 1053–83.

Baici, E. and Casalone, G. (2005) Can human capital be accounted for regional economic growth in Italy? A panel analysis of the 1980–2001 period; paper available from baici@eco.unipmn.it.

Bailey, D. and de Propris, L. (2002) The 1988 reform of the European structural funds: entitlement or empowerment?, *Journal of European Public Policy*, 9.3: 408–28.

Bairoch, P. (1976) Europe's Gross National Product 1800–1975, *Journal of European Economic History*, 5: 272–340.

Bairoch, P. (1981) The main trends on national economic disparities since the industrial revolution, in: Bairoch, P. and Serg-Leboyer, M. (eds), *Disparities in Economic Development Since the Industrial Revolution*, St. Martin's Press, New York.

Balducci, A. (2003) Cross border governance, inventing regions in a transnational multi-level polity, *DISP*, 152: 43–52.

Baldwin, R.E., Forslid, R. and Haaland, J.I. (1996) Investment creation and diversion in Europe, *The World Economy*, 19.6: 635–59.

Baldwin, R.E., Francois, J.F. and Portes, R. (1997) The cost and benefits of eastern enlargement: the impact on the EU and central Europe, *Economic Policy: A European Forum*, 24: 127–76.

Barr, D., Breedon, F. and Miles, D. (2003) Life on the outside, economic conditions and prospects outside Euroland, *Economic Policy*, 18.37: 573–613.

Barro, R.J. (1991) Economic growth in a cross section of countries, *The Quarterly Journal of Economics*, 106.2: 407–43.

Barro, R.J. (1997) *The Determinants of Economic Growth*, MIT Press, Cambridge, Mass.
Barro, R.J. and Sala-I-Martin, X. (1991) Convergence across states and regions, *Brookings Papers of Economic Activity*, 1991/1: 107–82.
Barro, R.J. and Sala-I-Martin, X. (1995) *Economic Growth*, McGraw Hill, New York.
Barry, F., Goerg, H. and Strobl, E. (2003) Foreign Direct Investment agglomerations and demonstration effects: an empirical investigation, *Review of World Economics*, 139.4: 583–600.
Basle, M. (2006) Strengths and weaknesses of European Union policy evaluation methods: ex post evaluation of Objective 2, 1994–1999, *Regional Studies*, 40.2: 225–35.
Baumol, W.J. (1986) Productivity growth, convergence and welfare; what the long-run data show, *American Economic Review*, 76: 1072–85.
Baumol, W.J. and Wolff, E.N. (1988) Productivity growth, convergence and welfare: reply, *American Economic Review*, 76.5: 1155–59.
Bayoumi, T. and Masson, P.R. (1995) Fiscal flows in the United States and Canada; lessons for monetary union in Europe, *European Economic Review*, 39.2: 253-74.
Bayoumi, T. and Masson, P.R. (1998) Liability creating versus non liability creating fiscal stabilisation policies: Ricardian equivalence, fiscal stabilisation and the EMU, *The Economic Journal*, 108: 1026–45.
BBR&P (2003) Integrated tools for European Spatial development, *Second interim report of the ESPON project 3.1*, www.espon.lu/online/documentation/projects/cross_ thematic/816/2ir-3.1.pdf.
Bean, Ch. (1994) European unemployment: a survey, *The Journal of Economic Literature*, 32.2: 573–619.
Bean, Ch., Bernholz, P., Danthine, J.P. and Malinvaud, E. (1990) *European Labour Markets: A Long-run View*, CEPR Macroeconomic Policy Group, Centre for European Policy Studies, Brussels.
Belessiotis, T., Levin, M. and Veugelers, R. (2006) *EU Competitiveness and Industrial Location*, EC Bureau of European Policy Advisors, Brussels.
Belke, A. and Hebler, M. (2002) Towards a European social union, impacts on labor markets in the acceding countries, *Constitutional Political Economy*, 13: 313–35.
Beugelsdijk, M. and Eijffinger, S. (2005) The effectiveness of structural policy in the European Union: an empirical analysis for the EU 15 during the period 1995–2001, *Journal of Common Market Studies*, 43.1: 37–52.
Blanchard, O. and Wolfers, J. (2000) The role of shocks and institutions in the rise of European unemployment: the aggregate evidence, *Economic Journal*, 110: 1–33.
Blankart, C. (2000) The process of government centralization: a constitutional view, *Constitutional Political Economy*, 11: 27–39.
Blatter, J. (2004) From 'spaces of place' to 'spaces of flows'? Territorial and functional governance in cross border regions in Europe and North America, *International Journal of Urban and Regional Research*, 28.3: 530–48.
Blazek, J. and Vozab, J. (2006) Ex ante evaluation in the new member states: the case of the Czech Republic, *Regional Studies*, 40.2: 237–48.
Blom-Hansen, J. (2005) Principals, agents and the implementation of EU cohesion policy, *Journal of European Public Policy*, 12.4: 624–48.
Blomstrom, M. and Kokko, A. (2001) Foreign direct investment and spillovers of technology, *International Journal of Technology Management*, 22.5/6: 435–54.
Blyde, J. (2005) Convergence Dynamics in Mercosur, Mimeo, IADB, Washington.
Bocconi (university of) (1997) EU foreign direct investments in Central and Eastern Europe, mimeo, Milan.

Böhning, W.R. (1993) *International Aid as a Means to Reduce the Need for Emigration*, ILO/UNHR, Geneva.

Boldrin, M. and Canova, F. (2001) Europe's regions: income disparities and regional policies, *Economic Policy*, 1.32: 207–53.

Boldrin, M. and Canova, F. (2003) Regional policies and EU enlargement, *CEPR Discussion Paper Series*, no. 3744.

Boltho, A. (ed.) (1982) *The European Economy: Growth and Crisis*, Oxford University Press, Oxford.

Boltho, A. and Holtham, G. (1992) The assessment: new approaches to economic growth, *Oxford Review of Economic Policy*, 8.4: 1–14.

Borchardt, K. (1968) Regionale Wachstumsdifferenzierung in Deutschland im 19.Jahrhundert unter besondere Berücksichtigung des West-Ost-Gefälles (Regional differentiation of growth in Germany in the 19th century under specific consideration of the West/East slope), in: Lütge, F. (ed.), *Wirtschaftliche und Soziale Probleme der gewerblichen Entwicklung im 15.-16. und 19. Jahrhundert*, GSWM, Stuttgart, 115–30.

Borensztein, E., De Gregorio, J. and Lee, J.-W. (1998) How does foreign direct investment affect economic growth?, *Journal of International Economics*, 45: 115–35.

Bornschier, V., Herkenrath, M. and Ziltener, P. (2004) Political and economic logic of western European integration: a study of convergence comparing member and non member states 1980–1998, *European Societies*, 6.1: 71–96.

Borts, G.H. (1960) The equalisation of returns and regional economic growth, *The American Economic Review*, 50: 319–47.

Bottasso, A. and Sembenelli, A. (2001) Market power, productivity and the EU single market programme: an ex post assessment of Italian firm level data, *European Economic Review*, 1: 167–86.

Bradley, J., Morgenroth, E. and Untiedt, G. (2004) Macro regional evaluation of the Structural funds using the HERMIN modelling framework, Paper for the Slovenia Conference.

Bradley, J., O'Donell, N., Sheridan, N. and Whelan, K. (1995) *Regional Aid and Convergence, Evaluating the Impact of the Structural funds on the European Periphery*, Avebury, Aldershot.

Braunerhjelm, P., Faini, R., Norman, V., Ruane, F. and Seabright, P. (2000) Integration and the regions of Europe: how the right policies can prevent polarization, *MEI 10*, CEPR, London.

Brenton, P., di Mauro, F. and Luecke, M. (1999) Economic integration and FDI, an empirical analysis of foreign direct investment in the EU and in Central and Eastern Europe, *Empirica*, 26.2: 95–121.

Breuss, F. (1998) Sustainability of the fiscal criteria in stage III of the EMU, *Working Papers*, no. 29, RIEA, Vienna.

Breuss, F. (2002) Benefits and dangers of EU enlargement, *Empirica*, 29.3: 245–74.

Breuss, F. and Eller, M. (2004) Fiscal decentralization and economic growth, is there really a link? *CESifo Report*, 2.1: 3–9.

Bris, A., Koskinen, Y. and Nilsson, M. (2006) The real effects of the euro: evidence from corporate investments, *Review of Finance*, 10.1: 1–37.

Brown, S., Button, K. and Sessions, J. (1996) Implications of liberalised European labour markets, *Contemporary Economic Policy*, 14.1: 58–69.

Bruelhart, M. (1998) Trading places: industrial specialisation in the European Union, *Journal of Common Market Studies*, 36.3: 319–46.

Brunnermeier, S.B. and Cohen, M.A. (2003) Determinants of environmental innovation in US manufacturing industries, *Journal of Environmental Economics and Management*, 45: 278–93.

Brusis, M. (2002) Between EU requirements, competitive politics and national traditions: re-creating regions in the accession countries of Central and Eastern Europe, *Governance: An International Journal of Policy, Administration and Institutions*, 15.4: 531–59.
Buchanan, J.M. (1991) *Constitutional Economics*, ME Basil Blackwell, Cambridge.
Buckley, P.J. and Artisien, P. (1987) Policy issues of intra-EC direct investment: British, French and German multinationals in Greece, Portugal and Spain, with special reference to employment effects, *Journal of Common Market Studies*, 26.2: 207–30.
Bukowski, J., Piattoni, S. and Smyrl, M. (eds) (2003) *Between Europeanization and Local Societies: The Space for Territorial Governance*, Rowman and Littlefield, Lanham, Md.
Camagni, R. (ed.) (1991) *Innovation Networks, Spatial Perspectives*, Belhaven Press, London.
Campos, N. and Kinoshita, Y. (2001) FDI as effective technology transferred, *Paper Dep. of Economics*, University of Newcastle upon Tyne, Newcastle.
Cantwell, J. and Randaccio, F.S. (1992) Intra-industry direct investment in the EC: oligopolistic rivalry and technological competition, in: Cantwell, J. (ed.), *Multinational Investment in Modern Europe*, Edward Elgar, Aldershot, 71–106.
Cappellen, A., Castellacci, F., Fagerberg, J. and Verspagen, B. (2003) The impact of EU regional support on growth and convergence in the European Union, *Journal of Common Market Studies*, 41.4: 621–44.
Carrubba, C.J. (1997) Net financial transfers in the European Union: Who gets what and why?, *Journal of Politics*, 59.2: 469–96.
Carson, M. (1982) The theory of foreign direct investment, in: Black, J. and Dunning, J.H. (eds), *International Capital Movements*, Macmillan, London, 22–58.
Carstensen, K. and Toubal, F. (2004) Foreign Direct Investment in Central and Eastern European countries, a dynamic panel analysis, *Journal of Comparative Economics*, 32.1: 3–22.
Casella, A. (2005) Redistribution policy; a European model, *Journal of Public Economics*, 89.7: 1305–31.
Casella, A. and Frey, B. (1992) Federalism and clubs; towards a theory of overlapping political jurisdictions, *European Economic Review*, 36.2/3: 639–46.
CE/ECORYS/UoC (2004) A study on the factors of regional competitiveness (preparatory study for the fourth cohesion report), Brussels.
CEEE (Centre for European Evaluation Expertise) (1995) *For Improved Evaluations of Community Programmes; Results of the 1995 Means Programme* (comprising seven handbooks), Brussels.
Chatterji, M. (1992) Convergence clubs and endogenous growth, *Oxford Review of Economic Policy*, 8: 57–69.
Chipman, J.S. (1965a) A survey of the theory of international trade, Part 1, *Econometrica*, 33: 477–519.
Chipman, J.S. (1965b) A survey of the theory of international trade, Part 2: The neoclassical theory, *Econometrica*, 33: 685–749.
Chipman, J.S. (1966) A survey of the theory of international trade, Part 3: The modern theory, *Econometrica*, 34: 18–76.
Chor, D. (2005) Institutions, wages, and inequality, the case of Europe and its periphery (1500–1899), *Explorations in Economic History*, 42.4: 547–66.
Christodoulakis, N. and Kalyritis, S. (2000) The effects of the second Community support framework, 1994–1999 on the Greek economy, *Journal of Policy Modeling*, 22.5: 611–24.

Cieslik, A. and Kawiewsk, M. (2004) Telecommunications, infrastructure and regional economic development: the case of Poland, *Regional Studies*, 38.6: 713–25.

Clark, C., Bradley, J. and Wilson, F. (1969) Industrial location and economic potential in western Europe, *Regional Studies*, 3 197–212.

Coats, D. and Wallace, H. (1984) European funds: how they are spent in the UK, in: Lewis, D. and Wallace, H. (eds), *Policies into Practice: National and International Case Studies inIimplementation*, Heinemann, London, 161–82.

College of Europe (1997) *The Impact of Community Policies, Other Than the Structural Policies, on Economic and Social Cohesion*, Bruges.

Collins, D. (1983) *The Operations of the European Social Fund*, Croom Helm, London.

Cooke, P. and de Laurentis, C. (2002) The index of knowledge economies in the European Union: performance rankings of cities and regions, *Regional Industrial Research Report*, 41, CAS, Cardiff University, Cardiff.

Cooke, Ph. (2002) *Knowledge Economies*, Routledge, London.

Cooke, Ph. (2003) Economic globalisation and its future challenges for regional development, in: *International Journal of Technology Management*, 26.2/2/4: 401–20.

Copus, A.K. (1999) A new peripherality index for the NUTS III regions of the European Union, *ERDF/FEDER Study 98/00/27/130*, CEC/DG XVI A.4, Brussels.

Corchon, L.C. (1996) *The Theory of Implementation of Socially Optimal Decisions in Economics*, Macmillan, Houndsmill/Basingstoke.

Cornelisse, P.A. and Goudswaard, K.P. (2002) On the convergence of social protection systems in the European Union, *International Social Security Review*, 55.3: 3–18.

Cornut, P. (1963) *Repartition de la fortune privee en France par departement et nature des biens au cours de la premiere moitie du XX eme siecle*, Armand Colin, Paris.

Costa-i-Font, J. and Tremosa-i-Bacells, R. (2003) Spanish regions and the macroeconomic benefits of the European Monetary Union, *Regional Studies*, 37.3: 217–26.

Council of Europe (2005) *Concerted Development of Social Cohesion Indicators; Methodological Guide*, Strasburg (can be downloaded from their website: www.coe.int).

CPB/SCP (2004) Sociaal Europa, *Europese Verkenning*, Vol. 1, Den Haag.

Crespo, J. and Velasquez, F.J. (2003) Multinationals and the diffusion of technology between developed countries, *Working Paper 26–2003*, FSEC/UCM, Madrid.

Crespo-Cuaresma, J., Dimitz, M.A. and Ritzberger-Gruenwald, D. (2003) The impact of European integration on growth: what can we learn from EU accession, in: Tumpell-Gugerell, G. and Mooslechner, P. (eds), *Economic Convergence and Divergence in Europe: Growth and Regional Development in an Enlarged Europe*, Edward Elgar, Cheltenham, 55–71.

Crozet, M., Mayer, T. and Mucchielli, J.-L. (2004) How do firms agglomerate?: a study of FDI in France, *Regional Science and Urban Economics*, 34.1: 27–54.

CSES (2003) Ex Post evaluation of 1994–1999 Objective 2 programmes, *Synthesis Report for the European Commission*, Brussels.

Cuadrado-Roura, J.-R., Garcia-Greciano, B. and Raymond, J.-L. (1999) Regional convergence in productivity and productive structure: the Spanish case, *International Regional Science Review*, 22.1: 350–53.

Dall'erba, S. and Le Gallo, J. (2003) Regional convergence and the impact of European Structural funds over 1989–1999; a spatial econometric analysis, ERSA Conference, Jyvaskyla (forthcoming in *Papers in Regional Science*).

Daveri, F. and Tabellini, G. (2000) Unemployment and taxes: Do taxes affect the rate of unemployment?, *Economic Policy: A European Forum*, 30: 47–104.

Dearden, S.J.H. (1995) European Social Policy and Flexible Production, *International Journal of Manpower*, 16.10: 3–13.

Degimbe, J. (1999) *La politique sociale Europeenne*, Institut Syndical Europeen, Bruxelles.
de Koning, J. and Mosley, H. (eds) (2001) *Labour Market Policy and Unemployment: Impact and Process Evaluations in Selected European Countries*, Edward Elgar, Cheltenham.
de la Fuente, A. and Vives, X. (1995) Infrastructure and education as instruments of regional policy: evidence from Spain, *Economic Policy*, 20: 13–51.
de la Fuente, A. (2003) Regional convergence in Spain, 1965–1995, in: Tumpell-Gugerell, G. and Mooslechner, P. (eds), *Economic Convergence and Divergence in Europe; Growth and Regional Development in an Enlarged Europe*, Edward Elgar, Cheltenham, 72–85.
de la Fuente, A. and Ciccone, A. (2003) *Human Capital in a Global and Knowledge Based Economy* (final report), EU Commission, Brussels.
Delors, J. et al. (1989) Report on Economic and Monetary Union in the European Community, *Report to the European Council by a Committee Chaired by J. Delors*, Brussels.
Deltas, G. and Van Der Beek, G. (2003) Modeling fiscal federalism, a decomposition analysis of changes in intra-European Union budgetary transfers, *The Quarterly Review of Economics and Finance*, 43: 592–613.
de Menil, G. (1999) Real capital market integration in the EU: How far has it gone? What will the effect of the euro be?, *Economic Policy: A European Forum*, 28: 167–204.
de Molina, J.L.M. and García Perea, P. (1992) European economic integration from the standpoint of Spanish labour market problems, in: Marsden, D. (ed.), *Pay and Employment in the New Europe*, Billing and Sons, Worcester, 99–122.
Demurger, S. (2001) Infrastructure development and economic growth: an explanation for regional disparities in China, *Journal of Comparative Economics*, 29: 95–117.
de Nardis, S. and Vicarelli, C. (2003) Currency unions and trade, the special case of EMU, *Review of World Economics*, 139.4: 625–49.
Devereux, M.B (2003) EU accession and alternative monetary policies, *Journal of Common Market Studies*, 41.5: 941–64.
Devereux, M.P. and Freeman, H. (1995) The impact of tax on foreign direct investment: empirical evidence and the implications for tax integration schemes, *International Tax and Public Finance*, 2: 85–106.
Djajic, S. (2001) Illegal immigration trends, policies and economic effects, in: Djajic, S. (ed.), *International Migration: Trends, Policies and Economic Impact*, Routledge, London/New York, 137–61.
Djarova, J. (2004) *Cross Border Investing: The Case of Central and Eastern Europe*, Kluwer, New York, Boston, Dordrecht.
Dobrinsky, R. (2003) Convergence in per capital income levels, productivity dynamics and the real exchange rate in the EU acceding countries, *Empirica*, 30.3: 305–34.
Dunning, J.H. (1979) Explaining changing patterns of international production: in defence of an eclectic theory, *Oxford Bulletin of Economics and Statistics*, 41: 269–95.
Dunning, J.H. (1980) A note on intra-industry foreign direct investment, *Banca Nazionale del Lavoro Quarterly Review*, 34: 427–37.
Dunning, J.H. (1988) The eclectic paradigm of international production: a restatement and some possible extensions, *Journal of International Business Studies*, 19.1: 6–12.
Dunning, J.H. (1993) *The Globalisation of Business: The Challenge of the 1990s*, Routledge, London.
Durán-Herrera, J.J. (1992), Cross direct investment and technological capability of Spanish domestic firms, in: Cantwell, J. (ed.), *Multinational Investment in Modern Europe*, Edward Elgar, Aldershot, 214–55.

EC (1961) *Document de la Conférence sur les Economies Régionales*, vol. II, Brussels.
EC (1964) *Reports by Groups of Experts on Regional Policy in the European Economic Community*, Brussels.
EC (1969) *A Regional Policy for the Community*, Brussels.
EC (1971) *Regional Development in the Community: Analytical Survey*, Brussels.
EC (1973) *Report on the Regional Problems in the Enlarged Community* (Thomson Report), COM 73/550, Brussels.
EC (1977) The Regional Policy of the Community, New Guidelines, *Supplement 2/77 to Bulletin of the European Communities*, Luxembourg.
EC (1979) The Regional Development Programmes, *Regional Policy Series*, no. 17, Brussels.
EC (1981a) *The Regions of Europe: First Periodic Report*, Brussels.
EC (1981b) *Proposal for a Council Regulation Amending the Regulation (EEC), no. 724/75, establishing a European Regional Development Fund*, Brussels.
EC (1983) *The Europeans and their Regions*. Commission DG XVI, Internal Document, Brussels.
EC (1984) *The Regions of Europe: Second Periodic Report on the Situation and Socioeconomic Evolution of the Regions of the Community*, Brussels.
EC (1985a) *The European Community and its Regions: 10 Years of Community Regional Policy and the ERDF*, Luxembourg.
EC (1985b) *Main Texts Governing the Regional Policy of the EC*, Collection Documents, Brussels.
EC (1987) *Regional Disparities and the Tasks of Regional Policy in the Enlarged Community* (Third Periodic Report), Brussels.
EC (1988) *La Dimension Sociale du Marché Intérieur*, Rapport d'etape du groupe interservices présidé par M.J. Degimbe, Brussels.
EC (1990a) *Guide to the Reform of the Community's Structural Funds*, OOPEC, Luxembourg.
EC (1990b) *An Empirical Assessment of Factors Shaping Regional Competitiveness in Problem Regions*, Luxembourg.
EC (1991a) *The Regions in the 1990's; Fourth Periodic Report on the Social and Economic Situation and Development of the Regions of the Community*, OOPEC, Luxembourg.
EC (1991b) *Eurobarometer*, no. 35, Brussels.
EC (1991c) *Eurobarometer*, no. 36, Brussels.
EC (1992) *Eurobarometer*, no. 38, Brussels.
EC (1993a) The economics of Community public finance, *European Economy, Reports and Studies*, no. 5, Brussels.
EC (1993b) *Eurobarometer*, no. 39/40, Brussels.
EC (1993c) Stable money, sound finances: Community public finance in the perspective of EMU, *European Economy*, no. 53, Brussels.
EC (1994a) *Eurobarometer*, no. 42, Brussels.
EC (1994b) *European Social Policy: Options for the Union*, Green Paper, Brussels.
EC (1995a) *Fifth Periodic Report on the Socioeconomic Situation and Development of the Regions of the Community*, OOPEC Brussels.
EC (1995b) Competitiveness and cohesion, trends in the regions, *Series: EC Regional Policies*, Brussels.
EC (1996a) *First Cohesion Report*, COM 96.542 final, Luxembourg.
EC (1996b) Economic evaluation of the internal market, *European Economy, Reports and Studies*, Luxembourg.
EC (1998) *Transport and Cohesion*, Brussels.

EC (1999a) *Sixth Periodic Report on the Social and Economic Situation and Development of Regions in the European Union*, Brussels.
EC (1999b) *European Spatial Development Perspective (EDSP), Towards Balanced and Sustainable Development of the Territory of the EU*, OOPEC, Luxembourg.
EC (1999c) *Reform of the Structural Funds 2000–2006: Comparative Analysis*, Brussels.
EC (1999d) *Means Collection*, 5 volumes, Evaluating Socioeconomic Programmes, Brussels.
EC (2000a) *Commission Report on the Measures to Implement Art. 299(2) the Outermost Regions of the European Union*, COM (2000) 147 final, Brussels/Luxembourg.
EC (2000b) *Eighth Survey on State Aid in the European Union*, Brussels.
EC (2000c) *The Cohesion Fund and the Environment: The Application of the 'Polluter Pays' Principle in Cohesion Fund Countries*, Brussels.
EC (2001) Unity, solidarity and diversity for Europe, its people and its territory, *Second Report on Economic and Social Cohesion*, Brussels/Luxembourg.
EC (2002a) *First Progress Report on Economic and Social Cohesion*, COM (2002) 46 final, Brussels.
EC (2002b) *Joint Report on Social Inclusion*, Brussels.
EC (2002c) *Eurobarometer*, no. 58.1, Brussels.
EC (2002d) *The Programming of the Structural Funds 2000–2006: The Initial Assessment of the Urban Initiative*, COM (2002) 308 final, Brussels.
EC (2002e) *Communication of the Commission on Impact Assessment*, Com (2002) 276 final, Brussels.
EC (2003a) *Ex Post Evaluation of Objective 1, 1994–1999*, Brussels.
EC (2003b) *Innovation Policy: Updating the Unions Approach in the Context of the Lisbon Strategy*, COM (2003) 112 final, Brussels.
EC (2004a) A new partnership for cohesion; convergence; competitiveness; cooperation, *Third Report on Economic and Social Cohesion*, Brussels.
EC (2004b) *Building Our Common Future: Policy Challenges and Budgetary Means of the Enlarged Union 2007–2013*, COM (2004) 101 final, Brussels.
EC (2004c) *Eurobarometer*, Brussels.
EC (2004d) The ex post evaluation 1994–1999 of ESF operations under Objectives 1, 3 and 4 and the Community initiatives employment and adapt, *EU Synthesis Report, Executive Summary*, available from www.europa.eu.int/comm./employment_social/esf_ex_post_exec_sum_only_eng.pdf.
EC (2004e) *Report of the High level Group on the future of social policy in an enlarged European Union, DG Employment and Social Affairs*, Brussels.
EC (2004f) *The Macro-economic Effects of the Single Market Programme After 10 years*, see: europa.eu.int/comm./internal_market/10years/background_en.htm.
EC (2005) The mid term review, performance reserve and mid term evaluation of ESF interventions, information paper, available from: www.europa.eu.int/comm./employment_social/esf.
EC (2006) *Joint Report on Social Protection and Social Inclusion*, Brussels.
Eckhaus, R.S. (1961) The north–south differential in Italian economic development, *Journal of Economic History*, 21: 285–317.
ECORYS (2004a) *Finalising the Structures and Measures to Increase the Absorption Capacity at the National and Regional Levels*, Final report on the ABCap projet to the Czech government, Prague.
ECORYS (2004b) *Ex Post Evaluation of a Sample of Projects Co-financed by the Cohesion Fund (1993–2002)*, Rotterdam.
ECORYS/NEI (2001) *Contribution to the Study of Agence Europeenne.*

ECORYS et al. (2005) *Promotion of Employment and Human Resource Development – Pomorskie Region*, Phare 2001/2 – Social and Economic Cohesion (PL01.06.09.01–02–11 – PL2002/000–580.06.04.10–01), Gdansk/Brussels.

ECORYS et al. (2006a) *Technical Assessment for the Development of the Inland Waterway Transport, Romania* (EA/115974/D/SV/RO; RO2002/000.586.04.09.02–3), Rotterdam.

ECORYS et al. (2006b) *Strategic Evaluation on Transport Investment Priorities Under Structural and Cohesion Funds for the Programming Period 2007–2013* (Report no. 2005.CE.16.AT.014), Rotterdam.

ECOTEC (2003a) *Ex Post Evaluation of Objective 1, 1994–1999*, a final report to the DG for Regional Policy, EC, Brussels.

ECOTEC (2003b) Territorial impact assessment: a scooping study, DETR, unpublished.

ECOTEC (2004) The territorial impact of EU research and development policies (available from the ESPON website www.espon.lu project 2.1.2), Luxembourg.

ECOTEC, with Nordregio and Eurofutures (2007) The state of European cities, mimeo.

Ederveen, S., Gorter, J., de Mooy, R. and Nahuis, R. (2002) *Funds and Games: The Economics of European Cohesion Policy*, CPB, The Hague.

Ehrlich, E. and Szigetvari, T. (2003) Transformation and Hungarian regional development: facts, trends, dilemmas and objectives, *Working Papers*, no. 137, Institute for World Economics, Budapest.

Eichengreen, B. and Leblang, D. (2003) Exchange rates and cohesion, *Journal of Common Market Studies*, 41.5: 797–822.

Elhorst, J.P. (1996) A regional analysis of labour force participation, participation rates across the member states of the European Union, *Regional Studies*, 30.5: 455–65.

Ernst and Young (1997) Ex post evaluation of the 1989–1993 Objective 2 programmes, *Evaluation Documents Series*, no. 4 DG Regional Policies, EC, Brussels.

Ernst and Young (2005) *European Attractiveness Survey*, www.ey.com/global/download.nsf/International/European_Attractiveness_Survey_May2005.

Esping-Andersen, G. (1990) *The Three Worlds of Welfare Capitalism*, Polity Press, Cambridge.

Esping-Andersen, G. (1999) *Social Foundations of Post-industrial Economics*, Oxford University Press, Oxford.

ESPON (2003) ESPON in progress, preliminary results by autumn 2003, available from ESPON website http://www.espon.lu.

ESPON (2004a) The territorial impact of the CAP and Rural Development Policy, available from the ESPON website http://www.espon.lu, project 2.1.3, Luxembourg.

ESPON (2004b) Telecommunication services and networks: territorial trends and basic supply of infrastructure for territorial cohesion, available from www.espon.lu project 1.2.2, Luxembourg.

ESPON (2004c) Territorial impacts of EU transport and TEN policies, available from www.espon.lu/online/documetation/projects/policy_impact/1867/fr-2.1.1.pdf.

ESPON (2005) The territorial effects of the Structural funds, available from www.espon.lu .

Esposto, A.G. (1992) Italian industrialization and the Gerschenkronan 'great spurt': a regional analysis, *Journal of Economic History*, 52: 353–62.

Esteban, J. (2000) Regional convergence in Europe and the industry mix: a shift share analysis, *Regional Science and Urban Economics*, 30: 353–64.

Etzkowitz, H. and Leydesdorff, L. (1997) Policy dimensions of the triple helix of university–industry–government relations, introduction to: Etzkowitz, H. and Leydesdorff, L. (eds), *Science and Public Policy*, Special Issue, 24.1: 2–52.

EU (2002) Our future; our choice; sixth environmental action programme, *Official Journal*, L 242.

EU (2005) *Financial Perspectives 2007–2013*, Doc 15915/05, Brussels.
EUMC (2005) *Majorities' Attitudes Towards Minorities; Key Findings from the Eurobarometer and the European Social Survey, Summary* (eumc.eu.int).
Eurostat (1990) *Poverty in Figures: Europe in the Early 1980s*, OOPEC, Luxembourg.
Eurostat (1994) Poverty statistics in the late 1980s: research based on micro-data, *Theme: Population and Social Conditions; Series: Accounts, Surveys, and Statistics*, 3 Series C, Luxembourg.
Eurostat (1999) *Social Protection: Expenditure and Receipts 1980–1996*, Luxembourg.
Eurostat (2006) *EU integration seen through statistics*, Luxembourg.
Evans, P. (1997) How fast do economies converge?, *Review of Economics and Statistics*, LXXIX: 219–25.
Ezcurra, R., Gil, C., Pascual, P. and Rapun, M. (2005) Regional inequality in the European Union: Does industry mix matter?, *Regional Studies*, 39.6: 679–97.
Fabbrini, S. and Brunazzo, M. (2003) Federalizing Italy; the convergent effects of Europeanization and domestic mobilization, *Regional and Federal Studies*, 13.1: 100–20.
Fahey, T. and Smyth, E. (2004) Do subjective indicators measure welfare? Evidence from 33 European Societies, *European Societies*, 6.1: 5–27.
Faini, R. (1996) Increasing returns, migrations and convergence, *Journal of Development Economics*, 49: 121–36.
Faini, R., Galli, G. and Giannini, C. (1992) Finance and development: the case of southern Italy, in: Giovanni, A. (ed.), *Finance and Development: Issues and Experience*, Cambridge University Press, Cambridge.
Faludi, A. (2004) Territorial cohesion; old French wines in new bottles?, *Urban Studies*, 7: 1349–65.
Faludi, A. and Waterhout, B. (2002) *The Making of the European Spatial Development Perspective: No Masterplan*, Routledge, London.
Fatas, A. (1998) Does EMU need a fiscal federation?, *Economic Policy*, 26: 165–203.
Ferrera, M. (1996) The southern model of welfare in social Europe, *Journal of European Social Policy*, 6.1: 17–37.
Ferrera, M. (2006) *The Boundaries of Welfare; European Integration and the New Spatial Politics of Social Protection*, Oxford University Press, Oxford.
Findlay, R. (1982) International Distributive Justice, a Trade Theoretic Approach, *Journal of International Economics*, 13: 1–14.
Fingleton, B. (1997) Specification and testing of Markov chain models: an application to convergence in the European Union, *Oxford Bulletin of Economics and Statistics*, 59.3: 385–403.
Franzmeyer, F., Hrubesch, P., Seiderl, B. and Weise, Ch. (1991) *The Regional Impact of Community Policies*, EP, Luxembourg.
Fremdling, R. and Tilly, R.D. (1979) *Industrialisierung und Raum; Studien zur regionalen Differenzierung im Deutschland des 19.Jahrhunderts* (Industrialization and Space: Studies into the Regional Differentiation in Germany in the 19th Century), Klett-Cotta, Stuttgart.
Gachet, F. and Le Gallo, J. (2005) The spatial dimension of segregation: a case study in four French urban areas, 1990–1999, *Cahier nr 2005–12*, GRES Bordeaux (gachet@u-bordeaux4.fr).
Gacs, J. (2003) Transition, EU accession and structural convergence, *Empirica*, 30.3: 271–303.
Gallie, P. and Paugam, S. (2002) Social precarity and social integration (Eurobarometer 56.1) EC, Brussels, available from: europa.eu.int/comm/public_opinion/archives/ebs/ebs_162_en.pdf.
Garcia-Mila, T. and MacGuire, T.J. (2001) Do interregional transfers improve the

economic performance of poor regions? The case of Spain, *International Tax and Public Finance*, 8.3: 281–96.

Gaspar, V. (1995) Cohesion and convergence: the economic effects of EC structural transfers, *Working Paper*, no. 257, Universidade Nova, Lisboa.

Gaspar, V. and Pereira, A.M. (1995) The impact of financial integration and unilateral public transfers on investment and growth in EC capital importing countries, *Journal of Development Economics*, 48.1: 43–66.

GHK (2003) *Ex post evaluation URBAN Community Initiative (1994–1999)*, Brussels.

Giannis, D., Liargovas, P. and Manolas, G. (1999) Quality of life indices for analyzing convergence in the European Union, *Regional Studies*, 33.1: 27–35.

Giersch, H. (1949) Economic Union between nations and the location of industries, *Review of Economic Studies*, 17: 87–97.

Glass, A.J. and Saggi, K. (1999) FDI policies under shared factor markets, *Journal of International Economics*, 49: 309–32.

Good, D.F. (1981) Economic integration and regional development in Austria-Hungary 1867–1913, in: Bairoch, P. and Levy-Leboyer, M. (eds), *Disparities in Economic Development Since the Industrial Revolution*, Macmillan, London, 137–50.

Gorzelak, G. (1996) *The Regional Dimension of Transformation in Central Europe*, Jessica Kingsley, London.

Gorzelak, G. and Kuklinski, A. (1992) Dilemmas of regional policies in Eastern and Central Europe, *Regional and Local Studies*, no. 8, University of Warsaw, Warsaw.

Gradstein, M. and Justman, M. (2001) Education, Social Cohesion and Economic Growth, *CEPR Discussion Paper*, no. 2723, London.

Grasland, C. and Hamez, G. (2005) Vers la construction d'un indicateur de cohesion territoriale europeen? *Espace Geographique*, 2: 97–116.

Gros, D. and Steinherr, A. (2004) *Economic Transition in Central and Eastern Europe: Planting the Seeds*, Cambridge University Press, Cambridge.

Gualini, E. (2004) *Multi-level Governance and Institutional Change: the Europeanization of Regional Policy in Italy*, Ashgate, Aldershot.

Guerrero, D.C. and Seró, M.A. (1997) Spatial distribution of patents in Spain: determining factors and consequences on regional development, *Regional Studies*, 31.4: 381–90.

Guimaraes, P., Figueiredo, O.G. and Woodward, D. (2000) Agglomeration and the location of Foreign Direct Investment in Portugal, *Journal of Urban Economics*, 47: 115–35.

Haaland, J.I., Kind, J.H., Midelfart Kvarnik, K.H. and Torstensson, J. (1998) What determines the economic geography of Europe? *Discussion Paper*, no. 19/98, Department of Economics, Norwegian School of Economic and Business Administration, Bergen.

Hall, R., Smith, A. and Tsoukalis, L. (eds) (2001) *Competitiveness and Cohesion in EU Policies*, Oxford University Press, Oxford.

Hallet, M. (2000) Regional specialisation and concentration in the EU, *Economic Papers*, no. 141 (EC DG Economic and Financial Affairs), Brussels.

Hantrais, L. (1995) *Social Policy in the European Union*, Macmillan, Basingstoke.

Hatzius, J. (2000) Foreign direct investment and factor demand elasticities, *European Economic Review*, 44: 117–43.

Hechter, M. (1971) Regional inequality and national integration: the case of the British Isles, *Journal of Social History*, 5: 96–117.

Heinelt, H. and Smith, R. (eds) (1996) *Policy Networks and European Structural Funds*, Avebury, Aldershot.

Henry, P. (1981) *Study of the Regional Impact of the Common Agricultural Policy*, CEC, Luxembourg.

Herve, I. and Holzman, R. (1998) *Fiscal Transfers and Economic Convergence in the EU: An Analysis of Absorption Problems and an Evaluation of the Literature*, Nomos, Baden-Baden.

Heylen, F. and van Poeck, A. (1995) National labour market institutions and the European economic and monetary integration process, *Journal of Common Market Studies*, 33.4: 573–95.

Hine, R.T.C. and Padoan, P.C. (2001) External trade policy, in: Hall, R., Smith, A. and Tsoukalis, L. (eds), *Competitiveness and Cohesion in EU Policies*, Oxford University Press, Oxford, 61–108.

Hirsch, S. (1974) Hypothesis regarding trade between developing and industrial countries, in: Giersch, H. (ed.), *The International Division of Labour*, Mohr, Tübingen, 65–82.

Hitchens, D. (1997) Environmental policy and the implications for competitiveness in the regions of the EU, *Regional Studies*, 31.8: 813–19.

HM Treasury (2002) *Spending Review, Public Service Agreements*, White Paper, London, Chapter 5.

Hofer, H. and Woergoetter, A. (1997) Regional per capita income convergence in Austria, *Regional Studies*, 31.1: 1–12.

Hollanders, H. and Rundel, A. (2004) *European Innovation Scoreboard, Methodology Report*, EC DG Enterprise, Brussels.

Holloway, J. (1981) *Social Policy Harmonisation in the European Community*, Gower, Aldershot.

Hooghe, L. (1996) *Cohesion Policy and European Integration: Building Multi-level Governance*, Oxford University Press, Oxford.

Hooghe, L. and Marks, G. (2001) *Multi Level Governance and European Integration*, Rowman and Littlefield, Lanham, Md.

Horvat, A. (2005) Why does nobody care about the absorption? *WIFO Working Papers*, no. 258, Vienna.

Huchet, M. (2003) Does the single monetary policy have asymmetric real effects in the EMU? *Journal of Policy Modeling*, 25: 151–78.

Hudson, R. and Williams, A. (1986) *The United Kingdom*, Harper and Row, London.

Hughes, J., Sasse, G. and Gordon, C. (2004) Conditionality and Compliance in the EU's Eastward Enlargement, *Journal of Common Market Studies*, 42.3: 523–52.

Hunt, E.H. (1986) Industrialization and regional inequality: wages in Britain 1760–1914, *Journal of Economic History*, 46: 935–67.

ILO (1956) *Social Aspects of European Economic Cooperation*, report by a group of experts, Geneva.

IRPUD (2000) *Towards a European Peripherality Index*, CEC, DG Regio, Brussels/Luxembourg.

Jaffe, A.B. and Palmer, K. (1997) Environmental regulation and innovation: a panel data study, *The Review of Economics and Statistics*, 79: 610–19.

Johannisson, B. (1998) Personal networks in emerging knowledge-based firms: spatial and functional patterns, *Entrepreneurship and Regional Development*, 10.4: 297–312.

Johnson, H.G. (1958) The gains from freer trade in Europe, an estimate, *Manchester School*, 26.3: 247–55.

Just, R.E., Hueth, D.L. and Schmitz, A. (2005) *The Welfare Economics of Public Policy: A Practical Approach to Project and Policy Evaluation*, Edward Elgar, Cheltenham.

Kaldor, N. (1966) *The Causes of the Slow Growth of the United Kingdom*, Cambridge University Press, Cambridge.

Kandogan, Y. (2000) Political economy of eastern enlargement of the EU: budgetary cost and then reform of voting rules, *European Journal of Political Economy*, 16: 685–706.

Kangasharju, A. and Pekkala, S. (2004) Increasing regional disparities in the 1990s: the Finnish experience, *Regional Studies*, 38.3: 255–67.

Karl, H. and Ranne, O. (1997) European environmental policy between decentralisation and uniformity, *Intereconomics*, 32.4: 159–69.

Kauppi, H. and Widgren, M. (2004) What determines EU decision making: needs, power or both?, *Economic Policy*, 39: 223–66.

Keeble, D., Offord, J. and Walker, S. (1988) *Peripheral Regions in a Community of Twelve Member States*, Office for Official Publications of the European Communities, Luxembourg.

Keeble, D., Owen, P.L. and Thomson, C. (1982) Regional Accessibility and Economic Potential in the European Community, *Regional Studies*, 16: 419–33.

Keune, M. (1998) *Regional Development and Employment Policy: Lessons for Central and Eastern Europe*, ILO, Geneva.

Kiesewetter, H. (1981) Regional disparities in wages: the cotton industry in nineteenth century Germany: some methodological consideration, in: Bairoch, P. and Levy-Leboyer, M. (eds), *Disparities in Economic Development Since the Industrial Revolution*, London: Macmillan, 248–59.

Klaassen, L.H. and Molle, W.T.M. (eds) (1982) *Industrial Migration and Mobility in the European Community*, Gower Press, Aldershot.

Kohler-Koch, B. and Eising, R. (eds) (1998) *The Transformation of Governance in the European Union*, Routledge, London.

Kozak, M.W. (2003) The consequences for Polish regions of integration with the EU, in Auctores Variie; *Cost and benefits of Poland's Membership in the European Union*, Natolin European Centre, Warsaw.

Krieger-Boden, C., Morgenroth, E. and Petrakos, G. (eds) (2007) *The Impact of European Integration on Its Regions*, Routledge, London.

Krugman, P. (1979) Increasing returns, monopolistic competition and international trade, *Journal of International Economics*, 9.4: 469–79.

Krugman, P. (1991) Increasing returns and economic geography, *Journal of Political Economy*, 99.3: 483–99.

Krugman, P.R. and Venables, A.J. (1990) Integration and the competitiveness of peripheral industry, in: Bliss, C. and Braga de Macedo, J. (eds), *Unity with Diversity in the European Economy*, Cambridge University Press, Cambridge, 56–75.

Labour Asociados SSL (2003) Impact of Community policies on social and economic cohesion, *Report for DG Regio*, Brussels.

Laffan, B. (1983) Policy implementation in the European Community: the European social fund as a case study, *Journal of Common Market Studies*, 21.4: 389–408.

Laffan, B. (2000) The big budgetary bargains: from negotiation to authority, *Journal of European Public Policy*, 7.5: 725–43.

Lahav, G. and Guiraudon, V. (2006) Actors and venues in immigration control: closing the gap between political demands and policy outcomes, *West European Politics*, 29.2: 201–23.

Layard, R., Nickell, S.J. and Jackman, R. (1991) *Unemployment*, Oxford University Press, Oxford.

Layte, R. and Whelan, C.T. (2003) Moving in and out of poverty; the impact of welfare regimes on poverty dynamics in the EU, *European Societies*, 5.2: 167–91.

Lenschow, A. (ed.) (2002) *Environmental Policy Integration: Greening Sectoral Policies in Europe*, Earthscan, London.

Letelier Saavedra, L.E. (2004) Fiscal decentralisation as a mechanism to modernise the state: truths and myths, *CESifo Dice Report*, 2.1: 15–21.

Levy, R. (2000) *Implementing European Union Public Policy*, Edward Elgar, Cheltenham.

Leydesdorff, L. and Meyer, M. (2006) Triple helix indicators of knowledge-based innovation systems, *Research Policy*, introduction to the Special Issue, 35.10: 1441–9.

Lin, J.Y. and Liu, P. (2005) Development strategies and regional income disparities in China, *Working Paper*, Series 2005/11, no. E200505, China Center for Economic Research.
Lion, C., Martini, P. and Volpi, S. (2004) Evaluation of European social fund programmes in a new framework of multinational governance: the Italian experience, *Regional Studies*, 38.2: 207–12.
Liu, T. and Li, K.-W. (2006) Disparity in factor contributions between coastal and inner provinces in post reform China, *China Economic Review*, 17.4: 449–70.
Lolos, S.E. (2001) European structural funds, their role in the growth of the Greek economy, *Bank of Greece Research Bulletin*, 17: 25–45.
Lopez-Rodriguez, J. (2002) Spatial structure and regional growth in the European Union, Doctoral thesis, A Coruna.
Lorz, O. and Willmann, G. (2005) On the endogenous powers in federal structures, *Journal of Urban Economics*, 57: 242–57.
LSE (1999) *The Socio-economic Impact of Projects Financed by the Cohesion Fund: A Modelling Approach*, study commissioned by the European Commission, Brussels.
Luebker, M. (2004) Globalisation and perceptions of social inequality, *International Labour Review*, 143.1/2: 91–128.
MacDougall, G.D.A. et al. (1977) *Report of the Study Group on the Role of Public Finance in European Integration*, CEC, Economy and Finance Series, vol. 1, General Report, Brussels.
McCann, Ph. (2001) *Urban and Regional Economics*, Oxford University Press, Oxford.
Mairate, A. (2006) The 'added value' of European cohesion policy, *Regional Studies*, 40.2: 167–78.
Mairate, A. and Hall, R. (2001) Structural policies, in: Hall, L.R., Smith, A. and Tsoukalis, L. (eds), *Competitiveness and Cohesion in EU Policies*, Oxford University Press, Oxford, 316–48.
Mankiw, N.G., Romer, P. and Weil, D.N. (1992) A contribution to the economics of economic growth, *Quarterly Journal of Economics*, 107: 407–38.
Mariotti, S. and Piscitello, L. (1995) Information cost and location of FDI within the host country; empirical evidence from Italy, *Journal of International Business Studies*, 26: 815–41.
Martin, C. and Saenz, I. (2003) Real convergence and European integration: the experience of the less developed EU members, *Empirica*, 30.3: 205–36.
Martin, C. and Turrion, J. (2003) Eastern enlargement of the European Union and Foreign Direct Investment adjustments, *Working Paper*, no. 24.2003, FSEE/UCM, Madrid.
Martin, P. (2003) Public policies and economic geography, in: Funck, B and Pizatti, L. (eds), *European Integration, Regional Policy and Growth*, World Bank, Washington, 19–32.
Martin, R. (1998a) Regional dimensions of Europe's unemployment crises, in: Lawless, P., Martin, R. and Hardy, S. (eds), *Unemployment and Social Exclusion: Landscapes of Labour Inequality*, Jessica Kingsley, London, 11–48.
Martin, R. (1998b) Regional incentive spending for European regions, *Regional Studies*, 32.6: 527–36.
Martin, R.L. and Sunley, P. (1998) Slow convergence? Post neo-classical endogenous growth theory and regional development, *Economic Geography*, 74: 201–27.
Martin, R.L. and Sunley, P. (2003) Deconstruction clusters: chaotic concept or policy panacea?, *Journal of Economic Geography*, 3.1: 5–35.
Martin, R. and Tyler, P. (2006) Evaluating the impact of the structural funds on Objective 1 regions, an exploratory discussion, *Regional Studies*, 40.2: 201–10.

Marques-Mendes, A.J. (1986a) The contribution of the European Community to economic growth, *Journal of Common Market Studies*, 24.4: 261–77.
Marques-Mendes, A.J. (1986b) *Economic Integration and Growth in Europe*, Croom Helm, London.
Massacesi, E. (1965) Regional economic development policies in Italy, in: Connor, J.T. and Batt, W.L. (eds), *Area Redevelopment Policies in Britain and the Countries of the Common Market*, United States Department of Commerce, Washington, 217–325.
Meen, G., Gibb, K., McGrath, T. and Mackinnon, J. (2005) *Economic Segregation in England: Causes, Consequences and Policy*, Joseph Rowntree Foundation, The Policy Press, Bristol.
Mendez, C., Wislade, F. and Yuill, D. (2006) Conditioning and fine tuning Europeanization: negotiating regional policy maps under the EU's competition and cohesion policies, *Journal of Common Market Studies*, 44.3: 581–605.
Messerlin, P.A. and Becuwe, S. (1986) Inter-industry trade in the long term, in: Greenaway, D. and Tharakan, P.K.M. (eds), *Imperfect Competition and International Trade: The Policy Aspects of Intra-Industry Trade*, Wheatsheaf, Brighton, 191–216.
Micco, A., Stein, E. and. Ordonez, G. (2003) The currency union effect on trade, early evidence from EMU, *Economic Policy*, 37: 315–56.
Midelfart-Kvarnik, K.H. and Overman, H.G. (2002) Delocation and European integration: Is structural spending justified?, *Economic Policy*, 35: 322–61.
Midelfart-Kvarnik, K.H., Overman, H.G. and Venables, A.J. (2000) Comparative advantage and economic geography: estimating the location and production in the EU, *CEPR Working Paper*, no. 2618.
Miller, M.H. and Spencer, J.E. (1977) The static economic effects of the UK joining the EEC, a general equilibrium approach, *Review of Economic Studies*, 44: 71–93.
Mitchell, B. (1981) *European Historical Statistics 1750–1975*, 2nd edn, Sijthoff & Noordhoff, Alphen a/d Rijn.
Modigliani, F. (1996) The shameful rate of unemployment in the EMS: causes and cures, *De Economist*, 144.3: 363–96.
Mold, A. (2003) The single market and US manufacturing affiliates, *Journal of Common Market Studies*, 41.1: 37–62.
Molle, W. (1983a) *Industrial Location and Regional Development in the European Community, the Fleur model*, Gower Press, Aldershot.
Molle, W. (2002) Globalization, regionalism and labour markets: Should we recast the foundations of the EU regime in matters of regional (rural and urban) development? *Regional Studies*, 36.2: 161–72.
Molle, W., Sleijpen, O. and Vanheukelen, M. (1993) The impact of an Economic and Monetary Union on social and economic cohesion: analysis and ensuing policy implications, in: Gretschmann, K. (ed.), *Economic and Monetary Union: Implications for National Policy Makers*, EIPA, Maastricht, 217–43.
Molle, W.T.M., with the assistance of van Holst, B. and Smit, H. (1980) *Regional Disparity and Economic Development in the European Community*, Saxon House, Farnborough.
Molle, W.T.M. (1986) Regional Impact of Welfare State Policies in the European Community, in: Paelinck, J.H.P. (ed.), *Human Behaviour in Geographical Space*, Gower Press, Aldershot, 77–90.
Molle, W.T.M. (1990) Will the completion of the internal market lead to regional divergence?, in: Siebert, H. (ed.), *The Completion of the Internal Market*, Institut fuer Weltwirtschaft, Kiel; Mohr Verlag, Tuebingen, 174–96.
Molle, W.T.M. (1995) The distribution of cost and benefits of economic integration: from empirical analysis to social reality, *Ecu*, 30.1: 31–5.

Molle, W.T.M. (1997a) The regional economic structure of the European Union: an analysis of long-term developments, in: Peschel, K. (ed.), *Regional Growth and Regional Policy within the Framework of European Integration*, Physica, Heidelberg, 66–86.

Molle, W.T.M. (1997b) Cohesion and fiscal federalism: the European experience, *The European Union Review*, 2.2: 61–85.

Molle, W.T.M. (2003) *Global Economic Institutions*, Routledge, London.

Molle, W.T.M. (2006) *The Economics of European Integration, Theory, Practice, Policy*, 5th edn, Ashgate, Aldershot.

Molle, W.T.M. and Boeckhout, I.J. (1995) Economic disparity under conditions of integration; a long-term view of the European case, *Papers in Regional Science, Journal of the Regional Science Association International*, 74.2: 105–23.

Molle, W.T.M. and Capellin, R. (eds) (1988) *Regional Impact of Community Policies in Europe*, Avebury, Aldershot.

Moreno, L. (2002) Decentralization in Spain, *Regional Studies*, 36.4: 399–408.

Morsink, R. and Molle, W.T.M. (1991a) European Direct Investment in Europe: an explanatory model of intra EC flows, in: Bürgermeier, B. and Mucchielli, J.M. (eds), *Multinationals and Europe 1992*, Routledge, London, 81–101.

Morsink, R. and Molle, W.T.M. (1991b) *Direct Investment and Monetary Integration, European Economy*, special edition, 1: 36–55.

Morsink, R.L.A. (1998) *Foreign Direct Investment and Corporate Networking: A Framework for Spatial Analysis of Investment Conditions*, Edward Elgar, Cheltenham.

Mortensen, J. (1992) The allocation of savings in a liberalised European capital market, in: Steinherr, A. (ed.), *The New European Financial Market Place*, Longman, London, 208–20.

Muntendam, J. (1987) Philips in the world, a view of a multinational on resource allocation, in: van der Knaap, B. and Wever, E. (eds), *New Technology and Regional Development*, Croom Helm, London, 136–44.

Musgrave, R.A. and Musgrave, P. (1989) *Public Finance in Theory and Practice*, McGraw-Hill, Auckland/New York.

Myrdal, G. (1956) *An International Economy, Problems and Prospects*, Routledge, New York.

Myrdal, G. (1957) *Economic Theory and Underdeveloped Regions*, G. Duckworth, London.

Nanetti, R. (1992) *Coordination in Development Planning an Evaluation of the Initial Implementation of the Community Support Frameworks*, EC Documents, Brussels.

NEI/ECORYS (2002) *Key Indicators for Candidate Countries to Effectively Manage the Structural Funds*, Report prepared for DG Regio/DG Enlargement, Rotterdam.

NEI/E&Y (1992) New location factors for mobile investment in Europe, *CEC Regional Development Studies*, no. 6, Brussels.

Neven, D. and Gouyette, C. (1995) Regional convergence in the European Community, *Journal of Common Market Studies*, 33: 47–65.

Nickell, S.J. and Layard, R. (1999) Labour market institutions and economic performance, in: Ashenfelterd, O. and Card, D. (eds), *Handbook of Labour Economics*, vol. 3E, North-Holland, Amsterdam, 3029–84.

NIESR (1996) *Capital Market Liberalization in Europe*, London.

Nolte, H.H. (1991) *Internal Peripheries in European History*, Muster-Schmidt, Göttingen.

North, D.C. (1991) *Institutional Change and Economic Performance*, Cambridge University Press, Cambridge.

North, D.C. and Thomas, R.P. (1973) *The Rise of the Western World*, Cambridge University Press, Cambridge.

Oates, W.E. (1972) *Fiscal Federalism*, Harcourt, New York.

Oates, W.E. (ed.) (1977) *The Political Economy of Fiscal Federalism*, Heath, Lexington.

OECD (1993) *Employment Outlook*, July, Paris.
OECD (1994a) *The OECD Jobs Study, Evidence and Explanations, Part II: The Adjustment Potential of the Labour Market*, Paris.
OECD (1994b) Labour standards and economic integration, *Employment Outlook*, July, Paris, 137–66.
OECD (1995) *The OECD Jobs Study: Investment, Productivity and Employment*, Paris.
OECD (2003) Trends in international migration 2003, www.oecd.org/document/17/0,2340,en_2649_33931_28703185_1_1_1_1,00.html.
OECD (2005) *Trends in International Migration*, Paris.
Okun, A. (1975) *Equality and Efficiency: The Big Trade Off*, Brookings Institution, Washington.
O'Loughlin, J. and Friedrichs, J. (eds) (1996) *Social Polarisation and Post Industrial Metropolises*, Walter de Gruyter, Berlin.
Overman, H. and Puga, D. (2002) Unemployment clusters across Europe's regions and countries, *Economic Policy*, 34: 117–47.
Owen, N. (1983) *Economies of Scale, Competitiveness and Trade Patterns within the European Community*, Clarendon, Oxford.
Paci, R. (1997) More similar and less equal, economic growth in the European regions, *Weltwirtschaftliches Archiv*, 133.4: 609–34.
Paci, R. and Usai, S. (2000) Technological enclaves and industrial districts: an analysis of the regional distribution of innovative activity in Europe, *Regional Studies*, 34.2: 97–114.
Padoa-Schioppa, T., Emerson, M., King, M., Millron, J.C., Paelinck, J.H.P., Papdemos, L.D., Pastor, A. and Scharpf, F. (1987) *Efficiency, Stability and Equity, a Strategy for the Evolution of the Economic System of the European Community*, Oxford University Press, Oxford.
Pain, N. and van Welsum, D. (2003) The multiple links between exchange rates and FDI, *Journal of Common Market Studies*, 41.5: 823–46.
Pain, N. and Young, G. (1996), Tax competition and the pattern of European direct investment, Paper of the Institute of Fiscal Studies Conference on Public Policy and the Location of Economic Activity, London.
Palfrey, T. (1998) Implementation theory, in: Aumann, R. and Hart, S. (eds), *Handbook of Game Theory*, vol. 3, North Holland, Amsterdam.
Paluzie, E., Pons, J. and Tirado, D.A. (2001) Regional integration and specialisation patterns in Spain, *Regional Studies*, 35.4: 285–96.
Papadopoulos, A. (2003) *Administrative Capacity Study: Phare Region (Phase 2)*, European Commission, Brussels.
Paraskevopoulos, C., Getimis, P. and Rees, N. (2006) *Adapting to EU Multilevel Governance; Regional and Environmental Policies in Cohesion and CEE Countries*, Ashgate, Aldershot.
Parkinson, M. (1998) *Combating Social Exclusion: Lessons from Area Based Programmes*, The Policy Press, Bristol.
Parkinson, M., Simmie, J., Clark, G. and Verdonk, H. (2004) *Competitive European Cities: Where Do the Core Cities Stand*, Report to ODPM, John Moores University, Liverpool (also Office of Deputy Prime Minister, London).
Patton, M.Q. (1986) *Utilization Focused Evaluation*, 2nd edn, Sage Publications, Beverley Hills, Calif.
Patton, M.Q. (2001) *Qualitative Research and Evaluation Methods*, 3rd edn, Sage Publications, Thousand Oaks, Calif.
Pelkmans, J. (1983) European Direct Investments in the European Community, *Journal of European Integration*, 7.1: 41–70.

Pelkmans, J. (1997) *European Integration: Methods and Analysis*, Longman/OUP, Harlow/Heerlen.

Pelkmans, J. (2006) *European Integration: Methods and Economic Integration*, 3rd edn, Prentice Hall, Harlow.

Pennings, E. and Sleuwaegen, L. (2000) International relocation: firm and industry determinants, *Economic Letters*, 67: 179–186.

Perin, D. and Semple, R. (1976) Recent trends in regional income inequalities in the US, *Regional Science Perspectives*, 6: 65–85.

Perkmann, M. (1999) Building governance institutions across European borders, *Regional Studies*, 33.7: 657–67.

Perroux, F. (1955) Note sur la notion de pole de croissance, *Economie Appliquee*, 1.2: 307–20.

Persson, J. (1997) Convergence across the Swedish counties 1911–1993, *European Economic Review*, 41: 1835–52.

Persson, T. (2001) Currency unions and trade, how large is the treatment effect?, *Economic Policy*, 33: 433–48.

Persson, T. and Tabellini, G. (1996) Federal fiscal constitutions: risk sharing and redistribution, *Journal of Political Economy*, 104: 979–1009.

Petith, H.C. (1977) European integration and the terms of trade, *Economic Journal*, 87: 262–72.

Petrakos, G. and Saratsis, Y. (2000) Regional inequalities in Greece, *Papers in Regional Science*, 79: 57–74.

Petrakos, G., Psycharis, Y. and Kollioras, D. (2004) Regional inequalities in EU accession countries, evolution and challenges, in: Bradley, J., Petrakos, G. and Traistaru, I. (eds), *Integration, Growth and Cohesion in an Enlarged European Union*, Springer, New York, Berlin, 45–64.

Petrochilos, G.A. (1989) *Foreign Direct Investment and the Development Process*, Avebury, Aldershot.

Pollack, M. (1995) Regional actors in an intergovernmental play: the making and implementation of EC Structural Policy, in: Mazey, S. and Rhodes, C. (eds) *State of the European Union*, Vol. 3, Longman, Harlow, 361–90.

Pollard, S. (1981) *Peaceful Conquest: The Industrialisation of Europe 1760–1970*, Oxford University Press, Oxford.

Porter, M. (1990) *The Competitive Advantage of Nations*, Free Press, New York.

Porter, M. (1998) Clusters and the new economics of competition, *Harvard Business Review*, 76.6: 77–90.

Puga, D. (1999) The rise and fall of regional inequalities, *European Economic Review*, 43.2: 304–34.

Pugliese, E. (1992) The new international migration and changes in the labour market, *Labour*, 6,1: 165–79.

Ravallion, M. and Chen, S. (2006) China's (uneven) progress against poverty, *Journal of Development Economics*, 82.1: 1–42.

Resmini, L. (2003) Economic integration, industry location and frontier economies in transition countries, *Economic Systems*, 27: 205–21.

Rhodes, C. and Marey, S. (eds), *The State of the European Union*, vol. 3, *Building a European Polity*, Longman, Harlow/Bolder, Col., 361–90.

Rhodes, R.A.W. (1986) *European Policy Making, Implementation and Subcentral Governments: A Survey*, EIPA, Maastricht.

Ritsilä, J.J. (1999) Regional differences in environments for enterprises, *Entrepreneurship and Regional Development*, 11: 187–202.

Roberto, B. (2004) Acquisition versus greenfield investment: the location of foreign manufacturers in Italy, *Regional Science and Urban Economics*, 34.1: 3–25.

Robinson, S. (1976) A note on the U hypothesis relating income inequality and economic development, *American Economic Review*, 66.3: 437–40.

Rodriguez-Fuentes, C. and Dow, S. (2003) EMU and the regional impact of monetary policy, *Regional Studies*, 37.9: 969–80.

Rodriguez-Pose, A. (1999) Convergence or divergence ? Types of regional responses to socio-economic change in western Europe, *Tijdschrift voor Economische en Sociale Geografie*, 90.4: 363–78.

Rodriguez-Pose, A. and Fratesi, U. (2004) Between development and social policies: the impact of European structural funds in Objective 1 regions, *Regional Studies*, 38.1: 97–113.

Roemisch, R. (2003) Regional disparities within accession countries, in: Tumpell-Gugerell, G. and Mooslechner, P. (eds), *Economic Convergence and Divergence in Europe: Growth and Regional Development in an Enlarged Europe*, Edward Elgar, Cheltenham, 183–208.

Rokkan, S. (1979) Gebietsgleichheiten in Europa: auf der Suche nach einem geo-ökonomischen, geo-politischen Modell zur Erläuterung verschiedenartiger regionaler Entwicklungen, in: Bonvicini, G. and Petrella, R. (eds), *Das ungleiche Europa: Region Europa 1*, Triest, 21–69.

Romer, P.M. (1986) Increasing returns and long run growth, *Journal of Political Economy*, 99: 500–21.

Romer, P.M. (1990) Endogenous technological change, *Journal of Political Economy*, 98.5: S71–102.

Rose, A. and van Wincoop, E. (2001) National money as a barrier to trade: the real case for currency union, *American Economic Review (Papers and proceedings)*, 91.2: 386–90.

Rose, A.K. (2000) One market, one money: the effect of common currencies on trade, *Economic Policy: A European Forum*, 30: 7–47.

Rose, A.K. (2001) Currency unions and trade, the effect is large, *Economic Policy*, 33: 433–62.

Rose, A.K. and Stanley, T.D. (2005) A meta analysis of the effect of common currencies on international trade, *Journal of Economic Surveys*, 19.3: 347–65.

Roses, J.R. and Sanchez-Alonso, B. (2004) Regional wage convergence in Spain, 1850–1930, *Explorations in Economic History*, 41.4: 404–25.

Sachs, J. and Sala-I-Martin, X. (1992) Fiscal federalism and optimal currency areas: evidence for Europe from the United States, in: Canconeri, M., Masson, P. and Grilli, V. (eds), *Establishing a Central Bank: Issues in Europe and Lessons from the US*, Cambridge University Press, London, 195–219.

Sack, R.D. (1986) *Human Territoriality, Its Theory and History*, Cambridge University Press, Cambridge.

Sala-I-Martin, X. (1996) Regional cohesion: evidence and theories of regional growth and convergence, *European Economic Review*, 40: 1325–52.

Sanchez-Albornoz, N. (1987) *The Economic Modernization of Spain 1830–1930*, New York University Press, New York.

Sapir, A., Aghion, Ph., Bertola, G., Hellwig, M., Pisani Ferry, J., Rosati, D., Vinals, J. and Wallace, H. (2004) *An Agenda for a Growing Europe*, Oxford University Press, Oxford.

Schmid, G., O'Reilly, J. and Schoemann, K. (1996) *International Handbook of Labour Market Policy and Evaluation*, Edward Elgar, Cheltenham.

Schneider, F. (2003) The development of the shadow economies and shadow labour force of 21 OECD and 22 transition countries, *Cesifo Dice Reports, Journal of International Comparisons*, 1.1: 17–23.

Scott, J.W. (2006) *EU Enlargement, Region Building and Shifting Borders of Inclusion and Exclusion*, Ashgate, Aldershot.
Seers, D., Schaffer, B. and Kiljunen, M.L. (1979) *Underdeveloped Europe: Studies in Core-Periphery Relations*, Harvester Press, Hassocks.
Seers, D., Vaitsos, C. and Kiljunen, M.L. (1980) *Integration and Unequal Development: The Experience of the EEC*, St. Martins Press, New York.
Sen, A.K. (1983) Poor, relatively speaking, *Oxford Economic Papers*, 35: 153–69.
Sharp, M. and Pereira, T.S. (2001) Research and technological development, in: Hall, R., Smith, A. and Tsoukalis, L. (eds) (2001) *Competitiveness and Cohesion in EU Policies*, Oxford University Press, Oxford, 147–78.
Siebert, H. (ed.) (1994) *Migration: A Challenge for Europe*, Mohr, Tübingen.
Simões, V.C. (1992) European integration and the pattern of FDI flows in Portugal, in Cantwell, J. (ed.), *Multinational Investment in Modern Europe*, Edward Elgar, Aldershot, 256–97.
Sindbjerg Martinsen, D. (2005) The Europeanisation of welfare; the domestic impact of intra European social security, *Journal of Common Market Studies*, 43.5:, 1027–54.
Sinn, H.W. and Ochel, W. (2003) Social Union, convergence and migration, *Journal of Common Market Studies*, 41.5: 869–96.
Skifter Andersen, H. (2002) *Urban Sores: On the Interaction Between Segregation, Urban Decay and Deprived Neighbourhoods*, Ashgate, Aldershot.
Sleuwaegen, L. (1987) Multinationals, the European Community and Belgium: recent developments, *Journal of Common Market Studies*, 26.2: 255–72.
Smarzynska-Javorcik, B. (2004) Does Foreign Direct Investment increase the productivity of domestic firms? In search of spill-overs through backward linkages, *American Economic Review*, 94.3: 605–27.
Smolensky, E. (1961) Industrialization and income inequality: recent US experience, *Papers and Proceedings of the Regional Science Association*, 7: 67–88.
Sokol, M. (2001) Central and Eastern Europe a decade after the fall of state socialism, regional dimensions of transition process, *Regional Studies*, 35.7: 645–55.
Solow, R.M. (1956) A contribution to the theory of economic growth, *Quarterly Journal of Economics*, 70: 65–94.
Steinle, W. (1988) Social policy, in: Molle, W. and Cappellin, R. (eds), *Regional Impact of Community Policies in Europe*, Avebury, Aldershot, 108–23.
Stewart, K. (2003) Monitoring social inclusion in Europe's regions, *Journal of European Social Policy*, 13.4: 335–56.
Stirboeck, C. (2002) What determines relative sectoral investment patterns in EU regions? *ZEW Discussion Papers*, no. 02–55, Mannheim.
Suarez-Villa, L. and Cuadrado-Roura, J.R. (1993) Regional economic integration and the evolution of disparities, *Papers in Regional Science*, 72.4: 369–87.
Talbot, R.B. (1977) The European Community's regional fund, *Progress in Planning*, 8.3: 183–281.
Tarditi, S. and Zanias, G. (2001) Common Agricultural Policy, in: Hall, R., Smith, A. and Tsoukalis, L. (eds) (2001) *Competitiveness and Cohesion in EU Policies*, Oxford University Press, Oxford, 179–216.
Tavistock Institute, with GKH and IRS (2003) *The Evaluation of Socio-Economic Development: The Guide*, Tavistock Institute, London, available at www.evlsed.info/.
Temple, J. (2001) Growth effects of education and social capital in the OECD countries, *OECD Economic Studies*, 33: 57–101.
Terrasi, M. (1999) Convergence and divergence across Italian regions, *The Annals of Regional Science*, 33: 491–510.

Teulings, A.W.M. (1984) The internationalisation squeeze: double capital movement and job transfer within Philips worldwide, *Environment and Planning*, A.16: 597–614.

Timar, L. (1992) Regional economic and local history or historical geography?, *Journal of European Economic History*, 21: 391–406.

Tondl, G. and Vuksic, G. (2003) What makes regions in Eastern Europe catching up? The role of foreign investment, human resources and geography, *Working Paper*, no. B12, ZEI, Bonn.

Toutain, J.C. (1981) The uneven growth of regional incomes in France from 1840–1970, in: Bairoch, P.P. and Levy-Leboyer, M. (eds), *Disparities in Economic Development Since the Industrial Revolution*, Macmillan, London, 302–15.

Tsakloglou, P. and Papadopoulos, F. (2002) Poverty, material deprivation, multi-dimensional disadvantage during four life-stages: evidence from the ECHP, in: Barnes, M., Heady, C., Middleton, S., Millar, J., Papadopoulos, F., Room, G. and Tsakloglou, P. (eds), *Poverty and Social Exclusion in Europe*, Edward Edgar, Cheltenham, 24–52.

Tsonias, E. (2002) Another look at regional convergence in Greece, *Regional Studies*, 36: 603–09.

Tsonias, E.G. and Christopoulos, D.K. (2003) Maastricht convergence and real convergence: European evidence from threshold and smooth transition regression models, *Journal of Policy Modeling*, 25: 43–52.

UNCTAD (2000) *World Investment Report*, UNO, Geneva.

UNDP (2004) Assessment of municipal and district capacities for the absorption of the EU structural and cohesion funds, mimeo, Sofia.

Vandamme, J. (ed.) (1986) *New Dimensions in European Social Policy*, TEPSA, Croom Helm, London.

Vaneecloo, C. (2005) *Economie Politique de la Solidarite Europeenne*, These de doctorat, Lille.

Vanhalewijn, E. and Simon, S. (1999) State aids and the single market, *European Economy*, 3: 53–6.

Vanhove, N. (1999) *Regional Policy: A European Approach*, 3rd edn, Ashgate, Aldershot.

Vanhove, N. and Klaassen, L.H. (1987) *Regional Policy: A European Approach*, 2nd edn, Ashgate, Aldershot.

van Marrewijk, C. (2002) *International Trade and the World Economy*, Oxford University Press, Oxford.

Vaughan-Whitehead, D. (2003) *EU Enlargement Versus Social Europe: The Uncertain Future of the European Social Model*, Edward Elgar, Cheltenham.

Vernon, R. (1979), The product cycle hypothesis in a new international environment, *Oxford Bulletin of Economics and Statistics*, 41.4: 255–67.

Vicente, M.R. and Lopez, A.J. (2006) Patterns of ICT diffusion across the European Union, *Economic Letters*, 93: 45–51.

Vickerman, R. and Armstrong, H.W. (eds) (1995) *Convergence and Divergence Among European Regions*, Pion, London.

Vinals, J. (1998) EMU and the single monetary policy, Paper for the 4th ECSA World Conference, Brussels.

Vleminckx, K. and Berghman, J. (2001) Social exclusion and the welfare state: an overview of conceptual issues and policy implications, in: Mayes, D.G., Berghman, J. and Slais, R. (eds), *Social Exclusion and European Policy*, Edward Elgar, Cheltenham, 27–46.

von Hagen, J. (1992) Fiscal arrangements in a monetary union, evidence from the US, in: Fair, D. and de Boissieux, Chr. (eds), *Fiscal Policy, Taxation and the Financial System in an Increasingly Integrated Europe*, Kluwer, London, 337–59.

Wallace, H. (1983) Distributional policies: dividing up the Community cake, in:

Wallace, H., Wallace, W. and Webb, C. (eds), *Policy Making in the European Community*, 2nd edn, Wiley, London, 81–114.

Wallace, H. (1984) Implementation across national boundaries, in: Lewis, D. and Wallace, H. (eds), *Policies into Practice: National and International Case Studies in Implementation*, Heineman, London, 129–43.

Whelan, C.T. and Maitre, B. (2005) Vulnerability and multiple deprivation perspectives on economic exclusion in Europe: a latent class analysis, *European Societies*, 7.3: 423–50.

WIFO (1999) Specialisation and (geographic) concentration of European manufacturing, Vienna, preparatory document for the European Commission: *The Competitiveness of European Industry*, 1999 report, Brussels/Luxembourg.

Williams, K., de Laat, B. and Stern, E. (2002) *The Use of Evaluation in the Commission Services*, final report, available on the EU website, Technopolis France and Tavistock Institute, Brussels.

Williamson, J.G. (1965) Regional inequality and the process of national development: a description of patterns, *Economic Development and Cultural Change*, 13: 3-45.

Williamson, J.G. (1976) The implication of European monetary integration for the peripheral areas, in: Vaizey, J. (ed.), *Economic Sovereignty and Regional Policy*, Gill and Macmillan, Dublin, 105–21.

Williamson, O.E. (1998) Transaction cost economics: how it works, where it is headed, *De Economist*, 146.1: 23–58.

World Bank (2006) EU 8 Administrative capacity in the new member states: the limits to innovation?, Report no. 36936-GLB, Washington.

Wu, Y. (2002) Regional disparities in China: an alternative view, *International Journal of Social Economics*, 29.7: 575–89.

Young, D., Leon, O., Kemos, A., Holmes, P. and Basle, M. (2001) Telecommunications policy, in: Hall, R., Smith, A. and Tsoukalis, L. (eds), *Competitiveness and Cohesion in EU Policies*, Oxford University Press, Oxford, 245–76.

Yuill, D., Bachtler, J. and Wislade, F. (1999) *European Regional Incentives*, 18th edn, Bowker/Saur, London.

Zhao, X.B. and Tong, S.P. (2000) Unequal economic development in China, spatial disparities and regional policy reconsideration, 1985–1995, *Regional Studies*, 34: 549–61.

Index

Figures are indicated by **bold** pages numbers, tables by *italic*.

absorption capacity *see* administrative absorption capacity
accession countries: appropriateness of interventions 240–1; effectiveness of interventions 241–2; *see also* new member states
Active Labour Market Policies (ALMP) 239–40
actors in the EU 125–7, *127*
additionality principle **150**, 150–1
administrative absorption capacity: in actioning programmes 204–8; in building partnerships 200–4, **202**; creation of institutions 197–200; for financial management and control 216–19; for managing implementation 208–14; for monitoring progress 214–16
agglomeration of industries 52–3
agriculture 255, 256–9, **257**
aid dependency 247
air connections *91*, 91–2
air transport 266
allocation: methods for support 149; as policy objective 104, 262
ALMP *see* Active Labour Market Policies
appropriateness of interventions 228–9, 235–8, 239, 240–1, 242–3
Association of Southeast Asian Nations (ASEAN) 294–5
Audit Authority 217–18
automatic de-commitment rule 219
automotive industry 58

Balkan states (western) 280
border problems 94, 96–8, 135–6
budget 255–6

CAP *see* Common Agricultural Policy

car industry 58
Certifying Authority 216–17
CF *see* Cohesion Fund
challenges for the future 277–82
change analysis, components of *see* shift-share analysis
CIs *see* Community Initiatives
cities: concentration of unemployment 66–7; education, level of 68
cluster theory 44, 302n9
cohesion: defined 4–5; economic 8, *283*; GDP/P as measure of 15; legal foundations 129–30; social 8, *283*; territorial 8, *283*; in treaties 109
Cohesion Fund (CF) 136, 137, 144; appropriateness of interventions 242–3; effectiveness of interventions 243–4
cohesion policy: added value through 244–6; benefits of 3; categories of expenditure 144; challenges for the future 277–82; contribution to widening and deepening of EU 248–50; criticisms of 3; development of 141–2, *143*; effect on other policies 290; elements of 6; EU added cost 246–8; evaluation of programmes 11–12; flexibility in the future 281–2; future increases in redistribution funds 281; implementation of 10–11; instruments of 10, 281; monitoring of programmes 11; objectives of 9–10, 281; partnership 10–11; problems and corresponding objectives 134–6; *see also* consistency with other EU policies
Commission (EU) 125, 127, 169–70, 201, 284
Committee of the Regions (CoR) 125–6

Index 343

Common Agricultural Policy (CAP) 249, 255, 256–9, **257**
common market 113, 115–16
Common Transport Policy (CTP) 265–8
Community Initiatives (CIs) 138
Community Method of coordination 164–5
compensation for effects of integration 136
competition rules for enterprises 261
competitiveness 7–8, 119, 135; allocation method for support 149; appropriateness of interventions 235–8; effectiveness of interventions 238; eligibility for funding 156–7; horizontal coordination 184–5
compliance with regulation 168–9
components of change analysis *see* shift-share analysis
concentration: of economic activity 42–5; effect of foreign direct investment (FDI) 47–8; expenditure according to 146
consistency with other EU policies: budget 255–6; Common Agricultural Policy (CAP) 255, 256–9, **257**; competition rules for enterprises 261; environment 268–9; European Monetary Union (EMU) 262–4; external trade 264–5; innovation 255–6, 270–1; internal market 259–62; International Monetary Fund (IMF) 261–2; overall impact of other policies 271–3, *272*; regulation 256; securing in the future 289–90; state aid 261; transport infrastructure 265–8, **267**
control systems for programmes 11
convergence: allocation method for support 149; appropriateness of interventions 232–3; consecutive with divergence 21; effect of sectoral change 39–40; effectiveness of interventions 233–5, **234**; eligibility for funding 154–5; inter-regional relations 18–19; and lagging regions 134–5; as objective for the future 7, 9, 16, **16**, 281; related theories 17–19, *23*; simultaneous with divergence 21–3
coordination: horizontal 10, 120–1, 178–87; of other EU and national policies 286–7; vertical 10, 119–20, 162–78; *see also* regulation
CoR *see* Committee of the Regions
core-periphery model 50, *51*, 52
cost estimates and plans 206
Council (EU) 125
Cross-border Business Cooperation for Central Europe project 158
cross border problems 96–7, 157
CTP *see* Common Transport Policy

cumulative causation 20
customs union 113, 115–16

de-localizations 57–8
delivery cycle 194
delivery framework for policy 128, **128**
delivery system, efficiency of 287–8
devolution: Brazil and China compared 291; within member states 124
disparities: appropriateness of interventions 228–9, 232–3; Association of Southeast Asian Nations (ASEAN) 294–5; Brazil 292; China 293–4; decreases in since integration 27–30, *28*; effectiveness of interventions 229–31, 233–5, **234**; efficiency of interventions 231–2; Hungary 35; Italy 35; Mercosur 292–3, *293*; national to 1950 23–5, *25*; between nations, current situation 26–7, **27**; regional, historical studies into 34–5; regional to 1950 25–6; regional within countries 30–4, **31**, **32**, *33*, 35; Spain 35; territorial 87–98, *93*, *95*; time needed to catch up 30, *30*; unemployment in regions 65; United Kingdom 34–5
divergence: consecutive with convergence 21; indicators **16**, 16–17; related theories 19–21, *23*; simultaneous with convergence 21–3

Economic and Social Committee (ESC) 126
economic cohesion: defined 37; environment 269; external trade 264; impact on of agricultural policy 258; impact on of internal market 260; impact on of other policies 273, *273*; International Monetary Fund (IMF) 261; legal foundations for policy 130; policy context 8
economic disparities: concentration 42–5; due to economic restructuring 38–42, *41*; foreign direct investment (FDI) 46–55, *48*, *51*; industrial migration 55–8
education, level of 67–9, *69*
effectiveness of interventions: competitiveness and employment 238; convergence 233–5, **234**; enhancement of 288–9; establishing 229–31; new member states **242**, 243–4; social deprivation 239–40
efficiency: of delivery system 287–8; of interventions 231–2; as policy objective 104; as reason for cohesion intervention 104, 106–7

344 Index

EGTC *see* European Grouping of Territorial Cooperation
eligibility for funding by objectives 154–8, **154**, 164–5
employment: allocation method for support 149; appropriateness of interventions 235–8; effectiveness of interventions 238; eligibility for funding 156–7; evaluation of interventions 235–9; horizontal coordination 185–6; *see also* labour market; unemployment
EMU *see* European Monetary Union
endogenous growth theory 22
enlargement of the EU: compensation for 136; upcoming 279–80
environment 98, 181, 186–7
equalization of factor returns theory 18
equity 151–2, **152**; *versus* 'juste retour' 147; as policy objective 104; as reason for cohesion intervention 104–5
European Grouping of Territorial Cooperation (EGTC) 171
European Monetary Union (EMU) 256, 262–4, 277–8
European Regional Development Fund (ERDF) 144
European Social Fund (ESF) 144
European Spatial Development Perspective (ESDP) 110–11
European Union (EU): actors in 125–7, *127*; background and development of 4, 298n4; challenges for the future 277–82; federation 278–9; future increases in redistribution 281; higher integration in the future 277–82; institutions of 125–6; objectives and instruments 183–4; optimization of institutions of 282, 284; solidarity in 108–9; standards 176–8, 187, 270
evaluation of cohesion policies: actors involved 227–8; appropriateness of interventions 228–9, 232–3, 235–8, 239, 240–1; contribution to widening and deepening of EU 248–50; development of model 224–5; effectiveness of interventions 229–31, 233–5, **234**, 238, 239–40, 241–2, **242**, 243–4; efficiency of interventions 231–2; EU added cost 246–8; EU added value 244–6; EU/SF model 225–6; improvement of 251–2; logic and structure of *226*, 226–7, **227**; use for other policies 250
evaluation of programmes 11–12, 206
expert committees 126

export related models 43
external trade 264–5

FDI *see* foreign direct investment
federation 116, 278–9
finance as instrument of cohesion policy 9, 109–10; eligibility and objectives 152–8, *153*; implementation of 137–44; match between objectives and resources 145–52, 285–6; problems and corresponding objectives 134–6
financial management and control 11, 216–19
'fire alarm oversight' 193
Fiscal federalism school 114
flexibility: of cohesion policy in the future 281–2; lack of in multi-annual framework 138
Fondo para la Convergencia Structural Del Mercosur (FOCEM) 293
foreign direct investment (FDI): and the characteristics of a country 47; defined 46; determinant factors for 52; effect on concentration 47–8; effect on new member states 53–5, **54**; effect on of membership of EU 50, 51; geographical (national) patterns of intra-EU 50, *51*, 52; geographical (regional) patterns of intra-EU 52–3; growth and composition of intra-EU 49–50; horizontal and vertical 47; welfare effects 55
framework for delivery of policy objectives 128, **128**
Full Union 278–9
functioning and absorption capacity: actioning programmes 207–8; building partnerships 203–4; creating institutions 199–200; management committees 216; managing implementation 213–14; monitoring progress 216; payment flows and budget commitments 219
future, challenges for 277–82

GDP/P: as indicator of disparities 16–17, 29; as measure of cohesion 15, 37, 299n5, 299n8
gender equality 64–5, *64*
general-purpose grants 114
Generalized Systems of Preference 181
geographical features as handicaps 84
grants 114, 117–18, 231–2, 281
growth theory 18–19, 20, 22

horizontal coordination: competitiveness

184–5; employment 185–6; EU model 182–3; EU objectives and instruments 183–4; global model 180–1; importance of 120–1; innovation and knowledge 186; national model 179–80; of other EU and national policies 287; sustainability and the environment 186–7
human resources and absorption capacity: actioning programmes 204; building partnerships 202–3; creating institutions 197, 199; financial management and control 218; managing implementation 210; monitoring progress 214–15

IMF *see* International Monetary Fund
implementation of cohesion policy: delivery cycle 194; human resources 210; institutional and administrative requirements 194, 196–7; intermediate bodies 209–10; Managing Authorities 208–9; monitoring devices 193; policy cycle stage 10–11; principal-agent relationship 192–4; projects 210–13; sanctions 193; structure 208–10; *see also* administrative absorption capacity
increasing returns models 20
indicators 16–17
industrial migration 55–8
industrial relations 61
industrial revolution 24
information systems 215–16
innovation: access to 92–4, *93, 95*, 255–6; consistency with other EU policies 270–1; and knowledge, horizontal coordination 186
institutions: creation of 197–200, *198*, 199; of the EU, optimization of 282, 284; history of Brazil and China compared 291
instruments of cohesion policy 10; finance 109–10; financial support through funds 137; proportionality principle 112; regulation 109–10; subsidiarity principle 111–12
integration: compensation for the effects of 136; effects of 120–1; of other countries and areas 291–6; *see also* stages of integration
inter-regional border problems 96
inter-regional redistribution 114
inter-regional relations 18–19, 158
intermediate bodies 209–10
internal market policies 256, 259–62
International Monetary Fund (IMF) 181, 261–2

international relations, theory of 17–18
interpersonal redistribution 114
intervention: design of systems for 8–9; reasons for 104–9; and stages of economic integration 107–8
investment and trade regimes 48–9, *48*

'juste retour' 147

knowledge: access to 92–4, *93, 95*; economy 40–2, *41*; horizontal coordination 186
Kyoto Protocol 181, 269; *see also* environment

labour market 55, 63; *see also* employment; unemployment
labour movements: effect on convergence 18; effect on divergence 20
legal foundations for cohesion policy 129–30
legitimization of EU institutions 124–5
lessons: for other countries and integration areas 291–6; from the past 282–90
life-cycle of the product 19, 20, 300n10
living conditions 77

management committees 216
Managing Authority 208–9, 210
manufacturing 40–1, *41*
markets, access to 87–92, **89**, *90, 91*
membership of EU, effect on FDI 50, 51
Mercosur 292–3
migration 55–8, 69–75, *73*
monetary union 113, 116–17
monitoring: committees 214; devices 193; of programmes 11; progress of programmes and projects 214–16
multiannual framework for funds 137–8
multilevel government 124–7
multinational firms: organization of 47; ownership, location and internalization (OLI) paradigm 46–7; reasons for multinationalism 47; and trade and investment regimes 48–9

N + 2 rule 219
National Action Plans (NAPs) 163, 183
national disparities to 1950 23–5, *25*
National Strategic Reference Frameworks (NSRFs) 170
necessities of life 77
needs, expenditure according to 145
network industries 260
New Economic Geography approach 43

new member states: administrative absorption capacity of 197, 199–200; appropriateness of interventions 240–1; effect of FDI 53–5, **54**; effectiveness of interventions 241–2, **242**; human resources in 197, 199; impact of internal market 260; implementation of rules 287–8; and policy management systems 199; sectoral changes 39–40; unemployment 62, 63
NMSs *see* new member states
nodes and networks 87

Objective 1 *see* convergence
Objective 2 *see* competitiveness; employment
Objective 3 and 4 *see* social deprivation
objective indicators 17
Objectively Verifiable Indicators (OVIs) 227
objectives: of cohesion policy 9–10; corresponding to problems 134–6; matching with finances 285–6; policy 104–5
OLI paradigm *see* ownership, location and internalization (OLI) paradigm
Open Method of Coordination (OMC) 162–3, 183–4
operational programmes (OPs) 171
OVIs *see* Objectively Verifiable Indicators
ownership, location and internalization (OLI) paradigm 46–7

Parliament (EU) 125
partnerships: building 200–4; and coordination 163; principle of 124, 251–2; as principle of cohesion policy 10–11; responsibilities of member states and regions 201; selection of partners 299n10
polarization 90
'police patrol oversight' 193
policy: competition 162; cycle 6–12, **7**, 127, *127*, 194, *195*; delivery framework for 128, **128**
policy objectives 104–5
political trade offs 140–1
polycentrism 85–6
poverty 75, 76
power politics 145
predictability for beneficiaries 137–8
preferential trade agreements 115
principal-agent relationship 192–4
privatization 124

problems and corresponding objectives 134–6
product, life-cycle of 19, 20, 300n10
production structure 37
productivity, impact of FDI 55
programmes, actioning of 204–8
programming 11
projects: pipelines 213–14; proposals 206; systems and tools 210–13
proportionality principle 112, 173, 288

railways 179
redistribution: form of and stages of integration 114–17, *115*; future increases 281; national or regional criterion 147–9, **148**; need for EU policies 112–13; as policy objective 104; scheme forms 113–14; via structural policies 117–19, **118**
regions: access to knowledge and innovation 94; actors in EU from 125, 126; disparity in unemployment 65; education, level of 68–9; France 35; Germany 35; Hungary 35; improved transport infrastructure 266; interregional border problems 96; Italy 35; lagging 134–5; negotiations on eligibility and area coverage 164–5; policies for 284; poverty 77–8; responsibilities for partnerships 201; restructuring of 135; role in vertical coordination 170–1; social protection 81; Spain 35; United Kingdom 34–5
regulation: and effect of other EU policies 256; forms and instruments of 121–2; as instrument of cohesion policy 109–10; instruments for 9; and level of finances needed 285–6; of other EU and national policies 286–7; social security 122–3; and territorial cohesion 110; *see also* coordination

sectoral change 39–40
segregation 71, 72–5
Services of General Interest (SGIs) 178
shift-share analysis 38
social cohesion: defined 60–1; environment 269; external trade 264–5; impact on of agriculture policy 258; impact on of internal market 260; impact on of other policies 273, *273*; International Monetary Fund (IMF) 262; legal foundations for policy 129; policy context 8
social deprivation: appropriateness of

interventions 239; effectiveness of interventions 239–40
social disparities: level of education 67–9, *69*; migration 69–75; segregation 71; social exclusion 75–8, *76*; social protection 78–81; unemployment 62–7, *64*
social exclusion 75–8, *76*, 167
social protection 78–81, *81*
social security regulation 122–3
social standards 176–7
solidarity, European and national 108–9
spatial planning 84–5
specific-purpose grants 114, 117–18, 231–2, 281
stability as policy objective 104
stages of integration: form of redistribution 114–17, *115*; increasing scope of EU policy 124; and intervention 107–8; and need for redistribution policies 112–13
standards, EU 176–8, 187, 270
state aid 172–6, *174*, 187, 261
Structural Fund 137
structure and absorption capacity: assignment of responsibilities 197, 200–2, 204; delegation to intermediate bodies (IBs) 209–10; monitoring committees 214; role of the Audit Authority 217–18; role of the Certifying Authority 216–17; role of the Managing Authority 208–9
subjective indicators 17
subsidiarity principle 111–12, 178, 232, 251, 284
sustainability and horizontal coordination 186–7
systems/tools and absorption capacity: actioning programmes 205–7; building partnerships 203; creating institutions 199; financial management and control 218–19; monitoring progress 215–16; for projects 210–13; used in previous programming periods 220

technology transfer via FDI 55
TEN *see* Trans European Network
territorial cohesion: concept of 83–5; environment 269; external trade 264; impact on of agriculture policy 258–9; impact on of internal market 260; impact on of other policies 273, *273*; indicators of 83–5; International Monetary Fund (IMF) 262; legal foundations for policy 130; policy context 8; and regulation 110; Services of General Interest (SGIs) 178; Territorial Impact Assessment 110; and vertical coordination 171
territorial cooperation 135–6, 157–8
territorial disparities: access to knowledge and innovation 92–4, *93*, *95*; accessibility to markets 87–92; border problems 94, 96–8
Territorial Impact Assessment 110
trade *48*, 48–9, 115, 181, 264–5
trade theory, new and traditional 42–3
Trans European Network (TEN) 266–8
transnational border problems 96, 97–8, 157–8
transport infrastructure 97, 98, 179, 243, 265–8, **267**
treaties, cohesion in 109

unemployment: appropriateness of interventions 239; concentration of in cities 66–7; concentration of in urban areas 66–7; decrease in as indicator of success 233; disparities between EU countries 5; disparity in regions 65; effectiveness of interventions 239–40; gender equality *64*, 64–5; historical trends 62; national differences 63–4, *64*; new member states 62, 63; theories concerning 62–3; *see also* employment; labour market
urban areas: concentration of unemployment 66–7; level of education 68; responses to problems in 159

vertical coordination: Community Method 164–5; coordination and regulation 119–20; EU standards 176–8; limits to state aid 172–6; need for and compliance with regulation 168–9; Open Method of Coordination (OMC) 162–3; operational programmes (OPs) 171; of other EU and national policies 286–7; rationale for stronger method of 166–8; regulation as major instrument 162; role of member states 170; role of regions in 170–1; role of the Commission (EU) 169–70; state aid *174*

water quality directives 268
welfare effects of FDI 55
welfare loss 247
welfare states, types of 79–80
World Trade Organization (WTO) 181

eBooks – at www.eBookstore.tandf.co.uk

A library at your fingertips!

eBooks are electronic versions of printed books. You can store them on your PC/laptop or browse them online.

They have advantages for anyone needing rapid access to a wide variety of published, copyright information.

eBooks can help your research by enabling you to bookmark chapters, annotate text and use instant searches to find specific words or phrases. Several eBook files would fit on even a small laptop or PDA.

NEW: Save money by eSubscribing: cheap, online access to any eBook for as long as you need it.

Annual subscription packages

We now offer special low-cost bulk subscriptions to packages of eBooks in certain subject areas. These are available to libraries or to individuals.

For more information please contact webmaster.ebooks@tandf.co.uk

We're continually developing the eBook concept, so keep up to date by visiting the website.

www.eBookstore.tandf.co.uk